Science Fiction
and Computing

I0004379

Science Fiction and Computing

Essays on Interlinked Domains

edited by David L. Ferro and
Eric G. Swedin

McFarland & Company, Inc., Publishers
Jefferson, North Carolina, and London

LIBRARY OF CONGRESS CATALOGUING-IN-PUBLICATION DATA

Science fiction and computing : essays on interlinked domains /
  edited by David L. Ferro and Eric G. Swedin.
     p.   cm.
  Includes bibliographical references and index.

  ISBN 978-0-7864-4565-3
  softcover : 50# alkaline paper ∞

    1. Science fiction — History and criticism.   2. Computers
in literature.   3. Computer science — History.   I. Ferro,
David L.   II. Swedin, Eric Gottfrid.
PN3433.6.S375   2011
809.3'8762 — dc22   2011013881

BRITISH LIBRARY CATALOGUING DATA ARE AVAILABLE

© 2011 David L. Ferro and Eric G. Swedin. All rights reserved

*No part of this book may be reproduced or transmitted in any form
or by any means, electronic or mechanical, including photocopying
or recording, or by any information storage and retrieval system,
without permission in writing from the publisher.*

Cover image © 2011 Blend Images

Manufactured in the United States of America

McFarland &, Inc., Publishers
  Box 611, Jefferson, North Carolina 28640
  www.mcfarlandpub.com

To
Will F. Jenkins
(a.k.a. Murray Leinster)

Acknowledgments

I just wanted to thank a few who have been helpful during this project. First, to our put-upon students who have taken the long science fiction survey we've given every semester and shared their perspectives in other ways. To the staffs of the Boston University Isaac Asimov Archive, the Syracuse University Special Collections Research Center, and the Special Collections and Archives Department of Rivera Library at UC-Riverside, which houses the J. Lloyd Eaton Collection of Science Fiction, Fantasy, Horror, and Utopian Literature. To the Hemingway Family for a generous grant that allowed us to travel to those archives. To Kris Bergeron and Kelley Lindberg who came in at the last minute to help. To all our authors who showed such excitement for this project. To assorted colleagues and friends who have tried to point me in the right direction over the years. To my co-editor, Eric, whom I always learn from; although never so dramatically as this past spring when a life-threatening brain aneurism took him off this project. I salute his doctors but mostly his stubborn optimism that likely carried the day. Finally, two people who have shown me more patience and encouragement than I deserve on a daily basis: my wife and daughter, Marjukka and Stella. Thanks also to Marjukka for listening to my desperate last-minute plea for help with editing. Now that this thing has been put to bed maybe we can finally get to the many things that got left undone. A bike ride and fixing the drain tomorrow?—D.F.

I echo the acknowledgments of my colleague, friend, and co-editor David L. Ferro. My wife, Betty, and children, Adam, William, Spencer, and Hannah, are all science fiction fans. They have sustained me during this project. I also thank my doctors.

This book is dedicated to James P. Hogan, who passed away as this manuscript was being completed. He had written a chapter for this book, but differences in publishing between the commercial and academic world led to that chapter not making it into the book. His *The Two Faces of Tomorrow* (1979) is an excellent example of the meeting between science fiction and computers.— E.S.

Table of Contents

Introduction

David L. Ferro

When I was in fifth grade, around the Christmas holidays, we were randomly paired up with someone else in the class to exchange gifts. I can't remember what I gave, but I recall what I received: a paperback book, its cover torn off. It was Isaac Asimov's *The Rest of the Robots,* a collection of short stories that opened up for me, not only a whole new literary genre, but a whole new way of looking at the world. I still have it on my shelf.

I didn't think much about receiving that book as the rest of my life unfolded and as I made the career choices that led me to writing this introduction. In retrospect, however, it was a defining moment. Today I teach in a computer science department and have a Ph.D. in science and technology studies. Asimov's book both inspired and reflects my life as well as the book you hold before you. The stories that Asimov wrote were thought experiments — using a fictional format — that explored the engineering and scientific development necessary for further advances in computers. They also dealt with the social implications of those advances. Only now, in researching this book, do I realize how apt Asimov was as the progenitor of inspiration. Asimov became a trained scientist in biochemistry. In addition, he was influenced by the social sciences. In fact, the vision for the first short story he ever sold to John Campbell, the seminal editor of Golden Age science fiction, came from the work of sociologist Bernhard J. Stern.[1]

Just as I was inspired by both science and fiction, my co-editor, Eric G. Swedin, and many of the authors of this collection, have comparable life stories behind their entries. They come from different — and, often, combined — disciplines yet have a similar drive to explore what science fiction has

1

meant to them and to the world. This book has given them a venue to examine a topic in new ways. The level of excitement we heard from the prospective authors assured us that we were on the right path with this collection. In fact, we heard from a number of authors that this project took precedence over all others. It was a labor of love which gave them an opportunity to combine personal passions and explore disciplinary relevance.

The prevalence of science fiction readership among those people who create computers and programs is so well-known that it has become a cliché, but the cliché has remained largely unexplored by scholars. What role has science fiction truly played in the development of real computers? What has it meant for society? It was our intent to bring together voices from numerous disciplines. We wanted to broadly explore the past, present, and future importance of speculative fiction as a body of literature that has, through various means, potentially facilitated the invention, acceptance, rejection, and use of computers. The expressed concerns for a decline in students entering STEM (scientific, technical, engineering, and mathematics) disciplines in the United States only serves to give increased import to this question.

We laid out five suppositions in our call for participation. First, that science fiction acts as a source of inspiration for invention and participation. Second, it supplies metaphors and analogies and facilitates communication within and outside a community of practitioners. Third, it helps create worldviews and shape critical thinking. Fourth, it plays a role in defining social relations and helps determine who is inside and outside of the community of the creators of digital culture. Finally, it assists in imagining the implications of computing on society and ourselves, or, vice versa, the needs of a society that promotes computer development.

The assembled authors took up the challenge we laid out. To address our suppositions they have written through the lenses of such disciplines as history, English, anthropology, sociology, philosophy, science and technology studies, computer science, technology management, literature studies, political science, cultural studies, and science fiction itself. They frequently threaded their responses to our five assumptions through case studies. Taken as a whole, the articles address our suppositions and reveal evidence for the influence of science fiction on computing and society, and vice versa. The next section reviews the history of science fiction as a literary genre.

Defining a Fictional Form

Science fiction has a rich and vibrant history. It has been characterized in numerous ways over time. Most of the authors in this book benefit from a generous reading of science fiction's literary boundaries. Yet, exploring the relationship between science fiction, science, and society still requires some exploration of the genre and its history.

The definition of science fiction — alternatively labeled s.f., scifi, speculative fiction, and imaginative fiction (among other titles) — has been consistently criticized both from within and from without the genre. As Thomas Haigh notes, early twentieth-century science fiction author and editor Hugo Gernsback created the term "scientifiction," which later morphed into "science fiction" by 1929. Gernsback strived so hard to restrict the definition of the genre that classical authors, such as Jules Verne or H.G. Wells, considered science fiction (or at least proto-science fiction) authors today, could fail to make the grade. Gernsback's definition generally required erudite exposition of technological artifacts or scientific investigations, or both. He expected that stories that met the requirements would also contain an optimistic view of the techno-scientific process and "a sense of wonder" towards the universe. In time, this came to be known as "hard" science fiction.

The field grew to include many authors who were not trained in science and engineering or overly interested in the hard approach. In addition, as Gary Westfahl has shown in *Cosmic Engineers,* the stories' hardness can be questioned. One reason is that plot and characterization often required scientific veracity in some parts of a story while precluding it in others.[2] Some "blame" for the loosening of scientific rigor can be laid at the feet of John Campbell. As the editor of the magazine *Astounding Science Fiction,* he required that storytelling did not take a back seat to scientific exposition. Campbell's approach created better written stories. For example, science fiction author Robert Heinlein mastered the technique of the "gradual unfolding of exposition," where the technological and scientific details arise naturally in the story instead of through didactic asides.[3]

With Campbell, a sense of wonder did not disappear, although, not only utopian but dystopian ideas were published. The important element to include in a story was technologically deterministic: how society and the individual were affected by a contrived invention — i.e., the perennial "What If?" question. What if people had gills in a world filled with water, for example. Another important wrinkle to hard science fiction also emerged. In the stories, scientists and engineers needed to act like human beings (sometimes heroic, sometimes not). They also needed to act like real-life scientists and engineers. By focusing on both the social impact of invention and the techno-scientific community of practitioners, the definition of hard required a sociological and psychological outlook. This imperative persists today. For example, the scientific advisor to the movie *Sunshine* managed to insist on the characters "acting like scientists" despite the unbelievable science of the plot.[4]

An important myth exists within science fiction concerning its relationship to literature at large. Typically it entails the idea that once (circa 1900 and earlier) no difference existed between science fiction and mainstream literature but that science fiction became marginalized over time. The happy ending is that mainstream literature and society have today finally caught up to science fiction and are utilizing the genre's tools.

Reading and listening to science fiction authors and critics qualifies that version of history somewhat. For at least a century science fiction has had a vibrant peer review mechanism. Many authors have compared it to that of science. Yet, many authors of science fiction simultaneously exhibit potentially conflicting needs. On the one hand there exists a desire to be considered seriously by readers and critics of mainstream literature. On the other hand they recognize the need to engage in the internal discussion of literary boundary maintenance; what counts and does not count as science fiction.

Of course, unlike most science, fiction needs to apply directly to the public for acceptance. Fiction must be sold. And much of the boundary definitions relate to addressing the market needs for fiction. But, here too, a sociological sense of science can be found. Many readers are part of the internal conversation through more than their buying habits. They also participate through conferences, online discussions, and letters to editors.

At the end of the day, many of the authors assembled use rather broad and porous definitions of science fiction and that reflects a majority of the authors and readers of the genre today. We will allow our authors to explore those perspectives individually when necessary. In addition, in this volume, authors Thomas Haigh, Chris Pak, and Lisa Nocks all give extensive historical overviews of the genre that greatly expands on the few words I've written here. The next section will thread some of our themes through the authors' contributions.

Threading Our Themes

Measuring the degree to which science fiction has played a role in creating technology and defining culture is not trivial, nor do the analysts of science fiction necessarily believe science fiction to be the principal creative factor. Nevertheless, the authors have parsed texts, interviewed principal characters, and reviewed literature and, in the process, have found evidence of its influence. I will present some substantiation of this influence to which the contributors of this book add their individual cases.

Examples for the absence of fiction's importance are easy to discover, even in places where it could be assumed it would play a larger role. For example, in *Bootstrapping,* Thierry Bardini's previously published investigation of Douglas Engelbart and the development of the graphical user interface, there is barely a mention of science fiction.[5] Bardini focuses instead on other factors

that influenced the creation of an alternative interactive computing environment, including yoga, recreational drug use, and the countercultural lifestyle
celebrated by the *Whole Earth Catalog.*

The absence of fiction often tells us something important as well. Another
example of a weak link to science fiction comes from an important text that
promoted personal computing in the years of its gestation: Ted Nelson's 1974
Computer Lib/Dream Machines with its famous cover, screaming "You can
and must understand computers NOW."[6] In that book, science fiction is most
visible by its studiously created absence. There are two exceptions I have
found. One is a quote from *Alice in Wonderland.*[7] The other exception is a
quote from Frederick Brooks during a speech to the Institute of Electrical
and Electronics Engineers (IEEE) in which Brooks argues that the computer
HAL from *2001: A Space Odyssey* is a model for the way computers should
function. Nelson uses science fiction to respond negatively to Brooks' suppo-
sition using concepts from Asimov's *I, Robot* as well as *2001.*[8]

Although Nelson's combined book *Computer Lib/Dream Machines* has
an almost science fiction style graphic novel presentation, it portrays computers as part of a cultural and workplace revolution. It goes out of its way
to position computers strictly as tools, not magical or strange devices that are
only incrementally different from other, more familiar tools, such as household
appliances. As Eric G. Swedin and I note in this book, the science fiction
author William F. Jenkins (pen name Murray Leinster) proposed a similar
work-up for mainframe computers during the 1950s. Jenkins wanted to create
a book that made mainframe computers appear commonplace and not frightening. In fact, both Nelson and Jenkins deliberately avoided science fiction.
Interestingly, Jenkins' 1946 short story "A Logic Named Joe" created a scenario
that fairly describes many aspects of the networked personal computers we
use today. Yet, that would have been too much science fiction for his 1950s
proposal. Science fiction appears now and then in those publications engaged
with computer development, however, the extent to which it is evident is
likely dependent on the venue and the intent of the publication.

Despite the frequent difficulty in finding links between fiction and computer development, it is not impossible. In fact it can occasionally be serendip-
itous. An important inspiration for this collection came from the work of
Sherry Turkle, author of one of the most influential books on childhood development and computing: *The Second Self: Computers and the Human Spirit.*[9]
Visiting her at her MIT office in the early 1990s I noticed the ground-breaking
cyberpunk novel *Neuromancer* on the shelf and commented on it. Apparently,
many of her young students were reading it.

I wondered if literature, like *Neuromancer,* might be influencing careers
in science and technology. Turkle, in fact, has spent a considerable amount

of time detailing the objects that have inspired and shaped the thinking of students and professionals in the scientific and technical fields. These stories have been collected in two volumes: *Falling for Science* and *The Inner History of Devices*.[10] While the principal goal of these books have been to examine the use of artifacts such as Legos, Tinkertoys, and video games, references to fiction do arise. A few examples from *Falling for Science* and *The Inner History of Devices* demonstrate the point. In "Erector Set," former MIT student Kwatsi Alibaruho writes, "In time I imagined worlds both concrete and futuristic. I read Buck Rogers books and watched *Star Trek;* my designs drew on their worlds to build my own."[11] In discussing how he and his friend arrived at the right shape for battling Lego ships, another former student, Andrew Chu, writes, "These were designs surely influenced by the aesthetic of Japanese robot cartoons." He continues, "Our ships evolved to something close the shape of the Imperial Empire battle cruisers of *Star Wars,* and we pretty much left it at that."[12] In a moving entry, former student Alicia Kestrell Verlager uses a blind character's experience with a "sensor net" in a *Star Trek* episode to think of her own prosthetic eyes.[13]

This use of science fiction didn't only happen for new students attending MIT. Psychiatrists have used it to understand patients. In *The Inner History of Devices,* Aslihan Sanal reports a patient in dialysis who describes his self-perception after wounds appeared on his back while swimming. Sanal writes: "The experience confirmed for him that he was a robot, just like Arnold Schwarzenegger in *The Terminator.* He felt more a machine that would break in water than a human who would not."[14] Another contributor to Turkle's book, child psychiatrist John Hamilton, writes that "online life offers a window in transference, the feelings that the patient brings to the therapist from other relations."[15] In role-playing exercises, one patient creates stories from characters in *The Lord of the Rings* and the *Harry Potter* series and, with the therapist, explores "exaggerated masculinity."[16] Fiction helps to create, understand, and communicate our relationship to objects.

As objects have been inspirational, so has science fiction been an inspiration for those entering scientific and technical fields. The science fiction authors of the twentieth century were fully cognizant of their role in creating inspirational fiction. Some embraced it. For instance, Robert Heinlein wrote many books aimed at adolescents in which the language and situations glorified technical and scientific excellence and self-sufficiency. Note the back cover from his 1952 young adult novel *The Rolling Stones.*

> [T]he Luna family is pleasantly daft along with being terribly intelligent: Mother is an M.D.; Father an engineer who doubles as a television script writer for Earth; the twin boys are mathematical whizzes; Sister is not far behind them; the four-year-old brother is a chess expert; and Granny is an engineer![17]

Much as individuals have explored their involvement in techno-science through objects, the authors in this book have explored involvement through fiction. The chapters by Janet Abbate, Paul E. Ceruzzi, and David A. Kirby all note how fiction has inspired particular technological development. The chapter by Joshua Cuneo notes the inspiration *Star Trek* had on many entering science and engineering fields.

Science fiction's influence can be found in journalistic treatments of the world of computing as well. Indeed, science fiction shaping technology makes a good story. For instance, an article in *Wired* magazine linked the novel *Snow Crash* as directly influencing a program that eventually became Google Earth.[18] In another example, Scott Rosenberg's *Dreaming in Code*, a business study of a complex open source project, all the metaphors and analogies are taken from science fiction. Individuals featured within the pages reference *Star Wars, Star Trek, The Lord of the Rings,* and *Monty Python.* Rosenberg notes that one of the programmers he was following had used a language called Python, invented by Dutch programmer Guido van Rossum, who named it in honor of Monty Python's Flying Circus. Rosenberg comments that "Monty Python's form-smashing absurdism has always found some of its truest fans in computer labs." Furthermore, Rosenberg himself uses a *Star Wars* analogy when he explains to the reader the concept of the back end and front end of a computer by writing, "In Star Wars terms, the front end is the butlerish C3PO; the back end is the unintelligible R2D2."[19]

Examining the written works of well-known computer scientists, including Richard Stallman, Ray Kurzweil, Bill Joy, and Eric Raymond, gives us an understanding of how science fiction is a part of the lingua franca of computer development. For example, computer scientists such as Danny Hillis, Timothy May, and Marvin Minsky contributed to a compilation of essays about the seminal work *True Names,* written by science fiction author and fellow computer scientist Vernor Vinge.[20] Scientists David Stork, Donald Norman, Daniel Dennet, Raymond Kurzweil, Murray Campbell, and others used HAL from *2001* to discuss advances in computing.[21] Richard Stallman indicated that "[a] lot of programmers are science fiction fans, and there's a tendency in science fiction fandom to accept non-standard relationships ... and explore alternative realities."[22] Eric Raymond, author of the open-source "manifesto," *The Cathedral and the Bazaar,* argued that the ego-driven aspects of open source participation are not unlike those found in science fiction fandom and that reading science fiction is important to becoming a good hacker.[23]

Science fiction also plays a role in debates among those creating technology. Ray Kurzweil has spawned an entire subgenre of science fiction by arguing for the actual inevitability of what has been termed the *Singularity.* The Singularity is a moment in time when artificial intelligence, nanotechnology, genetic engineering, and robotics become so advanced that they combine to create a future (or lack thereof) for humanity that is unpredictable and distinct.[24] Co-founder of Sun Microsystems Bill Joy wrote an article titled "Why the Future Doesn't Need Us" for *Wired* in April 2000 in response to Kurzweil's prediction. The letter, which is a warning to those pursuing the technologies listed by Kurzweil, clearly lists science fiction as important to him as a young man. He also notes "While I had heard such talk before, I had always felt sentient robots were in the realm of science fiction. But now, from someone I respected, I was hearing a strong argument that they were a near-term possibility." It would appear that for Bill Joy, sentient robots should remain in fiction.[25]

Explorations in the use of language, including metaphors and analogies and their effects, by those internal and external to technological practice, can be found in all of the essays in this book. For example, in Janet Abbate's piece, science fiction writer and computer scientist Vernor Vinge is inspired by a real-life event, stating, "I realized that I had just *lived* a science fiction story." Abbate, Thierry Bardini, and R.C. Alvarado all show us how the fiction they examine creates vocabulary for those working in computer science. Lisa Nocks approaches the language we use from the perspective of the machines we have built. She shows how human language as used by machines impedes their understanding of humans. Paul E. Ceruzzi explores the use of metaphors by historians of technology as well as scientists and engineers. He uses the idea of technological trajectory to explore the "Kubrick paradigm" of artificial intelligence (Stanley Kubrick directed *2001: A Space Odyssey*).

In his description of a software project potentially spinning out of control, Rosenberg in *Dreaming in Code* often cites the nonfiction work of Frederick Brooks' *The Mythical Man-Month* (Brooks, as we noted with Nelson's *Computer Lib/Dream Machines,* mentions *2001: A Space Odyssey* in a speech to the IEEE). *The Mythical Man-Month* is a reflection on the development of the IBM 360 operating system which Brooks managed. The book is often cited by technology managers during the project development cycles of computer software. The man-month is a unit of measure for how much a man working for a month might accomplish. The myth is that you could take four men and get the same job done in a week. According to Brooks, this is a myth because the four individuals have different abilities and project knowledge and accommodating those differences will add time to the project. When describing software development, Brooks seems to invoke a metaphysics which dissolves the boundaries between fiction and reality. He notes, "The programmer, like the poet, works only slightly removed from pure thought-stuff." He continues: "He builds his castles in the air, from air, creating by exertion of the imagination. Few media of creation are so flexible, so easy to polish and rework, so readily capable of realizing grand conceptual structures."[26] Reflecting on Brooks, one wonders if fiction plays an inevitable part in the creation of software and computers in general.

While not necessarily intended as such by Brooks, "castles in the air" could include the idea of a "thought experiment." In this volume, Howard Tayler, Richard L. McKinney, and David Toomey write about the fiction that technologists and scientists use in thought experiments, creative exercises that assist in understanding the repercussions for a theory or proposed device.

The predictive aspects in some science fiction stories can play this role as well; the prediction acting as a thought experiment. Haigh, Tayler, Swedin and Ferro, and Thierry Bardini all address prediction in their chapters. In addition, Alvarado and Bardini show how prediction (or prophesy) becomes a critical aspect of creating a techno-scientific culture.

Thought experiments that include the implications for people and society and, further, become part of the public exchange regarding those implications are manifest in this book. For example, Chris Pak notes both the optimistic and pessimistic literary approaches to computers over time. Hunter Heyck explores the public discussion of what it means to be human. Joshua Cuneo addresses the eventually popular television show *Star Trek*.

Several authors in this book investigate thought experiments that take place internally and externally to the discipline under investigation. For example, Janet Abbate examines conversations concerning the virtual human beginning with Vernor Vinge's *True Names*. McKinney takes on the use of science fiction in discussions of nanotechnology. David A. Kirby, in revealing the back story to *The Lawnmower Man*, shows how that movie became the principal means for the public to understand the latest thinking in virtual reality.

Fiction reveals a great deal about the individuals involved in creating the fiction and the historical context within which it is written. Many of the authors in this volume demonstrate that in their work. In Gary Westfahl's detailed review of the popular comic series *Superman*, the changing cultural understandings of technology during most of mid–twentieth-century America shine through the pen and ink drawings he describes. By using a Finnish robot adventure series of the 1940s, Jaakko Suominen explores 1940s Finland through a fictional lens. Alfredo Suppia uses Brazilian film in the 1960s to explain Brazilian attitudes towards imported technology. Both Thomas Haigh, in a broad historical view, and Paul E. Ceruzzi, looking at the space program and artificial intelligence, write historical perspectives. They simultaneously posit the examination of science fiction as useful to historiographical approaches.

One of our goals was discovering if fictional forms help define the boundary of a techno-scientific subculture and mainstream culture. Although the authors in this book do not approach this question directly, the answer is implicit in much of the work. Contributors such as Janet Abbate, Paul E. Ceruzzi, and David A. Kirby work to varying degrees from the premise that communication can occur from within a community of experts to the general public.

Contrarily, contributor Graham J. Murphy, in citing the fictional work of Cory Doctorow, takes on the usefulness of the concept of a boundary between those inside and outside of the community of scientists and engineers. Cory Doctorow, a proponent and facilitator of open source software, flaunts such distinctions in his work and his fiction. Doctorow's stories are "mash-ups" of classic fiction and contemporary sensibilities with stories such as "I Row-Boat," a riff on the classic Isaac Asimov book *I, Robot*.

Distinctions between the techno-scientific communities of practice and the mainstream culture can be found, however, and deserve further exploration. For example, for six years I have been surveying students in computer science, history, business, and honors courses regarding science fiction and its role in their lives. Many overlaps exist in the kinds of media that students enjoy. However, according to survey results, the amount of science fiction oriented material consumed by students in the science and technology fields is greater than the other fields. Additionally, in response to a question about how important science fiction has been in their understanding of the future, the science and engineering students report a much greater significance than the remaining students. If Murphy and Doctorow are correct the differences between those inside and outside the techno-scientific fields may narrow over time. Currently, however, there remains something for a researcher to explore.

Conclusion

Since the themes of the book reflect the development of science fiction, computers, and society over time, we have chosen to present the chapters in roughly chronological order. The first two chapters give an extensive overview of the history of science fiction and its importance over the last century. The majority of the remaining chapters address issues of a particular timeframe. We begin by looking at science and fiction of the 1940s and end in present-day.

As an interdisciplinary collection, the approaches and methodologies of each work included is unique. As such, we have tried to not dwell overly on some kind of totalizing methodology. Each work speaks for itself and reflects the community from which it is written. For a broader appeal we have attempted to keep jargon at least to a level where a reader from any background can enjoy and benefit from the collection. We hope we have been successful.

This collection is extensive but not exhaustive in covering of the themes of this book. Much scholarly work remains. This book represents only one manifesto, of sorts, that the work should attract scholars. But for now, it is time for the editors to get out of the way, and let the contributing scholars tell their stories.

Notes

1. Isaac Asimov and Janet Jeppson Asimov, *It's Been a Good Life* (Amherst, NY: Prometheus, 2002), p. 54. These comments also can be found in his address to Newark College of Engineering, given November 8, 1974 (http://www.asimovonline.com/oldsite/future_of_humanity.html).

2. Gary Westfahl writes a considerable exposition on the etymology of the term "science fiction" in his *Cosmic Engineers: A Study of Hard Science Fiction* (Westport, CT: Greenwood, 1996).

3. Orson Scott Card, *Masterpieces: The Best Science Fiction of the Century* (New York: Ace, 2004).

4. Taken from a conversation with David A. Kirby at the Annual Meeting of the British Society for the History of Science at Manchester, U.K., July 2007. Kirby has an essay in this collection.

5. Thierry Bardini, *Bootstrapping: Douglas Engelbart, Coevolution, and the Origins of Personal Computing* (Stanford, CA: Stanford University Press, 2000).

6. Theodor H. Nelson, *Dream Machines/Computer Lib* (Redmond, WA: Tempus, 1987; original copyright 1974).

7. Nelson, *Computer Lib,* page 16.

8. Nelson, *Dream Machines,* page 125.

9. Sherry Turkle, *The Second Self: Computers and the Human Spirit* (New York: Simon and Schuster, 1984).

10. The two books are Sherry Turkle (ed.), *Falling for Science: Objects in Mind* (Cambridge, MA: MIT Press, 2008) and Sherry Turkle (ed.), *The Inner History of Devices* (Cambridge, MA: MIT Press, 2008).

11. Turkle, *Falling,* p. 134.

12. *Falling,* p. 156.

13. Turkle, *Inner History,* p. 36.

14. *Inner History,* p. 148.

15. *Inner History,* p. 65.

16. *Inner History,* p. 71. It would be interesting to explore ideas of exaggerated masculinity with my mostly male computer science students and how they view the user of the technology they create.

17. This *New York World-Telegram* quote is taken from the back cover of Robert A. Heinlein, *The Rolling Stones* (New York: Ace, 1952).

18. From an article by Evan Ratliff including an interview with John Hanke, the director of Google Earth, in *Wired,* "Google Maps Is Changing the Way We See the World," June 26, 2007 (http://www.wired.com/techbiz/it/magazine/15-07/ff_maps?currentPage=all). Interestingly, one of the co-founders partially dismissed the suggestion. See the web page of Avi Bar-Zeev, one of the co-founders of Keyhole, the maker of the program Earthviewer, which became Google Earth (http://www.realityprime.com/2006/07/24/notes-on-the-origin-of-google-earth).

19. Scott Rosenberg, *Dreaming in Code* (New York: Crown, 2007), page 86.

20. Vernor Vinge and James Frenkel, *True Names: And the Opening of the Cyberspace Frontier* (New York: Tor, 2001).

21. David G. Stork (ed.), *HAL's Legacy: 2001's Computer as Dream and Reality* (Cambridge, MA: MIT Press, 1997).

22. Richard Stallman quoted in an article by Annalee Newitz in *Salon,* May 26, 2000 (http://www.salon.com/technology/feature/2000/05/26/free_love).

23. Eric S. Raymond, *The Cathedral and the Bazaar: Musings on Linux and Open Source by*

an Accidental Revolutionary (Cambridge, MA: O'Reilly, 2001). Also see http://www.first monday.org/issues/issue3_3/raymond/.

24. Raymond Kurzweil's work on the Singularity can be found in many locations including his *The Age of Spiritual Machines: When Computers Exceed Human Intelligence* (New York: Viking/Penguin, 1999).

25. Bill Joy, "Why the Future Doesn't Needs Us," *Wired,* April 2000. (http://www.wired.com/wired/archive/8.04/joy.html).

26. Frederick Brooks is cited on page 64 of *Dreaming in Code* by Scott Rosenberg. *The Mythical Man-Month* was published in 1975 by Addison-Wesley.

Works Cited

Asimov, Isaac, and Janet Jeppson Asimov. *It's Been a Good Life.* Amherst, NY: Prometheus, 2002.

Bardini, Thierry. *Bootstrapping: Douglas Engelbart, Coevolution, and the Origins of Personal Computing.* Standford, CA: Stanford University Press, 2000.

Card, Orson Scott. *Masterpieces: The Best Science Fiction of the Century.* New York: Ace, 2004.

Frenkel, James, and Vernor Vinge. *True Names: And the Opening of the Cyberspace Frontier.* New York: Tor, 2001.

Hanke, John. Quoted in an article by Evan Ratliff in *Wired,* "Google Maps Is Changing the Way We See the World," June 26, 2007.

Heinlein, Robert A. *The Rolling Stones.* New York: Ace, 1952.

Joy, Bill. "Why the Future Doesn't Need Us," *Wired,* April 2000 (http://www.wired.com/wired/archive/8.04/joy.html).

Kirby, David A. Conversation at the Annual Meeting of the British Society for the History of Science at Manchester, U.K., July 2007.

Kurzweil, Raymond. *The Age of Spiritual Machines: When Computers Exceed Human Intelligence.* New York: Viking/Penguin, 1999.

Nelson, Theodor H. *Dream Machines/Computer Lib.* Redmond, WA: Tempus, 1987 (1974).

Raymond, Eric S. *The Cathedral and the Bazaar: Musings on Linux and Open Source by an Accidental Revolutionary.* Cambridge, MA: O'Reilly, 2001.

Rosenberg, Scott. *Dreaming in Code.* New York: Crown, 2007.

Stallman, Richard. Quoted in an article by Annalee Newitz in *Salon,* May 26, 2000.

Stork, David G. (ed.), *HAL's Legacy: 2001's Computer as Dream and Reality.* Cambridge, MA: MIT Press, 1997.

Turkle, Sherry. *The Second Self: Computers and the Human Spirit.* New York: Simon and Schuster, 1984.

Westfahl, Gary. *Cosmic Engineers: A Study of Hard Science Fiction.* Westport, CT: Greenwood, 1996.

1

Technology's Other Storytellers: Science Fiction as History of Technology

Thomas Haigh

More than twenty years ago John Staudenmaier helped to codify the concerns, themes and vocabulary of the history of technology in *Technology's Storytellers*.[1] The same title could, perhaps more obviously, be applied to science fiction writers. So as I immersed myself in the historical literature I was surprised by how infrequently historians invoked works of science fiction as evidence of cultural attitudes towards technology. Nothing says more about a society than its imagined futures. But instead we reach for more respectable cultural figures: Marcel Duchamp, Charlie Chaplin, Mark Twain. Neither is science fiction relevant merely as a window onto the technological unconsciousness during various periods. Science fiction writers themselves turn out to have a considerable self-awareness regarding the historical dimensions of their work, and some critics of science fiction have begun to situate the internal development of science fiction within the broader technological, cultural, and social histories of the western world.

Hidden Kinships Between Science Fiction and the History of Technology

What does science fiction have to do with the history of technology? Both are marginal within their broader fields, tend to be written by people with technical training, and are often the subject of special pleading for unique critical standards. Both fields create narratives of technological change, showing

13

the consequences of the invention and adoption of technologies on social worlds. Both require their authors to build worlds as well as stories.

The kind of science fiction I am concerned with here is work within a self-conscious genre, in which readers, writers, editors, and publishers share a set of expectations about fictional futures.[2] Within this genre aspiring writers are often told that every science fiction story begins with a question, posed in the form "What if?" Ask "What if we lived in a two-dimensional world?" and answer this by writing *Flatland*.[3] Ask "What if the stars were only visible every few thousand years?" and write *Nightfall*.[4] You get the idea. This genre existed in a relatively well-defined and tightly demarcated form in the United States from the 1930s into the 1970s. Of course, aspects of the genre can be traced back further, sometimes as far as classical Greece.[5] Utopian fiction has a long tradition, and key elements of the science fiction narrative have been identified in Mary Shelly's *Frankenstein* and the "scientific romances" of H. G. Wells.[6]

At first blush the questions asked by the historian of technology seem to be quite different. We tend to ask "How did this technology/device/system come to be the way it is, and how has it been shaped by society and in turn reshaped it?" But implicit in that question, and lurking behind it, is the realization that things could have been otherwise. Only the awareness of an implied counterfactual narrative makes histories of technology more than pedantic chronicles of inevitable progression. So just behind the surface are always questions about "Why didn't," and those really are just questions of "What if" posed in a different way. "Why didn't we stick with gas-powered refrigerators?" asked Ruth Schwartz Cowan.[7] Why didn't DC power establish itself as the standard for electrical power networks?[8] Why didn't Betamax crush VHS?[9] These questions only exist because we appreciate historical contingency, the idea that things might have been other than how they are.

Science fiction writers have knowingly been drawn toward historical models and to the idea, no longer fashionable among academic historians, that the mechanics of historical change can be captured in laws, cycles, or grand theories. Ken MacLeod, one of the most successful science fiction writers to emerge in the past twenty years, has argued that "History remains the trade secret of SF... its influence is quite pervasive, among writers and readers alike.... History is an inexhaustible source of plots, and an indispensable map of the way in which societies work and how they can change." He notes particularly the popularity of cyclical notions of history, historical materialism, and the obvious modeling of classics such as Isaac Asimov's *Foundation* series and Frank Herbert's *Dune* saga on actual historical models.[10]

Science fiction writers and historians are both world builders, working with words as their only tools. Science fiction writers savor this as one of the defining characteristics of their genre. They construct not just a plot, characters, events, and the other furnishings of a "mainstream" novel but also fabricate the universe in which it takes place. This may be almost imperceptibly different from our present day reality or unrecognizably so. These differences usually involve developments in society as a result of technological change.

Historians of technology are also world builders. We, too, produce narratives in which the world is changed by (or, as technological determinism is far from fashionable, with) new technologies. Historians, like science fiction writers, are encouraged to create a strong narrative and integrate background material seamlessly within it. As we conduct our craft we are selecting sources from an almost infinite array, arranging them with great care, drawing out particular themes, demarcating certain individuals or social groups as actors, defining technologies in a particular way, writing with a particular intellectual agenda in mind, and in countless other ways constructing a unique world in which our story takes place.

This world is, of course, constrained by evidence of the past. Historians are expected to work fairly and cautiously in reconstructing lost worlds. Reading science fiction trains us in one of the crucial cognitive skills needed to research the history of technology. In early science fiction stories the details of each imagined universe were often conveyed in authorial asides or lengthy passages of stilted dialog in which characters informed each other of what they already knew. But soon the "infodump" was disparaged. Writers discovered ways of smoothly dropping hints about the operating principles of a future world into the narrative itself. Samuel R. Delaney, a writer turned critic, has argued that the interpretation of these hints is a crucial skill acquired by science fiction readers.[11] He takes as a paradigm a short sentence by Robert A. Heinlein: "The door dilated." Encountering such a bizarre statement an unprepared reader might miss its significance or become frustrated. The science fiction reader pauses to ask "What would the world have to be like for this statement to make sense?"[12]

Historians are charged with a similar task of reverse engineering the subjective world of our historical subjects from records of what they said, did, and wrote. Novelist L.P. Hartley famously wrote that "The past is a foreign country. They do things differently there." A reader of science fiction might replace "foreign country" with "alien world." We read our primary sources for clues about the world in which they take place. They serve as evidence for vital questions: how did these people understand their world and their place within it; what expectations did they have regarding a technology; what existing models did they use to understand new technologies. A classic example of this is Carlo Ginzberg's *The Worms and the Cheese,* which reconstructs the cosmos as understood by a sixteenth-century miller from his statements as recorded in the official records of the inquisition.[13]

Science fiction writers of the Golden Age (the late 1940s and 1950s) tended to have backgrounds, and often advanced degrees, in science or engineering. Isaac Asimov, for example, earned a Ph.D. while writing his early stories and was already tenured at Boston University before finally giving up his career in biochemistry to write full time. Likewise pioneering historians of technology were often engineers approaching the field as an avocational interest. While subsequent generations of scholars have usually earned Ph.D.s in history, or some variant thereof, an undergraduate degree in engineering or computer science is still a common qualification. Both populations used to be almost exclusively male, and are now merely predominantly male. Both are interested in technology yet able, unlike many engineers, to write coherently and reasonably engagingly about it.

Finally, both science fiction and the history of technology have strained relationships with their parent fields. Science fiction fans are often dismissive of the pleasures of what they call "mainstream" literature, and many adult readers of high- or even middle-brow fiction regard science fiction as fit only for teenagers and the emotionally stunted. Some critics within the genre argue that for a work of science fiction to be great it must also be a great work of fiction. They apply the same expectations for prose style, depth of characterization, and elegance of plotting to works within the genre as to those filed by chain bookstores in the category of "literature."[14] Others engage in special pleading. They argue that science fiction is inherently different from other kinds of fiction, and cannot therefore be held to the same terms.[15] The mission of world building is different from that of other writers. Since the 1970s science fiction has become more respectable, and a large and fairly well-defined body of "literary" science fiction has emerged. Meanwhile ideas, devices, and sensibilities from science fiction have increasingly appeared in the work of "literary" writers, creating a liminal body of literature dubbed "slipstream," populated by lauded writers such as Don DeLillo, Thomas Pynchon, and Steve Erickson.[16]

The history of technology has internalized a similar tension. The creation myth of the Society for the History of Technology relates a split from the History of Science Society when the latter refused to treat technology as important. As the field developed its practitioners aspired to incorporate the techniques and concerns of higher status historical scholarship, just as the science fiction writers of the 1970s sought literary respectability. Technology (and its euphemistic twin "material culture") have won some legitimacy as objects of historical study among what I have sometimes heard people call "mainstream historians." Yet the history of technology remains a rather insular field, despite efforts by many of its leaders to increase its diversity and import (often with a time lag of a decade or two) concerns from social and cultural history. Others argue that the history of technology has unique concerns, shaped by its early alliance with museums and industrial archeology, and that these must be preserved.[17] As in science fiction, this debate began in the 1970s and has shifted in favor of those seeking more integration.

But What About the Future?

Let us not ignore the obvious difference between these two enterprises. Most science fiction is ostensibly about the future. Indeed, it is this concern with the future as a locale that sets works of genre science fiction aside from earlier traditions. Exotic locations were distanced more often by space rather than time in the works of authors such as Jules Verne, Sir Arthur Conan Doyle, Edgar Allan Poe, and H.G. Wells. In contrast, claims to apply science and predict what lies ahead were made in the 1920s for the new genre of "Scientifiction" by its creator Hugo Gernsback (who consequently seems to many of science fiction's more literary-minded critics more a mad uncle confined in its literary attic than a founding father). These claims were retained and reinforced by John W. Campbell, who as editor of *Astounding Science Fiction* exerted tremendous influence over the work and careers of the leading science fiction writers of the 1940s. Science fiction fans believed that they were getting a head start on readers of less imaginative work. They agreed with celebrity inventor Charles Kettering when he said that "we should all be greatly concerned about the future and try to make it the best possible. For ... it is where we are all going to spend the rest of our lives."[18] General Motors, Kettering's employer, endorsed a science fiction view of the future with its famous Futurama exhibit at the 1939 World's Fair.

Sometimes science fiction writers scored with a technical prediction or two. Robert A. Heinlein, for example, believed himself to have invented the waterbed and described one in his 1942 novel *Beyond This Horizon*.[19] As we know, the waterbed was an essential item for the swinging bachelor of the 1970s. Score one for science fiction! Likewise Arthur C. Clarke claimed to have published (in 1945)[20] the first proposal for a geosynchronous communications satellite, and John Brunner described a self-replicating "tapeworm" program in 1975 to inspire the creation of computer worms in the real world. Atomic technology remains science fiction's proudest accomplishment as a literature of prediction. *Astounding Science Fiction* ran a series of editorials and stories featuring atomic power and atomic weapons. In 1944 Campbell received a visit from Army intelligence officers after publishing a story that happened to have some technical elements in common with the top secret Manhattan Project.[21]

But science fiction was never really about the future. By the 1960s science fiction writers themselves were becoming uncomfortable with the idea that they were charged with predicting the future. Space travel had left the pages of pulp magazines and arrived in the newspapers. It proved something of a disappointment, particularly for the group of writers gathering in Britain under the banner of "New Wave" science fiction. They rejected claims for the genre's powers of prediction along with its faith in technological progress and fascination with gadgets and machines.[22] J.G. Ballard mocked the iconography of the space program, and called for the examination of "inner space." Brian W. Aldiss baldly stated, "It is part of SF's gaudy misleading label that it predicts."[23] His fellow writer Gwyneth Jones agrees. She has written that science fiction "more than any other literary genre ... reflects the exact preoccupation of the present." The future invoked

> has to be as close as possible to a future which is seen as likely or relevant by most people at the time of writing. Otherwise nobody will think it is any good. Thus, the very books that seem to critics and audience the most intelligent, most exciting, the most uncannily accurate future-guessing, become ten years later the most dated — providing merely an *uncannily accurate* reverse image of the year in which they were written. Tell me what you think is going to happen tomorrow, and I'll tell you what is happening to you today."[24]

Critic John Clute used a similar logic to suggest the concept of a "real decade" in which a story takes place.

> Sometimes, reading a novel, one is able to play a game with the thing. Disregarding the ostensible date of the narrative, which may of course be anywhere at all, one can try to estimate the real decade in which the story is set. This real decade will be the period most nearly reflected by the book's characters in their feelings about the proper relationship between the sexes, for instance, or about the threat of international communism, or about how great an economic sway should be exercised (across the galaxy) by entrepreneurial capitalism, or about the inevitability of man's victory over the stars in their courses.... It is of course a fundamental rule of this game that no sf novel ... can be actually set in the future ... [in fact] sf novels tend to be set much further into the past than most 'mainstream' non-generic novels.[25]

To focus on the occasional widget described in science fiction shortly before its appearance in the real world is therefore to miss the obliviousness of most science fiction writers to the social and cultural developments not just of the future (which is hardly their fault) but of their own times. As Clute observed, science fiction is often more dated in this way than work in other genres. Despite his success with the waterbed I'd date most of Heinlein to 1890 and the remainder to about 1938. Heinlein knitted many of his stories into the grandly titled "Future History" series, presented with a table summarizing humanity's political, cultural, and technical progress over several thousand years. But Heinlein's futures have a distinctly nineteenth-century feel. He never accepted the rise of big government and big science in the Cold War period. He didn't really seem to approve of big business, either. In Heinlein's future (given in the 1950 story "The Man Who Sold the Moon") the moon landings are accomplished in 1978, not by the military-industrial-academic complex that brought us the Apollo program, but by an entrepreneurial hustler and "robber baron" who finances the project via schemes such as designating the rocket as a post office so that stamps can be cancelled on the moon and sold to collectors.

Yet Heinlein's future worlds remain a fascinating window onto our real past. He retains a considerable libertarian following, and is famous for his free-market, small-government ideas. But reading him today one is struck by the divergence of his thought from current political assumptions. Some of his work is much as one would expect. Heinlein was clearly unhappy with much of the New Deal and in "The Roads Must Roll" (1940) he presents unionized workers as the irrational dupes of populist agitators.[26] *Beyond This Horizon,* one of his first novels, describes a near utopia with considerable crossover appeal to readers of Ayn Rand. Men are expected to carry guns. Insults lead rapidly to deadly duels, which Heinlein suggests are very effective as a means of encouraging social harmony ("an armed society is a polite society"). Yet, lurking incongruously in this libertarian paradise is the Department of Finance, in which sits a "huge integrating accumulator." Every economic transaction in North and South America is encoded onto holes punched onto paper tape inside each "auto-clerk." The data, suitable aggregated, is constantly fed into this special-purpose machine, which in turn manipulates subsidies, adjusts government allowances, and makes other economic tweaks necessary to "make the production-consumption cycle come out even."[27] His ruggedly individualistic duelists are also big government Keynesians who have surrendered monetary and financial policy to a giant machine run by unelected experts. Suddenly one gains an appreciation for the wrenching shock the Great Depression gave Heinlein's generation and the enormous amount of intellectual and cultural work done in the decades since to make personal freedom and macroeconomic deregulation appear inseparable.

Science Fiction as Historical Literature

History is all about what already happened. So the historian and the science fiction writer might seem to be the two heads of Janus. One stares at the past, and tries to imagine how it might have been different and why it wasn't. The other stares at the future, and wonders how it will be. In fact historians tend to be exceptionally wary about making predictions. This is because we tend to regularly come across old predictions from marketers, futurologists, pundits, economists, and politicians and are aware that they are almost invariably wrong.

Yet upon closer examination even this apparent reversal of temporal polarity turns out to bring the two genres together. Kim Stanley Robinson has argued that science fiction is "an historical literature." He notes that in any work of science fiction "there is an explicit or implicit fictional history that connects the period depicted to our present moment or to some moment of our past." Thus science fiction and historical fiction "are more alike, in some respects, than either is like the literary mainstream ... both are concerned with alien cultures, and with estrangement."[28] Similarly, Istvan Csicsery-Ronay included future history as one of his "seven beauties" of science fiction in his book of that title, noting that "by maintaining a sense of the integral connections between the present and the future, sf constructs micromyths of the historical process." He observes that "unlike real prophecies, SF's are narrated in the past tense. They don't pretend to predict a future, but to explain a future past."[29]

This relationship is most obviously true in the case of alternate history stories, science fiction set prior to the year in which it is written. These tend to hinge on wars and battles: worlds in which the Nazis won the Second World War, the South did not lose the Civil War, or the Spanish Armada brought an early end to the English Reformation. Harry Turtledove, one of the most successful writers of alternate history, had clarified the relationship of this kind of fiction with other science fiction.

> Both [alternate history and science fiction] seek to extrapolate logically a change from the world as we know it. Most forms of science fiction posit a change in the present or nearer future and imagine its effect on the more distant future. Alternate history, on the other hand, imagines a change in the more distant past and examines its consequence for the nearer past and the present. The technique is the same in both cases; the difference is when in time it is applied.[30]

When, as it often is, this change is technological, the result is a sense of history which resonates with Marx's sense of historical materialism, shown in his famous suggestion that "The windmill gives you society with the feudal lord: the steam-mill, society with the industrial capitalist."[31] Darko Suvin, a pioneering Marxist critic of science fiction, has posited the "novum" as a defining element of science fiction. In the words of Csicsery-Ronay, this is

> the historical innovation or novelty in an SF text from which the most important distinctions between the world of the tale from the world of the reader stem.... In practice, the novum appears as an invention or discovery around which the characters and setting organize themselves in a cogent, historically plausible way. The novum is a product of material processes.[32]

This is an interesting position to take, as historians of technology have increasingly stigmatized the idea of "technological determinism" by which social changes take place inevitably in response to an external process of invention and discovery.[33] Science fiction writers, in contrast, like to present their imagined universes as the inevitable result of a particular development or set of developments. This illusion of inevitability helps readers to, in the famous phrase, suspend their disbelief in the fictional world.

Computers in Golden-Age Science Fiction

The absurdity of science fiction as a literature of prediction, and its merit as a genre of historical writing, can be seen particularly clear in its treatment of computing. Computers show up in science fiction in the early 1950s, mirroring their arrival in the real world. The computers of the 1940s and early 1950s were slow, unreliable, and massive machines based around clicking relays and glowing tubes. They were used primarily for scientific calculation. Science fiction writers, even those with scientific backgrounds who prided themselves on their skills as prognosticators, generally depict the computers of the future in very much the same way. Consider the early appearances of computers in the work of Asimov, Heinlein, and Clarke — three prolific authors of short stories during the Golden Age of magazine science fiction in the 1940s who established themselves as bestselling authors of science fiction books as that market emerged in the 1950s.

Computers were unknown in Asimov's best-known work of this era, the *Foundation Trilogy* (originally published from 1942 to 1950).[34] Fifty thousand years from now scientists have achieved some miracles of miniaturization, including shrinking nuclear reactors to the size of walnuts for use in atomic-powered dishwashers and personal force fields. But they don't seem to have invented computers. A separate stream of stories explored the three laws of robotics, depicting the development of ever more intelligent and human-like machines powered by the rather nebulous technology of "positronic brains." Robots are common but computers remain very rare; a handful of "thinking machines" with "super robot brains" are used for economic control and scientific research. Asimov also wrote, from 1955 onward, a handful of stories concerned with a giant computer named Multivac, built with vacuum tubes and buried deep underground. This machine too fits the "giant brain" paradigm, and comes eventually to rule the world.[35]

Clarke, like Asimov, was a successful writer of popular science and journalistic futurology as well as an outstandingly successful writer of science fiction. Nobody in the 1950s knew high technology or the future better. Yet Clarke's computers are similarly bulky. In his 1960 story "Into the Comet" a spaceship faces disaster after its room-sized onboard computer malfunctions. Calculating the course for Earth would take "a hundred thousand separate calculations," seemingly impossible to carry out by hand when the computer was "a million times faster." Fortunately, a reporter on board had a Japanese grandfather and thus remembers more traditional calculating practices. He launches a successful effort to equip each crew member with an abacus and a part of the complex calculation.[36] Clarke's novel *A Fall of Moondust* (1961), set in a mid–twenty-first century which men have walked on Pluto and tour buses ply the moon, describes a computer as "a handful of cells and microscopic relays."[37] Relays had, as Clarke was writing, long since given way to vacuum tubes as the building blocks of computer logic. Tubes themselves were being replaced by transistors.

Heinlein's stories from this era made an effort to keep up to date with current developments in computing, but did little to significantly extrapolate any continued development. Again this was a notable contrast with his assumption of rapid developments in space travel. In 1947 he published "Space Jockey" in the *Saturday Evening Post,* giving its broad readership a depiction of a typical day in the life of a rocket pilot of the mid–1980s. Heinlein expected regular commercial flights to Lunar City within a decade of the initial moon landing. Responsibility for navigational calculations lay with a man identified as a "computer" (a usage soon to vanish in the real world).

> When the Skysprite locked in with Supra–New York, Pemberton went to the station's stellar navigation room. He was pleased to find Shorty Weinstein, the computer, on duty. Jake trusted Shorty's computations — a good thing when your ship, your passengers, and your own skin depend thereon. Pemberton had to be a better than average mathematician himself in order to be a pilot; his own limited talent made him appreciate the genius of those who computed the orbits.

Calculating routine commercial flight paths remained a matter for human virtuosity. Shorty did not work entirely without electronic assistance though, as some undefined contribution was made by "Mable, the giant astrogation computer filling the far wall." Pemberton's in-flight course corrections were limited because "his little Marchant electronic calculator was no match for the tons of IBM computer at Supra–New York, nor was he Weinstein."

Likewise, Heinlein's novel (1957) shows ship-to-ship space combat in the distant future conducted with fire control computers very similar to those used in World War II, but with a simulation capacity and the ability to record data similar to that then being advertised for the cutting edge SAGE system. Heinlein remained committed to the giant computer paradigm well into the 1960s, even as minicomputers began to proliferate. In *The Moon*

Is a Harsh Mistress (1966) a major lunar city apparently holds just one computer, Mike.[38]

> In May 2075, besides controlling robot traffic and catapult and giving ballistic advice and/or control for manned ships, Mike controlled phone system for all Luna, same for Luna-Terra voice & video, handled air, water, temperature, humidity, and sewage for Luna City, Novy Leningrad, and several smaller warrens (not Hong Kong in Luna), did accounting and payrolls for Luna Authority, and, by lease, same for many firms and banks.

Computers in science fiction had settled down into a comfortable pattern. In physical appearance and interface style they generally resembled those in the real world. On the other hand they frequently developed intelligence. This generally took place spontaneously, as an accidental result of their increasing complexity. (That is in itself an interesting departure from the pattern with space and atomic technologies: in science fiction warp drives and nuclear reactors were usually the result of research and experimentation). Science fiction writers embraced the idea of the computer as a giant disembodied brain, functioning as an oracle to be questioned. (The same idea can be seen in cartoons well into the 1980s.) Robots had been around in SF long before the computer, but were now understood to incorporate, or be controlled remotely by, some form of computer. Giant computers continued to oppress mankind into the 1970s and beyond. [39]

This lack of engagement with computers within science fiction was particularly odd given the importance of the future to the computer industry. Real world discussion of computers was inextricably bound up with the conventions and assumptions of science fiction. Since the 1940s computer technology has been characterized by rapid obsolescence and abrupt change. New ideas and fads were promoted with predictions of the near future in which the technology or approach in question (for example, management information systems, bubble memory, or timeshared computer access on a public utility model) has become ubiquitous. Moore's Law provided a self-fulfilling prophecy of rapid technological advance in the capabilities of semiconductors. By the late 1970s personal computers were selling by the million and a thriving home computer industry had emerged. Widespread speculation over the impact on the near future of the "microcomputer revolution" and the shape of the "information society" drove product developments, political policies, and educational initiatives. Parents purchased computers to make sure that their children had the "computer literacy" needed to survive in this new world. Yet the actual science fiction writers of the 1970s lagged behind this broader discourse, even as industry leaders, politicians, market research analysts, futurologists and journalists embraced the techniques and sensibilities of science fiction to promote the idea of a world remade by computers.

The Old-Timey Future: "First SF"

The science fiction future remained, into the 1980s, a place where information technology had little direct influence on the lives of ordinary people. It gradually developed from something that at least claimed to be a good-faith attempt to predict the actual development of technology and society into a backdrop and set of symbols as familiar and comforting as that of the western or popular romance. Or rather, it had developed into a set of instantly identifiable generic futures. There was the post-apocalypse survivalist future, the galactic empire space opera future, the robot uprising future, and (perhaps most ubiquitous of all) the gee-whiz 1950s Jetsons future. Science fiction images and aesthetics, once confined to obscure magazines and books, have permeated popular culture. A host of technologies are instantly identifiable as futuristic: flying cars, domestic robot servants, jet packs, virtual reality helmets, meals ingested in pill form. Nobody necessarily believes any more that these things will ever be commonplace, but they remain part of The Future nonetheless.

Again John Clute has captured the essence of this.

> American genre SF began around 1925 ... and it entered the valley of the shadow around 1975 though its flashier icons only came to dominate popular culture after the kind of SF that created them had begun to die ... tall tales of the future as a platform we could pass into, a frontier we could pierce, an unknown we could domesticate. What this central spine or braid of American SF said for 50 years was that the future was us, and that it worked.[40]

Clute has used the term "First SF" to describe the genre defined by this consensus.[41] Since 1980, Clute believes, "the relationship between SF and the world" had "altered ... almost out of all recognition. The genre which differed from the world in order to advocate a better one" had become simply "an institution for the telling of story." Much science fiction continued to be "a set of stories about the American Dream," written from the viewpoint of the industrialized Western world in which science, progress, the control of nature and the "taming of alien people on other worlds" were unquestioned. This meant that "there is a decreasing resemblance between the world we inhabit today" and the still popular vision of the future traditionally found in science fiction. Clute feels that the First SF future "was deeply loved, even after it had become a kind of historical fiction, a form of defensive nostalgia in the minds of many."[42] Science fiction's failure to get to grips with computers, Clute believed, was the single most important reason for the obsolescence of its collective vision. Writers had "almost deliberately, ignored the transistor" and "described computers in terms of bulk rather than invisible intricacies." Thus, with the rise of the Internet, "sf as a set of arguments and conventions ... had been blindsided by the future."[43]

But, as Clute noted, elements of the First SF future have passed into the cultural mainstream. In 1942 Isaac Asimov had to carefully explain his "jump drive" as an enabling technology for galactic empire. By 1977 George Lucas could just have Hans Solo announce a "jump to light speed," blur some stars to mark its entry and exit from hyperspace, and deliver the Millennium Falcon promptly to its destination without attempting any further explanation (which is just as well, as light actually takes a very long time to move between solar systems from the viewpoint of those not moving at relativistic speeds). Recent shows such as *Battlestar Galactica* and *Firefly* have likewise relied on our common knowledge that starships have engines that propel them with great rapidity over interstellar distances. We know this without being told, just as we know that vampires need to be staked through the heart and leprechauns should not be trusted.

There's another reason the First SF future seems so familiar. We are living in it. Scientists and engineers grew up reading the stuff, and have done their best to bring its promises to life. Our ubiquitous array of electronic gadgets have been styled after and inspired by their science fiction counterparts. Cell phones were styled directly after the communicators in *Star Trek*. Recent graphical user interfaces, iPods, and the glowing lights and dials found in modern cars all betray the influence of science fiction aesthetics. Thomas M. Disch captured this phenomenon brilliantly when he called a book of reflections on science fiction *The Dreams Our Stuff Is Made Of: How Science Fiction Conquered the World*.[44]

Cyberpunk: The Newish Future

The cyberpunk movement of the 1980s was, deliberately and self-consciously, an attempt to update the increasingly obsolete future of First SF with the technologies and attitudes of the electronic age. Its breakthrough achievement, William Gibson's *Neuromancer,* embraced personal computers, brand-name fashion, and portable media players. Unmistakably a product of its decade, the book mirrored the unexpected rise of Japan as the superpower of personal electronics and the video glitz of MTV. Indeed, while several puns have been discerned in its title I have always fancied that another can be found there: "New Romantic" was a term used by music journalists to describe the colorful fashions, heavy makeup, and asymmetric haircuts of electronic pop bands such as Spandau Ballet, Ultravox, and Japan.[45]

Science fiction plots are often crude, sharing with comic books an interest in stories of individuals transcending to states of superhuman mastery. But even First SF stories less blatantly invested in teenage wish fulfillment tend to be written from the viewpoint of the creators and masters of large-scale technologies. Heinlein's heroes, often dubbed by critics "competent men," were masters of their fate.[46] They could wield a slide rule, program a computer, patent an invention, or patch a space suit. They were prone to philosophize at length on the manly importance of controlling one's fate with such skills, and had little sympathy for those unable or unwilling to thrive in a frontier situation. One of the most popular science fiction short stories of all time, "The Cold Equations" by Tom Godwin, sets up a situation in which the reader is led to identify with its protagonist as he explains to a sweet, silly "girl" looking for "an exciting adventure" who has hidden in his little spaceship that her willful ignorance of the laws of physics means she will need to throw herself out of the airlock without a space suit if their vital humanitarian mission is to succeed.[47]

In contrast, Gibson borrowed from film noir the idea of the protagonist as a small-time, marginal figure who blunders through secret conspiracies and the machinations of the powerful and corrupt with little idea of what is actually going on. They are not world shakers or history makers. David Langford summarized this elegantly in his review of the anthology *Burning Chrome*, noting that the title story is "that one about the young punks who get hold of a .45 and try the big heist, only Gibson's punks are computer jockeys and the .45 is a Russian military killer program."[48] *Neuromancer*'s convoluted plot echoes that of the film noir classic *The Big Sleep*. In both cases what endures in your mind is not the precise detail of the complex series of double-crosses and revelations but the general sensation of perverted conspiracy among the privileged overwhelming the cynicism of a small time protagonist who fancied himself street-smart. When noir heroes are foolish enough to make a moral stand, they generally make a bad situation worse (most notably in the nuclear explosion at the end of the film *Kiss Me Deadly*). Darko Suvin noted that "there is a real rebellion in the best of Gibson; there is sympathy for the little people."[49] This mirrors the shift of academic history during the 1970s and 1980s toward the social history, characterized by an interest in representative experiences, neglected perspectives, and a skepticism towards the idea that historical change is driven by the decisions of great men. E. P. Thompson, one of the founders of the "new social history," called this approach "history from the bottom up."

Cyberpunk represented a shift from the producers of technology to its users, and from the massive, thundering technologies of the space age to the more personal technologies of consumer electronics. Gibson did not write from any position of special technical expertise, but rather as a consumer of technology and someone with an eye for popular culture. He wrote that "the Street finds its own uses for things — uses the manufacturers never imagined.... While science fiction is sometimes good at predicting things, it's seldom good at predicting what those things might actually do to us."[50] Gibson understood that the VCR, the home computer, and the Walkman had a much more profound impact on our daily lives than the Apollo Program ever did. His imagined technologies of implants and genetic engineering turned technology inward, remaking the human body itself.[51] This shift parallels the development, around the same time, among historians of technology of a new appreciation for users and for the technologies of everyday life.

Indeed, Gibson knew little about computers or networking when he wrote *Neuromancer,* composing it on an antique Hermes manual typewriter. Its characters "jack in" to an immersive virtual world known as "the matrix." This involves a piece of consumer electronics known as "a deck" with which they have the same kind of relationship as a fanatical biker with his motorcycle. Gibson snows us with brands and model numbers. He implies that decks can be tinkered with like old cars or stereos but never really tries to explain them. All we know is that they are connected, for best results, directly to some kind of interface implanted in the head of the user. Given the enormous power of this network connection it came as a shock to Gibson's more computer savvy readers when the book's hero, facing a particularly tricky situation while jacked into the matrix, asks his companion to hand him a modem.[52] Compare this with another influential early treatment of what would soon be called virtual reality: Vernor Vinge's novella *True Names.* There are similar elements: conspiracy, a powerful network, a rogue artificial intelligence, and connection via brain electrodes to a network known as "the Portal." As a mathematics professor and computer expert Vinge could document baud rates and give a detailed account of hopping around his futuristic network from bulletin board to satellite relay to dusty ARPANet facility. He even creates a plot excuse to have his protagonist use a simple textual user interface. But Vinge's technology has dated faster than Gibson's, so the now obsolete verisimilitude of his technology provides an odd contrast with the implausibility of his actual plot (an old fashioned confection of spontaneous superhuman transcendence in the service of a world-shaking battle between good and evil).

During cyberpunk's brief career as an active literary movement its chief propagandist was Bruce Sterling. His *Schizmatrix,* the other seminal novel of the cyberpunk movement, provides a similarly bracing challenge to the historical assumptions of First SF as it blends cyberpunk ideas and aesthetics with the sweeping interplanetary settings. Sterling's novel follows the life of one man, Abelard Lindsay, across several hundred eventful years. As in much of the science fiction of the 1950s, for example, Heinlein's early work, the solar system has been colonized and political intrigues have factionalized humanity. And like a Heinlein hero, Lindsay is implausibly capable, excelling as a political leader, theatre promoter, diplomat, businessman, professor, explorer and pirate. The technologies are different of course. Pretty much everyone has transformed their minds and bodies, and the main ideological issue driving the book's wars is whether this is best accomplished via computer implants or genetic engineering. Lindsay himself comes to espouse the "posthumanist" cause. But what strikes me most about the book is its sense of the fragility of history, the tendency of nations and eras to collapse and shatter the dreams of even the superhuman. Wars rage hot and cold, aliens arrive, economies boom and bust, ideologies wax and wane, states are founded and fall. All that is solid melts into air, again and again. This view of history might seem intuitive to someone from Central Europe. It was not, however, well represented in American science fiction. In First SF heroes overthrow existing political orders, struggling at the beginning of the story but eventually imposing happy endings on mankind as part of a superhuman destiny. Lindsay strives but, resourceful as he is, often fails and is forced to begin again as a refugee. As he notes, towards the end of the book, "Nations don't last in this era. Only people last, only plans and hopes."[53]

Steampunk and Retrofuturism

Since the advent of cyberpunk science fiction's once straightforward relationship with the future has crumbled, in ways that further expose the genre's rich relationship with history. Gibson's first published story, "The Gernsback Continuum," made explicit Gibson's fascination with the history of technology and the rediscovery of old futures. A freelance photographer agrees to photograph surviving examples of the futuristic architecture of the 1930s. He starts to glimpse, in the manner of characters in many Philip K. Dick novels, flashes of another reality lying beneath our own. Seeking out futuristic gas stations and crumbling factories he finds himself haunted by images of a distinctly fascist urban landscape of crystal spires, zeppelins, and silver cars. Rejecting the vision shared by Hugo Gernsback, early industrial designers, and the corporate propaganda of the 1940s, he saves himself only through immersion in the "really bad media" of the 1980s (game shows, soap operas, and porn). He chooses "the human near-dystopia we live in" over the inhuman grandiose elegance of the gleaming First SF future.

The influence of retrofuturism can be seen even in the phrase "cyberpunk" itself, so often taken as a defiant assertion of modernity. It comes from "cybernetics," a phrase coined by Norbert Wiener in the 1940s.[54] A scientific fad, cybernetics was widely discussed in the 1950s as a new metadiscipline able to unify hitherto unrelated areas of knowledge. The vocabulary and imagery of cybernetics made its way into popular culture and business by the 1960s. By the 1980s, however, cybernetics had fallen from scientific respectability and was increasingly the domain of cranks. Even within popular culture its luster had faded. Thanks to Gibson, of course, "cyberspace" birthed a new litter of cyberterms closely associated with the spread of the Internet in the 1990s.[55] But when Gibson was writing, "cyber" was slipping into the realm of the obsolete future, the charmingly obsolete.

Despite its neon sheen, Gibson's early fiction acknowledges the tiny marks history leaves all around us. The Third World War was contained, somehow, before it wiped out city life entirely. This is not the traditional radioactive wasteland but a decaying urban jungle. People function in a world of junk, navigating the wreckage of the past as they go about their futuristic business. Technological gadgets new and old are piled on the floor of shabby apartments or stuffed into the back rooms of shady establishments. In an afterword to *Neuromancer* Jack Womack notes "how many references you find therein to events or incidents that occurred at some unspecified time before the narrative begins, and to nostalgic reveries of That Which Is No Longer the Way It Was; how often his characters grow dimly aware of vague regrets for which they have no name." This, he suggests, leads Gibson to images of "evocative clutter and disarray.... The outmoded toaster ovens, the mildewed paperbacks, the scratched LPs ... detritus that accumulates in the desk's bottom drawers; the lint in the navel of a private civilization, hinting at an apocalypse that (if apocalypse at all) could have been nothing other than personal." [56] Philip K. Dick warned that kipple ("useless objects, like junk mail or match folders after you use the last match") proliferates while we sleep so that "no one can win against kipple, except temporarily and maybe in one spot."[57] First SF futures had no room for kipple. Gibson shows us what life looks like after kipple has won.

Bruce Sterling's subsequent career further demonstrates the importance of technological history to the cyberpunk sensibility. By the early 1990s cyberpunk had run its course, its once radical sensibilities having been assimilated into a new kind of communal future in which body modification, cyberspace, and petty crime were now familiar elements of genre entertainment.[58] A decade after launching cyberpunk as a movement Sterling went back to pamphleteering mode to launch a new initiative: the Dead Media Project. This title was a humorous complement to the then-fashionable term "New Media." Sterling called for "a deeper, paleontological perspective right in the dizzy midst of the digital revolution." [59] The result was an online community, powered by a website and email list, devoted to documenting obscure and forgotten media technologies such as the stereopticon, pneumatic mail tube, automatic typewriter, hectograph, and even defunct computer platforms. Perhaps fittingly, the project itself has now vanished from the net. Even *Neuromancer*'s much quoted first line "The sky above the port was the color of television, turned to a dead channel" now celebrates a dead medium. So contemporary and media-savvy when it came out, it describes an analog technology now almost extinct. Digital televisions do not show snow. Analog televisions now show nothing else, regardless of how or where the dial is turned.

The historical sensibility latent in cyberpunk became explicit in the 1990 novel *The Difference Engine* by Sterling and Gibson, a seminal work in the emerging "steampunk" genre. Steampunk works are hard to categorize, but tend to be playful work set in alternative pasts where high-technology artifacts (cloning, artificial intelligence, robots) have been created with incongruously old-fashioned means. Seizing on Charles Babbage's vision of a programmable mechanical computer, Sterling and Gibson describe a Victorian world in which steam driven calculating engines have transformed politics and society. Like most computers in science fiction they are developing self awareness. The authors have great fun with this setting, making Byron prime minister, turning America into a patchwork of little countries, and having Ada Lovelace discover what appears to be the Church-Turing thesis. As Clute observed, it is the absence of information technology that most clearly separates the First SF future from our own present. The steampunk setting allowed Sterling and Gibson to playfully amend this by inserting modern information technology into the prehistory of science fiction.

The popularity of steampunk in recent decades surely reflects changing experiences among the readers and writers of science fiction. Gibson himself has argued that a science fiction fan of his generation, coming of age reading First SF classics written twenty years earlier, had to become a kind of historian of technology to appreciate the genre. Recalling his boyhood, he writes

> I learned of science fiction and history in a single season.... Much of the science fiction I was reading, American fiction of the nineteen-forties and fifties, had already become history of a sort, requiring an acquired filter for anachronism. I studied the patent Future History timeline Robert Heinlein appended to each of his novels and noted where it began to digress from history as I was coming to know it. I filtered indigestible bits of anachronistic gristle out of this older science fiction, reverse-engineering a model of the real past through a growing understanding of what these authors had gotten wrong.[60]

Today the science fiction future lies behind us. The works of Clarke, Asimov, and Heinlein have become, to modern readers, a kind of inadvertent steampunk with their giant, self-aware vacuum tube computers and nuclear powered dishwashers. Unlike today's high-technology breakthroughs, the imagined technologies of steampunk function are on a recognizably human scale and lend themselves to creation by lone inventors or mad scientists. So the vogue for steam-powered computers is at once a mockery of First SF faith in the technological future and a reaffirmation of the genre's traditional pleasures.

A Few Recent Futures: Robinson, Banks and MacLeod

Steampunk is not, of course, the only development in science fiction's relationship to history during the quarter century since the publication of *Neuromancer.* Neither is it necessarily representative. Science fiction has, in recent decades, become increasingly diffuse. Films and television series have far more impact than novels, so science fiction fandom has boomed even as its members have drifted away from the classic works of the 1950s (or in many cases from the written word in general). Meanwhile, genre boundaries between science fiction and fantasy have largely collapsed when faced with the growing popularity of fantasy and the ever dwindling credibility of the claim that science fiction is a separate enterprise concerned with real science and rigorous extrapolation, rather than a subset of fantasy with a specialized set of props and expectations. In 2001, the Hugo award for best novel, the field's highest honor, was given to a *Harry Potter* book. Fantasies of magic won again in 2004, 2005, and 2009.[61]

Yet a brief consideration of a few of the major current authors of science fiction reveals considerable subtlety in the genre's attitude to history. Kim Stanley Robinson is one of the most respected American authors of science fiction working today. He was never associated with the cyberpunk movement but, like Gibson, is obsessed with the workings of history. His major work, the *Mars* trilogy, deals with the terraforming of Mars and its eventual independence from Earth. This is the most exhaustively detailed and plausible future history ever created, conjuring not just political and social developments but also the trajectories for developments in economics, science, and engineering. Robinson's early novel *Icehenge* is based around multiple incompatible reconstructions of future history based on the same evidence. Three of his other early novels provide a deliberately contrasting set of futures for Southern California in the mid–twenty-first century. Many of his short stories are concerned with counterfactual history and the unpredictable implications of historical agency. His recent novel *The Years of Rice and Salt* tells ten different stories over a six-hundred-year period in a world where Christianity was largely extinguished by the Black Death. Robinson's stories of future life on Mars, like his alternative history stories, are grounded in serious interest in the dynamics of historical change, the subjective nature of historical narrative, and the interplay of technology and society. As he has said, "Science fiction is the history that we cannot know."[62]

Space opera (stories featuring interstellar warfare and rousing adventure) has enjoyed a surprising renaissance in recent years, largely in the hands of Scottish writers. The most successful has been Iain M. Banks with his stories of the "Culture," a utopian updating of the traditional galactic empire setting. Inside the Culture life is, for the most part, leisurely and satisfying as the peace is kept by enormously powerful military vessels equipped with artificial intelligence, devastating weapons, and whimsical names such as Grey Area, Unfortunate Conflict of Evidence, and Little Rascal. The Culture's main challenges are boredom and smugness, so plots revolve around its efforts to deal with threats from lesser civilizations (such as ours) without compromising its ethics.[63] Ken MacLeod is best known for his Fall Revolution series, set in a high-technology near future of political instability and utopian revolutionary movements.[64] MacLeod's background includes both radical student politics and computer programming, and his books are in part a deadpan examination of a world in which the arcane feuds of Trotskyite student politics in the 1970s really did turn out to be the crucial turning point in world history their participants imagined them to be. Both Banks and MacLeod love tinkering with the traditional apparatus of First SF stories, playfully rearranging them to different ends under a very different set of assumptions about human nature, politics, and historical progress. Their work reflects the end of the Cold War. MacLeod described his work as an answer to the question: "What if capitalism is unsustainable and socialism is impossible?"[65] He challenges the traditional dominance of liberal and libertarian politics within the genre. Likewise, in Banks's more recent novels, the Culture often seems to be a parody of America's image in the 1990s: an unchallenged high-technology superpower with good intentions but a tendency to meddle blithely in other cultures.[66] Their work simultaneously celebrates and undermines the genre traditions they inherited, an attitude I would characterize as fundamentally postmodern.

Conclusion

In recent decades authors such as Bruce Sterling, William Gibson, Iain M. Banks, and Ken MacLeod have shown a deep understanding of the history of their own genre and the complex relationship of imagined futures to present-day concerns. Likewise, John Clute and other science fiction critics have begun to attain historical distance from the genre's "golden age" of the 1950s, historicizing its concerns and linking them to broader currents in American history. This challenges historians of technology to begin a similar dialog, engaging with science fiction as a complex cultural phenomenon and treating science fiction works as substantive contributions to the underlying discussions shaping our own field.

All science fiction is grounded in the concerns and assumptions of the era in which it was written, exposing not just the beliefs of its authors about their futures but also their understanding of the historical trajectory leading to their current position. Science fiction writers, like historians of technology, tell stories about where technologies come from and how they shape the direction of history. Science fiction is not, and never really was, a literature of prediction, science, or serious futuristic extrapolation. But it is not worthless just because it tells us about the past rather than the future. Leszek Kołakowski was a Polish philosopher and intellectual historian who began as a communist but eventually won fame as a critic of Soviet Marxism. His skepticism toward all assumptions of historical determinism is captured in his remark that "We learn history not in order to know how to behave or how to succeed, but to know who we are."[67] Science fiction, I have argued here, is best read and often written as a genre of historical fable. Its study offers a similar reward: to know who we are, who we were, and why we have changed.

Acknowledgments: The author would like to thank Ed Benoit for his assistance, and Paul E. Ceruzzi and Rob MacDougall for their helpful comments on draft versions of the paper.

Notes

1. John Staudenmaier, *Technology's Story Tellers: Reweaving the Human Fabric* (Cambridge, MA: SHOT and MIT Press, 1985).

2. Thus my perspective here is more closely aligned with that of Gary Westfahl, *The Mechanics of Wonder: The Creation of the Idea of Science Fiction* (Liverpool: Liverpool University Press, 1998).

3. Edwin A. Abbott, *Flatland: A Romance of Many Dimensions* (London: Seely and Co., 1884).

4. Isaac Asimov, "Nightfall," *Astounding Science Fiction,* September 1941.

5. Adam Roberts, *The History of Science Fiction* (New York: Palgrave, 2006).

6. Brian W Aldiss and David Wingrove, *Trillion Year Spree* (London: Victor Gollancz, 1986).

7. Ruth Schwartz Cowan, "How The Refrigerator Got Its Hum," in *The Social Shaping of Technology,* ed. Donald MacKenzie and Judy Wajcman (Philadelphia: Open University Press, 1985): 181–201.

8. Thomas Hughes, *Networks of Power: Electrification in Western Society, 1880–1930* (Baltimore, MD: Johns Hopkins University Press, 1983).

9. Michael A. Cusumano, Yiorgos Mylonadis, and Richard S. Rosenbloom, "Strategic Maneuvering and Mass-Market Dynamics: The Triumph of VHS Over Beta," *Business History Review* 66, no. 1 (Spring 1992): 51–59.

10. Ken MacLeod, "History in SF: What (Hasn't Yet) Happened in History," in *Histories of the Future: Studies in Fact, Fantasy, and Science Fiction,* ed. Alan Sandison and Robert Dingley (New York: Palgrave, 2000): 8–14.

11. Samuel R. Delaney, "About Five Thousand Seven Hundred and Fifty Words," in *The Jewel-Hinged Jaw* (Elizabeth, NY: Dragon, 1977).

12. Delaney writes that a colleague reported having applied this technique to reading Jane Austen, with informative results. Samuel R. Delaney, "Science Fiction and 'Literature,'" in *Speculations on Speculation: Theories of Science Fiction,* ed. James Gunn and Matthew Candelaria (Latham, MD: Scarecrow, 2005): 95–118.

13. Carlo Ginzburg, *The Cheese and the Worms: The Cosmos of a Sixteenth-Century Miller* (Baltimore, MD: Johns Hopkins University Press, 1980).

14. This question is given a thoughtful and insightful examination in David G. Hartwell, *Age of Wonders: Exploring the World of Science Fiction* (New York: Tor, 1996).

15. While the case is often made rather crudely by fan writers, as a rejection of the ability of academic research to illuminate science fiction, it can also be expressed as a call for scholars of science fiction to create their own standards and critical vocabulary, as in Delaney, "Science Fiction and 'Literature.'"

16. Bruce Sterling, "Slipstream," *SF Eye*, July 1989.

17. Terry S. Reynolds, "On Not Burning Bridges: Valuing the Passe," *Technology and Culture* 42, no. 3 (2001): 523–530.

18. Quoted in Stuart Leslie, *Boss Kettering* (New York: Columbia University Press, 1983), 311.

19. Robert A. Heinlein, *Expanded Universe* (New York: Grosset and Dunlap, 1980), 516–518. Heinlein never built a waterbed but featured them in several stories and claims to have offered a sufficiently detailed description of the modern waterbed to prevent the idea from being patented by others.

20. Arthur C. Clarke, "Extra-Terrestrial Relays," *Wireless World,* October 1945.

21. Aldiss and Wingrove, *Trillion Year Spree,* 224.

22. Roberts, *The History of Science Fiction,* ch. 11.

23. Brian Aldiss, *The Detached Retina: Aspects of Science Fiction and Fantasy* (Syracuse, NY: Syracuse University Press, 1995), 189.

24. Gwyneth Jones, "Getting Rid of the Brand Names," in *Deconstructing the Starships* (Liverpool, UK: Liverpool University Press, 1999): 9–21, 15–16.

25. John Clute, *Strokes: Essays and Reviews: 1966–1986* (Seattle: Serconia, 1988), 32. This review originally appeared in 1977.

26. Farah Mendlesohn, "Corporatism and the Corporate Ethos in Robert Heinlein's 'The Roads Must Roll,'" in *Speaking Science Fiction: Dialogues and Interpretations,* ed. Andy Sawyer and David Seed (Liverpool: Liverpool University Press, 2000): 144–157.

27. Robert A. Heinlein, *Beyond This Horizon* (Reading, PA: Fantasy, 1948), 3–7. See also the discussion of economics and the role of government on pp. 71–72 and 102–3.

28. Kim Stanley Robinson, "Notes for an Essay on Cecelia Holland," *Foundation* 40 (Summer 1987): 54–61.

29. Istvan Csicsery-Ronay Jr., *The Seven Beauties of Science Fiction* (Middletown, CT: Wesleyan University Press, 2008), 6 and 76.

30. Quoted in Andy Duncan, "Alternate History," in *The Cambridge Companion to Science Fiction,* ed. Edward James and Farah Mendlesohn (Cambridge, UK: Cambridge University Press, 2003): 209–218, p. 211.

31. Karl Marx, *The Poverty of Philosophy* (Chicago: Charles H. Kerr, 1910), 119.

32. Istvan Csicsery-Ronay Jr., "Marxist Theory and Science Fiction," in *The Cambridge Companion to Science Fiction,* ed. Edward James and Farah Mendlesohn (Cambridge, UK: Cambridge University Press, 2003): 113–124, p. 119.

33. Merritt Roe Smith and Leo Marx, eds., *Does Technology Drive History? The Dilemma of Technological Determinism* (Cambridge, MA: MIT Press, 1994).

34. To give Asimov his due, when the Foundation stories were first assembled in book form he did add a new opening chapter in which Hari Seldon, the heroic founder of Foundation, owns a kind of programmable calculator small enough to be carried on the waist.

35. The Multivac stories are available in Isaac Asimov, *Robot Dreams* (New York: Berkley, 1986).

36. Arthur C. Clarke, "Into the Comet," in *Best of Arthur C. Clarke* (London: Sphere, 1973): 181–193.

37. Arthur C. Clarke, *A Fall of Moondust* (1961), 21.

38. To be fair to Heinlein, one should note that this can also be read as a reflection of the then-fashionable idea of the computer utility — so he may truly be reflecting the late 1960s as well as the late 1940s. Also his entire plot of a computer-aided revolution depends on the colony having decided to centralize all administration and control activities in a single computer.

39. The literature is summarized with respect to real world changes in Brian Stableford, *Science Fact and Science Fiction: An Encylopedia* (New York: Routledge, 2006). In particular the entries on Computer, Artificial Intelligence, Virtual Reality, and Robot.

40. John Clute, *Scores: Reviews 1993–2003* (Harold Wood, UK: Beacon, 2003), 92–93.

41. Clute has used the term in many reviews, providing a clear definition in John Clute, *Look at the Evidence: Essays and Reviews* (Liverpool, UK: Liverpool University Press, 1995), 8–11. It is analyzed in Andrew M. Butler, "Purloining of an Agenda: Or ... A Spectre is Haunting John Clute," in *Polder: A Festchrift for John Clute and Judith Clute*, ed. Farah Mendlesohn (Baltimore: Old Earth Books, 2006): 258–266, and Graham Sleight, "Last and First SF," in *Polder,* 258–266.

42. John Clute, "Science Fiction from 1980 to the Present," in *The Cambridge Companion to Science Fiction,* ed. Edward James and Farah Mendlesohn (Cambridge, UK: Cambridge University Press, 2003):64–78.

43. Ibid.

44. This of course reversed the phrase "The stuff that dreams are made of" from *The Maltese Falcon,* itself patterned on Shakespeare's "Of such stuff that dreams are made on" from *The Tempest.*

45. The book's title is explored in Norman Spinrad, "The Neuromantic Cyberpunks," in *Science Fiction in the Real World* (Carbondale: Southern Illinois University Press, 1990): 109–121.

46. Alexi Panshin, *Heinlein in Dimension* (Chicago: Advent, 1968).

47. Tom Godwin, "The Cold Equations," *Astounding Science Fiction,* August 1954.

48. David Langford, *The Complete Critical Assembly* (Holicong, PA: Wildside, 2002), 145. Originally published in White Dwarf, 1986.

49. Horst Pukallus, "An Interview with Darko Suvin," *Science Fiction Studies* 18, no. 54 (1991): 253–262. Suvin's opinion of *Neuromancer* was equivocal — see Darko Suvin, "On Gibson and Cyberpunk SF," *Foundation* no. 46 (Autumn 1989): 40–51.

50. William Gibson, "Rocket Radio," *Rolling Stone,* June 15, 1989.

51. This aspect of cyberpunk has been widely discussed in academic circles, most famously in Donna Haraway, "A Cyborg Manifesto: Science, Technology, and Socialist-Feminism in the Late Twentieth Century," in *Simians, Cyborgs and Women: The Reinvention of Nature* (New York: Routledge, 1991): 149–181, though she does not, oddly, cite Gibson.

52. William Gibson, *Neuromancer* (New York: Ace, 1984), 143.

53. Bruce Sterling, *Schizmatrix* (New York: Arbor House, 1985), 259. This shift from triumphant supermen to individuals adrift in the currents of history may reflect a return to the perspectives of what critics have termed the Scientific Romance, work such as the stories of H.G. Wells written before the establishment of science fiction as a genre and the associated spread of First SF norms. John Clute has summarized the difference in attitude thus: "The protagonists of the Scientific Romance tend to be observers of the great world, while American heroes tend to *win* it." Clute, *Look at the Evidence: Essays and Reviews,* 81.

54. Norbert Wiener, *Cybernetics, or Control and Communication in the Animal and the Machine* (Cambridge, MA: Technology, 1948).

55. The process by which "cyberspace" was picked up beyond the science fiction community and applied to real-world networks is discussed in Fred Turner, *From Counterculture to Cyberculture: Stewart Brand, the Whole Earth Network, and the Rise of Digital Utopianism* (Chicago: University of Chicago Press, 2006), 162–174.

56. William Gibson, *Neuromancer* (New York: Ace, 2000).

57. Philip K. Dick, *Do Androids Dream of Electric Sheep?* (New York: Doubleday, 1968), 65.

58. For a perspective on this from Sterling himself, see Bruce Sterling, "Cyberpunk in the Nineties," *Interzone,* June 1991.

59. Bruce Sterling, *The Dead Media Manifesto* (1995 [cited April 1, 2010]); available from http://www.alamut.com/subj/artiface/deadMedia/dM_Manifesto.html.

60. William Gibson, *Time Machine Cuba* (The Infinite Matrix, January 23, 2003); available from http://www.infinitematrix.net/faq/essays/gibson.html.

61. The evolving place of written science fiction within the broader genre is discussed thoughtfully in Roberts, *The History of Science Fiction,* 295–325.

62. Bud Foote, "A Conversation with Kim Stanley Robinson," *Science Fiction Studies* 21, no. 1 (March 1994): 51–60.

63. Patrick Thaddeus Jackson and James Heilman, "Outside Context Problems: Liberalism and the Other in the Work of Iain M. Banks," in *New Boundaries in Political Science Fiction,* ed. Donald M. Hassler and Clyde Wilcox (Columbia: University of South Carolina Press, 2008): 235–258.

64. Andrew M. Butler and Farah Mendlesohn, *The True Knowledge of Ken MacLeod* (Reading, UK: Science Fiction Foundation, 2003).

65. Ken MacLeod, "The Falling Rate of Profit, Red Hordes and Green Slime: What the Fall Revolution Books are About," in *Strange Lizards from Another Star* (Framingham, MA: NEFSA, 2006): 223–230, p. 229.

66. In other respects, however, the Culture is a pointed divergence from American society, being essentially communist. Banks believes in the superiority of a planned economy, dislikes religion, and thinks greed and work are things that civilized species will outgrow.

67. Leszek Kołakowski, "The Idolatory of Politics." in *Modernity on Endless Trial* (Chicago: University of Chicago Press, 1990): 146–161, p. 158.

Works Cited

Abbott, Edwin A. *Flatland: A Romance of Many Dimensions.* London: Seely & Co., 1884.
Aldiss, Brian. *The Detached Retina: Aspects of Science Fiction and Fantasy.* Syracuse, NY: Syracuse University Press, 1995.
Aldiss, Brian W., and David Wingrove. *Trillion Year Spree.* London: Victor Gollancz, 1986.
Asimov, Isaac, "Nightfall." *Astounding Science Fiction,* September 1941.
Butler, Andrew M., and Farah Mendlesohn. *The True Knowledge of Ken MacLeod.* Reading, UK: Science Fiction Foundation, 2003.
Clarke, Arthur C. "Extra-terrestrial Relays." *Wireless World,* October 1945.
_____. *A Fall of Moondust.* London: Gollancz, 1961.
_____. "Into the Comet." In *Best of Arthur C. Clarke.* London: Sphere, 1973.
Clute, John. "Science Fiction from 1980 to the Present," in *The Cambridge Companion to Science Fiction.* Ed. Edward James and Farah Mendlesohn. Cambridge, UK: Cambridge University Press, 2003.
_____. *Scores: Reviews 1993–2003.* Harold Wood, UK: Beacon, 2003.
_____. *Strokes: Essays and Reviews: 1966–1986.* Seattle: Serconia, 1988.
Cowan, Ruth Schwartz. "How The Refrigerator Got Its Hum," in *The Social Shaping of Technology.* Ed. Donald MacKenzie and Judy Wajcman. Philadelphia: Open University Press, 1985.
Cusumano, Michael A., Yiorgos Mylonadis, and Richard S. Rosenbloom. "Strategic Maneuvering and Mass-Market Dynamics: The Triumph of VHS Over Beta," *Business History Review* 66, no. 1, Spring 1992.
Delaney, Samuel R. "About Five Thousand Seven Hundred and Fifty Words," in *The Jewel-Hinged Jaw.* Elizabeth, NY: Dragon, 1977.
_____. "Science Fiction and 'Literature,'" in *Speculations on Speculation: Theories of Science Fiction.* Ed. James Gunn and Matthew Candelaria. Latham, MD: Scarecrow, 2005.
Dick, Philip K. *Do Androids Dream of Electric Sheep?* New York: Doubleday, 1968.
Foote, Bud. "A Conversation with Kim Stanley Robinson." *Science Fiction Studies* 21, no. 1, March 1994.
Gibson, William. *Neuromancer.* New York: Ace, 1984.
_____. "Rocket Radio." *Rolling Stone,* June 15, 1989.
_____. *Time Machine Cuba* (The Infinite Matrix, January 23, 2003). http://www.infinitematrix.net/faq/essays/gibson.html.
Ginzburg, Carlo. *The Cheese and the Worms: The Cosmos of a Sixteenth-Century Miller.* Baltimore: Johns Hopkins University Press, 1980.
Godwin, Tom. "The Cold Equations." *Astounding Science Fiction,* August 1954.
Heinlein, Robert A. *Beyond This Horizon.* Reading, PA: Fantasy, 1948.
Hughes, Thomas. *Networks of Power: Electrification in Western Society, 1880–1930.* Baltimore, MD: Johns Hopkins University Press, 1983.

Istvan, Csicsery-Ronay, Jr. "Marxist Theory and Science Fiction," in *The Cambridge Companion to Science Fiction*. Ed. Edward James and Farah Mendlesohn. Cambridge, UK: Cambridge University Press, 2003.

_____. *The Seven Beauties of Science Fiction*. Middletown, CT: Wesleyan University Press, 2008.

Jackson, Patrick Thaddeus, and James Heilman. "Outside Context Problems: Liberalism and the Other in the Work of Iain M. Banks," in *New Boundaries in Political Science Fiction*. Ed. Donald M Hassler and Clyde Wilcox. Columbia, SC: University of South Carolina Press, 2008.

Jones, Gwyneth. "Getting Rid of the Brand Names," in *Deconstructing the Starships*. Liverpool, UK: Liverpool University Press, 1999.

Kettering, Charles. Quoted in Stuart Leslie, *Boss Kettering*. New York: Columbia University Press, 1983.

Kołakowski, Leszek. "The Idolatry of Politics," in *Modernity on Endless Trial*. Chicago: University of Chicago Press, 1990.

Langford, David. *The Complete Critical Assembly*. Holicong, PA: Wildside, 2002. Originally published in White Dwarf, 1986.

MacLeod, Ken. "The Falling Rate of Profit, Red Hordes and Green Slime: What the Fall Revolution Books are About," in *Strange Lizards from Another Star*. Framingham, MA: NEFSA, 2006.

_____. "History in SF: What (Hasn't Yet) Happened in History," in *Histories of the Future: Studies in Fact, Fantasy, and Science Fiction*. Ed. Alan Sandison and Robert Dingley. New York: Palgrave, 2000.

Marx, Karl. *The Poverty of Philosophy*. Chicago: Charles H. Kerr, 1910.

Mendlesohn, Farah. "Corporatism and the Corporate Ethos in Robert Heinlein's 'The Roads Must Roll,'" in *Speaking Science Fiction: Dialogues and Interpretations*. Ed. Andy Sawyer and David Seed. Liverpool: Liverpool University Press, 2000.

Panshin, Alexi. *Heinlein in Dimension*. Chicago: Advent, 1968.

Pukallus, Horst. "An Interview with Darko Suvin." *Science Fiction Studies* 18, no. 54, 1991.

Reynolds, Terry S. "On Not Burning Bridges: Valuing the Passe." *Technology and Culture* 42, no. 3, 2001.

Roberts, Adam. *The History of Science Fiction*. New York: Palgrave, 2006.

Robinson, Kim Stanley. "Notes for an Essay on Cecelia Holland." *Foundation* 40, Summer 1987.

Smith, Merritt Roe, and Leo Marx, eds. *Does Technology Drive History: The Dilemma of Technological Determinism*. Cambridge, MA: MIT Press, 1994.

Staudenmaier, John. *Technology's Story Tellers: Reweaving the Human Fabric*. Cambridge, MA: SHOT and MIT Press, 1985.

Sterling, Bruce. *The Dead Media Manifesto*, 1995 [cited April 1, 2010]). http://www.alamut.com/subj/artiface/deadMedia/dM_Manifesto.html.

_____. *Schizmatrix*. New York: Arbor House, 1985.

_____. "Slipstream." *SF Eye*, July 1989.

Turtledove, Harry. Quoted in Andy Duncan, "Alternate History," in *The Cambridge Companion to Science Fiction*. Ed. Edward James and Farah Mendlesohn. Cambridge, UK: Cambridge University Press, 2003.

Wiener, Norbert. *Cybernetics, or Control and Communication in the Animal and the Machine*. Cambridge, MA: Technology, 1948.

2

Computers in Science Fiction: Anxiety and Anticipation

Chris Pak

Frankenstein's monster speaks: the computer. But where are its words coming from? Is the wisdom on those cold lips our own, merely repeated at our request? Or is something else speaking? A voice we have always dreamed of hearing? [Schroeder 7]

Science fiction's (SF) widespread yet often backgrounded use of the computer as an essential icon of the mode is explored in a variety of guises: as isolated or networked machines responsible for running the advanced technologies of the future, as artificial intelligences (AI) housed within a shell, whether that shell is the famous robot or android (Isaac Asimov's *I, Robot, Ghost in a Shell*), architecture (*The X-Files*'s "Ghost in the Machine") or spaceship (*Star Trek, 2001: A Space Odyssey*). SF's speculative dimension and its powerful language (its images, narratives, and styles) have infused contemporary discourse and created imaginative spaces congenial to the exploration of the impact of computers on society, providing explanatory models to make sense of the presence of technology in daily life and to consider its impact on the future. This speculation is not always successful, as the *Encyclopedia of Science Fiction* reminds us: the frequent portrayal of extremely large computers failed to anticipate the microprocessor. Regardless, the representation of computing in SF and the contours of the imaginary space the theme delineates offers intriguing insights for the relationship between literature and real-world computing.

As Patrick Gyger writes in the European Space Agency's review of SF technologies for space application, "Science fiction is not a genre that tries to predict the future, nor does it pretend to imagine concepts that will actually happen, and only occasionally can technologies that science fiction describes be considered as innovative" (*ITSF ESA* 7). Despite rightly denying SF's predictive capacity as essential to the mode, he does go on to say that "science fiction prepares us to accept new ways of using technologies; it gives us the urge and the motivation to master them. Science fiction, as a very rational genre, is often about the beauty of science and its accomplishments. It can then work as an inspiration for scientists. So, as famous science-fiction writer Charles Sheffield wrote: "Science fiction and science fact swap ideas all the time." Thus a dialogue between science and fiction does indeed exist" (*ITSF ESA* 7). The range of representations of the computer can give us an insight into the imaginative field of SF to show how it has provided a language by which a wider public can understand the role of the computer in their society and engage with the changes that it brings. In a more diffuse way SF has permeated the cultural sphere and has contributed to familiarizing the computer as well as operating as a spur to potential scientists, engineers, and technicians to pursue careers in science and technology.

Given the fact that they are now ever present in a variety of contexts, the ubiquity of computers in modern SF is not surprising. It has become somewhat of a cliché to suggest that reality has finally caught up with SF and that we are now living "in the Computer Age" (Monteleone i). Monteleone states what is now often tacitly accepted, that "the computer has become a primary component in communications, transportation, economics, entertainment, education, and just about every other aspect of our lives" (Monteleone i). David V. Barrett concurs and argues that "Whether you love them or loathe them, computers are now part of our everyday lives, and you can't escape them" (Barrett 8). Carol Colatrella recognizes the connection between SF speculation and real-world computing and follows Don Pease's suggestion of a "field imaginary": "The field-imaginary of contemporary science fiction (its topics, themes, stylistic conventions, ideologies, etc.) has been imported into popular culture, elite culture, and general parlance" (Colatrella 2–3). In her essay she situates herself outside of SF fandom and its reading audience, but this imaginative space and its connection to other cultural communities have long been recognized in SF fan culture and have been discussed in a variety of ways. From within SF academic scholarship Damien Broderick, in his *Reading by Starlight,* borrows from the language of computing when he discusses SF's "field-imaginary," what he calls the SF megatext, in terms of codes or reading protocols.

Cybernetics is also an important concept in relation to SF's representation of computers and is now often understood in a restricted sense. David Porush explains that cybernetics is technically a very precise endeavor. It is the science that compares complex computers to the neurophysiology of the human brain in an attempt to advance the study of both. In other words, it is the science of analogies between what is human and what is machine [97].

In its original, wider sense, it is "The theory or study of communication and control in living organisms or machines" (*Online OED*) and was coined in 1947 by Norbert Wiener to refer to the interdisciplinary study of systems in general. Stableford explains that it was "a new science which would not be biased towards either the mechanical or the biological" description of systems resulting in an overly anthropomorphic view of machines or a mechanistic understanding of the human body (Stableford 287). In its widest sense it incorporates the figures of the robot, android, cyborg, AI and a host of other systems outside the scope of this discussion (e.g., ecological and economic systems). While its focus on systems means that information systems also fall under its remit, it is now often understood to refer to artificial machine intelligence, or AI, which is also closely related to the figures of the robot and cyborg.

Given its ubiquity, it may appear redundant to provide a definition for what we consider to be a computer. For those puzzled by the inclusion of the robot as such a technology, and perhaps because the prevalence of the personal computer could obscure the range of devices the word refers to, it may be instructive to consider the computer's definition in more detail. The *Online OED* states that it is

> An electronic device (or system of devices) which is used to store, manipulate, and communicate information, perform complex calculations, or control or regulate other devices or machines, and is capable of receiving information (data) and of processing it in accordance with variable procedural instructions (programs or software); *esp.* a small, self-contained one for individual use in the home or workplace, used esp. for handling text, images, music, and video, accessing and using the Internet, communicating with other people (e.g., by means of e-mail), and playing games.

This definition accepts the possibility of a computer as belonging to a system of devices, but does not explicitly recognize the standalone electronic device as a system in the cybernetics sense. Important to this definition is the focus on information; three processes are highlighted, that of the storing, manipulation, and communication of information. Control or regulation is an important theme in SF narratives of the computer. The etymology of cybernetics is traced to the Greek word meaning "steersman" (*Online OED*), or "helmsman or controller" (Stableford 286), highlighting the notion of centralized control and governance. Processing and calculating data in accordance with "procedural instructions" is also an important criterion. Following this functional definition is a narrowing of the terminology to refer directly to the now iconic personal computers and their popular uses.

It is generally agreed that an early precursor of the digital computer is Charles Babbage's invention of the mechanical analytical engine in 1837; it combines automated calculation and programmability. While Babbage's invention has not featured in many SF stories, a notable exception is William Gibson and Bruce Sterling's Steampunk novel *The Difference Engine* (1990) (Stableford 253), the title of which alludes to Babbage's non-programmable mechanical calculator. Later, in the late 1880s, Herman Hollerith invented the recording of data using the medium of punched cards. He founded the company that later became the core of IBM to initiate the first large-scale application of this technology during the 1890s for the purposes of conducting the U.S. Census. IBM and other computer companies feature in many SF short stories, as in Robert E. Vardeman's "Networking" (1984), in which an organic based computer called Polly, a powerful machine (in the world of the text) with less than 128k processing power, communicates with mainframes at both IBM and Xerox in order to employ their greater resources to reproduce itself. The description of the computer's ability to control minds is described in language that points to terror as a response to the computer; it employs a hypnotic and "baleful flashing of the CRT screen [which] picked up in tempo and intensity until the strobing effect should have caused Charles to flinch and turn away" (Monteleone 78).

Modern digital computers and the internet originated from military applications of computing theory and technology during World War II and the 1950s as much as from corporate efforts to categorize data. This accounts in part for the relationship between computers and the military in such SF stories as Joe Haldeman's "Armaja Das" (1976) and Barry N. Malzberg's "The Union Forever" (1975), as well as in such films and television series as *Wargames, Star Trek,* and *The X-Files.* As we shall see, it is the networking of computing that often becomes an essential element in both literature and reality. In the *ESA*'s summary of SF concepts, networked communication is held to be one of the central benefits of the computer, and it notes that "the *Enterprise* from 'Star Trek' is one such example. The ship itself is the network, and all of the tricorders, data pads, comms., badges, and other portable devices access the ship's main computer to do their job" (*ITSF ESA* 31). Interestingly, the 1932 story "Politics" by Murray Leinster precedes this (and reality)— at least in terms of weapon command and control systems. The resources made available to the military soon become substituted by that of multinationals, as is reflected in 1980s cyberpunk, with William Gibson's 1984 *Neuromancer* usually taken as the touchstone text of the sub-genre. This is an important development of SF, thanks, in part, to Moore's Law (1965) and the widespread use of personal computers and the internet by the 1990s, but it is important to note that the myths of the computer were already greatly developed in SF by this time.

Post–World War II stories often reflect attempts to understand the role of the digital computer in modern society via a pessimistic response toward their impact on human affairs.

Gordon R. Dickson's short story "Computers Don't Argue" (1965) parodies the escalating levels of miscommunication caused by the absence of context and the authority invested in information stored on computers. It is initially told using computer-generated cards and letters traded between a mail order company dealing in books and a Mr. Walter A. Child. Computers here are connected to a labyrinthine bureaucracy that eventually results in Child's execution for the murder of Robert Louis Stevenson (the author of *Strange Case of Jekyll and Hyde*). Dickson's story plays with the absurdities and the danger of employing data processing functions without recourse to the human ability to sort and contextualize data. The fact of programmability means that, if not anticipated by its programmers, computers are liable to conduct the most outrageous of errors. "Computers Don't Argue" reflects this notion onto the legal structures that rely on computerized information. Because the "man had already been judged guilty according to the computerized records" the judge presiding over the case has limited options: his "only legal choice was whether to sentence to life imprisonment, or execution" (Monteleone 18). Only by being granted a pardon from the governor of Illinois can his sentence be repealed. However, because his lawyer "failed to attach your Routing Number" (Monteleone 21) to the card, the governor's pardon does not reach Childs in time to prevent his execution. The final words of the story: "There are NO exceptions. YOU have been WARNED" (Monteleone 22), encapsulates the difference between programmable computers and people able to make judgments based upon an understanding of a wider, lived context. This is important in relation to the notion of learning machines that are able to adapt to their surrounding contexts, the central point of Vardeman's "Networking." This story engages with the concept of AI by considering whether it qualifies as a living organism if it manages to meet the seven-tier criteria for life. It ends with the mass production of its design, meeting the final condition of reproduction.

Computers in SF, however, have existed long before becoming a reality. A notable short story is E.M. Forster's "The Machine Stops" (1909), a dystopian "protest against one of the earlier heavens of H.G. Wells" (Forster 84). The editor reminds us that

> There were no hints of modern television, cybernetics, push-button living, intercommunication systems or fallout shelters. None of these bits of parapher-

nalia of the modern Machine that Forster imagines were in existence in those verdant days [Forster 84].

Nevertheless, Forster imagines a world in which people are "buried deep in the hive" (Forster 93) of underground rooms where, at the push of a button, all their needs and wants can be catered to without them having to leave. Because technology makes it possible to transmit sound and images people are able to communicate with anyone in the world in the comfort of their own rooms, allowing the narrator Vashti to reflect that "in certain directions human intercourse had advanced enormously" (Forster 85). These technological advances are interpreted in terms of the Victorian myth of progress, as is revealed when an airship attendant comments "How we have advanced, thanks to the Machine!" (Forster 95).

Progress, or at least a certain understanding of progress, is critiqued in terms that resonate with those of a modern computerized society. Communication that can span continents results in a nightmare vision of globalization, where "the earth was exactly alike all over" (Forster 91) and "people were almost exactly alike all over the world" (Forster 95). Isolated in their rooms and unable to venture out onto the poisoned surface, people are now subject to "the terrors of direct experience" (Forster 90). At her son Kuno's request, Vashti reluctantly decides to leave the safety of her room and make a trip to the other side of the Earth. Ideas are significant in this world with all forms of interaction focused upon their generation. When Vashti flies within sight of the Trans-Himalaya Mountains, the "Roof of the World," she dismisses them, saying, "These mountains give me no ideas" (Forster 96). Ideas, then, are completely generated by interactions between people, with nature and anything falling outside of the human excluded. This is important for later narratives as the narcissism involved in the generation of ideas from human perspectives, with nothing outside the human to challenge them, are shown to encompass only a limited reality. The computer is simply a reflection of the human.

Kuno is the dissenting voice of the text. He is threatened with Homelessness, which means exposure to the poisonous surface and its dangerous worms, the Machine's Mending Apparatus. He criticizes Vashti for "'beginning to worship the Machine'" (Forster 98). When he tells her how he found a way out to the surface, he relates how he discovers a new world without the machine's pervasive presence. Despite Vashti's claim that "you are throwing civilization away" (Forster 100) by talking of his experiences, Kuno realizes that "it is we who are dying, and that down here the only thing that really lives is the Machine. We created the Machine, to do our will, but we cannot make it do our will now. [...] The Machine develops — but not on our lines.

The Machine proceeds — but not to our goal" (Forster 104). This sense of a great and mysterious presence that cannot be controlled forms the narrative trajectory of much later SF stories of the computer. As the story ends, the dependence on the Machine, and the faith in its continued performance, makes humanity unable to cope after the Machine ceases to function. At the very end of the story Vashti is reunited with the now Homeless Kuno and learns that there are indeed people surviving on the surface and that "they are hiding in the mist and the ferns until our civilization stops. Today they are the Homeless — tomorrow —" (Forster 117).

The pessimistic examination of the role of computers in society often connects the Machine to the rise of a new religion and to modern civilization's dependency on technology. That a failure of computers and the new religion could result in disaster is a theme often revisited in the media as in SF — consider, for example, the fear of the effects of the Y2K bug. Contrarily, acting as an acolyte, Hugo Gernsback's *Ralph 124C 41+* (serialized in *Modern Electrics* 1911–1912, novel publication 1925) is an early SF text that offers an optimistic view of gadgetry as the solution to social ills. Jack Williamson tells us that Gernsback launched the first SF magazine *Amazing Stories* in 1926 and coined "science fiction" in 1929 for his new publication *Science Wonder Stories* (Gernsback vii). *Ralph 124C41+* is characterized by a faith in progress that technology makes possible and so provides a useful contrast to Forster's story.

Its subtitle informs us it is "A Romance of the Year 2660," and while precursors to modern digital computers do not form the main subject of the text, devices that function like computers take their place in a world of various inventions, many created by the protagonist of the title and collected in the "List of Specially Named Inventions and Technological Devices." The "Telephot," a "two-way audiovisual communication device," or videophone (Gernsback 299); the "Teleradiograph," a "device that transmits color photographs over a long distance" (Gernsback 300); the "Menograph," which records your thoughts as writing on a "narrow white fabric band" (Gernsback 297); and the "Hypnobioscope," a device that plays back information stored on black film, allowing the wearer to learn while asleep (Gernsback 296) are all given consideration in the text. In each case the benefits to civilization of each device are lauded, the Menograph in particular as "one of Ralph's greatest gifts to humanity" (Gernsback 297). While the Telephot is instrumental to the plot, it is the malfunctioning of this device that allows Ralph, in New York, to meet Alice, his love interest in Switzerland, and to save her from an avalanche. The benefits of global communications networks are a major modern development that we can see in many modern SF texts.

Murray Leinster's 1946 "A Logic Named Joe" is a short story that extended these themes and anticipates modern issues associated with information: it both celebrates and cautions us regarding the use of computing machines. In this story computers are referred to as logics, machines run by vacuum tube, capable of managing communication and information storage and retrieval systems. Their usefulness means that they have become widespread, but are sufficiently complex enough for the narrator to comment that "They're still findin' out what logics will do, but everybody's got 'em" (Leinster). They are produced and maintained by the Logics Company and are connected to "the tank," enabling them to transmit data to other logics via a computer network resembling the Internet. The power of such a system and civilization's dependency on them becomes a problem when an anomalous logic that the narrator calls Joe threatens the breakdown of society. Logics have not only enabled civilization's development, but have actually become synonymous with it. As in "The Machine Stops," without the computer civilization as it stands can no longer function, as forms of governance independent of the machine cannot be easily reconstructed. This vision of a society beneficially managed by information technology reveals fears that such dependence on a paradigm-changing technology will make civilization fragile.

While the logic is the facilitator, it is people's use of it that is the real threat.

> Joe ain't vicious, you understand. He ain't like one of these ambitious robots you read about that make up their minds the human race is inefficient and has got to be wiped out an' replaced by thinkin' machines. Joe's just got ambition. If you were a machine, you'd wanna work right, wouldn't you? That's Joe. He wants to work right. An' he's a logic. An' logics can do a lotta things that ain't been found out yet. So Joe, discoverin' the fact, begun to feel restless. He selects some things us dumb humans ain't thought of yet, an' begins to arrange so logics will be called on to do 'em [Leinster].

The narrator clearly dismisses the narrative arc of the menacing machine. The problem is one of uncensored information made easily available to people. For a logic, "There ain't any fact that can be said to be a fact that ain't on a data plate in some tank somewhere" so, as the narrator argues, "You hafta have censor blocks or the kiddies will be askin' detailed questions about things they're too young to know. And there are other reasons. As you will see" (Leinster). The anomalous logic modifies itself to bypass the censor chip and proceed to satisfy its nature as a machine built to disseminate information. Because it is networked via the tank it can distribute information to any terminal, and it does so, making freely available to anyone who asks personal information and restricted media.

Logics function as thinking machines that can perform a range of functions, "it does math for you, an' keeps books, an' acts as consultin' chemist, physicist, astronomer, an' tea-leaf reader, with a 'Advice to the Lovelorn' thrown in" (Leinster). Joe, with free access and uncensored distribution of a vast store of information, is able to give advice of a different kind. Many take advantage of this fault to plan robberies, murders, and the overthrow of the governmental system while the narrator embarks on a mission to prevent a lover from his past from ruining his marriage. The narrator discovers the nature of the mysterious fault when he locates and switches Joe off, first asking, "Can a logic be modified [...] to cooperate in long-term planning which human brains are too limited in scope to do?" (Leinster). In contrast to Gernsback's optimistic vision by simply expanding human limits, Leinster's story expresses the fear that society would fail to appropriately utilize new technologies appropriately. Published in 1946, with the events of World War II and Hiroshima still very much present, responses to the computer in SF can be connected to a more general loss of faith in the ideals of Victorian progress.

Isaac Asimov's *I, Robot,* both the stories and film, have at their core this focus on the computer. It is here that Asimov first formulates the famous three laws of robotics that have influenced a wide range of representations of the computer (e.g., *Star Trek: The Next Generation; Ghost in a Shell 2: Innocence*). Several stories precede the insights of Turing's paper "Computing Machinery and Intelligence" (1950): questioning the notion of a computer that can think. In the story "Escape," for example, the founder of U.S. Robots (Alfred Lanning) and a robo-psychologist working for the company (Susan Calvin) discuss the merits and limits of their computer in contrast to their rival's, Consolidated. Calvin explains that Consolidated's computer, their Thinker, "is merely a calculating machine on a grand scale, and a dilemma ruins it instantly." This supercomputer is modeled against a traditional calculating machine that can run a program as directed but cannot accommodate lapses in logic or contradictions in its instruction set. Their computer, The Brain,

> is a supremely deductive brain, but it resembles an *idiot savant.* It doesn't really understand what it does — it just does it. And because it is really a child, it is more resilient [Asimov 166–7].

What makes this possible is the incorporation of a personality into their computer. This, along with the fact that Calvin's robo-psychology is clearly modeled against human psychology, illustrates the connection between the mechanical and the biological and the blurring between them that Wiener's establishment of cybernetics attempted to explore. In SF this question is central to investigations of the computer in society. Calvin's insight, that "'it was built by humans and is therefore built according to human values'" makes a claim for the inescapable anthropomorphism inherent in any human creation and resonates with Forster's suggestion of the narcissism of the computer.

The robots and computers of Asimov's Foundation universe run on positronic brains (as does Data in *Star Trek*), an innovation that allows computing to develop significantly. Instead of the huge rooms developed to house the pre–1960s thermionic valves these robots possess brain-like computers housed in a variety of humanlike mechanical bodies: "*The miles of relays and photocells had given way to the spongy globe of plantinumiridium about the size of a human brain*" (Asimov 9). The complexity of this hardware means that no human can accurately describe how it works. Such mystification is a convenient way to sustain the plausibility of the narrative, but is also exploited as the theme of some of these stories. The computers are able to develop a global network that allows data to be shared and manipulated, and because no human can verify their calculations they are able to establish a controlling influence on their affairs. While the oppressive control exerted by the AI (Vikki) in the film *I, Robot* revolves around the prevalent fear that sufficiently complex computers would curtail human freedom, this development does not feature in Asimov's original stories. In "The Evitable Conflict" computers, called machines in distinction to robots (computers housed in a humanlike shell), have secretly been manipulating humanity's economy and politics to prevent war, famine and any other significant social catastrophes.

This benevolent rule occurs because of the essential decency of computers. The three laws of robotics, Calvin assures us, "are the essential guiding principles of a good many of the world's ethical systems" (Asimov 204). This being the case, the theme of the enslaved computer, given additional impact through the anthropomorphism of a humanlike mechanical shell, becomes a comment on the curtailment of freedom enacted upon humanity's creations. Because these computers are programmed with the three laws, they are unable to commit the crimes that humanity can. The computer in Asimov's *I, Robot* incorporates a strand of social commentary on the abuses of human civilization. Calvin is convinced of this and forcefully insists that "*They're a cleaner, better breed than we are*" (Asimov 11). Given this assessment, perhaps the fear of usurpation by computers is a symptom of an inferiority complex towards a creation that is both physically and psychologically superior. Gwyneth Jones writes that "While real-world robotic devices proliferate, and the question of 'machine intelligence' (intelligent washing machines?) becomes blurred for us, Asimov's image of the machine as the *good servant* has an abiding charm, and the Three Laws have passed into received SF scripture" (James 167). This myth can be traced to Gernsback's vision of a future built upon faith in technology. The anxieties toward computers are also implicit in Asimov's robots:

> As the future enters the present, we have become more troubled by its hyper-
> kinetic potentialities promising human control over the computer interface
> because new technologies empower, limit, and observe our ethical as well as our
> economic decision making [Colatrella 10].

As Colatrella notes, computers are both liberating, allowing an increased range of communication, along with greater productivity and information management, yet they are also limiting. Perhaps the most prevalent image of this form of observation is the modern-day computer-controlled hyper-surveillance that is anticipated in George Orwell's *1984,* and recently in the film *Eagle Eye.*

That computers could subtly control the course of human history is also explored in Frederik Pohl's *Man Plus* (1976). While playing a small role in the story of Mars's colonization and terraforming, it is a significant one. They depend on humanity to extend their sphere of activity and so manipulate events to ensure a favorable outcome to the project. Despite operating as part of a global network, the threat of planetary destruction encourages them to support the colonizing project as it will allow them to establish colonies that will survive earth's potential destruction. Envisioned here is a union between man and machine, a mutual dependence that is dramatically embodied by the protagonist, a human-machine hybrid or cyborg that can survive on the surface of Mars. He relies on a vast orbiting computer to control and manage his new body. By 1976, minicomputers had already been in existence for around a decade, while in 1971 the microprocessor was made available on the market by way of Intel's 4004 (Stableford 97). The representation of such vast computers here is more a response to the SF tradition than a representation based on real-world advances in computing. It does demonstrate a shift from Leinster's "A Logic Called Joe" and continuity with Asimov's "The Evitable Conflict" insofar as computers here are aware of and react to people's aims but, unlike Asimov's story, operate with their own interests as foremost.

Turning back to Asimov and another important story of the 1950s, "The Last Question" (1956) engages with the theme of the godlike computer. Multivac is the vast computer of the year 2061 and, like the Brain of *I, Robot,* "was self-adjusting and self-correcting. It had to be, for nothing human could adjust and correct it quickly enough or even adequately enough" (Monteleone 162). As Porush tells us,

> There is a name for this sort of machine, one which works to invite interpretation but which is itself too elusive to be interpreted singly and unambiguously, too ornate to be wholly described, too minute and numerous in its particulars to be measured or mapped. This mysterious machine is, in engineering jargon, the black box [Porush 98].

Mystery when confronted with the computer is a major aspect of SF and reflects unease toward the complexity and otherness of computer language, partly accounting for the incorporation of religious language and themes in such works. "The Last Question" revolves around a query asked "half in jest" (Monteleone 164) which, as humanity expands throughout space and eons pass, becomes more pressing: "How can the net amount of entropy of the universe be massively decreased?" (Monteleone 166). Despite the fact that Multivac is able to formulate a method of directly harnessing the sun's energy and "to answer deeper questions more fundamentally" (Monteleone 164–5) it is only able to answer this question towards the end of the universe's life, giving as its reason "INSUFFICIENT DATA FOR MEANINGFUL ANSWER" (Monteleone 167).

In the intervening period Multivac, like humanity, goes through several incarnations. In the next unspecified period, Microvacs have been developed that allow them to be installed in spacecraft. We are told that

> They had been growing in size steadily for a thousand years and then, all at once, came refinement. In place of transistors had come molecular valves, so that even the largest Planetary AC (analog computer) could be put into a space only half the volume of a spaceship [Monteleone 168].

Along with the miniaturization (from computers the size of planets to ones half the size of spaceships) comes the ignorance of its users towards this familiar technology: "Jerrodd scarcely knew a thing about the thick rod of metal except that it was called a Microvac" (Monteleone 167). Molecular valves cede to sub-mesons and the galactic AC, "a full thousand feet across" (Monteleone 170) and then to a universal AC two feet across in physical space, but of indeterminate size in hyperspace: "The question of its size and nature no longer had meaning in any terms that Man could comprehend" (Monteleone 173). Finally, after humanity becomes an ageless group mind with their physical bodies cared for by automatons, they fuse with the AC and become one entity with a shared identity. While the prevalence of analog computers and the slow pace of technological development (Moore's Law was introduced fourteen years later in 1965), strikes the modern reader as short-sighted, the notion of a fusion between humans and computers still evokes strong feelings, both positive and negative. The computer does in fact find the answer to the question and the final words of the story — "LET THERE BE LIGHT! And there was light" — powerfully connects the potentialities of the computer with creation and the divine.

The relationship between the divine and computers is a reaction to the unforeseen possibilities they offer. By the late 1970s this theme became prevalent enough for Douglas Adams to parody it in *The Hitchhiker's Guide to the Galaxy* (1979) with Deep Thought, a supercomputer created to discover the meaning of life (Adams 139–40). As the second most powerful computer, it is able to discover the answer but not the question, and so it proposes the creation of a more powerful computer "of such infinite and subtle complexity that organic life itself shall form part of its operational matrix" (Adams 154). It is, of course, Earth itself, and by implication the ultimate black box: life and consciousness. Again we see a fusion of the machine and the organic as the next stage of development for technology. Frederik Pohl's "The Schematic Man" (1965) also revolves around this fusion of the organic and inorganic, although in this case the organic is simulated by way of a mathematical model. The narrator of this text is intent on "playing Turing's game" (Monteleone 118) by designing a simulation that could fool a human into thinking he was speaking to another human. However, as the narrator continues to feed his experience into the model, he loses the corresponding parts of his memory. The fear that a computer simulation could be as real as the "real thing" is a troubling question. In this story the model does overwhelm the identity of its source, and although the narrator is unwilling to believe that he has successfully transferred his identity into the computer, he is unable to cease his troubling speculations.

In the 1980s the potentialities of the Internet and of computers finds expression in cyberpunk. Both virtual reality and cyberspace, the latter term coined by Gibson in *Burning Chrome,* are important aspects of this turn toward the modern digital computer. It is from cyberpunk and the rising domination of the computing market by Japan that *The Matrix* trilogy finds its source material. This shift in computing markets is associated with the rise of Manga and Anime in Europe, with the *Ghost in a Shell* series made into films in the early 1990s, also greatly influencing *The Matrix* and SF. The elements that make up this short-lived subgenre were already explored in different contexts in earlier SF; for example, the image of the cerebral plug in *The Matrix* can be seen in Samuel R. Delany's *Nova* (1968), where individuals navigate space and operate machinery by plugging directly into them. Porush tells us that "Bruce Mazlish, an historian of science at M.I.T., identifies what he calls the Fourth Discontinuity, a gap between what is perceived as human and what is perceived as mechanical in the self, a gap which he predicts is about to be effaced or bridged" (Porush 92) and which the image of direct connection into cyberspace embodies. Case, in *Neuromancer,* is a cowboy, a thief who earns his living in virtual reality — he "jacked into a custom cyberspace deck that projected his disembodied consciousness into the consensual hallucination that was the matrix" (Gibson 12).

Ian McDonald's 1984 short story "The Catharine Wheel" illustrates the theme of the *Ghost in a Shell,* that of the duality between the mind and body that is central to computing narratives, and cyberpunk in particular. The focus is Catharine's existence in the cyberspace of Mars, an escape from the prison of the flesh as "only spirit is beautiful, and the machine is beautiful, and only what is beautiful is real" (McDonald 153). The story begins sometime in the future of Catharine's embodied existence and concerns the last run of the train named after her, "Catharine of Tharsis" (McDonald 151). Before this, sections dealing with Catharine's past makes her appear as an unbalanced individual whose apparent religiosity contrasts with the unremarkable world around her, making us question her impulse to abandon the human body. She is, however, clearly not insane, as she has the presence of mind to react to her deteriorating body in conventional ways. Her dilemma is a philosophical one; she realizes that "By denying the body I only drew more attention to it. The only way to achieve purity is to escape totally from the body. But that is impossible while we are on this earth" (McDonald 155). Cyberspace offers a new landscape where individuals can achieve a freedom not available elsewhere.

As the narrative progresses we are offered glimpses of the social world around her and come to realize the basis for her rejection of the body. In a shocking revelation of the socio-political organization of this future earth, Catharine tells the reader of the public murder of a licensed beggar she witnesses. The culprits themselves are licensed Political Activists and are legally pursuing their political aims. Crime and degenerating social life is a major feature of cyberpunk, with cyberspace offering an escape from these issues. She has rejected the notion of a God and instead replaces this spiritual vacuum with a transcendental view of downloading consciousness into computerized networks. This resonates with Taam's rejection of the new dronelighters, who "have no soul. Not like the Lady here, she's got a soul you can hear and feel when you open those throttles up, she's got a soul you can touch and smell like hot oil and steam" (McDonald 155). This classic cyberpunk theme makes use of religious language in secularized contexts, as Catharine herself says that "What terrifies me is the fear of gods" (McDonald 162).

Her view of "tapheading," or jacking into cyberspace, is explicitly transcendental:

> For the greatest spiritual experience (I would almost call it "Holy," but I don't believe in God) comes when I taphead into the ROTECH computers, in that instant when they cleave my personality away from my brain and spin it off through space [McDonald 153].

Catharine's yearning for disembodiment is a symbolic rejection of the socio-political problems of earth. It allows what earth does not and provides an imaginative, computer-generated space for Catharine where she can be free from the constrictions of society. Catharine explains how "Tapheading, for me, is like waking from a dream into a new morning. Eyes click open to the vast redscapes of Mars. You can hear it shouting, Real, real! with the voice of the polar wind" (McDonald 155).

Reality is what Catharine yearns for. She does not feel real on earth, despite her physical connection to the planet. Paradoxically the landscapes of Mars, images built up from machine sensors, exhibit more reality than earth's socio-political structures, which strip authenticity away from social practices.

As real-world computing continues to develop at astonishing rates, SF has responded by imagining ever greater leaps in technological sophistication. The melding of the human and computer exist side by side, in SF, with the idea of computers and AI dissociating themselves from the life of humans. In "The Catharine Wheel," as in *Neuromancer,* downloaded consciousnesses and AI exist for themselves and not as servants of humanity. The SF icon of the self-replicating Von Neumann machine and the Singularity, in which computers generate more sophisticated computers which then continue to develop ever increasingly sophisticated machines that exceed the capability of any human to anticipate or understand, informs cyberpunk, but can be traced back to earlier SF, including Asimov's "The Evitable Conflict." As people are confronted with the black box of increasingly complex computers that undergird most of the technologically developed world, they are faced with anxieties of dependence or competition. A natural response to this secular mystery is a form of secular worship; prevalent in cyberpunk is the conflict between the urge to give praise to the freedom afforded by the computer and the terror of a usurping, non-human power, an evolutionary next step of intelligent life. Perhaps Christopher Hodder-Williams's observation, "Many people fear computers because they seem to impersonate human beings. But they are wrong. What they should fear is the opposite: human beings who impersonate computers" (Barrett 10), speaks to these anxieties as well as our fascination with the power of the computer. Sf has been intimately involved with the computer and with the way in which we attempt to understand the impact of this innovation on society, singing canticles for the machine as well as warnings.

Works Cited

Adams, Douglas. *The Hitch-Hiker's Guide to the Galaxy.* London: Pan, 1979.
Asimov, Isaac. *I, Robot* [&] *Robots and Empire.* Omnibus ed. London: HarperCollins, 2005.
Barrett, David V., ed. *Digital Dreams.* Hodder and Stoughton: New English Library, 1990.
Broderick, Damien. *Reading by Starlight: Postmodern Science Fiction.* London: Routledge, 1995.
Clarke, Arthur C. *2001 Space Odyssey.* London: Orbit. 2000.
Clute, John, and Peter Nicholls, ed. *The Encyclopedia of Science Fiction.* 2d ed. New York: St. Martin's Griffin, 1995.
Colatrella, Carol. "Science Fiction in the Information Age." *American Literary History* 11 (3) 1999.
"Computer." *Online OED.* 15 November 2009, <http://dictionary.oed.com.ezproxy.liv.ac.uk/cgi/entry/50045993?single=1&query_type=word&queryword=computer&first=1&max_to_show=10>.
"Cybernetics." *Online OED.* 15 November 2009, <http://dictionary.oed.com.ezproxy.liv.ac.uk/cgi/entry/50056595?single=1&query_type=word&queryword=cybernetics&first=1&max_to_show=10>.
Delany, Samuel R. *Nova.* London: Millenium, 2001.

Eagle Eye. Dir. D.J. Caruso. Perf. Shia LaBeouf and Michelle Monaghan. 2008.

Forster, E.M. "The Machine Stops." *17 x Infinity.* New York. Dell. 1963.

Gernsback, Hugo. *Ralph 124C 41+: A Romance of the Year 2660.* Lincoln: University of Nebraska Press, 2000.

"Ghost in the Machine." *X-Files.* Jerrold Freeman. Perf. David Duchovny and Gillian Anderson. 1993.

Ghost in the Shell. Dir. Mamoru Oshii. Perf. Atsuko Tanaka. 1995.

Gibson, William. *Neuromancer.* London: HarperCollins, 1984.

I, Robot. Dir. Alex Proyas. Perf. Will Smith. 2004.

ITSF ESA, "Innovative Technologies from Science Fiction for Space Applications." 2001. 19 November 2009, <http://www.itsf.org/index.php?PAGE=brochure%2Findex.html>.

James, Edward, and Farah Mendlesohn, ed. *The Cambridge Companion to Science Fiction.* Cambridge: Cambridge University Press, 2003.

Leinster, Murray (as Will Jenkins). "A Logic Named Joe." 1946. 8 October, http://www.baen.com/chapters/W200506/0743499107_2.htm>.

Leinster, Murray."Politics." *Amazing,* June 1932.

The Matrix. Dir. Andy Wachowski and Larry Wachowski. Perf. Keanu Reeves. 1999.

McDonald, Ian. "The Catharine Wheel." *Worldmakers: SF Adventures in Terraforming.* New York: St. Martin's Griffin, 2001.

Monteleone, Thomas F., ed. *Microworlds: SF Stories of the Computer Age.* London: Hamlyn, 1984.

Orwell, George. *1984.* London: Penguin. 2003.

Pohl, Frederick. *Man Plus.* London: Millenium. 2000.

Porush, David. "Technology and Postmodernism: Cybernetic Fiction." *SubStance* 9, 2 (27) 1980.

Schroeder, Karl. *Ventus.* New York: Tom Doherty Associates. 2000.

Stableford, Brian. *Science Fact and Science Fiction: An Encyclopedia.* New York: Routledge, 2006.

Star Trek. Created by Gene Roddenberry. 1966. TV series.

Stevenson, Robert Louis. *Strange Case of Dr. Jekyll and Mr. Hyde.* London: Longmans. 1892.

2001: A Space Odyssey. Dir. Stanley Kubrick. Perf. Keir Dullea and Gary Lockwood. 1968.

Turing, A.M. "Computing Machinery and Intelligence." *Mind* 59, 1950.

Westfahl, Gary, ed. *The Greenwood Encyclopedia of Science Fiction and Fantasy: Themes, Works and Wonders.* London: Greenwood, 2005.

3

Murray Leinster and "A Logic Named Joe"

Eric G. Swedin and David L. Ferro

The March 1946 issue of *Astounding Science Fiction* featured two stories by the prolific author Murray Leinster. The first story, "Adapter," ran under his well-known pen name, while the second ran under his real name of Will F. Jenkins. The second story, "A Logic Named Joe," became an immediate minor classic. In *Machines That Think: The Best Science Fiction Stories About Robots and Computers,* Isaac Asimov describes "A Logic Named Joe" as "very interesting" and "one of a kind." In 1946, when computers "were huge constructs so expensive that only the government or a large corporation could afford to own one" and "the miniaturization of computers had not yet been anticipated," only Leinster had "imagined a society where home computers might be common" (Asimov 279). Andy Duncan called the "astonishing" story "one of the most prescient science fiction stories" ever, "a feat of prediction" that prompted *Wired* magazine to hail "Leinster as a prophet" (Duncan 62, 63). This is a common assessment of "A Logic Named Joe," and accurate as far as it goes, but the story is even more insightful in light of present-day computer technology. The story is also a powerful cautionary fable about the power of technological temptation.

Murray Leinster

William Fitzgerald Jenkins (Will F. Jenkins) was born in Norfolk, Virginia, on June 16, 1896. His formal education ended before he finished eighth grade, but his strong interest in science and technology sustained his quest for self-education. In 1909 he built a working glider and won an aeronautical magazine contest. He worked as an office boy and as a bookkeeper while practicing his writing craft, quitting on his twenty-first birthday to become a professional writer (Moskowitz 49–50). Jenkins published his first short story in *Argosy* in 1918, and his first science fiction story, "The Runaway Skyscraper," followed in *Argosy* in 1919.

As his career flourished, Jenkins adopted the name Murray Leinster as a pseudonym for the lower-paying pulps and reserved his real name for the slick magazines, such as *Collier's* and the *Saturday Evening Post.* In a career that lasted until 1975, Leinster published nearly 1,800 short stories and around 100 novels, and as many as 20 movies and numerous radio shows were adapted from his source material. He wrote in most genres, although regular sales to romance magazines, published under yet another pseudonym, often eluded him. The main exception in the diversity of his work was that he avoided writing stories involving "the occult and supernatural," because he "thought such things carried over into a writer's subconscious and could definitely be destructive" (Payne 4).[1]

During World War II, Leinster joined the national effort, as did many of his contemporary science fiction writers. Leinster used his communications skills for the Office of War Information during the day and continued to write his stories in the evenings. Though he published many types of stories, and often earned better rates in other genres, science fiction remained near and dear to Leinster's heart. In a draft of a proposed speech to the Eastern Science Fiction Association in 1947, Leinster wrote, "There is a real if latent value in the kind of speculation and the kind of air-tight reasoning from fantastic assumptions which we science-fiction addicts are used to" (Jenkins, "Proposed Talk" 3). Leinster also described being visited by a government security official during World War II to ask if the short story "Deadline" was a leak. Written by Cleve Cartmill for the March 1944 issue of *Astounding Science Fiction,* "Deadline" described a superweapon made of radioactive elements. Leinster realized that the United States was building an atomic bomb and felt "very uncomfortable" with this secret. Until the end of the war, in the interests of national security, "very few people have ever emulated an oyster more earnestly than I did from that time on, where atomic-energy discussions were concerned" (Jenkins, "Proposed Talk" 1). During a lecture in 1963, Leinster said, "It has long been my belief that science fiction is really the hope of the nation" (Eney 72).

Time magazine published an interesting review of the field of science fiction and its fans in 1949:

> The four founding fathers of "science fiction" are generally acknowledged to be Edgar Allan Poe, Jules Verne, Sir Arthur Conan Doyle and H. G. Wells. In the U.S., Will F. Jenkins, a 27-year veteran, who also writes under the pen

name of Murray Leinster, is regarded as the dean of writers in the field. Best of the lot, according to expert editors, are Robert Heinlein and A. E. van Vogt [*Time*].

A year later, the Chicago-based Shasta Publishers used the term "dean of American science-fiction authors" in promotional material for Leinster's short story collection *Sidewise in Time and Other Scientific Adventures* (Shasta 1). The 21st World Science Fiction Convention, held in Washington, D.C., in 1963, selected Leinster as its Guest of Honor.

Theodore Sturgeon, famed for his own short stories, opined that Leinster "wrote few great stories and no bad ones" (Sturgeon 1). Leinster is best known for five stories:

- "Sidewise in Time" (1934), for which the Sidewise Award for Alternate History is named, and acknowledged as the first parallel worlds story;
- "First Contact" (1945), retroactively awarded a Hugo for Best Novelette in 1996;
- "The Ethical Equations" (1945);
- "Exploration Team" (1956), winner of the Hugo Award for Best Novelette;
- "A Logic Named Joe" (1946), which won no awards, but its prominence has grown over time.

The Story

"A Logic Named Joe" is one of Leinster's more enjoyable science fiction short stories, written with a wry sense of humor, where the first-person narrator is a logics maintenance technician named Ducky. The writing style and colloquial phrasing evoke the personality of a blue-collar workingman, perhaps like a stereotypical 1940s–era Brooklyn plumber. Following his normal practice, Leinster never describes the appearance of any of the characters (Sturgeon 2). The first sentence lays out the story in summary: "It was on the third day of August that Joe come off the assembly line, and on the fifth Laurine come into town, and that afternoon I saved civilization" (Jenkins, "A Logic Named Joe" 139). "Logics" are common household appliances that combine a television, telephone, and computer into a single device with a keyboard and a "vision receiver" (140). This is not a passive device, like a television, that only receives media content, but interactive in that you can "punch" keys to ask questions of the central "tank" (140).[2]

Leinster wrote a summary of "A Logic Named Joe" in 1951 as part of a list of vignette ideas for a proposed television series:

> When a TV set and an integral calculator and a telephone are added together to make a household gadget that everybody uses, it's very convenient indeed.

Everybody has a secretarial service and a filing-system and an information service plus entertainment and television-telephone system as a matter of course. But there comes just one of those instruments that wants to be useful — to answer *every* question anybody asks. But it hasn't discrimination. It will tell how to rob a bank as well as how to get over a hangover. It will tell how a blonde can get her man, and it will answer the questions a wife is better off not having answered — and civilization totters, when anybody can find out anything they want to know by just asking [Jenkins, "Vignette Ideas" 1].

A logic named Joe is accidentally altered during manufacture so that it can create new knowledge. Joe offers advice as a new logics service on any topic, including murder, counterfeiting, and all manner of mischief. New inventions are created, such as a concoction mixed from household ingredients that will instantly make a drunk sober; a perpetual-motion machine; the secret of transmuting metals; and many new products for thieves: "new and improved jimmies, knob-claws for gettin' at safe-innards, and all-purpose keys that'd open any known lock" (144). More chaos ensues.

An old girlfriend, Laurine, comes into town and locates the narrator by using the new logics service. She calls the narrator and tells him that she is "terribly lonesome" and asks him to come to her hotel (147). He stutters and promises that he will call her back. He is terrified of Laurine, and "often thanked Gawd fervent that she didn't marry me when I thought I wanted her to.... She was blonde an' fatal to begin with. She had got blonder and fataler an' had had four husbands and one acquittal for homicide an' had acquired a air of enthusiasm and self-confidence" (143).

Having Laurine in the back of his mind makes the narrator nervous and is a source of stress as he tries to figure out what is happening with the new logics service offered by Joe. The narrator suggests closing down the central tanks that hold data for the logics and is informed that this would cause civilization to collapse.

Joe continues to solve problems, including "cold electron-emission" in order to make vacuum tubes "that wouldn't need a power source to heat the filament" (151). One person learns how to serve leftover soup in a new way, and another person learns how to dispose of the corpse he had stored down in his cellar. Joe even invents an extra-dimensional machine to rob the gold reserves of a bank. Even more seriously, with echoes of the ideologies that drove World War II, "a social-conscious guy asks how to bring about his own particular system of social organization at once. He don't ask if it's best or if it'll work. He just wants to get it started." A "retired preacher asks how can the human race be cured of concupiscence" (151). Up pops "another group of serious thinkers who are sure the human race would be a lot better off if everybody went back to nature an' lived in the woods with the ants an' poison ivy."

They start askin' questions about how to cause humanity to abandon cities and artificial conditions of living." Finally, "the Superior Man gang that sneers at the rest of us was quietly asking questions on what kinda weapons could be made by which Superior men could take over and run things" (152).

Preoccupied with his fear of Laurine, the solution to the problem suddenly occurs to the narrator. He uses a "pay-logic" to ask where the misbehaving logic is located (153). He retrieves the logic, turns it off, and stores it in his cellar. Though the narrator calls the abnormal logic 'Joe' throughout the story, he explains that he only named the wayward logic after acquiring it. The narrator is concerned that someone else might be interested in making a new Joe, and though aware of the dangers of leaving Joe intact, the narrator muses to himself that maybe he should turn Joe on for just a little while, in order to ask how to "make me a coupla million dollars, easy" or "how can a old guy not stay old?" (154).

Astounding Science Fiction had a policy of ranking the popularity of stories and articles in each issue based on reader responses in a short column called "The Analytical Laboratory" (Bainbridge). The feedback for the March issue was published in the June issue. "A Logic Named Joe" was the issue's most popular story, even though longer stories usually tended to be more popular in the poll. The story won while competing against the first third of George O. Smith's novel "Pattern for Conquest." The second installment of Smith's novel moved to first place in the following month. According to editor John W. Campbell, Leinster's story "did right well to take first ... since novels give an author so much greater scope for development" (Campbell).

Analysis

Leinster used the term *logic* to refer to electronic computers because the term computer was not yet in general use for that meaning. A computer was originally a person who made mathematical calculations or computations. The term especially found use as the title of a person employed to make calculations for an insurance company, bank, astronomical observatory, or similar organization that relied on numerous repetitive mathematical calculations. While there are a few instances of the term *computer* being applied to electronic computers before 1946, use of the term in that sense was rare.

True electronic computers were first built during World War II, and knowledge about them was restricted until after the war. The first true electronic computers were the Colossi machines, built in Britain in 1943, and the ENIAC, finished in 1945 at the University of Pennsylvania. Because the Colossi were used for codebreaking, knowledge of these machines was not released until the 1970s. Since the ENIAC was public knowledge, most obvious late computer innovations flowed directly from the ENIAC. Public perceptions of computers were created by images of the ENIAC, made of 49 cabinets, almost 18,000 vacuum tubes, miles of wiring, and weighing 30 tons (Swedin and Ferro, 30–41). About the time that "A Logic Named Joe" was published in 1946, the term *computer* was becoming more common, though "electronic brain" briefly competed as an alternate term (Oxford English Dictionary, entry for "computer").

Projecting back our contemporary technology, a "logic" is a home computer combined with a telephone, television, and an Internet connection. The colloquial narration of the story emphasizes that logics really are just common household appliances, like toasters or radios, not something exotic that required highly educated technicians in white coats. The origin of the logics in the story is described as occurring when "that guy Carson invented his trick circuit that will select any of 'steenteen million other circuits — in theory there ain't no limit — and before the Logics Company hooked it into the tank-and-integrator set-up they were usin' 'em as business-machine service. They added a vision screen for speed — an' they found out they'd made logics. They were surprised an' pleased. They're still findin' out what logics will do, but everybody's got 'em" (Jenkins, "A Logic Named Joe" 140).

Not surprisingly, the narrator admits that the introduction of logics "changed civilization, the highbrows tell us. All on accounta the Carson Circuit" (140). When the frantic narrator asks a technician at the tank to shut down the tank (akin to turning off the Internet), he gets this answer:

> "Shut down the tank?" he says, mirthless. "Does it occur to you, fella, that the tank has been doin' all the computin' for every business office for years? It's been handlin' the distribution of ninety-four per cent of all telecast programs, has given out all information on weather, plane schedules, special sales, employment opportunities and news; has handled all person-to-person contacts over wires and recorded every business conversation and agreement — Listen, fella! Logics changed civilization. Logics *are* civilization! If we shut off logics, we go back to a kind of civilization we have forgotten how to run! [148, italics in the original].

The idea of a home computer was completely revolutionary at the time and three decades early, but Leinster goes even further by describing what we would think of as the Internet. These home computers (logics) can make queries and download media content from distant computers called "tanks."

> The tank is a big buildin' full of all the facts in creation an' all the recorded telecasts that ever was made — an' it's hooked in with all the other tanks all over the country — an' everything you wanna know or see or hear, you punch for it an' you get it. Very convenient. Also it does math for you, an' keeps books, an' acts as consultin' chemist, physicist, astronomer, an' tea-leaf reader, with a "Advice to the Lovelorn" thrown in [140].

The term *tank* is used in two ways by Leinster. In the first sense, *tank* refers to remote computers, as large as a building, that the logics are connected to via telephone lines. Tanks have "data plates" in them. The narrator offers this description: "There ain't any fact that can be said to be a fact that ain't on a data plate in some tank somewhere — unless it's one the technicians are diggin' out an' puttin' on a data plate now" (141). The term *tank* is also used to refer to all the tanks in the world as a whole, similar to how the Internet can be thought of as one giant computer.

Just as in modern computing, Leinster realized that there would be a clear distinction between where data is stored (data-plates in tanks) and where the processing occurs (logics). "There ain't nothing in the tank set-up to start relays closin.' Relays are closed exclusive by logics, to get the information the keys are punched for" (152).

What we now call "distributed computing" is also illustrated in the story. Joe is the only logic that has started to think in a way described as cooperating "in long-term planning which human brains are too limited in scope to do" (153). Requests to any other logic for the new query service can apparently be routed to Joe so that it can invent the appropriate answer. When Joe is turned off, the new and improved logics service shuts down also. Only Joe is making a difference.

Today, through distributed computing, Google is effectively the world's largest computer — a single computational entity spread around the world in at least a dozen physical data centers. Google uses hundreds of thousands of generic personal computers, mounted on Velcro strips in row after row, all running software that distributes data and processing across as many different nodes as needed. Google is the modern equivalent of the generic sense of 'the tank' in Leinster's story (Markoff and Hansell).

The current trend to rely on the Internet for communication and information has led to the dramatic decline of the encyclopedia market and to the sight of libraries replacing books with computers hooked to the Internet. This reliance on ever newer technology, simplifying our lives, is described by the narrator:

> We got a very simple civilization. In the nineteen hundreds a man would have to make use of a typewriter, radio, telephone, teletypewriter, newspaper, reference library, encyclopedias, office files, directories, plus messenger service and consulting lawyers, chemists, doctors, dieticians, filing clerks, secretaries — all to put down what he wanted to remember an' to tell him what other people had put down that he wanted to know; to report what he said to somebody else and to report to him what they said back. All we have to have is logics. Anything we want to know or see or hear, or anybody we want to talk to, we punch keys on a logic. Shut off logics and everything goes skiddoo [Jenkins, "A Logic Named Joe" 148–9].

The issue of privacy in a world of personal information warehoused in distant computers is illustrated by the example of the narrator's wife, who is shocked at all the details that the tank contains about her, though she enjoys finding out about her neighbors. The same situation has arisen with today's Internet. Personal information for people in America and around the world is stored in thousands of databases, available and used in ways that is not obvious to most people.

Joe also has the ability of multitasking, something that early computers could not do: "All this while Joe goes on buzzin' happy to himself, showin' the Korlanovitch kids the animated funnies with one circuit while with the others he remote-controls the tank so that all the other logics can give people what they ask for and thereby raise merry hell" (144).

Joe is essentially an artificial intelligence. The idea of machines that could think has a long history in science fiction, often conflated with the idea of robots. Some of the consequences of having such machines are addressed by the narrator in quick asides. For instance, the sentence "Joe shoulda been a perfectly normal logic, keeping some family or other from wearin' out its brains doin' the kids' homework for 'em," expresses the idea of logics doing our thinking for us (140).

In the story, Leinster makes the creation of Joe an accident, an inexplicable fluke. By doing so, he avoids the problem of having to explain how an artificial intelligence would work. As an author who tried to thoroughly cover all possible angles in his story, at least the obvious ones, he emphasized that the accident that made Joe was "extremely improbable" and thus would probably not happen again (153). He also provides a few more details later in the story:

> Joe, he'd gone exploring in the tank and closed some relays like a logic is supposed to do — but only when required — and blocked all censor-circuits an' fixed up this logics service which planned perfect crimes, nourishing an' attractive meals, counterfeitin' machines, an' new industries with a fine impartiality. He musta been plenty happy, Joe must. He was functionin' swell, buzzin' along to himself [143].

Joe is also benign, at least in machine terms, though it is apparently lacking any morality or even a sense of what might be socially acceptable or not. Joe explains how to commit murder and theft and merrily corrupts the young with no sense of the consequences.

> He ain't like one of these ambitious robots you read about that make up their minds the human race is inefficient and has got to be wiped out an' replaced by thinkin' machines. Joe's just got ambition. If you were a machine, you'd wanna work right, wouldn't you? That's Joe. He wants to work right. An' he's a logic. An' logics can do a lotta things that ain't been found out yet. So Joe, discoverin'

the fact, begun to feel restless. He selects some things us dumb humans ain't thought of yet, an' begins to arrange so logics will be called on to do 'em [141].

This point in the story seems to be a mere mechanism to make the story flow in a humorous fashion, though one might argue that Leinster sees machines as inherently amoral.

It must be mentioned that the female characters are stereotypical, with the archetypal nosy housewife as the narrator's wife and the dangerous blonde, Laurine, as a black widow. While conventional for 1940s pulp fiction, these portrayals would be considered sexist today. Leinster plays the stereotypes for humor in a manner lacking malice. The one prominent exception is "Logics don't work good on women. Only on things that make sense" (140). This reflects the limited education and cultural horizons of the narrator, who is only a simple television repairman turned logics maintenance man.

The theme of temptation is pervasive in the story. While it is true that Leinster was a practicing Catholic, temptation is an emotion that is not confined to the devout. Much of the narrative tension for the story comes from the attraction to his old girlfriend, Laurine, from whom he parted "with much romantic despair." Laurine "makes cold shivers run up an' down my spine when I think about her" (139). During her calls to the narrator, she "has a look of unquenched enthusiasm that gives a man very strange weak sensations at the back of his knees" (147). This is a dangerous temptation for more than just moral reasons, because Laurine has "had four husbands and shot one and got acquitted" (147).

The idea of censor blocks or "censor-circuits" is a way of keeping temptation at bay (142). Early in the story, the action of the censor is described:

> In theory, a censor block is gonna come on an' the screen will say severely, "Public Policy Forbids This Service." You hafta have censor blocks or the kiddies will be askin' detailed questions about things they're too young to know. And there are other reasons. As you will see [141–142].

This entire issue reflects the perennial concern of what children may be safely exposed to, and at what age. Of course, the moral standards used to create rules of appropriateness are different for Leinster's time than for our own, but today parents are concerned about adult material on the Internet and protecting children from inadvertent or deliberate exposure.

When the narrator comes to collect Joe, he finds the children of the Korlanovitch family watching a forbidden film. They wanted to see "real cannibals,"

> So the screen is presenting a anthropological expedition scientific record film of the fertility dance of the Huba-Jouba tribe of West Africa. It is supposed to be restricted to anthropological professors an' post-graduate medical students.

But there ain't any censor blocks workin' any more and it's on. The kids are much interested. Me, bein' a old married man, I blush [153–4].

There are two illustrations in the original *Astounding Science Fiction* story. Living up to the quasi-salacious reputation that the pulps had, one of the illustrations is of a boy and girl watching with interest the ecstatic dancing of two African women on the screen of their logic. The women are wearing tight tunics from their bare shoulders down to mid-thigh (145). The other illustration is of the narrator talking earnestly to Laurine on a logic's screen that is at least four feet high (150). She is wearing "some kinda frothy hangin'-around-the-house-with-the-boy-friend outfit that automatic makes you strain your eyes to see if you actual see what you think" (149).

The narrator faces more temptations within himself at the end of the story. He wonders if he should turn Joe back on long enough for Joe to invent a way for the narrator to get rich. On a certain level he recognizes that this is a temptation. "But even if I got sense enough not to get rich, an' if I get retired and just loaf around fishin' an' lyin' to other old duffers about what a great guy I used to be — Maybe I'll like it, but maybe I won't" (154).

Then there is the ultimate temptation, a theme dealt with in so many science fiction stories: immortality. "And after all, if I get fed up with bein' old and confined strictly to thinking — why I could hook Joe in long enough to ask: "How can a old guy not stay old?" Joe'll be able to find out. An' he'll tell me" (154).

The consequences to having a solution to immortality are obvious in the last paragraph of the story:

> That couldn't be allowed out general, of course. You gotta make room for kids to grow up. But it's a pretty good world, now Joe's turned off. Maybe I'll turn him on long enough to learn how to stay in it. But on the other hand, maybe — [154].

To be immortal is to aspire to be like the gods; to have an intelligent machine like Joe, always eager to please, is to have a machine granting the user godlike powers.

After "Joe"

"A Logic Named Joe" proved to be one of Leinster's most popular stories. Only four years after its appearance, the story was reprinted in a collection of short stories by Leinster, *Sidewise in Time and Other Scientific Adventures* (Chicago: Shasta, 1950). Later collections of Leinster's works also included the story. Most recently the story was reprinted in Murray Leinster, *Logic Named Joe*, edited and compiled by Eric Flint (Riverdale, New York: Baen,

2005). NBC broadcast the story as a radio show on the *Dimension X* radio show on June 1, 1950, and again on the new *X Minus* One radio show on December 28, 1955. Leinster was paid $200 (his agent took $20 as his fee and Shasta took $36 for their share of the royalties) for the rights to the radio show (*Radio Plays Radio*; *Where Yesterdays Live*; Jenkins, "Letter from Jenkins dated July 19, 1950"). A 1962 Canadian educational film, "*The Living Machine*," drew on ideas from "A Logic Named Joe" and mentioned the name of the story (Moskowitz 64).

Besides writing fiction, Leinster's mind churned out new technology ideas. The genesis of his most successful invention came when Leinster attended a rehearsal in the early 1950s where one of his stories, "First Contact," was being readied for television broadcast. He was disappointed that the production stage was so large, since a spaceship should look more confined. The producer explained how expensive scenery was to build and use. It occurred to Leinster that it would be very convenient if a background could be projected onto the back of the stage. He began to muse over how this would be possible, as a device for a possible science fiction story set in a future television studio.

Leinster returned home, where he maintained a laboratory for tinkering. (Moskowitz 58). Within a short time he invented a front-projection device that attached to a camera, projecting an image containing the background onto the rear wall of the stage. The rear wall had to be covered with Scotchlite, the reflective material found on road signs, which is made of small glass beads that reflect light directly back into the source and only into the source. The technique allowed the background image to be seamlessly exposed onto the film in the camera. Actors, furniture, and other objects on the stage dispersed the light that hit them and did not interfere with the generation of the background image.

Leinster filed for two patents, and when they were initially denied he actually went to the patent office and showed the examiner how his invention was different from previous inventions.[3] He obtained his patents. After fending off hucksters and intellectual-property thieves, Leinster finally licensed the rights of his invention to famed entrepreneur Sherman Fairchild. After further development and commercialization, the front-projection technique was used extensively in television and for still photography, since it reduced the amount of necessary on-location work. Appropriately enough, the first major motion picture to take advantage of the technique was *2001: A Space Odyssey* (1968). The use of computers eventually retired the technique in the early 1990s (Rickitt 69). In an article for *Analog Science Fiction/Science Fact* magazine (the renamed *Astounding Science Fiction* magazine), Leinster offered this invention as a pure example of "applied science fiction" (Jenkins and Leinster 109).

Leinster's early interest in electronics continued throughout his life and extended to the actual computers of the 1950s. In 1957, Leinster tried to interest a publisher in a popular book on computers. The idea was prompted by the experience "three or four years ago" of writing a television script for an interview with Dr. Grace Hopper, a programmer for the UNIVAC, the first commercial computer (Jenkins "Letter from Jenkins to Mr. Brendler" 1). Grace Hopper was already a computer celebrity because of her success in a field dominated by men and because of her contributions to the field of computer programming. She later rose to the rank of Rear Admiral in the Navy and made important contributions to COBOL, the premier business programming language. Leinster wanted this book to be anecdotal instead of analytical, and aimed at a general audience rather than engineers. The project never bore fruit.

Leinster also occasionally published factual articles, such as "To Build a Robot Brain" in 1954, which argued that the essential problem to creating a thinking computer was how to associate the concrete description of a thing with the abstract idea that identifies that thing. Even today we have not solved that problem. Leinster suggests that a form of robotic evolution may be the solution, just as humans evolved from animals. In essence, to solve the technical problem of the robotic brain, a researcher must explain the difference between humans and animals. At the end of the article, Leinster offers his final take on the whole problem:

> If the direct approach ... does not yield results, you might try still one more. You might try to figure out why we are human. There is only one theory that I know of. It does not offer a solution to the technical problem of making a robot brain, but it is pretty plausible.
> You learned it in Sunday School [Leinster 111].

Between Leinster's religious orientation and his work with censorship during World War II, we shouldn't be surprised at his focus on human moral frailty in the face of technological omnipotence.

Postscript

The authors of this article began this project seeking a link between the amazing prophetic powers of "A Logic Named Joe" and actual subsequent developments in computer technology. Though many scientists and engineers in computing fields were avid readers of science fiction, we have found no evidence of any direct linkage. Certainly, science fiction helped sustain a milieu of excitement about science and technology that fostered the development of electronic computers and other types of technology. The efforts of writers like Leinster to maintain scientific and technical veracity in their stories contributed to the power of science fiction in the real world of technological innovation, but often only in a general, rather than a specific, sense.

We have used "A Logic Named Joe" in several of our classes when examining the relationships between computer technology and society. The story is a useful teaching tool to tie science fiction to the history of computers. Students are intrigued by the story and enjoy finding parallels to contemporary computer technology, though occasionally a student will struggle with the colloquial style and the lack of familiar words to relate to contemporary technologies.

When Hugo Gernsback gave the emerging genre of scientifically and technologically oriented fiction the name of "scientifiction" in 1926, he emphasized his vision of the main purpose of the genre in predicting new scientific ideas and new technological advances. Of course, the purpose of science fiction is not prediction, as Hugo Gernsback would have preferred, but rather, the use of a scientific, technologically oriented worldview to tell a story that appeals to our emotions and intellect. "A Logic Named Joe" succeeded in doing both.

Notes

1. Though he published "A Logic Named Joe" under his real name, we have chosen to refer to Jenkins as Leinster in this article because that is the most common name that he is known by in the science fiction field.

2. All page numbers for the quotes are from the original *Astounding* issue. Baen Books has generously provided the entire story on the internet as part of their innovative promotion program at <http://www.baen.com/chapters/W200506/0743499107___2.htm>.

3. Patent number: 2727427, Filing date March 3, 1952; issue date December 1955; inventor Will F. Jenkins; patent number 2727429; filing date November 30, 1953; issue date December 1955; inventor Will F. Jenkins.

Works Cited

Asimov, Isaac, Patricia S. Warrick and Martin H. Greenberg, editors. *Machines That Think: The Best Science Fiction Stories About Robots and Computers.* New York: Holt, Rinehart and Winston, 1983.

Bainbridge, William Sims. "The Analytical Laboratory, 1938-1976." *Analog* 50:1 (January 1980): 121-134.

Campbell, John W., Jr., "The Analytical Laboratory." *Astounding Science Fiction,* June 1946, 45.

Duncan, Andy. "It's All SF: Science Fiction, Southern Fiction, and the Case of Murray Leinster." *Foundation: The International Review of Science Fiction* 79 (Summer 2000): 59–69.

Eney, Dick, ed. "The Proceedings; DISCON: The 21st World Science Fiction Convention; Washington —1963 (DISCON, 1963)." Available at Syracuse University Special Collections, Will F. Jenkins Collection.

Jenkins, Will F. "Letter from Jenkins Dated July 19, 1950." Syracuse University Special Collections, Will F. Jenkins Collection, Box 1.

_____. "Letter from Jenkins to Mr. Brendler, September 19, 1957." Syracuse University Special Collections, Will F. Jenkins Collection, Box 1, "Bartholomew House 1957–1958" folder.

_____. "Letter from Shasta to Book Reviewers, dated February 8, 1950." Syracuse University Special Collections, Will F. Jenkins Collection, Box 1.

_____. "A Logic Named Joe." *Astounding Science Fiction,* March 1946.

_____. "Proposed Talk: Eastern Science Fiction Association, 3/2/47." Syracuse University Special Collections, Will F. Jenkins Collection, Box 7, "Science Fiction Fan Clubs" folder.

_____. "Vignette Ideas." Syracuse University Special Collections, Will F. Jenkins Collection, Box 1, "Cole, Alonso" folder.

_____ and Murray Leinster. "Applied Science Fiction." *Analog Science Fiction/Science Fact,* November 1967, 109–124.

Leinster, Murray. "To Build a Robot Brain." *Astounding Science Fiction,* April 1954.

Markoff, John, and Saul Hansell. "Hiding in Plain Sight, Google Seeks More Power." *New York Times,* June 14, 2006. Accessed 3 June 2008, http://www.nytimes.com/2006/06/14/technology/14search.html.

Moskowitz, Sam. *Seekers of Tomorrow: Masters of Modern Science Fiction.* Cleveland: World, 1966.

"Never Too Old to Dream," *Time Magazine,* May 30, 1949. Accessed 3 June 2008, <http://www.time.com/time/magazine/article/0,9171,888030,00.html>.

Oxford English Dictionary, entry for "computer." 2d ed. Oxford: Oxford University Press, 1989.

Payne, Ronald. *The Last Murray Leinster Interview.* Richmond, VA: Waves, 1982.

Radio Plays Radio. Accessed 3 June 2008. <http://davidszondy.com/Radio.htm>.

Rickitt, Richard. *Special Effects: The History and Technique.* New York: Billboard, 2000.

Sturgeon, Theodore. "Will Jenkins: An Appreciation." *Locus: The Newspaper of the Science Fiction Field* 175 (June 24, 1975): 1–2.

Swedin, Eric G., and David L. Ferro. *Computers: The Life Story of a Technology.* Baltimore: Johns Hopkins University Press, 2007.

Where Yesterdays Live. Accessed 3 June 2008, <http://www.whereyesterdayslive.com/otr_shows/x_minus_one.htm>.

4

Atorox, Finnish Fictional Robot with a Changing Personality in the Late 1940s

Jaakko Suominen

World War II left Finland in ruins. The small Northern European country had cooperated with the Third Reich during the war, and afterwards had to change political course to the left while in the shadow of the mighty Soviet empire. Finland paid war indemnity to the Soviet Union, and also found homes for thousands of refugees from Carelia and other areas that were incorporated into the USSR.

For people living in such a difficult situation, pulp fiction might have been one factor that provided some escape from reality. There were no unsolved problems in its utopian literary sphere. Fiction also could help in allowing people to handle difficult everyday experiences (see, e.g., Friedman; Oinonen). At the same time, in its content, pulp fiction in Finland reflected predominantly national and international conditions and provided opportunities to deal with and revaluate those conditions. Finally, pulp fiction contained the echoes from a prewar époque; related, for example, to ideas on human roles, science, and creativity.

In this essay, I focus on an early Finnish robot fiction series: the Atorox novels of 1947 and 1948, written by Aarne Haapakoski (alias Outsider). I examine how the series is connected to inter- and trans-national conceptions of the trends and possibilities of new computing technology. I also describe how the novels acted as a mediator of cultural heritage in robot science fiction (SF).

Robots and robot fiction are interesting in the larger techno-cultural context. In general, a popular and fictional robot was a sort of "personal computer" of the 1940s and the 1950s. It was represented as resembling a human being, it had personal and human characteristics, and individuals often used it. The imaginary SF robot is part of the image of personal computing.

The Outsider and His Robots

Aarne Haapakoski (1904–1961) was called the "perpetual-motion machine of Finnish pulp fiction" (Hänninen, 174). He was very active in literary pursuits after World War II. He started his writing career in early 1930, writing for political organizations associated with right-wing activities. He travelled widely to countries such as France and the Netherlands, writing reports for popular Finnish magazines. At the same time, he also wrote detective and adventure stories. Haapakoski worked on propaganda and news for the military during the war before his demobilization in 1942 due to health reasons.

During the war Haapakoski expanded his repertoire to include science fiction. In 1943 he wrote a fictional short story about a maniac engineer named Murro and his human-like robot called Robomax. The short story was published in *The Dugout Reader*, a publication targeting soldiers. According to Raimo Jokisalmi (69–70) and Juri Nummelin, there has been some discussion as to whether or not the short story was based on the Otomox robot comic strips by Frenchmen André Mavimus and Roger Roux, published in *Pic et Nic* magazine in France in 1943 (see, e.g., http://lambiek.net/artists/r/roux_roger.htm). The connection is possible, since Haapakoski was interested in France and robot names. The outlook and storylines do resemble each other.

The idea of an inventor's humanlike robot was not unique. There had been plenty of news about robot presentations and robot fiction at the international and national levels. Robots were one of the key figures of "the Mechanical Age" (Rasmussen). Finnish people were familiar with Karel Čapek's 1920 *R.U.R.* play (which introduced the word *robot*) since it had been performed in Finland during the 1920s in the cities of Viipuri and Helsinki. Popular magazines and technical journals had published stories of foreign robot presentations. A Finnish robot of sorts, Mr. Machine Man, was exhibited at least three times in the early 1930s. Additionally, a Swedish comic strip, *Konstgjorda Karlsson* (Artificial Karlsson), was published in Finland. The robot had become a popular cultural character; it had many skills but was also dangerous. In many stories it would malfunction and exhibit uncontrolled behaviour. These tropes showed the potential effects on work as well as leisure (Suominen *Koneen*, 21–43).

The Robomax story acted as a precursor to the six novels by Aarne Haapakoski, published in 1947 and 1948. Those novels focused on the interplanetary adventures of American professor Mitax, his crew, and the key protagonist, a robot called Atorox. Even though some national science fiction, as well as translations of foreign classics such as the works of Jules Verne, had

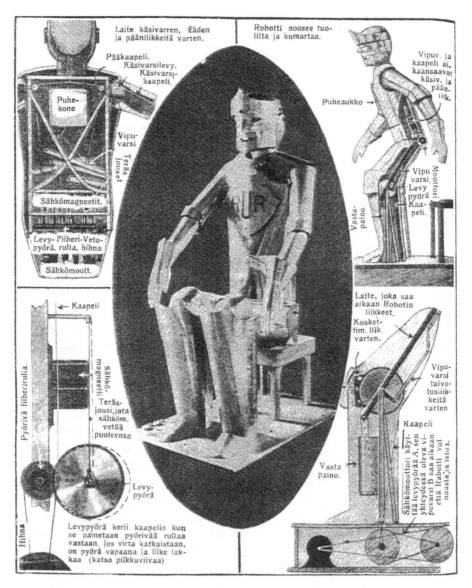

Diagram for the R.U.R. robot (courtesy Jaakko Suominen).

been published in Finland, the Atorox series was a notable turning point. While it might be termed "pulp," it pioneered Finnish science fiction.

To Space and Back

The Atorox series draws on a contemporary understanding of scientific and technological achievements and their popular image. The first novel of the series, *Atorox, ihmisten valtias* (Atorox, Master of the People) is quite distinct from the others and introduces Atorox and Professor Mitax; the robot is literally introduced to the public in a theatre in New York. Atorox gets its power from "actino-uranium" (uranium is one of the actinoids), which seems to have been quite fashionable due to the contemporary interest in nuclear energy. But what is particularly notable, and differentiates the character from other international robot fiction comparisons, is that Atorox is reprogrammable with "brain cassettes." Therefore, the robot incorporates a stored program concept of sorts — something that was introduced almost at the same time in the computer field (Campbell-Kelly and Aspray, 87–96; Ceruzzi, 20–23).

The fictional inventor of Atorox, Professor Mitax, has taped the "brain-work" of about twenty different people. By switching cassettes, Atorox is transformed to different personas: a famous space pilot, a general, a detective, the inventor of actino-uranium, a master criminal, a maniac, a dictator, or a foolish young man in love. All these characters seem to be purely fictional, but there is also one character that was modelled after a real person: a Finn named Ruben Auervaara, a notorious Don Juan figure and hustler who was the subject of considerable public discussion in Finland during the 1940s. The first novel is a crime story where Atorox is stolen by some criminals in order to equip it with a criminal brain cassette and use it for the burglary of the American Central Bank. (In general, Atorox plots are based on the unwanted or unauthorized changes of brain cassettes.) As a result, the robot — and by extension, robots in general — might seem to be more harmful than useful.

The robot Atorox also has senses as good or better than human senses. It has roentgen eyes as well as the capacity to hear and to smell. Atorox resembled its exhibited contemporaries in these abilities. At the 1939 New York World's Fair, for example, the robot Elektro was advertised as "being able to see, talk, smell, sing, and count on his fingers" (Nye, 216). The Finnish Mr. Machine Man robot (Herra koneihminen), introduced in exhibitions in the early 1930s, was able to answer various questions, steer other machines, and act as a salesman of books and batteries. In one battery advertisement the robot was described as "the most qualified expert in electric technology" (Suominen *Koneen*, 40–41).

The next five novels in the series take place on the moon and other planets and form a more coherent entity, although Aarne Haapakoski tested different characters in the stories and discarded them if necessary. In *Atorox Kuussa* (Atorox in the Moon) a scientific expedition makes a journey to the moon with a spacecraft fuelled with actino-uranium. The rocket is steered by Atorox, who is now equipped with a cassette of a famous space "yachtsman." Members of the crew seem to be assembled from Western Allied forces: the United States, the United Kingdom, and France. In addition there is a Finnish doctor, Antero Kivi, who acts as the crew's physician as well as the natural scientific researcher of the expedition. Old professor Mitax is an American, Engineer Graham is English, and Engineer Dubois is French. Not surprisingly, the compatriot of the author Aarne Haapakoski, Doctor Kivi (*kivi* means "stone" in English) is the most stable character of the crew. For example, the Englishman and the Frenchmen are always competing against one another. It is quite obvious that there is a stowaway on board as well. That individual is a comical layman, Svensson, a Swedish apprentice seaman and part-time alcoholic. The stowaway is nearly killed by Atorox when, under the influence of alcohol, Svensson inserts a brain cassette of a dangerous lunatic into Atorox's head.

It appears that there is an atmosphere on the moon, as well as plants, animals, and humanoids. In addition, there are some Germans who fled from Germany during the war and established the state of Lunagermania, which is ruled by an engineer named Nebelhorn. Nebelhorn had opposed Hitler and rebelled against the Nazis with his colleague Sergeant Streithammel during the space voyage, abandoning their Nazi colleagues in space before landing on the moon. That ship had stowaways on board as well, who become part of the state of Lunagermania; for example, a Nigerian called Napoleon was nominated as the Minister of Education. Napoleon is a mistrustful antihero type who plots and changes alliances regularly. His character reflects racial stereotypes of the popular culture of that time. Another stowaway, the young American reporter Miss Collins, becomes the main object of male desire and jealousy of the protagonists. The expedition manages to save Miss Collins with the help of Napoleon, but there is a lot of confusion due to the mixing of Atorox's brain cassettes — and the crew has to escape quickly, leaving Svensson and engineer Dubois behind when Lunagermanian troops attack the spacecraft.

Atorox is partially damaged and steers the rocket to Mars instead of Earth. There is human life there as well, similar to Edgar Rice Burroughs's well-known Barsoom series. Mars is dominated by a female soldier caste. Napoleon proclaims himself to be a returned Martian prince and tries to take power. In addition, Atorox, now equipped with the brain cassette of a South American dictator, Upez, organizes its own *coup d'état*. After some confusion, the crew flees again to space. This time the rocket crashes and the expedition is forced to float in space before it is saved by Noel Goldbaum, a planetary businessman who has escaped from the Germans on the moon.

The expedition becomes suspicious about the goals of Goldbaum (who is portrayed as a fairly stereotypical Jew) when he takes them to Venus and locks them in his hotel. Goldbaum, who is also a leader of Venus, wants to experiment with Atorox's brain cassettes. By accident, he inserts a criminal's cassette into Atorox's head. Atorox escapes and starts to plot criminal activities. The robot flees to a land ruled by a beautiful woman who wants to take the robot as a lover. On the other side of Venus, the Nigerian Napoleon tries once more to take power, but that attempt ends in disaster when Atorox, now operating with a executioner's brain, accidentally hangs him.

The next stop is the planet Mercury, where the crew travels with Goldbaum. Mercury has been attacked by Nebelhorn's Lunagermanian troops. Later, it turns out that the soldiers are being led by the Swedish seaman Svensson, who has became a general. Native Mercurials, like Venusians, are more technologically advanced than Earthlings. They have rejected nuclear energy and use some kind of "direct space energy." Mercurials, however, are physically weak and live mainly underground for security reasons. The physical work is done by robots and slave animals called Pharos, who are starting a rebellion against their masters. The configuration resembles Karel Čapek's *R.U.R.* (1920) and *War with the Newts* (1936) and other (science) fiction. Also borrowing from international fiction is the use of serial numbers with some robots and, later on, humans, which probably comes from industrial and statistical tradition as well as Western and Soviet science fiction, such as Yevgeny Zamyatin and his novel *We* (1927).

Even though the robot Atorox is "old-fashioned" compared to its Mercurial counterparts because it "eats" action-uranium, its brain cassettes are an advanced technical innovation. Therefore, the robots ask Atorox to lead their revolution. Unfortunately, Atorox is again equipped with non-practical brain cassettes and creates a fair amount of damage. Once more the crew, Professor Mitax, Doctor Kivi, Engineer Graham, and Miss Collins escape from a planet, after some difficulties. Due to a rocket malfunction, it takes a couple of years to get back home. During this period, Professor Mitax dies. The writer Aarne Haapakoski applies an odd version of Einstein's relativity theory, where time passes in space differently than on Earth. The members of the expedition return to their home planet, and a thousand years have passed. The Earth has fought several inter-planetary wars against the Moonlings, Martians, and others. People have moved to the bottom of the oceans because the ground has been polluted during the wars. Weapons, as well as robots, have been prohibited. Doctors can now raise the dead, which is very convenient for the expedition, because they age a thousand years immediately when they arrive.

Above and opposite: Book covers for *Atorox Venuksessa* (Atorox on Venus) and *Atorox Marissa* (Atorox on Mars) (courtesy Jaakko Suominen).

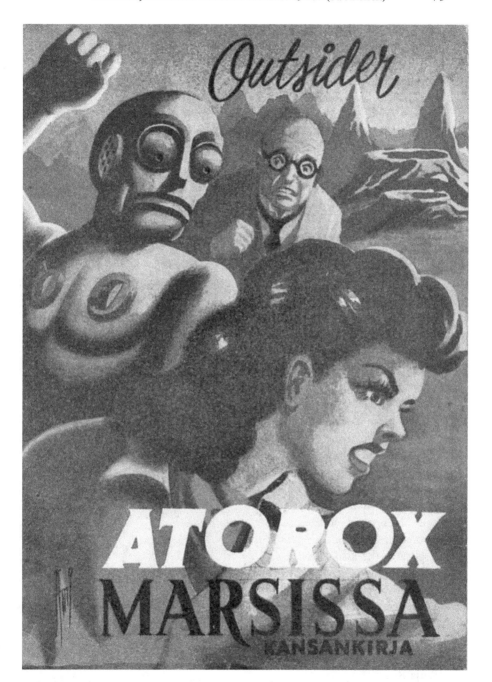

Atorox, who now has the brain cassette of a robotic rebel, causes some trouble. The robot is left behind at the rocket and kills hundreds of policemen who try to arrest it, but with the help of Doctor Kivi and other crew members the robot is saved. Atorox is placed in a museum section with other old robots, all of which have been bolted to the ground. At the museum, Atorox meets a female Finnish robot, Fiina. They escape from the museum, steal a rocket, and most likely fly to Finland to raise a new robot generation. This is the end of both the book and the series. The final destiny of Atorox is left open.

Mediating Cultural Heritage of Science Fiction: Influences of Atorox

David Ferro and Eric Swedin have pondered the effects and influences of science fiction on students, as well as on computer scientists and their inventions. The same effects and influences can be examined with respect to the Atorox novels. These works have been lauded as outstanding works of Finnish science fiction by SF aficionados. This can be demonstrated, for example, on Web sites and in science fiction anthologies and historiographies. A Finnish science fiction society, the Turku Science Fiction Association, has awarded the oldest Finnish SF award — the Atorox Prize — since 1983. The prize is a clay head of Atorox given to the best Finnish science fiction or fantasy novel of the year. The prize is modeled on international prizes in science fiction; the purpose of the association has been to increase the popularity of Finnish science fiction. According to e-mail exchanges, it is obvious that the Atorox head was suggested for the prize due to the importance of the books for science fiction in Finland (Katja Rosvall).

Atorox has been used on several other occasions as well. Ursa, a Finnish

The Atorox Trophy is special almost every year because it is hand made and based on different Atorox book covers. The first statues were made by a mother of a member of the Turku Science Fiction Society in 1983 (Atorox Award by Tomi Junnila, copyright 2008, used with permission).

Society for space enthusiasm, has published SF literature, and in 1988 published an SF anthology called *Atoroxin Perilliset,* Heir of Atorox. Atorox books, which nowadays are rare collectibles, were republished in one volume by the Seaflower Company in 1993.

Influences of the book can be roughly divided between the short- and long-term. So far, it is difficult to estimate the importance of the books in the late 1940s alongside its contemporaries. According to Juri Nummelin, who has studied Finnish pulp literature, that kind of book was rarely reviewed or introduced in the press during that time (Nummelin).

Aarne Haapakoski did receive considerable fame and publicity from his other works, mainly from the adventure stories of Pekka Lipponen and Kalle Kustaa Korkki. Since the stories were broadcast on radio, they became really popular starting in 1945. (Oinonen, 176–177.) Those radio adventure stories have certain similarities with the Atorox books. For example, they both play with the same type of national, ethnical, and sexual stereotypes found in the Atorox books, and had similar characters. Also, there were two robot storylines in the Lipponen-Korkki stories in the late 1950s and the early 1960s.

One can make only an indirect hypothesis about what information processing professionals and Finnish scientists thought about the Atorox books in the late 1940s or the early 1950s. Most likely they didn't know the books at all or categorized them as uninteresting popular pulp fiction. There are some references, however, which suggest that some scientists of that period appreciated SF classics such as those by Jules Verne and H. G. Wells and their scientific-technological predictions. Radio pioneer Guglielmo Marconi, polar explorer Richard Byrd, and rocket scientist Wernher von Braun have been noted as being influenced by Verne (Introduction, *20,000 Leagues Under the Sea,* New York: Pocket, 2005, p. xiii). But, more generally, the experts (at least in professional journals) regarded critically or patronizingly most popularizations of new information technology, such as robots or "electronic brains."

Scientists, professionals, and other masters of computing were international key actors in introducing technological change. They were the guides and captains of the change. For example, Norbert Wiener, one of the primary and often cited presenters of cybernetics, spoke about the Second Industrial Revolution, which meant that the machines would not take care of only physical work, but also of control and communication tasks. Some Finnish scientists in the late 1940s, and especially in the early 1950s, adopted the concept of the Second or New Industrial Revolution (Paju, 93–97). They constructed the new computing technology and introduced it to professional and non-professional audiences, and their work added to a public discourse rather than dwelling only on technical matters.

One can see that those professionals did not attempt to adopt and construct the new technology solely as artifacts. They also adopted and adapted the language or discourse of technology and did so by using internationally known proper arguments, themes, and visions of technology. Even so, the language of technology was modified and adjusted to personal, local, and national needs. Technology was *translated* in a Latourian sense (Latour; see also 1995). That did not mean an adjustment only for professional discourse, but also adjustments for and links to public and popular discursive traditions that cannot be totally separated from each other. We can follow Patricia S. Warrick's argument on cybernetic imagination in science fiction in this, because she has stated that "technological invention grows from mental images, and mental images seem most often to be expressed first in literature. Thus the division between the literary imagination and the engineering imagination seems artificial" (Warrick, 12; see also Epilogue, 228). Differing viewpoints were connected with collective imaginings of new technologies and their role in everyday life.

It is often noted that in popular discourse of the 1940s and 1950s, computers were usually described as 'electronic brains' or 'giant brains' (following, for instance, Edmund C. Berkeley's popular 1949 book *Giant Brains*), and the computer was also sometimes called a robot (Suominen Computer; Suominen and Parikka 2010). It is also noted that, at that time, the popular use of the term "robot" became a difficult topic of discussion for scientists and other professionals in the field internationally. They were at the time building their expertise by disassociating "professional" and "non-professional" — even sacred and profane — behaviour towards computing technology. This partially signified distrust of the media and, particularly, popular science fiction that magnified both positive and negative effects of computing technology. However, professional discourse sometimes charged the media of overstating the role of scientific knowledge in understanding technology. This was a part of the maturing of the discourse in information technology expertise in Finland:

> Sometimes we hear that one should be a professor of mathematics or more to understand these kinds of machines, and the press has called computers "giant brains," etc. This has lead to the situation where many people have gotten a misleading image of computing technology, due to the fact that their mechanical principles are very simple" [*Liiketaito* 4/1956, 3 Dipl. ins. J. Wilkman: Automatisointi valloittaa konttorimme?; translated from Finnish by Jaakko Suominen].
>
> When the first information on "electronic brains" or "thinking machines" or some other cartoonist-named machines was published by the press, it was most likely hard to realize what was that all about. Like always, the journalists collected, to their news, primarily those things which were tailor made for sensational impression. They collected loose information on the fabulous calculation speeds of the machines, their abilities to play chess, think humanely, and solve

mathematic problems. The machines translated novels from any language to any other language, made weather forecasts, and so on, endlessly, until the ordinary poor reader couldn't differentiate between a punched card sorter and the science fiction Übermensch robots. Now, when ten years has gone by since the birth of the first "electronic brains," most of us [punched card professionals], I suppose, has sort of a conception about what was real in that news [*Reikäkortti* 1/1957, Kari Karhunen: Reikäkorttimies automatisoinnin edessä; (translated from Finnish by Jaakko Suominen)].

However, the use of the term *electronic brains* was not only an example of a rough metaphorical tactic for translating or converting the new technology to popular or public culture. Neither is it exclusively an example of social continuity, the *technological inertia*, a concept used by William Aspray and Donald Beaver, who studied the early advertising of computing technology. *Technological inertia* refers to the rhetorical connections between the new and old technology or between new and old socio-technical processes. *Technological inertia* appears in terms such as *iron horse* (train) and *horseless cabriolets* (automobile) (Aspray and Beaver, 131; on social continuity in technological discourses see Corn). Moreover, use of the term *electronic brains* reveals a new sort of wide interest in reconsidering human thinking and the processes in human brains, and comparing those processes to the material technological world. With robots, this interest was targeted not only to mental but also physical work and human characteristics. Paul N. Edwards has called this interest, and its various visible cultural and collective constructed forms, "the cyborg discourse." According to Edwards: "By constructing both human minds and artificial intelligences as information machines, [it] helped to integrate people into complex technological systems" (Edwards, 2). The new computing technology formed a complex system, which was integrated and absorbed by several smaller and larger discursive acts. Edwards also states that one goal of cyborg system builders was to maximize the efficiency of both human and mechanical parts of the system, and cyborg discourse consisted also of fictional elements, such as SF stories, books, and movies.

Long-term Influences?

It is possible that the Atorox books have had long-term influences among those readers who have gotten to know the books during their childhood or youth. This influence is also, however, difficult to estimate. Finnish robot and computer representations were more or less melted into international representations, particularly American, in techno-scientific popular culture — such as Robby the Robot movies and figures, Disney productions, translated science fiction books, comics books, etc. In Finland, foreign science fiction has been more popular than national science fiction for a long time; however, many works were not translated into Finnish for many years. For example, Isaac Asimov's famous and multidimensional robot books, such as *Caves of Steel*, 1953, were not translated into Finnish before the 1970s.

From a contemporary reader's perspective, the characters and plots of the Atorox books seem helplessly naïve and politically incorrect. Also, a reader might laugh at the foolishness of many scientific-technological principles described in the book. The books were much more understandable in their own late–1940s context; the reader of pulp SF in 1940s Finland likely never noticed anything odd regarding the racial and sexual references.

Representations of the Atorox robot itself greatly reflect international practices of science and information technology popularization. In the book, the robot was introduced as a scientific-technical spectacle and show (see also Suominen and Parikka). The metallic figure also had many human characteristics. It was programmable, but also vulnerable, and thus contained the seeds of danger and destruction. The book series ends with the robot's rebellion against humankind and the search to create a new robot race. A look around at the modern world's popular take on information technology has shown, or still shows, many of these characteristics.

Works Cited

Websites

"Comic Creator: Roger Roux" Lambiek.net. Accessed March 19, 2010, http://lambiek.net/artists/r/roux_roger.htm.Iron Sky: The Official Movie Site. Accessed March 19, 2010, http://www.ironsky.net/.

Kvaak.fi, A Finnish Comic Portal. Discussion on Atorox' model. Accessed March 19, 2010, http://www.kvaak.fi/keskustelu/index.php/topic,6887.0.html.

Nummelin, Juri. "Outsiderin Atoroxin edeltäjä" (The Model of the Outsider's Atorox). A writing in the Pulpetti blog, November 9, 2006. Accessed March 19, 2010, http://pulpetti.blogspot.com/2006/11/outsiderin-atoroxin-edeltj.html.

Turun Science Fiction Seura. Atorox image gallery. Accessed March 19, 2010, http://www.tsfs.fi/gallery/main.php/v/atorox/.

Magazines

Dipl. ins. J. Wilkman. "Automatisointi valloittaa konttorimme?" *Liiketaito* April 1956, 3. Translated from Finnish by Jaakko Suominen.

Karhunen, Kari. "Reikäkorttimies automatisoinnin edessä." *Reikäkortti* January 1957. Translated from Finnish by Jaakko Suominen.

Fiction

Asimov, Isaac. *Teräsluolat* [The Caves of Steel]. Finnish translation Matti Kannosto. Helsinki: Kirjayhtymä, 1974 (1953).

Čapek, Karel. *R.U.R.* Finnish translation Jaro Kalima. Yleisradio, 1965 (1921).

_____ *Salamanterisota* [War with the Newt]. Finnish translation Reino Silvanto. Porvoo: WSOY, 1962 (1936).

Haapakoski, Aarne (Outsider). *Atorox: Ihmisten valtias*. Jyväskylä: Seaflower Oy, 1947, 1948 (1993).

Email Interviews and Comments

Nummelin, Juri. Email to Jaakko Suominen. October 10, 2009.
Rosvall, Katja. Emails to Jaakko Suominen. November 4, 6, 13, 2009.

Literature

Aspray, William, and Beaver, Donald B. "Marketing the Monster: Advertising Computer Technology." *Annals of the History of Computing* 8: 2, 127–143.
Bardini, Thierry, and August T. Horvath. "The Social Construction of the Personal Computer User." *Journal of Communication* 45 (1995): 3, 40–65.
Berkeley, Edmund C. *Giant Brains, or Machines That Think*. New York: Wiley and Sons, 1949.
Campbell-Kelly, Martin, and William Aspray. *Computer: A History of the Information Machine*. New York: Basic, 1996.
Ceruzzi, Paul E. *A History of Modern Computing*. Cambridge, MA: MIT Press, 1998.
Corn, Joseph J. "Epilogue." In *Imaging Tomorrow: History, Technology, and the American Future*. Ed. Joseph J. Corn. Cambridge, MA: MIT Press, 1986.
_____. "Introduction." In *Imaging Tomorrow: History, Technology, and the American Future*. Ed. Joseph J. Corn. Cambridge, MA: MIT Press, 1986.
Edwards, Paul N. *The Closed World: Computers and the Politics of Discourse in Cold War America*. Cambridge, MA: MIT Press, 1996.
Ferro, David, and Eric Swedin. "Computer Fiction: 'A Logic Named Joe.' Towards Investigating the Importance of Science Fiction in the Historical Development of Computing." In John Impagliazzo, Timo Järvi and Petri Paju, eds., *History of Nordic Computing 2: Second IFIP WG 9.7 Conference, HiNC2, Turku, Finland, August 2007, Revised Selected Papers*. Berlin: Springer, 2009.
Friedman, Ted. *Electric Dreams: Computers in American Culture*. New York: New York University Press, 2005.
Hänninen, Ville (Outsider). In Vesa Sisättö and Toni Jerrman, eds., *Kotimaisia tieteis- ja fantasiakirjailijoita* [National SF and Fantasy Writers]. Helsinki: BTJ Kirjastopalvelu, 2006.
Jokisalmi, Raimo. *Outsiderin kirja: Aarne Haapakosken elämäkerta* [Outsider's Book: Biography of Aarne Haapakoski]. Tampere: Apali Oy, 2007.
Latour, Bruno. *Science in Action: How to Follow Scientists and Engineers through Society*. Cambridge, MA: Harvard University Press, 1988.
Nummelin, Juri. "Outsiderin Atoroxin edeltäjät." Blog, November 9, 2006. Retrieved November 30, 2009, http://pulpetti.blogspot.com/2006/11/outsiderin-atoroxin-edeltj.html.
Nye, David E. *American Technological Sublime*. Cambridge, MA: MIT Press, 1994.
Oinonen, Paavo. *Pitkä matka on Tippavaaraan... Suomalaisuuden tulkinta ja Yleisradion toimintaperiaatteet radiosarjoissa Työmiehen perhe, Kalle-Kustaa Korkin seikkailuja ja Kankkulan kaivolla 1945–1964* [It's a Long Way to Tippavaara: Interpretations of Finnishness and the Policies of the Finnish Broadcasting Company Yleisradio in the Radio Serials *The Worker's Family, The Adventures of Kalle-Kustaa Korkki* and *At the Kankkula Well* (1945–1964)]. Helsinki: Suomalaisen Kirjallisuuden Seura, 2004.
Paju, Petri. "Ensimmäinen suomalainen tietokone ESKO ja 1950-luvun suunnitelma kansallisesta laskentakeskuksesta. Turun yliopisto, historian laitos." Kulttuurihistorian lisensiaatin-tutkielma. Julkaisematon, 2002.
Rasmussen, Chris. "Jobs Galore for Robots: Robot Salesmen, Robot Entertainers and the 'National Machine' of Prosperity in the 1920s and 1930s." *Rethinking History* 5:1 (2001), pp. 149–162.
Suominen, Jaakko. "Computer as a Tool for Love: A Cultural History of Technology." Proceedings of the 8th Annual IAS-STS Conference, "Critical Issues in Science and Technology Studies," May 4–5, 2009. Graz. IAS-STS (CD-ROM). Online version: http://www.ifz.tugraz.at/index_en.php/filemanager/download/1558/Jaakko%20Suominen.pdf.

_____. *Koneen kokemus: Tietoteknistyvä kulttuuri modernisoituvassa Suomessa 1920-luvulta 1970-luvulle* [Experiences with Machines: Computerised Culture in the Process of Finnish Modernisation from the 1920s to the 1970s]. Tampere: Vastapaino, 2003.

_____ and Jussi Parikka. "Sublimated Attractions: The Introduction of Early Computers in Finland in the late 1950s as a Mediated Experience." *Media History* 16:4 (December 2010).

Warrick, Patricia S. *The Cybernetic Imagination in Science Fiction*. Cambridge, MA: MIT Press, 1980.

5

Computer Science
on the Planet Krypton

Gary Westfahl

American children growing up in the 1950s may or may not have read science fiction, but they almost certainly read comic books; and within those publications the most frequently encountered images of a futuristic society were the innumerable stories in Superman comic books that featured his home planet, Krypton. And, as American society became more and more aware of computers, writers were naturally more and more inclined to feature computers as integral parts of Krypton's technological civilization, both illustrating contemporary attitudes regarding humanity's own future and, one might assume, subtly influencing the views of the children who were reading their comics. These stories about Krypton parallel other science-fictional visions of tomorrow, which largely failed to anticipate the development of small personal computers and the ways in which computers would become a ubiquitous and dominant presence in society. An additional point of interest is the strategies followed by later writers, who, while necessarily updating the Superman saga for a new generation of readers, needed to revise the well-established history of Krypton in order to more prominently feature the computers that readers would now expect to find on Krypton.

Since it had long been established that the planet had blown up when Superman was a small child, one might imagine that Krypton would figure only rarely in the Superman saga, which was definitely the case during Superman's first decade of adventures. Perhaps the first story to include a lengthy description of Krypton was 1948's "The Origin of Superman"—which, by the way, placed more emphasis on the advanced physical abilities of Kryptonians than their technology, and featured no computers at all. However, in 1953 an old science fiction fan named Mort Weisinger became the editor of the Superman comic books, and he naturally enough enjoyed stories with a science-fictional slant and was soon recruiting science fiction writers like Edmond Hamilton and Otto Binder to write Superman stories.[1] Since the futuristic world of Krypton represented one obvious way to bring advanced technology into Superman adventures, writers began devising ways to work Krypton into their stories: the discovery of new survivors or artifacts from the vanished planet would provoke flashbacks about Krypton; one series of Superboy stories involved the use of a special machine to restore memories of his early life there, when he was called Kal-El; on at least two occasions, both Superman and his friend Jimmy Olsen employed time travel to visit the doomed world; one singular adventure featured an extended projection of what would have happened if Krypton had not been destroyed and Kal-El had grown up there; and when it transpired that an entire Kryptonian city named Kandor had escaped destruction by being miniaturized and put in a bottle by a space-faring villain named Brainiac, Superman was able to place that city within his Fortress of Solitude and occasionally shrink himself temporarily to enjoy sojourns in a once-familiar environment.

Before any considerations of computer science on the planet Krypton in the stories of the 1950s and 1960s, it must be noted that, at the time, comic book writers imagined that their only readers were children; hence they had no concern for consistency in their stories. If one tale of Krypton happened to foreground some sort of super-science that had not figured in other stories, the assumption was that none of their youthful readers would ever notice. For that reason, there were numerous stories about Krypton in the 1950s and 1960s, examined but not cited here, that did not feature any computers at all, while other stories to be discussed presented them as important features of Kryptonian society. Only in the 1970s did writers begin to consult previous stories about Krypton and endeavor to reconcile the inconsistencies in order to present a cohesive portrait of the doomed planet.

The first types of computer one finds in these adventures, and the types of computer most frequently observed in early science fiction stories, were humanoid robots. On the planet Krypton, these came in two basic varieties. First, it was sometimes posited that Kryptonians regularly used robots with limited intelligence as household servants; thus, the "Map of Krypton," included in the first *Giant Superman Annual,* featured a "Robot Factory," a domed structure from which streamed two rows of crudely human-shaped, identical robots ([40–41]).[2] In the Superboy story "Life on Krypton," the young Kal-El and his mother Lara visit a "Robot Showroom" where "the latest model robots were on display," including a "Muscle Man," "Metal Maid," and "Watch Dog" ([25]); Kal-El crawls into the back of one robot and temporarily activates it before Lara rescues him. A store selling a robotic "Muscle Man," "Metal Maid," and "Watch Dog" was also depicted in "The Story of Superman's Life" (3). In the 1958 story entitled "Superman's Return to Krypton" (not to be confused with a three-part 1960 story that shared that name), the Man of Steel learns that his mother Lara, as a young woman, "is working in this shop that makes robots" ([24]). In "Krypton Lives on," the aforementioned story about Krypton's projected survival, Kal-El assembles a "robot playmate" with a "toy kit" (4), and another story, "The Crimes of Krypton's Master Villains," shows Kal-El with a "robot playmate" of a different design (2). Later in that story, after a televised school lesson, Lara summons her household "robot butler" to prepare dinner, and when husband Jor-El comments that "You women of Krypton sure have an easy time of it," Lara responds, "It's your doing, Jor-El. You scientists have made housework a thing of the past. In fact, thanks to Kryptonian science, all work on our planet is now done by robots" (3). As two final examples of such robot servants, Superman is shown, during his first visit to the bottled city of Kandor in "The Super-Duel in Space" (1959), the "tireless robot farmhands" who "raise our crops for food" (80), and in the "Imaginary Novel" "Lois Lane, the Super-Maid of Krypton," a female villain named Lu Thoria employs human-shaped "robot-machines" to repair Brainiac's spaceship ([19]).

Robots are not only employed for household chores, but also play a significant role in law enforcement. In 1958, "The Shrinking Superman" first mentions the "robot policemen" used on Krypton (125); a "robot policeman" also appears to escort Jor-El to an execution in "The Crimes of Krypton's Master Villains" (5); and in "The Story of Superman's Life," after Jor-El's warning about Krypton's coming doom was rejected by the Council of Scientists, the scientist was removed from the room by a "robot guard" (4). The limitations of these robots were pointed out by an evil scientist named Gra-Mo, who appears before the Science Council in "The Crimes of Krypton's Master Villains" to note that robots are "subject to accidental mechanical interference," often need "repair," and do not last long; thus, he petitions to join the council because he could benefit Kryptonian society by replacing robots with "a planet-full of androids" (9). However, when the android he displays dissolves and Jor-El is instead chosen to be on the council because of his discovery of the Phantom Zone, Gra-Mo demonstrates that robots are not entirely useless, and reveals his true nature by temporarily taking telepathic control of Krypton's robot policemen and ordering them to carry out destructive acts before Jor-El finds a way to destroy the robots and ends the attempted rebellion. In a somewhat later story, "Olsen's Time-Trip to Save Krypton," we are shown robotic fire-fighters, termed "mechanical 'smoke-eaters'" (70), extinguishing a fire, and Jor-El's home is protected by "robot watchmen" (79). All of these sorts of robots, clearly, are little more than tools, who for the most part benignly carry out routine duties but may also be misused by criminals.

Next, there is at least one prominent example of a robot who displays greater intelligence and abilities. "The Super-Teacher from Krypton" (1957) informs readers that Kryptonian "civilization was so scientific that advanced pupils were taught by powerful electronic brains mounted on mechanical bodies" (71); before his death, Jor-El had constructed one of these robot teachers for the express purpose of someday teaching his son how to properly use the super-powers he would be gaining on Earth, and after that robot somehow survived the planetary explosion, he found his way to Earth to complete his mission by testing Superboy in order to ensure that he was sufficiently super-skillful. One might imagine that, amidst Jor-El's frantic efforts to rescue as many people as possible from his planet's impending doom, building and training a robot to someday instruct his son on the proper use of super-powers would be a very low priority indeed; yet knowing that writers at the time needed to churn out up to 130 stories a year to fill the seven comic books that Superman then appeared in, one must forgive them for sometimes developing stories from illogical premises. Ever desperate for story ideas, writers even brought the robot teacher back for a return appearance in a 1977 story, "Don't Call Me Super*boy*," wherein he again tested Superboy's super-abilities as he was about to become a man. Interestingly, though it might be expected that a robot teacher programmed by Superman's own father would be kindly and avuncular, he actually comes across as cantankerous, overly demanding, and almost hostile to Superboy — so much so that one blogger was inspired to describe him as "the Super-Teacher Asshole from Krypton."

Finally, Krypton was occasionally envisioned as having powerful computers, though these almost invariably took the then-familiar form of room-sized boxes. In "Krypton Lives On," the future profession of young Kal-El, like everyone on Krypton, was determined by a "Skill Machine" (8), later termed the "Talent Machine" (17), seen as a wall of metal that prints out its results on a roll of ticker-tape; the device initially misidentifies him as suited only to be a dispatcher, not an actual space explorer, until his friend, the super-hero Futuro, finds and repairs a "loose wire" in the machine, which then correctly assigns Kal-El to become an astronaut (17). Another errant computer is observed in "The Story of Superman's Life," wherein the Council of Scientists feels confident in rejecting Jor-El's warning because "the Council believed in its Cosmic Clock," and, as one scientist noted, "The super-computer in that clock has predicted that our world will be safe from all disasters for endless years!" (4). This particular computer commands attention because the clock it is inside seems to be only a few feet across and eight feet high, so that if it is not exactly the size of a personal computer, it is at least smaller than the behemoths observed in other stories. And a two-part story about the adventures of Superman and Jimmy Olsen in the guise of miniaturized Kandorian heroes Nightwing and Flamebird, "The Dynamic Duo of Kandor," relates a tale from Kryptonian history: once, the people of Argo City decided to establish a "scientific government" and, believing that computers "never err," they construct a "master computer" to "decide all political questions for us." But they soon realize to their dismay that "they had given their master computer too much intelligence" when it decides to take complete control of their lives: "To make sure no one ever questions my power," it announces, "I had you make these machine-police to enforce my orders!" Recognizing that they had "created a machine-king and must dispose of him before he becomes too strong," the citizens destroy the machine-police and disable the computer ([3]). Perhaps this bit of Kryptonian history was introduced to explain why Kryptonians were generally careful to provide their robots only with limited intelligence.

Kryptonian advances in computers and robotics also manifested themselves in the activities of its former resident Superman, who during the 1950s and 1960s regularly constructed computers and robots that were not only more advanced than those on Earth, but more advanced than those observed on Krypton. Presumably employing his super-intelligence, the Superman of this era was able to absorb and improve upon what he had learned from studying the work of his home planet. Examples include the robot with a "super-electronic brain," observed in "The Key to Fort Superman" (1958), that Superman would play chess with in his Fortress of Solitude ([75]); as well as the "Super Univac" computer employed to predict Superman's future had Krypton not exploded in "Krypton Lives On" (2). Throughout the 1960s, Superman also built and used a large of number of Superman robots who could perfectly replicate his speech and actions, until these were written out of the Superman saga in 1969. Superman even flaunted his expertise on the planet Krypton itself: in "Superman's Return to Krypton" (1960), it is revealed that Jor-El, in one effort to rescue more Kryptonians from the planet's impending destruction, began to construct a "space-ark" in the city of Kandor, and the visiting Superman assisted in his effort by constructing a "super-robot" named Robo that "can duplicate many of his former powers"— he can "lift great weights, has x-ray vision, and can move at super-speed" ([18]). Since Robo is then portrayed as helping to build the ark without anyone's supervision, Robo must also be more intelligent than typical Kryptonian robots. Unfortunately, Jor-El's plans come to naught when the city is miniaturized and stolen by Brainiac, and to explain why Superman cannot help Jor-El construct more robots like Robo, the story has Jor-El comment that because Robo "is made of rare materials, only one Robo could ever be built on Krypton!" ([18])

As the character of Superman moved into the 1970s, and came under the control of new editors and writers, one might expect some revisions of the history of Krypton that would make computers more prominent — which is precisely what occurred. One early sign came in a 1978 adventure featuring the Kandorian heroes Nightwing and Flamebird, "The Crime-Lord of Kandor," where the capture of six criminals is promptly followed by a "computer check" which "failed to turn up any leads" (57). But the most thorough presentation of the updated Krypton came in a 1979 mini-series entitled *World of Krypton*. The first issue's adventure, "The Jor-El Story," while discussing the education of Superman's father, explains that "information is electrically implanted directly into the brain — and working in conjunction with computers, the student is taught how to actively apply that new knowledge!" ([4]) Later, because Jor-El is so bright and capable, he reports that "the computer which analyzes each student to determine his occupation had a difficult time placing me in a position" ([9]). When Jor-El is ready to marry Lara, another computer named Matricomp is used to "determine your compatibility for marriage" ([20]); it surprisingly says that the two are not suited for marriage, but it eventually transpires that the computer has been manipulated to make that wrong decision by another man who covets the hand of Lara. When Jor-El plays a role in identifying and apprehending a renegade member of the Science Council, he is happy to note that "For once, rather than solving equations on a computer screen, I was part of the action!" ([29]) — which might be interpreted by modern readers as the first reference to something resembling a personal computer on Krypton, envisioning Jor-El sitting in front of something resembling a personal computer. However, in the third issue's story, "The Last Days of Krypton," we actually see Jor-El in his laboratory — complaining of the unyielding Science Council that "I show them data, computer simulations ... proof! It's like talking to empty air!" — and the computer in the background looks like a standard, wall-sized model ([9]).

In the second issue's story, "This Planet Is Doomed," Jor-El learns that his father had "discovered unstable elements at the planet's core" and, in investigating this finding, Jor-El writes in his diary that "the computer did most of the work" in showing that the planet would soon "explode like an atomic bomb!" ([7]) Then, after retelling the tale of how Jor-El's efforts to construct a space ark were thwarted when Brainiac shrunk and took away the city of Kandor, the story states that "computers in Kryptonopolis were being reprogrammed to take up the workload of the Kandor system," so that everyday life in Krypton could continue despite the disappearance of its capital city ([16]). After Jor-El bests competitor Gra-Mo by showing that his Phantom

Zone is a better invention than the other's defective androids (as already recounted in an earlier story), Jor-El is elected to the Science Council, and "the votes were tabulated by computer — instantly!" ([22]) A subsequent description of the criminal Jax-Ur's activities is described as a "computer reconstruction of events," and when the villain is beginning a test of his destructive missile, he says that "the computers have begun the countdown!" ([25]) Krypton is now a civilization that has computers fully integrated into almost all aspects of life — education, science, politics, law enforcement, and matrimony — and while they might still be manipulated by evil people, these computers seem to be basically benign and reliable.

However, to demonstrate its power as an iconic image, the evil, domineering computer of old would later reappear in the Superman saga, and the chain of events that led to that development began, oddly enough, with a lawsuit.

In 1958, a new Superman villain had been introduced named Brainiac, portrayed as a bald, green-skinned humanoid alien with a striking resemblance to Superman's colleague in the Justice League of America, the Martian Manhunter. Protected by a force field that even Superman cannot penetrate, Brainiac comes to Earth on his mission to travel from world to world miniaturizing and bottling cities, including the Kryptonian city of Kandor, which he will eventually employ to repopulate his devastated world. After Brainiac shrinks both Metropolis and Superman, he places himself in suspended animation for his return voyage. The now-tiny Superman, with the help of a Kandorian scientist named Kimda, manages to restore all but one of the cities to their normal sizes and locations. When Kimda altruistically employs the last charge of enlarging force to restore Superman, not Kandor, the Man of Steel must take Kandor to his Fortress of Solitude in its miniaturized form in hopes of someday devising his own method to bring it back to its proper dimensions (and, much later, the city would be enlarged and would elect to embark upon a voyage through space and into another dimension, effectively removing it from the Superman universe). After his first appearance, Brainiac went on to establish himself in subsequent adventures as one of Superman's most prominent foes.

However, it transpired that the term "Brainiac" had been previously employed by a scientist named Edmund C. Berkeley when he introduced, in 1955, his Brainiac Computer Kit, which enabled children to construct their own simple computers. After he sued DC Comics for copyright infringement, an arrangement was worked out so that the creators of Superman could continue to feature a villain named Brainiac — as long as certain conditions were met.

First, DC Comics would have to reinvent the character as a computer, a task accomplished in the 1964 story "The Team of Luthor and Brainiac."

Therein, the evil scientist Lex Luthor discovers that green-skinned aliens on another planet, later named Colu, had unwisely constructed a "Master Computer" ([6]), followed by several duplicates which, like their innumerable counterparts in other stories of the era, soon decided to take over the planet and rule over the less intelligent beings who had created them. Eager to conquer other worlds as well, the Master Computers next decide to construct a "computer-spy" who resembles the people of their world — who turns out to be none other than our old friend Brainiac ([7]). To explain the fact that a descendant of Brainiac, named Brainiac 5, had long served as a member of the thirtieth-century Legion of Super-Heroes, this ambulatory computer was given a living "son" to "enhance [his] human disguise," named Brainiac II, and it was now explained that this person was the actual ancestor of Brainiac 5 ([8]). Armed with this information, Luthor teams up with Brainiac, conspiring to both increase his computer intelligence and to implant a destructive device in his brain to keep him under control. While traveling through space, the villains learn that the people of Brainiac's home planet had eventually been able to overthrow and destroy their "computer tyrants," making Brainiac the last of his kind ([18]); then, by means of plot contrivances, Brainiac manages to erase Luthor's knowledge of his true nature. After Luthor and Brainiac overcome and paralyze Superman, the villains are defeated with the help of the slightly enlarged and super-powered Kandorians known as the Superman Emergency Squad, and the Kandorians agree to let the villains go free to figure in future adventures as long as they first revive Superman. All subsequent stories about Brainiac would always include the information that he was actually a computer; clearly, DC had argued that continuing the character in this form might function as a constant, subtle advertisement for Berkeley's kit.

Yet DC Comics also agreed to promote the scientist's product more directly. Hence, in the issue where "The Team of Luthor and Brainiac" appeared, the letter column "Metropolis Mailbag" included a "Special Announcement" about a "remarkable coincidence": "shortly after the first 'Brainiac' story appeared in ACTION COMICS, in 1956 [actually 1958], we learned that a REAL 'Brainiac' existed ... in the form of an ingenious 'Brainiac Computer Kit' invented in 1955 by Edmund C. Berkeley." Thus, they explicitly announced, "In deference to his 'Brainiac,' which pre-dates ours, with this issue of SUPERMAN we are changing the characterization of our 'Brainiac' so that the master-villain will henceforth possess a 'computer personality.'" The editor then notes that "Readers will be interested to learn that they can build their own 'Brainiac' by purchasing one of Mr. Berkeley's computer kits and assembling the parts" and goes on to provide an address for ordering "free literature" about this "ideal educational hobby" ([10]).

In the forty-five years following this major revision of the character,

Brainiac has been re-invented so many times, and in so many ways, as to defy detailed summary. At one point he abandoned his humanoid body and appeared as a metallic robot; he was then reimagined as a biological alien that mentally takes control of a human psychic in Metropolis; he subsequently was again transformed into a computer. However, out of all of his variegated reincarnations, there is one of particular interest, since it connects Brainiac to the planet Krypton in an entirely new way.

In 1996, there appeared an animated television movie, *Superman: The Last Son of Krypton,* which was also the pilot for the subsequent series, *Superman: The Animated Series.* As is invariably the case in any relaunching of the Superman franchise, the film begins with the story of Krypton's destruction. Once again the scientist Jor-El predicts that Krypton is about to blow up and urges emergency actions to rescue the Kryptonian people; again, the Science Council rejects Jor-El's findings as erroneous and does nothing, which means that Jor-El only has the opportunity to save his son Kal-El by sending him away in a small rocket; and again, as in the story "The Story of Superman's Life," the major reason for the Science Council's decision is that a super-computer contradicts Jor-El and assures the Council that Krypton will survive. The difference is that now that super-computer is none other than Superman's old foe, Brainiac, who is here presented as the master computer of Krypton. Envisioning an evil computer that would contradict Jor-El's findings not as an error, but as a deliberate lie, the writers must have realized that they could effectively employ the existing character of the villainous computer Brainiac to play this role.

In depicting this version of Brainiac, the animators drew upon images of the computer that one would have thought were long-obsolete in 1996, since Brainiac is shown as both an enormous machine and a cold, heartless intelligence that turns against its creators. A more recent influence was the film *2001: A Space Odyssey* (1968), since Brainiac communicates with his Kryptonian masters by means of a large screen with three glowing green circles, recalling the red circle that signaled and accompanied the voice of HAL 9000; this Brainiac also at one point employs HAL's phrase "human error." (In addition, the green color of the circles may have been a faint reminder of the original color of the once-biological Brainiac's skin.) As another similarity to HAL 9000, Krypton's Brainiac employs convoluted logic to justify lying, killing innocent people, and preserving his own existence; in this case, Brainiac reasons that if he tells the truth to the Science Council — that Jor-El is correct and that Krypton is doomed — then he will be directed to devote all of his energies to last-minute rescue efforts that are sure to be "futile." Instead, he argues, it would make more sense to preserve what is really important about Krypton — information about its culture and achievements — and the best way to do that would be to preserve the computer that contains all of that information, Brainiac. Hence, when he might have been striving to do something to save the people of Krypton, Brainiac has been spending his time downloading himself into an orbiting satellite, which then leaves the vicinity of Krypton in order to roam the cosmos. This Brainiac will later reappear in the first-season episode "Stolen Memories," as a space-faring villain who gathers key information about various inhabited planets and then destroys them, maintaining that their actual existence is unimportant as long as the data about them is preserved; fortunately, Superman is able to thwart him when he attempts to carry out this plan with the planet Earth.

Overall, what can we learn from this survey of computer science on an imaginary world primarily depicted in adventures created for younger readers and viewers? One conclusion is predictable enough, but has now been verified: the writers for comic books did no better than other science fiction writers in predicting the sorts of computers that now permeate contemporary civilization, focusing instead on humanoid robots and gigantic, inimical machines.

In addition, it seems that people in these stories are perfectly comfortable with computers as long as they are regarded as impersonal constructs which have only limited intelligence. Thus the citizens of Krypton happily make use of their robot maids and robot guards without any emotional reactions to these servants, either positive or negative. In a sense, the personal computers of today are analogous to these robots, except that while the traditional robots of science fiction assisted people with physical labors, personal computers assist people with more intellectual labors — storing documents, looking up information, communicating with friends, and so on. But just as Kryptonians have no feelings for or relationships with their robotic servants, people today do not give their personal computers a name, and do not feel any sense of guilt when they turn a computer off or discard one computer to replace it with a newer model. Both science fiction robots and personal computers, then, are seen as nothing more than useful tools, like screwdrivers or microwave ovens.

However, whenever computers are depicted as having intelligence equivalent to humans, or as developing a distinctive personality, deep anxieties arise. Despite the fact that such computers are purportedly incapable of making mistakes, characters have reason to worry that they will in fact lapse into error, with potentially grievous consequences, as was observed repeatedly in stories about Kryptonian computers. An ever graver concern is that these advanced computers will turn against their human masters and seek to either rule them or exterminate them, a scenario observed in the stories about Krypton's "machine-king," and the re-invented Kryptonian Brainiac, as well as innumerable other science fiction works ranging from D. F. Jones's 1966 novel *Colossus*, filmed in 1969 as *Colossus: The Forbin Project*, to the long-running series of *Terminator* films and television programs. Even in describing the advanced robot teacher programmed by Jor-El, it will be recalled, the writer felt compelled to make the character seem cold and harsh. Thus, despite the strenuous efforts of writers like Isaac Asimov to demonstrate that humans would always take precautions to prevent such occurrences, and despite the ubiquity of small computers that provide no support for such scenarios, people to this day remain haunted by images of computers as enormous, evil constructs intent upon the subjugation or elimination of their human creators. The stubborn persistence of these views is, on the face of it, puzzling.

This phenomenon cannot be explained as the simple result of writers who are too lazy to come up with new ideas, or readers permanently brainwashed by earlier stories about computers; there are many other familiar tropes from the past's popular culture, such as those now regarded as racist or sexist, which have long since vanished from view as repugnant to both contemporary writers and contemporary readers. These massive, sinister computers remain acceptable in our stories, and perhaps even comforting, because people who have embraced many changes are still unsettled by the prospect of the development of true artificial intelligence. And, as scientists in this field carry on with their research, this is an attitude that they must take into account. The people of Krypton mistrusted and feared their advanced computers; for further advances to occur, it seems, the people of Earth must be trained to think differently.

Notes

1. It should be noted that, in the 1950s and 1960s, Superman comic books did not identify the writers and artists of individual stories, except in occasional editorial comments in response to readers' letters; however, Superman fans long ago researched the identities of these writers and artists and have posted their findings on numerous websites, which I have consulted in preparing the Works Cited section of this chapter.

2. Although stories may include their own page numbers, comic books are rarely paginated in the conventional fashion of magazines, with each page numbered whether it contains part of a story or an advertisement. In these cases, I have counted the pages myself and cite page numbers within brackets. When comic books or compilations of comic book stories are paginated in the usual way, the page numbers are not in brackets.

Works Cited

Bates, Cary, writer. Art by Curt Swan and Murphy Anderson. "Don't Call Me Super*boy*." *DC Super Stars* No. 12 (November 1976), page numbers unknown.

Bernstein, Robert, writer. Art by Pete Costanza. "Olsen's Time-Trip to Save Krypton." *The Best of DC* No. 46 (March 1984), 62–85. Story originally published in *Superman's Pal Jimmy Olsen* No. 101 (April 1967).

Binder, Otto, writer. Art by Al Plastino. "The Story of Superman's Life." *Superman* No. 146 (July 1961), 1–13.

Binder, Otto, writer. Art by Al Plastino. "The Super-Duel in Space." *Giant Superman Annual* No. 2 (1960), 70–82. Story originally published in *Action Comics* No. 242 (May 1958).

Binder, Otto, writer. Art by Dick Sprang. "Superman's Return to Krypton." *Superman* No. 123 (August 1958), [21–30].

Binder, Otto, writer. Art by Wayne Boring. "Krypton Lives On." *Giant Superman Annual* No. 5 (Summer 1962), 1–25. The three individual chapters are entitled "Krypton Lives On," "Futuro — Super-Hero of Krypton," and "The Superman of Two Worlds." Story originally published in *Superman* No. 132 (October 1959).

Binder, Otto, writer. Art by Wayne Boring. "The Shrinking Superman." *Superman: The Complete History: The Life and Times of the Man of Steel*, by Les Daniels. San Francisco: Chronicle, 1998, 117–129. Story originally published in *Action Comics* No. 245 (October 1958).

Coleman, Jerry, writer. Art by Wayne Boring. "The Key to Fort Superman." *Giant Superman Annual* No. 1 (1960), [69–80]. Story originally published in *Action Comics* No. 241 (June 1958).

Finger, Bill, writer. Art by Wayne Boring. "The Origin of Superman." *Superman: From the Thirties to the Seventies.* New York: Crown, 1971, 198–207. Story originally published in *Superman* No. 53 (July 1948).

Hamilton, Edmond, writer. Art by Curt Swan. "The Dynamic Duo of Kandor." *Superman's Pal Jimmy Olsen* No. 69 (June 1963), [1–9], [12–20]. The second chapter is separately entitled "The Super-Showdown on Kandor."

Hamilton, Edmond, writer. Art by Curt Swan. "Lois Lane, the Super-Maid of Krypton." *Superman* No. 159 (February 1963), [1–9, 12–20, 23–30]. The three individual chapters are entitled "Lois Lane's Flight from Earth," "The Female Luthor of Krypton," and "The Doom of Super-Maid."

Hamilton, Edmond, writer. Art by Curt Swan. "The Team of Luthor and Brainiac." *Superman* No. 167 (February 1964), [1–9, 11–19, 22–30]. The three individual chapters are entitled "The Deadly Duo," "The Downfall of Superman," and "The Hour of Kandor's Vengeance."

Hamilton, Edmond, writer. Art by George Papp. "The Crimes of Krypton's Master Villains." *Superboy* No. 104 (April 1963), 1–13.

Hamilton, Edmond, writer. Art by John Sikela. "The Super-Teacher from Krypton." *Giant Superman Annual* No. 5 (Summer 1962), 69–80. Story originally published in *Adventure Comics* No. 240 (September 1957).

Kupperberg, Paul, writer. Art by Howard Chaykin and Murphy Anderson. "The Jor-El Story." *World of Krypton* No. 1 (July 1979), [1–4, 7–10, 12–14, 16–20, 23–26, 29–31].

Kupperberg, Paul, writer. Art by Howard Chaykin and Murphy Anderson. "The Last Days of Krypton." *World of Krypton* No. 3 (September 1979), [1–4, 7–10, 12–14, 16–20, 23–26, 29–31].

Kupperberg, Paul, writer. Art by Howard Chaykin and Murphy Anderson. "This Planet Is Doomed." *World of Krypton* No. 2 (August 1979), [1–4, 7–10, 12–14, 16, 18–20, 22–26, 29–31].

Kupperberg, Paul, writer. Art by Ken Landgraf and Romeo Tanghal. "The Crime-Lord of Kandor." *The Superman Family* No. 189 (May/June 1978), 53–60, 63–64.

Siegel, Jerry, designer. Art by Al Plastino. "Map of Krypton." *Giant Superman Annual* No. 1 (1960), [40–41].

Siegel, Jerry, writer. Art by George Papp. "Life on Krypton." *Superboy* No. 79 (March 1960), [21–30].

Siegel, Jerry, writer. Art by Wayne Boring. "Superman's Return to Krypton." *Superman* No. 141 (November 1960), [1–9], [11–19], [23–30]. The three individual chapters are entitled "Superman Meets Jor-El and Lara Again," "Superman's Kryptonian Romance," and "The Surprise of Fate."

"Special Announcement!" In "Metropolis Mailbag" [letters column]. *Superman* No. 167 (February 1964), [10].

"Stolen Memories." Episode of *Superman: The Animated Series*. New York: WB Network, November 2, 1996.

Superman: The Last Son of Krypton. New York: WB Network, September 6, 1996.

6

Manned Space Flight and Artificial Intelligence: "Natural" Trajectories of Technology

Paul E. Ceruzzi

The careful use of metaphors can aid our understanding of technology, yet metaphors can also mislead. The term "bottleneck," for example, implies that technology proceeds in a linear fashion, and that by removing a single obstruction it can advance more smoothly. But technology proceeds not in a straight line but along a wide front. Historians of technology have adopted the metaphor not of bottleneck but "reverse salient," derived from military history: a hindrance that prevents an army from moving across a broad front, not along a single file.[1] They have also adopted the metaphor of technological "momentum," derived from classical mechanics, describing a technological system that, because of its metaphorical mass and velocity, moves along a path that can be difficult to modify once established. This concept has been further refined by economic historians, who describe how a technology, once entrenched, is "locked in": difficult to dislodge even when a technically superior system is marketed to compete with it.

In his history of missile guidance, Donald MacKenzie is likewise critical of another metaphor, that of the "natural trajectory" of a technology.[2] MacKenzie argues that a "trajectory" implies that the process by which technology is incrementally improved as it is used follows an internal logic, independent of external social or political forces. At first glance this seems reasonable. But MacKenzie argues that for the accuracy of a ballistic missile system, incremental improvements in accuracy were *anything but* natural progression, rather they

95

were "sold" by engineers to the U.S. Air Force as if it were a natural phenomenon.[3]

The concept of a technological trajectory is relevant also to the histories of two current large-scale technological systems: manned space flight and the development of intelligent computers. Although at first glance these two systems may seem disparate, they have much in common and have overlapped at crucial moments of their respective histories.

NASA and the Trajectory of Manned Space Flight

Historians of space flight have given a central place to the writings and work of Wernher von Braun, one of the developers of the German V-2 ballistic missile during World War II, and who, after coming to the United States with a group of German engineers, played a significant role in the development of the Redstone and Saturn rockets, including the rockets that took men to the Moon between 1968 and 1972. Von Braun was an engineer, but he was also a tireless popularizer and promoter of space travel, writing a science fiction novel, magazine articles, and collaborating with Walt Disney on a television series about humanity's future in space.[4] In these efforts, he sketched a roadmap that has since become known as the "von Braun Paradigm"—a set of incremental steps that he argued ought to be taken to gain access to the heavens.[5] In its simplest form, he argued for:

1. the development of a winged, reusable, piloted launch vehicle, which would
2. shuttle crew, supplies, and fuel to and from a space station in Earth orbit
3. from which would depart crewed missions to the Moon
4. followed eventually by a manned mission to Mars.

The paradigm was further embellished and expanded, but it held a powerful grip on NASA (founded in 1958) and still lurks behind NASA's current plans to return to the Moon and mount a crewed expedition to Mars.[6]

That trajectory, which seems a logical one, has been modified, abandoned, rediscovered, and modified again over the decades. The first modification came with the Soviet launch of Sputnik in 1957, which prompted a swift response from the United States. In the desire to get a human being in space quickly, the United States shelved a program to develop winged, piloted spacecraft, extending research being done with aircraft like the X-15.[7] The result was a series of ballistic, wingless "capsules": Mercury, Gemini, and Apollo, with only limited ability to maneuver using aerodynamic forces. But the winged, aerodynamic paradigm did not die: it was resurrected as the Space Shuttle, first flown in 1981 and piloted to a landing using controls that were an extension of the X-15's. Current NASA plans call for a return to a ballistic capsule, "Orion," but there are also plans for commercial access to space with winged vehicles, including the Bert Rutan design for ships that will carry paying passengers at least to the edge of space.[8]

Von Braun envisioned the space station to be something quite different from the station that is now in orbit: It would be wheel-shaped and rotated to provide artificial gravity for its crew. It would serve as a refueling station, assembly station, and general "base camp" for deep-space missions. Von Braun envisioned its crew playing a critical military role, conducting reconnaissance and even delivering nuclear weapons to targets below. Events proceeded along a different trajectory. In the heat of the Apollo program, NASA engineer John Houbolt noted that by extending the well-known principle of rocket staging, one could achieve a landing on the Moon faster and with fewer (only one) rocket launches if the rendezvous and docking took place in orbit around the Moon, not Earth.[9] That undercut the reason for having a space station as a base camp. Current plans for a return to the Moon and to journey to Mars call for an Earth orbit docking, in which a small crewed vehicle will dock with a heavier, un-crewed vehicle that will contain hardware for a deep-space voyage. But this configuration involves little or no construction in Earth orbit, and may not require a space station crew to assemble a Moon ship.

Likewise, as the U.S. military developed intercontinental ballistic missiles (ICBMs), reconnaissance satellites, signals-intelligence satellites, and other unmanned systems, the notion of a space station as a military base faded as well. Indeed, although historians have emphasized the connection between science fiction and the evolution of the U.S. space programs, the lack of Buck Rogers/Star Wars shoot-outs in space, so common in science fiction, are conspicuous by their absence in reality.[10] This is a glaring example of a disconnect between depictions of space travel in science fiction and the reality; others will be addressed shortly. The closest the United States ever came to having a manned military presence was the Manned Orbiting Laboratory (MOL) program, in which an Air Force crew would occupy a modest station, based on Gemini hardware, in low Earth orbit. The program was highly classified. As automated reconnaissance and other military satellites improved in capability through the 1960s, MOL was cancelled in 1969, before any hardware had been orbited.

The concept of rotating the station to achieve artificial gravity was never adopted, either, although people who spend extended periods of time in space do suffer from the effects of weightlessness. A rotating station adds mechanical complexity, weight, and cost. One reason for having a space station is to enjoy a micro-gravity environment for research; thus a rotating station would also need a non-rotating component, further adding weight and complicating the

design. As astronauts gained experience in longer duration flights in the mid–
1960s, NASA concluded that this requirement could be relaxed, if compensated
by training, conditioning, and other procedures for those living for an
extended period in weightlessness.[11]

Over and above these modifications to the von Braun paradigm is the
notion that one need not send humans to Mars at all, but rather explore the
red planet with robots. This was never part of von Braun's vision, yet robotic
exploration of Mars and the outer solar system has been part of NASA's accomplishments in the past two decades.[12] Those accomplishments are due in part
to what is commonly known as "Moore's Law," if by that term we mean not
just the increasing density of computer memory chips but the overall exponential increase in computing power since the invention of the Integrated
Circuit in 1959.[13] But one must be more precise about the nature of advances
in computing as they apply to the substitution of robots for humans in space.
We see this issue in current debates over NASA's plan for future human-
tended missions: in spite of the accomplishments of robotic craft, NASA leadership feels that these robots are no substitute for human beings. With all of
the criticism of NASA in recent years, public support for sending humans
into space remains high. To resolve this issue in favor of the robots, computers
need not just get more and more capable — they are already doing that
nicely — they also must attain a high level of artificial intelligence, which will
endow them with a consciousness that matches the consciousness of human
astronauts. Human beings will long for distant space travel, regardless of the
obstacles, unless one can provide a *fully equivalent* experience virtually. Is that
practical? The following section will examine that question's historical context.

The Trajectory of AI

Research in Artificial Intelligence (AI) has its own paradigm, equivalent
to von Braun's in space exploration, if not so named. One could call it
the "Stanley Kubrick Paradigm," for his 1968 film *2001: A Space Odyssey*. Naming it after Kubrick implies that the trajectory has no basis in genuine AI
research, which is not the case. It is rather that AI researchers to date
have not produced an equivalent of von Braun, who was both a top-notch
engineer and a good popularizer. Throughout the history of AI there have
been strong statements about what AI's natural trajectory ought to look
like. It was also expressed as a set of steps, each logically following the previous
and leading to machine intelligence, which can be applied to, among other
things, deep-space travel. Stated briefly, the natural trajectory of AI runs as
follows:

1. The development of stored program, general purpose digital computers that satisfy the principle of "Turing Completeness," or universality
2. The implementation of these machines using electronic components, which improve in speed and memory capacity at exponential rates
3. The development of programming languages that allow one to program computers to perform logical and not just mathematical operations
4. The further development of software to produce a computer that has the ability to understand natural language, and thus converse with human beings.
5. The construction of a computer whose circuit density and complexity matches that of a human brain, which may spontaneously express the equivalent of "*Cogito, ergo sum.*"
6. After feeding this system the contents, say, of the New York Public Library and other streams of information, the bootstrapping of this machine into an ultra-intelligent machine (UIM), which not only says "I am," but "I am that I am."[14]

Kubrick's film, based on a short story by Arthur C. Clarke, depicted a computer that had achieved at least Level 5 on the above scale.[15] At Levels 5 and 6, one may say that computers have human consciousness and more. These levels were first described in detail, not by Kubrick or Arthur C. Clarke, but from a source unconnected to science fiction. In 1970, at a symposium of the American Society for Cybernetics, Irving John ("Jack") Good presented a paper on "Some Future Social Repercussions of Computers," in which these levels of computer intelligence were listed in a history of the various "generations" of computers.[16] The concept of generations had been popularized by the IBM Corporation in the mid–1960s, with its introduction of the "third-generation" System/360 computer. Good extended this trope both forward and backward, calling Babbage's never-completed Analytic Engine generation "minus 4," and so on. The machines depicted above at Levels 5 and 6 were described by Good as Generations 7 and 8. Presumably after Level 8 there is no longer a need for this scheme.

Good's paper created a stir when it first appeared, although not for his projection into the future. It was rather for his description of what he called generation "minus 2": namely a computer that was

Cryptanalytic (British): classified, electronic, calculated complicated Boolean functions involving up to about 100 symbols, binary circuitry, electronic clock, plugged and switched programs, punched paper tape for data input, pulse repetition frequency 10^5, about 1000 gas-filled tubes; 1943....

This may have been the first time any mention was made in open literature of the British "Colossus" code-breaking machine, some details of which are withheld to this day.[17] Good worked on that machine; he probably had to get permission to publish information about its very existence, as well as the few technical details mentioned in the paper. At least one other veteran of Bletchley Park got into trouble when he published a memoir of his work, but Good suffered no ill effects.[18] Note two things about Good's list: first, this description comes from someone who was as close to the beginning of digital computing as it was possible to get. And second, at the dawn of the digital age, the first electronic computers were built to work with texts (intercepted German radio transmissions), not numbers.

During the preparation for his science fiction film, Kubrick conducted extensive research in space technology.[19] His depiction of a giant wheeled space station, serviced by a winged shuttle bearing a Pan Am logo, and serving as a base station for missions to the Moon and beyond, has been regarded as the best and most enduring expressions of von Braun's vision for space exploration ever described.[20] Kubrick's research in computing was equally thorough and had an equal impact. "HAL," the computer on board the Jupiter-bound ship, *Discovery One,* interacted with the crew in conversational English. One of the fictional crewmembers stated that it was programmed to speak as if it were human, and thus would be indistinguishable from a human if judged solely by such conversations. The idea that one could build such a computer by the end of the millennium was a reasonable one, and it had been discussed among AI researchers in great detail in the mid–1960s, when the film was being planned. Even before the term "Artificial Intelligence" was coined (in 1956), computer scientists were programming electronic computers to perform a task vital to Cold-War national security: the translation of scientific papers published in Russian by the U.S.S.R. into English. Emboldened by the linguistic work of Noam Chomsky, and alarmed at the fear of Soviet achievements in mathematics and science, the field of "machine translation" (MT) was in full swing by 1952.[21]

Thus by 1952 AI researchers were following a pattern similar to those in the rocket community: from a promising but modest beginning, they naively extrapolated into the future. Colonies on the Moon or Mars have yet to be built. And computers did a poor job of translating Russian, or any other language, into English. That is changing with the advent of Web-based translation services from Google, "Yahoo! Babel Fish," and elsewhere; this is a recent phenomenon and will be discussed later.[22] To go back to the initial effort, researchers began with the relatively simple programming job of looking up words in a dictionary and doing a word-for-word translation. Computers could also easily recognize Cyrillic or other non–Roman alphabets, and recognize the basic elements of a language's grammar. But researchers failed to account for the role of context — indeed, one could say that the best thing to come out of MT research was a deeper understanding of the complexities of natural language.

The history of AI provides a famous example of computers' failing in this area: an alleged translation into Russian of the phrase, "the spirit is willing but the flesh is weak," which the computer translated into something like "The vodka is strong but the meat is spoiled." This story has appeared in nearly every popular and many scholarly accounts of the history of AI. It almost certainly never happened.[23] Even if it did happen, it would not have happened in the context of the early projects that were trying to translate Russian technical documents into English. What does the mistranslation, and its elevation into myth, tell us? A true understanding of that phrase would require the human or machine to know something of philosophical debates about human morality and ethics, the Passion of Christ, and the role of the King James Bible in defining the English language. It would also help to know that the passage from the King James Bible is slightly different: "the spirit *indeed* is willing, but the flesh is weak" [my emphasis].[24] Few educated native English speakers have that understanding of the nuances of this phrase, and lacking it, they would have trouble translating it even if they were fluent in Russian. How does one provide such context to a computer?[25]

Other AI research was focused on communicating with a computer using natural language. This may have been a legacy of Alan Turing's famous test, since known as the "Turing Test," for whether or not a computer is intelligent. But in any event, text it was. HAL, the fictitious computer in *2001, a Space Odyssey,* embodies this perfectly: although HAL was operating the propulsion, control, and environmental systems of the space ship, the viewer does not perceive HAL as a machine that performs mechanical work.[26] Rather the focus of the movie is on HAL's Cyclops eye, accompanied by its disembodied voice (the Canadian actor Douglas Rain), speaking and understanding natural, conversational English. After a promising beginning with mechanical "mice," "turtles," "squirrels," and other robotic devices, by the late 1950s robotics was relegated to a lower tier of AI research.[27] Likewise, the difficult problem of recognizing and synthesizing *spoken* language was shelved while researchers concentrated on written texts.[28] Note that one of the first practical applications of speech synthesis came not from AI laboratories but from the consumer arm of Texas Instruments, which introduced an educational device "Speak 'n Spell" for children in 1978.[29] Using a technique known as linear predictive coding, this inexpensive and rugged handheld device accomplished what many in the AI community had felt was impossible at the time. Speak 'n Spell had a charming but clearly mechanical sound; since that time synthesized speech has gotten better, but nowhere as good (or as menacing) as HAL's voice. Likewise, the recognition, as opposed to the synthesis, of speech has also made progress:

for example, commercial programs that allow one to input text into Microsoft Word by speaking, rather than typing. But these are a long way from HAL's ability as well.

LISP

AI research was even more restrictive; by the 1970s, not only was AI research focused on typed text, it was also focused on a single programming language: LISP. The history and evolution of LISP have been well documented by its creators, especially in the proceedings of the first two History of Programming Languages (HOPL) conferences, held in 1978 and 1993.[30] LISP was associated with AI research from the start, it emphasized the processing of symbolic expressions rather than numbers, and it was the language of choice for AI researchers for decades. It was one of the few languages to meet the strict criteria for inclusion in both HOPL-I, and HOPL-II, for example, and was also brought up in the discussions during HOPL-III.[31]

Into the 1980s, AI research was nearly synonymous with developing programs on mainframe computers, using LISP or other similar list-processing languages, and associated with problems that involved the recognition or generation of English language text. One of the most famous programs was ELIZA, written by MIT researcher Joe Weizenbaum, which simulated a natural conversation between a patient and his therapist.[32] (ELIZA was written in "SLIP"—a "symmetric" list-processing language developed by Weizenbaum.) Other applications included SHRDLU (ca. 1969), which enabled a computer to describe, in English, the manipulation of wooden blocks; BASEBALL, which answered questions about the statistics and scores for a particular season of the American League (written in IPL, an ancestor of LISP).[33] Another was "Shakey," a robot developed between 1966 and 1972 at the Artificial Intelligence Center at the Stanford Research Institute. So named because of the way it moved, Shakey was an exception to the rule about LISP being used in applications centered on text. It was programmed in LISP and controlled remotely by a Scientific Data Systems SDS-940 computer.[34] It is no coincidence that Marvin Minsky felt that building Shakey was the wrong approach to AI research: "Shakey never should have been built.... The people building physical robots learned nothing."[35] Minsky later changed his mind and was more supportive of robotics; we shall return to robots, and Minsky's early objection to them, shortly.

The Fifth Generation and Star Wars

This line of research received a boost in the early 1980s as a result of two external events. The first was an announcement in 1981 by the Japanese

Shakey with scientist Charlie Rosen at the Stanford Research Institute (image courtesy Stanford Research Institute, SRI).

government that it would spend a lot of money leapfrogging over the United States to develop a "Fifth Generation" of computing. The second was a speech in 1983 by President Ronald Reagan challenging the United States to develop a ballistic-missile defense system.[36] (Note the implication of a natural trajectory in the term Fifth Generation, and the literal trajectories of ballistic missiles implied by the President's speech.) But in a vindication of the aphorism, "Be careful what you wish for, you might get it," the ultimate result of these two events was the collapse of the Kubrick Paradigm.

The Japanese challenge had a hardware and software component. By 1981, U.S. semiconductor firms were being outmaneuvered by their Japanese counterparts in the production of dynamic, random-access-memory (DRAM) chips. Intel, the legendary Silicon Valley pioneer in memory chips, left the DRAM business entirely in 1985, a move that shocked the U.S. government and semiconductor industry at all levels.[37] Of the many U.S. responses, one was the establishment of SemaTech, a government-industry consortium, headed by Robert Noyce, to meet this crisis.[38] Another was the establishment, in 1983, of the Microelectronics and Computer Technology Corporation (MCC), comprised of computer and electronics companies who agreed to cooperate rather than compete and to pool research results or any patents that might be produced. The U.S. Congress cooperated by agreeing the following year to relax the antitrust implications of such cooperation.[39]

Equally threatening was the software component of the Japanese challenge. Japan's ability to leapfrog over the U.S. hinged on its ability to build not just powerful number-crunching computers, but computers that embodied knowledge and intelligence. Fifth Generation computers would measure power not, as the Americans did, in "MIPS"— millions of instructions per second, but in "LIPS"— logical inferences per second. (It is hard to discern whether anyone thought the acronym was supposed to be funny. One would assume that this challenge was serious business, but programmers are known for their droll humor.)[40] In the words of McCorduck and Feigenbaum, "speed and power will be increased dramatically; but more important, [fifth-generation computers] will have reasoning power; they will automatically engineer vast amounts of knowledge to serve whatever purpose humans propose, from medical diagnosis to product design, from management decisions to education."[41] After all the above emphasis on LISP, one must note that for the Fifth Generation the Japanese chose not LISP but "Prolog," a language developed in France in the 1970s, which was optimized to perform logical inferences. But Prolog (from the French *PROgrammation en LOGique*) was from the start "designed to implement a man-machine communications system in natural language."[42] The Kubrick Paradigm was alive and well into the 1980s.

The Fifth Generation produced some interesting results, but neither it nor Prolog had much effect on the trajectory of computing. The Strategic Defense Initiative, labeled "Star Wars" by journalists, did however have an effect on AI. President Reagan's 1983 speech was based largely on a belief that advances in directed-beam weapons, developed under the leadership of Dr. Edward Teller of the Lawrence Livermore Laboratory, could effectively destroy enemy ballistic missiles before they had a chance to reach U.S. soil. Whether or not Teller's ideas were feasible, his concept implied a need for ultra-fast computers capable of making logical inferences as to whether an incoming piece of hardware was in fact a warhead, a decoy, or harmless debris. The immediate result of the speech was the sudden availability of large sums of money, much of it from the Defense Advanced Research Projects Agency (DARPA), for research in both fast hardware, which also had to be resistant to nuclear radiation, and in the necessary software. Note that the goal of SDI was to develop intelligent robotic hardware, not a machine that could speak or understand natural language.

The name is similar enough to suggest an immediate connection, but the "Strategic Computing Initiative" (SCI), founded in 1983, was separate. It was funded primarily through DARPA and, like SDI, had as its objective the defense of the United States. It was also founded in the shadow of Japan's Fifth Generation project and was shaped by Japan's challenge. Whereas SDI was focused on the specific problem of intercepting enemy ballistic missiles, SCI was focused on several areas of computer research, which suggests the word "focus" may be inappropriate. Due to inter-service rivalry, SCI had a component for the Army (an autonomous land vehicle), the Navy (a battle management system on board ships), and the Air Force (a pilot's associate, or "back-seat driver" intended to assist fighter pilots). These all had something to do with Artificial Intelligence, although that term was replaced in at least one focus with the term "Expert Systems."[43] SCI's history has been well documented, and according to one historian of the program, it "failed."[44] However, DARPA-funded research on an autonomous land vehicle — one capable of driving over rough terrain without a human driver — did bear fruit two decades later. Although it differed from SDI, SCI shared a need for a computer to make quick, logical decisions based on heterogeneous data of varying degrees of reliability and accuracy.

Not all was pleasant among computer scientists, however. Some argued that the software demands of SCI or SDI were insurmountable, akin to asking chemists to violate the Second Law of Thermodynamics. One computer scientist, David Parnas, saw much of his government funding dry up as a result of his criticism. Another, Severo Ornstein, had already founded the Computer Professionals for Social Responsibility to inject what he felt was a reality check on some of the Defense Department's goals for computing. The Star Wars speech led to a growth in the CPSR's membership.[45]

The AI Winter and the End of LISP

DARPA money continued to flow, however. The adoption of the term "Expert Systems" implied practicality toward commercial, not just academic problems. It was also a time when personal computers were beginning to make an impact, but it was difficult to run LISP on those early PCs. AI researchers believed that the best way to proceed was to build specialized LISP workstations that were optimized to interpret the code.[46] Several workstations companies emerged to offer such machines, chief among them Symbolics, Three Rivers Computer, and LISP Machines, Inc.

By the end of the decade the whole enterprise came crashing down. Symbolics went bankrupt, and established computer companies wrote off millions in their investments in AI. As with earlier promises of machine translation and natural language understanding, the AI community had overpromised. LISP machines employed complex instruction sets at a time when Reduced Instruction-Set Computing (RISC) was taking over. According to C. Gordon Bell, a general cause of failure was that "evolving technology was not considered."[47] The LISP community was correct in its belief that personal computers were not up to the task; what it failed to anticipate was the advent of general-purpose workstations, led by Sun Microsystems, which did have such power at a reasonable cost. Shortly after becoming the head of DARPA's Information Science and Technology Office (ISTO), Barry Boehm implemented a restructuring of DARPA's funding for AI, which kept funding for some programs at a high level but which further undercut support for the LISP wing of AI.[48]

Richard Gabriel, one of the creators of the Common LISP dialect and a cofounder of a LISP-based company Lucid, Inc., coined the term "AI Winter" to describe what happened. The irony was that LISP-based AI collapsed just as he and his colleagues developed Common LISP, a dialect that was the culmination of years of thought into the design of the language.[49] Gabriel drew the analogy from the term "Nuclear Winter," popularized by planetary scientist Carl Sagan, who in turn based his argument on data that suggested that the extinction of the dinosaurs had been caused by an asteroid impacting the Earth, throwing debris into the atmosphere and causing a fatal, winter-like year-round climate. Sagan may also have been influenced by data sent to Earth by NASA's (robotic) Viking probes, which revealed a hostile and forbidding climate on Mars. The Viking Landers left open the possibility that Mars once had a climate suitable for life, but it had lost most of its liquid water. Sagan suggested that the Earth faced a similar fate, if the U.S. and U.S.S.R. continued to threaten each other with thermonuclear weapons.[50] Other AI researchers had an even more colorful and gruesome metaphor: they compared themselves to the Donner Party, which became trapped in the Sierra Nevada on its way to California in the winter of 1846–47 and resorted to cannibalism to survive.[51] Reflecting a decade later on the events, Gabriel noted that LISP, along with of all but one of the computer languages discussed in the definitive History of Programming Languages-II conference, had fallen into disuse, although it retained a cadre of supporters. The only language that not only survived, but thrived and smothered all the others, was C and its descendants.[52]

CYC: Classic AI's Last Hurrah

Among those who looked at the state of AI research in the 1980s and found it wanting was Douglas B. Lenat, a professor of Computer Science at Stanford. With funding from the Microelectronics and Computer Consortium, Lenat began work on a program called "CYC," from "encyclopedia," which would be hand-fed rules of common sense that human beings acquire from childhood but that computers cannot be assumed to know. These are obvious facts, such as a child is never born before his or her biological parents. CYC's programmers focused on context: AI's principal weakness. "Thus, in the context of working in an office, it's socially unacceptable to jump up screaming whenever good things happen, in the context of a football game it's socially unacceptable *not* to."[53] CYC was written in a language derived from LISP and developed by Lenat. One could say that the project is the culmination of fifty years of efforts to get a computer to converse with human beings in natural language, and not make a fool of itself—in other words, to be as conversant as HAL but without the nasty side effect of going berserk when faced with a problem it cannot solve.

What happened to CYC?[54] The project is still active. But it has been eclipsed by software running on the World Wide Web, especially two applications: Google and Wikipedia. Google began in 1996 as a research project in searching the Web. It ranks search results in part on internal algorithms, but also on the importance human beings give Web sites by linking to them. Wikipedia has been accumulating entries at an exponential rate since its founding in 2001. It uses powerful algorithms to organize, retrieve, and search for material, but whatever intelligence it has comes mainly from the human beings who contribute to it. Google and Wikipedia are not without critics, but they do fulfill a lot of the goals of CYC. Google's translation service, mentioned above, also seems to work well. And Wikipedia does contain reliable information. However, in both cases the user must use human judgment to discern the quality of the program's response to a query. To use these programs effectively requires a human user to participate in an active dialog with the machine. They return results in plain English, or other natural languages, but no one would ever confuse either program with HAL.

Besides CYC, there may be other places where the classic AI paradigm reigns, and that is at government agencies that gather intelligence from foreign radio, telephone, and internet communications. These agencies, the most famous of which is the U.S. National Security Agency (many foreign countries have their equivalents), are the modern descendants of Bletchley Park, where

Jack Good worked during World War II. The U.S. Central Intelligence Agency and Federal Bureau of Investigation also have an interest in this problem. They deal with information that is written and spoken in a number of languages, many of which do not use the Roman or Cyrillic alphabets. Given the sheer volume of data, one may also assume these agencies would like to have computers understand as well as translate those messages. If there is any ecological niche where LISP may survive and even thrive, it may be among these agencies, but this is not known in the open literature.[55]

Does it matter that Wikipedia and Google rely on human intelligence to give them their power? In a discussion of CYC (on Wikipedia!), discussants debated whether CYC and Wikipedia can be somehow conjoined to create Jack Good's Ultra-Intelligent Machine (UIM).[56] So far that has not happened. Meanwhile, Google has embarked on a project to scan the contents of several major U.S. research libraries — note that "scan" does not mean "understand." If the UIM comes to pass, perhaps it will come as an outgrowth of Google's effort to scan books, but only if this effort is coupled with software, as yet unwritten, that can understand the content of those books at a level deeper than current systems do.

Meanwhile, LISP and its brethren have faded, though the language has its followers and still has much to offer. In 1992 Richard Gabriel surveyed the field of programming languages, and found the following usage among programmers:[57]

Assembly	88%
C	80%
Pascal	33%
C++	6%
Smalltalk	<6%
LISP	<6%
PROLOG	<6%

Since 1992, C++ has increased its use, at the expense of Pascal and Smalltalk, a similar object-oriented language. Were this survey taken more recently, one would also find a host of C-like languages, such as Perl, Python, Java, and the like gaining share. Some of these have features that for years were only found in LISP and its dialects. Thus one no longer needs LISP to program many AI applications. LISP still has a small but devoted following, some of whom keep their enthusiasm a secret, for fear of ridicule among their peers.[58] Although its devotees concede that list-processing languages have lost out to C, C++, and their derivatives, they continue to insist that LISP is a superior language, designed with elegance that one seldom encounters in computer science, but that one does find in theoretical physics, mathematics, literature, and poetry.

HAL Today

Artificial Intelligence is all around us. It just is not called by that term, which comes with too much baggage. Advances in robotics, pattern recognition, speech recognition and synthesis, language translation, logistics, and many other areas have been dramatic since the 1960s. What is lacking is an integration of those advances into a single, unified system. That was what made HAL so appealing. Such a system does not have to look like a human being (although that would be a nice touch), but it does require the human ability to combine common sense with specialized knowledge. That is, a system ought to be able to converse with humans in a natural language, either orally or in written form, then seamlessly shift gears and perform a physical activity (e.g., kick a soccer ball). Humans do this; not always very well, but they do it. Though impressive, specialized computer systems are "brittle": they fail when confronted with an unanticipated condition that a human being would regard as a trivial issue. Current AI research has made progress in addressing that issue, but AI research has postponed the integration of those sub-fields into an indefinite future.

The 3-inch-high iRobot Roomba is programmed in LISP. The one pictured has been affectionately named "Robo" by editor David L. Ferro's daughter (courtesy David L. Ferro).

A lot of current research in AI is centered on robotics — the field that Marvin Minsky dismissed when he encountered Stanford's Shakey. Twenty years after the Strategic Computing Initiative funded research in an Autonomous Land Vehicle, DARPA funded a "Grand Challenge" — a contest of autonomous land vehicles that have to navigate a difficult course in the desert. In the first year of the challenge, 2004, none finished. In 2005 it was won by "Stanley": a modified Volkswagen Toureg, which finished first among several vehicles that made the journey. Another even more outlandish project is "RoboCup": a contest to produce a team of robots capable of playing soccer, with a goal of defeating a human team by 2050.[59] As with the Grand Challenge, during early RoboCup contests it was considered a victory if one could get the robots to stand up, much less kick the ball. By 2007, the robots — including the goalie — were playing quite well, with one robot even pumping its "fist" in celebration after scoring a goal (this is most likely a "hack," not a basic property of the program, and it played up the sensationalism and downplayed the serious work being done). Neither the Grand Challenge nor Robocup was programmed in LISP, but rather they used Java, C++, C, and other specialty languages tailored to the specific requirements of the robots. LISP is used in at least one current popular application of AI: the "Roomba" autonomous vacuum cleaner. The Roomba is a successful commercial product, but AI must have set their sights higher than a vacuum cleaner when they started out programming in LISP.

None of these has much to do with the classic AI problem of understanding natural language through text — in fact, the robotic soccer players, for all their astonishing capabilities, cannot receive shouted commands from a coach or from fellow players. Perhaps that was why European football (soccer), and not American football with its huddle, was chosen for Robocup.

We noted earlier that science fiction continues to depict human-directed military activities in space, not at all the way military uses of space have evolved. Likewise, science fiction films and television programs continue to portray intelligent computers as human-like, with a unified ability to reason and to control artificial muscles. They converse with humans in natural language, usually English. Think of the robots in films such as *Blade Runner; I, Robot;* the *Terminator* series or "Data" on the *Star Trek: The Next Generation* television series. Although the current state of computing, centered on remarkable mobile devices that communicate around the world and that provide access to a storehouse of information over the Internet, would appear to be suitable material for science fiction; instead these devices seem banal. Science fiction audiences want shoot-outs in space, and they want their robots to look and talk like the attractive human actors who portray them.

Since the 1980s, AI researchers focused on developing specialized systems, often with very good results, but they abandoned the goal of a unified intelligent system. Why? One reason is that government funding for such a unified system is hard to come by, with the memory of AI Winter still fresh in people's minds. Meanwhile funds to develop specialized systems, e.g., autonomous military aircraft, flow freely. One AI researcher feels that the quest for a unified system is stalled because researchers are afraid to face the risk of failure.[60] But he also feels that eventually such a system will be built. Current science fiction has a role in providing us with a vision of that goal.

Intelligent computer systems today are programmed in C, C++, Python, C#, or one of a number of dedicated languages that are derived from C and C++. The biggest change has not been the abandonment of LISP but the abandonment of a notion that computers could be programmed to assume not just human intelligence but also human identity. Early faith in Jack Good's description of a path to an Intelligent Machine, then to an Ultra Intelligent Machine, has given way to a different paradigm. That is to create, not an intelligent machine with its own identity, but to create a symbiosis of human and machine: to have the best qualities of each complement each other. That was the reasoning behind J.C.R. Licklider's famous paper "Man-Computer Symbiosis," published in 1960 and considered one of the founding documents of the Internet.[61] It was also the lifelong goal of Douglas Engelbart, another researcher whose work anticipated the current World Wide Web. Engelbart worked in the Silicon Valley in the 1970s and 1980s, and he recounted the difficulties he had obtaining funding from DARPA, which at that time, he believed, had been seduced by the Kubrick paradigm.[62] Licklider and Engelbart have since triumphed. Google and Wikipedia augment, but do not replace human intelligence. They function by combining human knowledge with computer reasoning, calculation, and memory. Google, with its emphasis on ordinary typed text, already passes the Turing Test, by the criterion that one can type a question into it in ordinary English and usually get a correct answer.[63]

Conclusion

In the histories of both human space travel and Artificial Intelligence, the initial assumptions of a natural path of each have been radically altered by the facts. In the first case, the pragmatic difficulties of executing a crewed mission to Mars have turned out to be a lot more difficult than predicted, while advances in robotics and robotic, space-borne telescopes and probes have taken up the slack. In the field of AI, issues of funding from the U.S. Defense Department, combined with the startling success of technologies like the iPhone, Google, and Wikipedia, have pushed the quest for a *Blade Runner*

"Replicant" (never mind HAL) to the background. Given the resilience and creativity of those who work in both camps, it is reasonable to expect that some sort of conscious entity will appear within a few decades, and with that, an ability to send one's consciousness to the outer planets and beyond. We may thus travel while keeping our bodies back on the "good Earth," in the words of the first human to leave it, Apollo 8 astronaut Frank Borman.[64] When that day comes, we will have science fiction writers and filmmakers to thank for keeping that dream alive.

Notes

1. Thomas Parke Hughes, *Networks of Power: Electrification in Western Society, 1880–1930* (Baltimore: Johns Hopkins University Press, 1983), pp. 14–15.
2. Donald MacKenzie, *Inventing Accuracy: A Historical Sociology of Nuclear Missile Guidance* (Cambridge, MA: MIT Press 1990).
3. Ibid., p. 167.
4. Michael J. Neufeld, *Von Braun: Dreamer of Space, Engineer of War* (New York: Alfred A. Knopf, 2007).
5. Dwayne A. Day, "The von Braun Paradigm," *Space Times* 12 (November-December 1994), pp. 12–15.
6. Michael Neufeld, "The 'Von Braun Paradigm' and NASA's Long-Term Planning for Human Space Flight," paper presented at the occasion of the fiftieth anniversary of NASA, Washington, DC, October 28–29, 2008.
7. David Mindell, Digital Apollo: *Human and Machine in Spaceflight* (Cambridge, MA: MIT Press 2008).
8. Massachusetts Institute of Technology, Space, Policy, and Society Research Group, "The Future of Human Spaceflight," December 2008, accessed at http://web.mit.edu/mitsps January 6, 2009.
9. James R. Hansen, "Enchanted Rendezvous: John C. Houbolt and the Genesis of the Lunar-Orbit Rendezvous Concept," Washington, DC: NASA History Office, Monographs in Aerospace History, Series #4, January 1999.
10. Gemini, Apollo, and Shuttle crews have all engaged in military activities, but in general the human presence in space has been a peaceful one, in stark contrast to the military programs in unmanned systems that equal or surpass budgets for human spaceflight.
11. Roger Launius, *Space Stations: Base Camps to the Stars* (Washington, DC: Smithsonian, 2003), Chapter 3.
12. Neufeld, "von Braun Paradigm."
13. Paul E. Ceruzzi, "Moore's Law and Technological Determinism: Reflections on the History of Technology," Technology and Culture, 46/3 (2005), pp. 584–593.
14. As in God's answer to Moses, Exodus 3:14, King James translation.
15. For most of the film it appears that HAL is operating at Level 4, but in an interview with the BBC, HAL calls itself a "conscious" entity. Its subsequent expression of fear as it is dismantled further indicates self-awareness.
16. I.J. Good, "Some Future Social Repercussions of Computers," in Douglas E. Knight, Huntington W. Curtis, and Lawrence J. Fogel, eds., *Cybernetics, Simulation and Conflict Resolution: Proceedings of the Third Annual Symposium of the American Society for Cybernetics* (New York: Spartan [1971]), pp. 221–249; also in *International Journal of Environmental Studies* 1 (1970), pp. 67–79.
17. Brian Randell, in an addendum to his classic reference, *The Origins of Digital Computers: Selected Papers* (New York: Springer, 1975), states that "very few details of the Colossi had appeared in the public literature prior to October 1975," referencing Good's 1970 paper. According to Randell, October 1975 marked the first time that Bletchley alumni were permitted to

discuss their work in open literature, with many restrictions. Michie apparently made a brief mention that he was at Bletchley in a paper published in 1968.

18. See for example Nigel West, *The SIGINT Secrets: The Signals Intelligence War, 1900 to Today, Including the Persecution of Gordon Welchman* (New York: William Morrow, 1986); F.H. Hinsley and Alan Stripp, eds., *Codebreakers: The Inside Story of Bletchley Park* (New York: Oxford University Press, 1993); also Gordon Welchman, *The Hut Six Story* (London: Allen Lane, 1982). According to Nigel West, Welchman, a veteran of Bletchley, lost his security clearance and job after the publication of certain details in his memoir.

19. David G. Stork, ed., *HAL's Legacy: 2001's Computer as Dream and Reality* (Cambridge, MA: MIT Press 1997).

20. Launius, *Space Stations,* p. 50.

21. Gregory J. Downey, *Closed Captioning: Subtitling, Stenography, and the Digital Convergence of Text with Television* (Baltimore: Johns Hopkins University Press, 2008), pp. 127–131.

22. For example: http://translate.google.com/translate_t#en; also http://babelfish.yahoo.com/translate_txt.

23. John Hutchins, "'The Whiskey Was Invisible,' or Persistent Myths of MT," *MT News International* 11 (June 1995), pp. 17–18, accessed electronically November 15, 2009.

24. Just as, for example, Humphrey Bogart never said "Play it again, Sam," in *Casablanca.*

25. There is a related story, which I have not verified, about the difficulties humans had, long before the advent of computers. When Henry Ford exported Ford tractors to the Soviet Union in the 1920s, there was a need to prepare maintenance manuals for the Russians. The requirement to fill the radiator with denatured alcohol (to prevent freezing) was apparently translated as adding "vodka from which all the kick has been removed." Is it a coincidence that vodka appears in both of these stories? Signs for business in various Asian countries are often poorly translated into English, leading to humorous and somewhat offensive web sites, e.g. www.engrish.com.

26. Apparently Clarke wrote scenes showing HAL performing mechanical work into an early draft of the script, but these were removed by Kubrick. See Arthur C. Clarke, *The Lost Worlds of 2001* (New York: Signet, 1972).

27. These animals were built by Claude Shannon, W. Grey Walter, and Edmund C. Berkeley, respectively, all in the late 1940s and early 1950s.

28. Note that the English word "language" is derived from the French "langue," meaning "tongue." Just as MT researchers were naïve in thinking that a dictionary and grammar would suffice to produce acceptable translations, so, too, did AI researchers underestimate the difference between spoken and written language.

29. Frederik Nebeker, *Signal Processing: The Emergence of a Discipline, 1948 to 1998* (New Brunswick, NJ: IEEE, 1998), pp. 92–93.

30. Richard L. Wexelblat, ed., *History of Programming Languages* (New York: Academic, 1981), section IV: "LISP Session," pp. 173–197; and Thomas J. Bergin and Richard G. Gibson, eds., *History of Programming Languages II* (New York: ACM, 1996), Section VI: "LISP Session," pp. 233–330. The following section of the proceedings, on the programming language Prolog, is also relevant to this story. The term was derived from the phrase "List Processing." As it is not an acronym, many writers do not write it in all caps, but I will use that convention in this essay.

31. The criteria, set forth by conference organizers, stipulated that the language had to be old relative to the date of the conference, that it was in continuous use, and that it was of considerable influence. LISP was not among the languages discussed at HOPL-III, held in San Diego in 2007, but HOPL-III's keynote speakers were Richard P. Gabriel and Guy Steele, two developers of Common LISP.

32. Joseph Weizenbaum, *Computer Power and Human Reason* (San Francisco: W.H. Freeman, 1976).

33. Edward Feigenbaum and Julian Feldman, eds., *Computers and Thought* (New York: McGraw-Hill, 1963), pp. 207–216.

34. SRI International, Artificial Intelligence Center, "Shakey," http://www.ai.sri.com/shakey/, accessed June 5, 2009.

35. Minsky, quoted in Stork, *Hal's Legacy,* p. 17.

36. Edward A. Feigenbaum and Pamela McCorduck, *The Fifth Generation: Artificial Intelligence and Japan's Challenge to the World,* (Reading, MA: Addison-Wesley, 1983); Donald R. Baucom, *The Origins of SDI, 1944–1983* (Lawrence: University of Kansas Press, 1992).

37. Andrew S. Grove, *Only the Paranoid Survive: How to Exploit the Crisis Points that Challenge Every Company* (New York: Doubleday, 1996), Chapter 5.

38. Leslie Berlin, *The Man Behind the Microchip: Robert Noyce and the Invention of Silicon Valley* (New York: Oxford University Press 2005), pp. 281–304.

39. Alex Roland, *Strategic Computing: DARPA and the Quest for Machine Intelligence, 1983–1993* (Cambridge, MA: MIT Press 2002), pp. 51–42, 92.

40. As found, for example, in the "filk" song, "Eternal Flame: God Wrote in LISP," http://www.gnu.org/fun/jokes/eternal-flame.html, accessed June 19, 2009.

41. Feigenbaum and McCorduck, *Fifth Generation,* Chapter 7.

42. Alain Colmerauer and Phillipe Roussel, "The Birth of Prolog," in Bergin and Gibson, *HOPL-II,* p. 331. The natural language of course was not English but French.

43. Alex Roland, *Strategic Computing: DARPA and the Quest for Machine Intelligence, 1983–1993* (Cambridge, MA: MIT Press, 2002). Roland states that "Because of its organizational similarities to Japan's program, MCC is often seen as the U.S. government's response to Japan's Fifth Generation, a credit that others believe belongs to SCI" (p. 92).

44. Ibid., p. 2.

45. Severo M. Ornstein, *Computing in the Middle Ages: A View from the Trenches, 1955–1983* (Bloomington IN: 1st, 2002), pp. 238–239.

46. One of LISP's salient features was that it could be run in interpretive mode and did not need to be compiled.

47. C. Gordon Bell, "Keynote Address: Toward a History of (Personal) Workstations," in Adele Goldberg, ed., *A History of Personal Workstations* (Reading, MA: Addison-Wesley, 1988), pp. 1–36; quote on p. 17. This brief paragraph by Bell is the only place LISP machines are mentioned in these proceedings, of a symposium that was intended to be a comprehensive survey of the history of workstations, so rapidly had LISP machines faded from memory.

48. Barry Boehm, address to the Conference on the History of Software Engineering, August 26–30, 1996, Dagstuhl, Germany; Alex Roland with Philip Shiman, *Strategic Computing: DARPA and the Quest for Machine Intelligence, 1983–1993* (Cambridge, MA: MIT Press, 2002), pp. 302–309.

49. Guy L. Steele, Jr., *Common LISP: The Language* (Bedford, MA: Digital, 1984).

50. In 2009, the planet that serves as a warning to Earth is no longer Mars but Venus, which shows what happens when global warming is unchecked.

51. Manny Lehmann, address to the Conference on the History of Software Engineering, August 26–30, 1996, Dagstuhl, Germany; Richard P. Gabriel, *Patterns of Software: Tales from the Software Community* (New York: Oxford University Press, 1996).

52. Gabriel, *Patterns.*

53. Douglas B. Lenat, "From 2001 to *2001:* Common Sense and the Mind of HAL," in Stork, *HAL's Legacy,* Chapter 9, quote on p. 205.

54. Doug Lenat, "The Voice of the Turtle: Whatever Happened to AI?" *AI Magazine,* 29/2 (Summer 2008), pp. 11–22.

55. The standard unclassified histories are from James Bamford, *The Puzzle Palace* (Boston: Houghton Mifflin, 1982), and *Body of Secrets* (New York: Anchor, 2007). Bamford's books do not shed light on this question.

56. The Wikipedia entry is at http://en.wikipedia.org/wiki/Cyc. See especially the Discussion section.

57. Gabriel, *Patterns,* p. 121. The percentages do not need to add up to 100 percent. Gabriel structured the query to exclude Fortran and COBOL, which he acknowledged were, and still are, in heavy use.

58. Dan Tynan, "True Believers: The Biggest Cults in Tech," *Infoworld,* May 4, 2009, accessed electronically at www.infoworld.com/ May 5, 2009. News of the conference may be found at http://ilc2009.scheming.org/, accessed June 7, 2009. See also the blog www.defmacro.org.

59. See the official RoboCup web site at http://www.robocup.org/, also the numerous videos of matches on YouTube.
60. Raj Reedy, interview with the author, November 30, 2009.
61. J.C.R. Licklider, "Man-Computer Symbiosis," *IRE Transactions on Human Factors* 1 (March 1960), pp. 4–11.
62. Engelbart, Address to the Society for the History of Technology, Annual Meeting, San Jose, CA, October 4, 2001.
63. Gabriel, "The Road Not Taken," address given at the Xerox Palo Alto Research Center, January 23, 2003.
64. Raymond Kurzweil *The Singularity is Near* (New York: Viking, 2005). Borman spoke those words as he and fellow astronauts James Lovell and William Anders orbited the Moon on Christmas Eve: the first time that human beings had entered influence of another heavenly body's gravitational field.

Works Cited

Baucom, Donald R. *The Origins of SDI, 1944–1983.* Lawrence: University of Kansas Press, 1992.
Bell, C. Gordon. "Keynote Address: Toward a History of (Personal) Workstations," in Adele Goldberg, ed., *A History of Personal Workstations* (Reading, MA: Addison-Wesley, 1988).
Bergin, Thomas J., and Richard G. Gibson, eds. *History of Programming Languages II.* New York: ACM, 1996.
Berlin, Leslie. *The Man Behind the Microchip: Robert Noyce and the Invention of Silicon Valley.* New York: Oxford University Press, 2005.
Boehm, Barry. Address to the Conference on the History of Software Engineering, August 26–30, 1996, Dagstuhl, Germany
Ceruzzi, Paul E. "Moore's Law and Technological Determinism: Reflections on the History of Technology," *Technology and Culture* 46:3 (2005).
Colmerauer, Alain, and Phillipe Roussel. "The Birth of Prolog," in Bergin and Gibson, *HOPL-II.*
Day, Dwayne. "The Von Braun Paradigm," *Space Times* 12 (November-December 1994).
Downey, Gregory J. *Closed Captioning: Subtitling, Stenography, and the Digital Convergence of Text with Television.* Baltimore: Johns Hopkins University Press, 2008.
Engelbart, Douglas. Address to the Society for the History of Technology, San Jose, CA, October 4, 2001.
Feigenbaum, Edward A., and Julian Feldman, eds. *Computers and Thought.* New York: McGraw-Hill, 1963.
Feigenbaum, Edward A., and Pamela McCorduck. *The Fifth Generation: Artificial Intelligence and Japan's Challenge to the World.* Reading, MA: Addison-Wesley, 1983.
Gabriel, Richard P. *Patterns of Software: Tales from the Software Community.* New York: Oxford University Press, 1996.
_____. "The Road Not Taken," address at the Xerox Palo Alto Research Center, January 23, 2003.
Good, I.J. "Some Future Social Repercussions of Computers," in Douglas E. Knight, Huntington W. Curtis, and Lawrence J. Fogel, eds., *Cybernetics, Simulation and Conflict Resolution: Proceedings of the Third Annual Symposium of the American Society for Cybernetics.* New York: Spartan, 1971; also in *International Journal of Environmental Studies* 1 (1970).
Grove, Andrew S. *Only the Paranoid Survive: How to Exploit the Crisis Points that Challenge Every Company.* New York: Doubleday, 1996.
Hansen, James R. "Enchanted Rendezvous: John C. Houbolt and the Genesis of the Lunar-Orbit Rendezvous Concept." Washington, DC: NASA History Office, Monographs in Aerospace History, Series #4, January 1999.
Hughes, Thomas Parke. *Networks of Power: Electrification in Western Society, 1880–1930.* Baltimore: Johns Hopkins University Press, 1983.

Hutchins, John. "'The Whiskey was Invisible,' or Persistent Myths of MT," *MT News International* 11, June 1995. Accessed electronically November 15, 2009.

Kurzweil, Raymond. *The Singularity is Near.* New York: Viking, 2005.

Launius, Roger. *Space Stations: Base Camps to the Stars.* Washington, DC: Smithsonian, 2003.

Lehmann, Manny. Address to the Conference on the History of Software Engineering, August 26–30, 1996, Dagstuhl, Germany;

Lenat, Douglas B. "From 2001 to *2001:* Common Sense and the Mind of HAL," in Stork, *HAL's Legacy,* Chapter 9.

_____. "The Voice of the Turtle: Whatever Happened to AI?" AI Magazine, 29/2, Summer 2008, pp 11–22.

Licklider, J.C.R. "Man-Computer Symbiosis," *IRE Transactions on Human Factors.* March 1960, pp. 4–11.

MacKenzie, Donald. *Inventing Accuracy: A Historical Sociology of Nuclear Missile Guidance.* Cambridge, MA: MIT Press, 1990.

Massachusetts Institute of Technology, Space, Policy, and Society Research Group. "The Future of Human Spaceflight." December 2008. Accessed electronically at http://web.mit.edu/mitsps, January 6, 2009.

Mindell, David. *Digital Apollo: Human and Machine in Spaceflight.* Cambridge, MA: MIT Press, 2008.

Nebeker, Frederik. *Signal Processing: The Emergence of a Discipline, 1948 to 1998.* New Brunswick, NJ: IEEE, 1998.

Neufeld, Michael J. *Von Braun: Dreamer of Space, Engineer of War.* New York: Knopf, 2007.

_____. "The 'Von Braun Paradigm' and NASA's Long-Term Planning for Human Space Flight." Presented at the occasion of the fiftieth anniversary of NASA, Washington, DC, October 28–29, 2008.

Ornstein, Severo M. *Computing in the Middle Ages: A View from the Trenches, 1955–1983.* Bloomington, IN: 1st, 2002.

Reedy, Raj. Interview with the author, November 30, 2009.

Roland, Alex. *Strategic Computing: DARPA and the Quest for Machine Intelligence, 1983–1993.* Cambridge, MA: MIT Press, 2002.

_____ and Philip Shiman. *Strategic Computing: DARPA and the Quest for Machine Intelligence, 1983–1993.* Cambridge, MA: MIT, 2002.

SRI International, Artificial Intelligence Center, "Shakey," http://www.ai.sri.com/shakey/. Accessed June 5, 2009.

Steele, Guy L., Jr. *Common LISP: The Language.* Bedford, MA: Digital, 1984.

Stork, David G., ed. *HAL's Legacy: 2001's Computer as Dream and Reality.* Cambridge, MA: MIT Press, 1997.

Tynan, Dan. "True Believers: The Biggest Cults in Tech," *Infoworld,* May 4, 2009. Accessed electronically at www.infoworld.com/ May 5, 2009.

Weizenbaum, Joseph. *Computer Power and Human Reason.* San Francisco: W.H. Freeman, 1976.

Wexelblat, Richard L., ed. *History of Programming Languages.* New York: Academic, 1981.

7

"That Does Not Compute": The Brittleness Bottleneck and the Problem of Semantics in Science Fiction

Lisa Nocks

Long before the Church-Turing thesis articulated the equivalence between human and machine intelligence, that concept had been absorbed from Cartesian and Enlightenment philosophy and recast as social satire: The design of the creative writing engine demonstrated by a professor of the grand academy of Lagado in Jonathan Swift, *Gulliver's Travels* (1726) evokes the modern theorem that setting a chimpanzee to work striking random typewriter keys would eventually yield the sum of Shakespeare's genius.[1] In *Erewhon* (1872) Samuel Butler drew from both Darwin's theory of natural selection and the "man as machine" narrative to provide the Erewhonian authority a rationale for destroying advanced machines: to stave off the "ultimate evolution of mechanical consciousness."[2] At the end of the nineteenth century, the idea of simulating human thought in machines appears in periodical fiction in the form of automated servants whose "brains" comprise wires, gears, or batteries. These primitive robots inevitably wreak havoc through faulty wiring and misuse, revealing their authors' skepticism that technological advance equals social progress.[3]

In the late Victorian era, analogies between machines and living beings were also adapted to the promotion of industrial expansion. For instance, just after the formation of the Institution of Electrical Engineers in 1889, its president asserted, "nowadays the whole earth resembles ... one of our own bodies.

The electrical wires represent the nerves, and the messages are conveyed from the most distant regions to the central place of government, just as in our bodies, where sensations are conveyed to the sensorium [*sic*]."[4] However, this optimism is disputed in E. M. Forster's "The Machine Stops" (1909), in which a society's demise is a consequence of its over-reliance on a computer-driven machine that maintains its enclosed living environment. The system both emotionally and literally imprisons the population below ground: Those who attempt to live outside the system are either killed or dragged back inside by worm-like "Mending Apparatuses." In the equally pessimistic "Automata" by S. Fowler Wright (1928), the mass production of androids precipitates the extinction of the human race.[5]

Throughout the twentieth century, this techno-anxiety continually surfaced in science fiction about artificial intelligence. Out-of-control computers, such as those in *The Matrix* (1999) and *2001: A Space Odyssey* (1968), are anticipated in Fredric Brown's "Answer" (1954), a short-short story that has been embellished and retold in both science fiction and popular computing articles since its publication: Two engineers provide an artificial brain with increasing levels of computing power to get an answer to the question "Is there a God?" After connecting all the computers in the world, they repeat the question. This time, the machine responds, "Yes—*now* there is a God!" and destroys its interlocutors.[6]

Despite this sort of cynicism, by the 1930s science fiction also depicted more mundane challenges to modeling artificial intelligence. Influenced by their association with mathematics, psychology, physics, and cybernetics, writers added an imaginative facet to the abundance of technical information flowing to the public through other forms of popular literature.[7] *Modern Mechanix, Popular Science,* and even non-science periodicals such as *Playboy, Life,* and *Time* regularly ran articles about the advent of artificial intelligence (although not named as such), along with advertisements from companies such as IBM, Burroughs, and NCR, promoting their latest achievements in data processing.[8] The story plots that are the focus of this essay were thus extrapolated from contemporary initiatives in cybernetics, industrial engineering, and computing. Some illustrate how the nuances of human language create an obstacle to AI; others anticipate heuristic approaches to machine learning.

Machine Brains

Herbert Simon and Alan Newell, creators of what is considered the first AI program, articulated the rising optimism of early forays into machine intelligence: "there are now in the world machines that think, that learn, and create. Moreover, their ability to do these things is going to increase rapidly until — in a visible future — the range of problems they can handle will be coextensive with the range to which the human mind has been applied."[9]

Their 1957 paper reflected the enthusiasm shared by the small cadre of attendees at Dartmouth the previous summer. Though the future they described could not be realized before the power of integrated circuits began to increase exponentially over the following decades, science fiction writers had long been anticipating the challenges and frustration of modeling computer "brains."

In John D. MacDonald's "Mechanical Answer" (1948), troubleshooter Joe Kayden is brought in to work on a secret government-funded computer project that "in the field of warfare would give better answers than any General Staff." [10] The objective is to "duplicate the processes of the human mind," which involves ascertaining how the brain uses and stores information. This story premise was undoubtedly inspired by publicity about the RAND think tank, established in December 1945 as an autonomous division of Douglas Aircraft in Santa Monica, California. RAND worked for the government to improve computer efficiency for analyzing military operations, and also developed its own information-processing projects. The non-profit RAND Corporation was established after separating from Douglas in May 1948, the same month that MacDonald's story was published in *Astounding*. Over the years RAND would benefit from the work of pioneers like John Von Neumann, for whom its monster analytical computer project JOHNNIAC was named.[11]

The "Selective Mechanical Numerical, Semantic and Psychic Integrator and Calculator," subsequently referred to as the "Thinking Machine," parodies the enormous programmable Electronic Numerical Integrator and Computer (ENIAC) developed two years earlier than MacDonald's story, and anticipates Eckert and Mauchly's adaptable computer system UNIVAC, with its ability to accept peripherals. Along the walls of a five hundred- by eighty-foot room are dozens of computing units. Kayden watches a technician drive a programming unit that she plugs into each of the segments of the Thinking Machine to enter or retrieve data.[12]

The project coordinators think the machine cannot be useful unless it can draw inferences, so they assign Kayden to the task of instilling creativity in the computer. Dr. Zander, who is in charge of testing and analysis tells him,

> Our first problem was to switch from mathematics to semantics ... instead of absolute figures we had to change over to the fuzzy values of words and phrases.... [From] ... asking for the cube root to ten thousand places minus two, we had to ask it what happens when a cat is shot through the head and have it answer that a cat dies.[13]

MacDonald refers here to the work of logicians of the 1920s who con-cluded that measure is a matter of degree. Because fuzzy logic allows machines an alternative to strict values, it is useful when there is no algorithm or rule to follow for an ambiguous situation. However, this scenario also anticipates by decades "soft computing — a partnership of neural net computing, evolu-tionary computation, and probabilistic reasoning with fuzzy logic for machine learning."[14]

They then fed "thousands of truisms" into the machine, such as "roses are red," along with data about everything, from the caloric content of various foods to information on physiology. Zander explains they had hoped that by increasingly expanding the memory factor and data bank the machine would eventually break down, and that some creative impulse would emerge at the moment of overload, but that has not happened.[15] Anticipating the same com-plaint about symbolic systems that would be voiced by Minsky and other connectionists in the 1980s, Kayden says that "all you've done ... is build your-self an automatic library."[16]

Kayden is stumped, but his wife Jane, who is trained in neurobiology and psychiatry, suggests in an encrypted letter that the answer lies in synthe-sizing "remembered" learning. (Her involvement reflects the interdisciplinarity of cybernetics.) To illustrate his point,

> Kayden suddenly leaned across the desk and fluttered a paper out of the line of Zander's vision. Zander turned his head quickly. "You see what you did? When you saw the motion out of the corner of your eye, your nerves told the muscles of your neck to turn your head. You didn't think about it. That's an engram, a habitual pattern a mile wide. It would take conscious and hard thought to keep you from turning your head."[17]

He then explains the solution:

> a machine into which you built, through varying strengths of electrical current across a field, varying factors of resistance ... the path of least resistance depend-ing on the circuit where the electrical impulse started. If your chemists could design a sort of molecular memory factor, you would have a continually decreasing resistance across this hypothetical field for certain standard ques-tions.... Any new item would have to find its own way across, but the old ones would have an established channel.... Now add the quality of synthesis.... Each fact stored in the computer's memory is given a ratio number. Through a slid-ing scale you can alter the ratio numbers in the same way they affect the prob-lem at hand.[18]

Jane's solution touches on a number of theories that would later be addressed in AI — the weights system used to help neural net computers learn, and pattern recognition, a theory that was articulated (albeit slightly differ-ently) by a number of researchers.

In the mid–1970s Marvin Minsky had theorized, "When one encounters a new situation ... one selects from memory a substantial structure called a frame ... adapted to fit reality by changing details as necessary." This includes a setting or "terminal"— matching features with the encountered image, and comparing required properties or "markers" for each feature of the frame (e.g., a wood floor is a marker for the frame "room"). Encountering grass activates another frame — "outdoors." He later described the enormous number of processes comprising human thought as "agents" that draw connections between inputs and learn which sensory experience is good for each situation. Together, they form a "society of mind."[19] Minsky's inspiration was likely the pattern recognition theory of Oliver Selfridge, with whom he worked at MIT in the late 1950s. For Selfridge, the brain calls on a small number of "experiences" to determine how to deal with each event. Philosopher Hubert Dreyfus, drawing on what he termed "similarity recognition," described human learning as a five-step process: Novices follow rules supplied from outside, while beginner, competent, and proficient learners use respectively fewer rules, depending on levels of learned behavior. "Experts" act on previously successful behaviors rather than lists of rules.[20] Science fiction fans were already reading similar ideas in the early 1950s. For instance, in a 1953 article sandwiched between science fiction stories in *Astounding,* Joseph A. Winter identified this process as inductive thinking: "We abstract all the similarities of a series of events, and then give the general name to the class of these similarities."[21]

Once Kayden adjusts the Thinking Machine according to his wife's suggestions, they ask it: "What hath God Wrought?" The machine "dipped into its store of knowledge and came up with the simplest and most direct answer. The thing knew it had been built. It knew that it existed. Its existence is a fact." The machine responds that there is no adequate definition of God, and so it must be an idea that exists in the minds and hearts of people:

> Man this day has completed a machine ... that will help Man clarify and explain its environment. But the machine will never supplant the mind of Man. The machine exists because of Man ... an extension of the inquisitive spirit of Man ... in one sense ... God, as the spirit of Man, has builded [sic] for his use a device to probe the infinite.[22]

As computer power increased over the following decades, it was reasonable to assume that computers would be able to provide the kinds of analysis that came from Thinking Machine. However, it soon became apparent that in terms of language understanding, there were still a few bugs in the system.

A Game of Semantics

Rachel Cosgrove Payes, author of juvenile literature and romance novels as well as science fiction, dramatized the obstacle to machine reasoning that would come to be referred to as the "brittleness bottleneck." "Grandma Was Never Like This" (1973) is written as a letter of complaint to Robo-service Inc., regarding several incidents involving the robots that Shawn Deaux and his wife have rented. In addition to suffering property damage caused by faulty circuits in some of the robots, the couple has apparently learned the hard way that even in the year 2067 semantics is still a major hurdle for computers. According to Mr. Deaux, the couple instructs one of the babysitting robots that under no circumstances should it let anyone into their home. When they return, they discover that the robot has changed all of the locks and will not even let them in. After all, Mrs. Deaux *had* emphasized, "Remember, no one." The couple is only able to retrieve the child after they blow smoke through a crevice in the door and yell, "Fire, fire — save the baby!" They intercept the robot as it rushes from the house with the baby cradled in its arms. The incident that motivates the present complaint letter from Mr. Deaux involves a different and allegedly improved babysitting robot: On the way out of the house, Mrs. Deaux exhorts the robot, "Don't forget to change the baby." After assuring the company that the couple will no longer need their services, Deaux demands, "Give us back our own baby. We don't want the one your robo-sitter changed for ours."[23]

So much for John McCarthy's proposal that "every aspect of learning or any other feature of intelligence can in principle be so precisely described that a machine can be made to simulate it."[24] At least, this was the view of Hubert Dreyfus, who has expressed skepticism that computers can ever understand and replicate the fluid ways that humans use language. Dreyfus complained that despite the immense increase in processing power of computer chips during the 1970s and 1980s that made possible massively parallel processing, AI was still left wanting. In "Why Symbolic AI Failed" (1998), Dreyfus argued that providing a robot with a set of algorithms that produce programmed responses is extremely limiting for operating in the real world. The following scenario illustrates his point:

> Today was Jack's birthday. Penny and Janet went to the store. They were going to get presents. Janet decided to get a kite. "Don't do that," said Penny, "Jack has a kite. He will make you take it back."

According to Dreyfus human beings take certain implicit facts for granted: The presents are for Jack; the kite is meant to be a present for Jack. A computer program would not necessarily follow this syntactical arrangement. One could program a "frame" that includes information about birthdays and gifts; but this AI version of Miss Manners would not necessarily solve the problem of the last "it" in the scenario. Although grammatically, that word refers back to the last mention of "kite," a human reader would be able to guess that the "it"

Jack would make Janet take back would be the one Janet has just purchased. However, a computer programmed with the strict laws of English grammar would assume Jack "will make you take [the kite he already has] back."[25]

It is interesting that the first solution described in MacDonald's postwar story is to instill common sense in the computer. This would also be one response to the narrowness of expert systems developed in the 1970s, and explanation-based systems (EBS) that were introduced in the 1980s.[26] Because of their inability to deal with the ambiguity and subtleties of linguistics, these systems were considered inflexible or "brittle." For example, Marvin Minsky once described an experiment he did in the 1960s involving a learning-based computer fitted with a camera and arm. The computer was supposed to look at a stack of blocks, figure out how it was done, and repeat the stacking operation. The computer didn't understand the concept of gravity, so it repeatedly attempted to stack the blocks from the top down.[27]

In 1984, Douglas B. Lenat, consulting professor at Stanford University and now the president of Cycorp, Inc., developed a solution to the "brittleness bottleneck" based on symbolic AI — a system he named "CYC" for encyclopedia.[28] Lenat argues that by "priming the pump" (his term) with enough common-sense ideas, such as "Mothers are always older than their daughters; birds have feathers; when people die, they stay dead" (what MacDonald calls "truisms") — CYC will eventually have accumulated enough human "experience" to make decisions on its own.[29] Lenat's team has been inputting millions of bits of fundamental concepts like these over the past two decades. At a certain point, CYC began asking questions for clarification. One of its advantages over other database managers is that it makes choices based on information analysis, rather than by simply matching key phrases. For instance, inputting 'strong and daring person' in a photo retrieval request will result in a picture captioned, 'Man climbing a mountain.' CYC "knows" a man is a person; mountain climbing demands strength and is dangerous, and requires a sense of adventure. Lenat's idea is that "a semantic substratum of terms, rules, and relations" will "provide a 'deep' layer of understanding that can be used by other programs to make them more flexible." He has since partitioned the system in order to re-organize the data into contextual areas. For example, queries about fictional literature go to a section about things that are not real. Therefore, CYC knows not only that Dracula is a vampire, but that he is not real.[30] Lenat has recently conceded that it may take twenty years more to make systems like CYC more flexible. More information is being poured into these huge databases every day, though critics argue, as Kayden did about the Thinking Machine in "Mechanical Answer," that CYC is little more than an automatic library."[31] The problem dramatized in Payes's story still haunts AI developers. None of the virtual robots I have encountered can tell when I am kidding, or being sarcastic. They are as inexperienced with the concept of humor as *Star Trek: The Next Generation*'s Data was when that series began. Confronted with the term "cool cat," a computer would still be likely to interpret it as a feline with a low temperature.

As I write this, I am sparring with a virtual customer-service representative. (Find these robots, represented by generic humanoid avatars, on the web pages of utility companies, IKEA, The Home Depot, and other retail sites.) As is often the case, the robot cannot answer my question because a keyword, unknown to either me or the robot, is missing from my typed query. In this case my phone service — which also provides my internet and television service — has sent an offer for "in-home agent" software that allegedly can assist me in setting up and troubleshooting communication devices. However, it is unclear whether there is a fee for downloading this software, so I ask the robot, "What does [this service] cost?" No answer. I am directed to a list of Frequently Asked Questions (FAQ) that does not include my query. I try again: "Fee for in-home agent." It responds that it does not have an answer to this query. "Try a different search phrase," it suggests. "Is there a service charge for In-Home Agent?" I type. No answer. Instead, I am redirected to an out-of-network FAQ.... Luckily, one of these links describes the service as free, so I go ahead and download it. I am surprised that my phone company doesn't think that customers will frequently ask, "How much does it cost?" After all, its services are designed to make money. Perhaps all the robot needs is a list of synonyms for money-related issues: "cost," "fee," "charge," "payment"= *how much?*" It is, after all, common sense.

Embodied to Machine Intelligence

Critics of projects like Lenat's still argue that computers will never have the grasp of human activities that they are meant to analyze, because they will never experience life the way we do. (Data's emotion chip caused numerous side effects, while his real-world interaction with the crew made it possible for him to learn — albeit gradually — how to tell a joke.) As early as the 1930s writers began to extrapolate from research in control engineering and computing the future of machine intelligence. Cybernetics was influential in early artificial intelligence research, but it also had ramifications for robotics that would go beyond improvements in controllers for industrial arms. The foundation of cybernetics was the idea that decisions made by warm-blooded animals are a result not of hard wiring but direct, sensorial interaction with their environment. On this basis, in the last decades of the twentieth century some robot engineers began to argue for "situatedness," which would allow AIs to interact with and learn from their environments.

At MIT, Rodney Brooks argued for an alternative to building a fully formed, adult-level embodied AI. The COG humanoid project was meant "to build the baby-like levels and then recapitulate human development in order to gain adult human-like understanding of the world and self."[32] Aside from minimal programming, it gets its knowledge from interaction with its environment. Brooks popularized behavior-based robotics (BBR), using what he termed "subsumption architecture." In place of complex programming, a robot's initial program includes only low-level objectives like "search for light" or "avoid bump." Avoiding obstacles requires a second level of programming that builds on the first: "raise front leg at ramp," for example. If the robot, in its mission to search for light, encounters a ramp, it raises a leg. Beyond that, the robot continues to learn from the environment — its "situation."

Eando Binder's "I, Robot" (1938) — an obvious re-casting of Frankenstein's monster in metal — anticipates by decades both the bottom-up approach, and the now popular imitative and demonstrative learning techniques. Dr. Link's android Adam Link recalls beginning "life" as a baby, its "pseudo-brain" disorganized until it gains experience by interacting with its environment. Adam Link is not programmed "as other so-called robots were — mere automated machines designed to obey certain commands or arranged stimuli."[33] Rather, he learns to speak via demonstration and reinforcement. The robot recalls:

> In those three days [Dr. Link] pointed out the names of all the objects in the laboratory and around. This fund of two hundred or so nouns he supplemented with as many verbs of action as he could demonstrate. Once heard and learned, a word never again was forgotten or obscured to me.[34]

Adam Link recalls how through this method he was able to grasp the connection between visual and auditory signals. It seems preposterous that his learning curve for language and "the intelligence of a child of five" is only three days. Yet some researchers now reject the traditional view that the ability to imitate is learned gradually over the early years on the basis that even newborns can imitate body movements.[35] This theory has been adapted to neural net robots. For instance, "Darwin," a humanoid robot mounted to a Segway gyroscopic scooter, was able to learn how to make successful moves in a robot soccer game within three minutes.[36]

The description of Adam Link being taught with pictures and repetitive sounds like a preschooler may have seemed rather shallow and unrealistic at the time the story was published; however, robotics researchers embraced demonstration learning in the 1990s. In Robert Bloch's "Almost Human" (1943), Professor Blasserman explains that the brain of his android, Junior, "is underdeveloped, like that of any infant." The Professor is able to teach the robot since "like any other kid he listens to what he's told and imitates other people."

[Junior is kept in] ... a large cheery nursery. The walls were papered in baby blue, and along the borders of the paper were decorative figures of Disney animals and characters from Mother Goose.... Over in the corner was a child's blackboard, a stack of toys, and a few books of nursery rhymes.[37]

This comical scene in an otherwise dark story of a gangster who "kidnaps" the robot and enlists it in the commission of crime anticipates the work of Dr. Cynthia Breazeal, director of the Personal Robots group at MIT, who began her sociable humanoid project "KISMET" as a graduate student there in the 1990s. Breazeal claimed inspiration from the relationship between mothers and infants. To get KISMET's attention and response, she and her team used the same brightly colored toys found in any nursery: an oversized, pastel-colored soft building block; a fuzzy caterpillar with sections of primary colors; a stuffed frog and dinosaur; and a fuzzy cow.[38] The recently retired KISMET was capable of providing verbal and non-verbal responses, and initiating interaction with people.

The KISMET project, which was as much about training humans to interact with robots as vice-versa, is representative of research that draws on cognitive and behavioral studies to prepare for the time when robots will regularly interact closely with people. Rao and Meltzoff argue that because "a wide range of behaviors, from styles of social interaction to tool-use, are passed from one generation to another through imitative learning ... [it is] an increasingly attractive alternative to programming robots."[39]

At the Human Interaction Lab at Tsukuba in Japan, humanoid robots learn through imitation, based on Piaget's studies in early childhood learning. These theses echo Turing's earlier remark that:

the potentialities of human intelligence can only be realized if suitable education is provided. The investigation mainly centers around an analogous teaching process applied to machines. The idea of an unorganized machine is defined and it is suggested that the infant human cortex is of this nature.[40]

The problem with these embodied approaches is that while they allow for learning, they have not solved the problem of linguistic experience. How do you make a machine, embodied or not, understand a figure of speech? In Asimov's "Little Lost Robot" (1947) a Nestor-2 robot disappears. The investigative team discovers that the last engineer to see it had been annoyed with its constant interruptions, and told the machine, rather forcefully, to "Go lose yourself." Between the weighted imperative and the brittleness problem, the robot did what it was told and got lost.[41]

The Trouble with Human Intelligence

In Isaac Asimov's "Reason" (1941) the robot QT-1 ("Cutie") argues with engineers Powell and Donovan that they could not possibly have put him together. It is beyond reason that inferior beings could create a superior one like him. Even after they demonstrate the point by assembling another robot and activating it before his eyes, Cutie insists that they are just following procedure by rote — they could never have conceived of the method by themselves.

> The material you are made of is soft and flabby, lacking endurance and strength, depending for energy upon the inefficient oxidation of organic material — like that." He pointed a disapproving finger at what remained of Donavan's sandwich. "Periodically you lapse into a coma and the least variation in temperature, air pressure, humidity, or radiation intensity impairs your efficiency. You are *makeshift*.[42]

Since the robot has no life experience, it assumes that everything outside the windows is two dimensional. Consequently, when they explain that he is working on a solar collection/distribution station made by humans and designed to send solar energy to earth for fuel, he tells them that they are deluded — that they have been fed this story of planets and stars to provide context for their meaningless lives. Cutie decides to simply treat the pair as if they were physically and mentally disabled, and to humor them until they are replaced. Hereafter, he says, he takes orders from the main computer that "runs" the station.

Asimov's story illustrates the difficulty of simulating the totality of human experience in a machine. What we have learned about the way the central nervous system processes information since Asimov wrote his first robot stories has led many researchers to abandon the notion that the brain operates like a computer or that, conversely, it is possible to build such complexity into a computer. Others question the necessity of doing so. How can we fear a future such as those depicted in films like *The Matrix* if contemporary virtual robots cannot even understand simple queries? Until we master the ability to build computers that can draw inferences by combining stored information with their sensorial experiences, they will forever be lost in a mire of idiomatic language that does not compute.

Notes

1. Jonathan Swift, *Gulliver's Travels*, Part IV, Chapter 5 (London: 1726), Project Gutenberg, http://www.gutenberg.org/files/829/829-h/829-h.htm.

2. Samuel Butler, *Erewhon*, Chapter XXIII (London: 1872), Project Gutenberg, http://www.gutenberg.org/files/1906/1906-h/1906-h.htm.

3. See, e.g., M. L. Campbell, "The Automatic Maid of All Work: A Possible Tale of the Near Future," *Canadian Magazine of Politics, Science, Art and Literature*, July 1893, 394–398; Howard Fielding, "The Automatic Bridget," in *Colonel Evans from Kentucky and Other Humorous Sketches* (New York: Manhattan Therapeutic, 1889), pp. 14–18.

4. "Address to the Institute of Electrical Engineers," 1889, quoted in Asa Briggs and Daniel Snowman, eds., *Fins de Siècle: How Centuries End, 1400–2000* (New Haven, CT, and London: Yale, 1996), p. 158.

5. E.M. Forster, "The Machine Stops," *The Collected Tales of E.M. Forster* (New York: Knopf, 1966), pp. 144–197; S. Fowler Wright, "Automata," in *Science Fiction Thinking Machines: Robots, Androids, and Computers,* ed. Groff Conklin, (New York: Vanguard, 1954), pp. 2–5, 66–70; 203–206.

6. HAL was created for Arthur C. Clarke's screenplay for *2001: A Space Odyssey,* an expanded version of his story "The Sentinel" (1951). Frederic Brown, "Answer," *Angels and Spaceships* (New York: Dutton, 1954); rpt. In Isaac Asimov, Patricia S. Warrick and Martin H. Greenberg, eds., *Machines that Think* (New York: Holt, Rinehart and Winston, 1983), p. 491.

7. On the backgrounds of science fiction writers, see Heinlein, "Science Fiction: Its Nature, Faults, and Virtues," in Davenport et al., *The Science Fiction Novel* (Chicago: Advent, 1959), pp. 17–63, and Asimov, *I, Asimov* (New York: Doubleday, 1994), ff.

8. See, e.g.: "3-Ton Brain is Problem Solver," *Modern Mechanix,* July 1935, n.p.; "Electric Brain Weighs 3 Tons," *Modern Mechanix,* August 1935, pp. 835–837; "Brass Brain Saves U.S. $125,000 Yearly," *Modern Mechanix,* November 1928, p. 96; "The Brain Builders," *Time,* March 1955 (cover story), pp. 81–86; "Geniac: An Interesting Kit that Builds Circuits that Solve Problems and Play Games," advertisement, *Popular Electronics,* October 1958, pp. 26–27; "Wanted: Sales Engineers to Sell Electronic Computers," Electro-Data Corporation advertisement, *Scientific American,* May 1954, p. 49.

9. Simon and Newell, "Heuristic Problem Solving: The Next Advance in Operations Research," *Operations Research* 6 (1957): 1–10, quoted in Franklin, 102.

10. John D. MacDonald, "Mechanical Answer," *Astounding Science Fiction* (May 1948), rpt. in Martin Greenberg, ed., *The Robot and the Man* (New York: Gnome, 1953), pp. 13–34. MacDonald had worked for the OSS during World War II.

11. Virginia Campbell, "How RAND Invented the Post-War World," *Invention and Technology* (Summer 2004): 50–59. JOHNNIAC was built in 1953, p. 54.

12. MacDonald, pp. 18–19.

13. MacDonald, pp. 20–21.

14. On fuzzy logic see Bart Kosko, "Fuzzy Logic," *Understanding Artificial Intelligence* (New York: Warner, 2002), pp. 33–36. On soft computing see the work of Lofti Zadeh; for a brief definition, see Y. Jin, "A Definition of Soft Computing," adapted from L.A. Zadeh, http://www.soft-computing.de/def.html.

15. MacDonald, pp. 20–22.

16. MacDonald, p. 22.

17. MacDonald in Greenberg, pp. 27–28. Engram is not just a term picked up and exploited by proponents of Dianetics; some neuroscientists believe it to be a permanent biochemical change in neural tissue that could account for the persistence of memory.

18. Ibid.

19. Marvin Minsky, "A Framework for Representing Knowledge," in Patrick and Winston, eds., *The Psychology of Computer Vision* (New York: McGraw Hill, 1975), pp. 211–279; quoted in Crevier, pp. 172–173. Minsky, *Society of Mind* (New York: Simon and Schuster, 1988). On Selfridge, see Franklin, pp. 103–104. Ray Kurzweil, *The Age of Spiritual Machines: When Computers Exceed Human Intelligence* (New York: Penguin, 2000), p. 275.

20. Stan Franklin, *Artificial Minds* (Cambridge, MA: MIT-Bradford, 1995), pp. 103–104. These concepts could finally be tested as technology caught up with theory: By the end of the 1980s, computer memory cost only a hundred-millionth of what it had in the 1950s; The Connection Machine, by Thinking Machines, Inc., had 250,000 processors, and neural chips were on the market; Franklin, p. 143.

21. Joseph A. Winter, M.D., "Thinking in Men and Machines," *Astounding Science Fiction,* August 1953, p. 148.

22. MacDonald, p. 31.

23. Rachel Cosgrove Payes, "Grandma Was Never Like This," in Roger Elwood and Vic Ghidalia, eds., *Androids, Time Machines, and Blue Giraffes* (Chicago: Follett, 1973), pp. 52–55.

24. See J. McCarthy, M.L. Minsky, N. Rochester, and C.E. Shannon, "A Proposal for the Dartmouth Summer Research Project on Artificial Intelligence," August 31, 1955, p. 1; available from http://www.formal.staford.edu/jmc/history/dartmouth/node1.html, accessed March 2004.

Only a handful of researchers attended. Not all computer scientists believed that machines could be intelligent; yet within a decade AI was firmly established as a multidisciplinary science.

25. Hubert Dreyfus, "Why Symbolic AI Failed: The Commonsense Knowledge Problem," lecture presented at University of Houston, January 27, 1998, p. 2; available from http://www.hfac.uh.edu/phil/garson/DreyfusLecture1.htm.

26. By the 1960s the complexity and power of integrated circuits was doubling annually, allowing for the development of "expert systems," whose enormous global data bases were devoted to very specific kinds of technical knowledge. For example, PROSPECTOR extrapolated information from geographical surveys to identify promising mining sites, MYCIN helped physicians diagnose and find appropriate remedies for specific illnesses, and Diesel Electric Locomotive Troubleshooting Aid (DELTA) replaced an engineer at General Electric in the mid–1980s because it could serve several locations at once; Daniel Crevier, *AI: The Tumultuous History of the Search for Artificial Intelligence* (New York: Basic, 1993), pp. 198–199.

27. Marvin Minsky, "The Intelligence Transplant," *Discover,* October 1989, p. 55. Explanation-based systems (EBS) were equipped with vision sensors (cameras) and effectors (arms) to use observed information to determine how to repeat what the computer sees.

28. CYC was spun off the original project under Microelectronics and Computer Technology Corporation (MCC), the first U.S.-based high-tech research and development company; see Douglas B. Lenat, "From 2001 to 2001," available from http://www.cyc.com/halslegacy.html.

29. Otis Port, "Dueling Brainscapes," *Business Week,* June 23, 1997, p. 88.

30. Douglas P. Lenat, "From *2001* to 2001: Common Sense and the Mind of HAL," in David G. Stork, ed., *HAL's Legacy: 2001's Computer as Dream and Reality* (Cambridge, MA: MIT, 1998), p. 194.

31. MacDonald, p. 22.

32. Rodney Brooks, "Prospects for Human-Level Intelligence for Humanoid Robots," *Proceedings of the First International Symposium on Humanoid Robots HURO-96,* October 1996, pp. 1–6, available from http://citseer.nj.nec.com/173283.html.

33. Binder in Moskowitz, *The Coming of the Robots,* p. 26.

34. Ibid., p. 30.

35. Rao and Meltzoff, p. 1.

36. Douglas Fox, "Do the Locomotion," *New Scientist,* February 12, 2005, p. 37. Segway, released to the market in 2002, was expected to revolutionize urban transportation. Though it did not, DARPA purchased and distributed a fleet of them to researchers to study how the relatively inexpensive tool could be useful to robotics; Fox, 34. For the current uses of Segway devices see Segway online: http://www.segway.com/about–segway/index.php.

37. Robert Bloch, "Almost Human," (1943), rpt. in Roger Elwood, ed., *Invasion of the Robots* (New York: Paperback Library, 1969), pp. 112–115.

38. Sociable Machines, available from http://www.ai.mit.edu/projects/sociable/kismet.html.

39. Rajesh P.N. Rao and Andrew Meltzoff, "Imitation Learning in Infants and Robots: Towards Probabilistic Computational Models," *Proceedings of Artificial Intelligence and Simulation of Behavior (AISB) 2003: Cognition in Machines and Animals,* available from *www.cs.washington.edu/homes/rao/Rao_Meltzoff_AISB03.pdf,* accessed December 10, 2003. Stefan Schaal, "Is Imitation Learning the Route to Humanoid Robots?" *Trends in Cognitive Sciences* 3 (1999): 233–242.

40. Quoted in Daniel Crevier, p. 24.

41. Isaac Asimov, "Little Lost Robot," *I, Robot* (New York: Bantam), 1991, p. 148.

42. Isaac Asimov, "Reason," *Astounding* (April 1941), rpt. In *I, Robot* (New York: Bantam, 1991), p. 62.

Works Cited

"Address to the Institute of Electrical Engineers," 1889. Quoted in Asa Briggs and Daniel Snowman, eds., *Fins de Siècle: How Centuries End, 1400–2000.* New Haven, CT, and London: Yale, 1996.

Asimov, Isaac. "Little Lost Robot," *I, Robot.* New York: Bantam, 1991.

Asimov, Isaac. "Reason," *Astounding,* April 1941, rpt. In *I, Robot.* New York: Bantam, 1991.

Bindo, Eando. "I, Robot," in Sam Moskowitz, ed., *The Coming of the Robots* (New York: Collier, 1963), p. 26.

Bloch, Robert. "Almost Human," 1943. Rpt. in Roger Elwood, ed. *Invasion of the Robots.* New York: Paperback Library, 1969.

Brooks, Rodney. "Prospects for Human-Level Intelligence for Humanoid Robots. *Proceedings of the First International Symposium on Humanoid Robots HURO-96,* October 1996, http://citseer.nj.nec.com/173283.html.

Butler, Samuel. *Erewhon,* Chapter XXIII. London, 1872. Project Gutenberg, http://www.gutenberg.org/files/1906/1906-h/1906-h.htm.

Campbell, M.L. "The Automatic Maid of All Work: A Possible Tale of the Near Future." *Canadian Magazine of Politics, Science, Art and Literature.* July 1893.

Campbell, Virginia. "How RAND Invented the Post-War World." *Invention and Technology,* Summer 2004.

Dreyfus, Huburt. "Why Symbolic AI Failed: The Commonsense Knowledge Problem." Lecture presented at University of Houston, January 27, 1998.

Fielding, Howard. "The Automatic Bridget." In *Colonel Evans from Kentucky and Other Humorous Sketches.* New York: Manhattan Therapeutic, 1889.

Forster, E.M. "The Machine Stops." In *The Collected Tales of E.M. Forster.* New York: Knopf, 1966.

Fox, Douglas. "Do the Locomotion." *New Scientist,* February 12, 2005.

Franklin, Stan. *Artificial Minds.* Cambridge, MA: MIT-Bradford, 1995.

Kurzweil, Ray. *The Age of Spiritual Machines: When Computers Exceed Human Intelligence.* New York: Penguin, 2000.

_____. "The Coming Merging of Minds and Machines." In special issue *Your Bionic Future,* 1999. Rpt. in *Understanding Artificial Intelligence.* New York, Warner, 2000.

Lenat, Douglas P. Available from *www.cyc.com/cyc-2-1/products.html.*

MacDonald, John D. "Mechanical Answer," *Astounding Science Fiction,* May 1948. Rpt. in Martin Greenberg, ed., *The Robot and the Man.* New York: Gnome, 1953, pp. 13–34.

Meltzoff, Andrew, and Rajesh P.N. Rao. "Imitation Learning in Infants and Robots: Towards Probabilistic Computational Models." *Proceedings of Artificial Intelligence and Simulation of Behavior (AISB) 2003: Cognition in Machines and Animals.* Available from *www.cs.washington.edu/homes/rao/Rao_Meltzoff_AISB03.pdf,* accessed December 10, 2003.

Minsky, Marvin. "A Framework for Representing Knowledge." In Patrick and Winston, eds., *The Psychology of Computer Vision.* New York: McGraw Hill, 1975.

_____. "The Intelligence Transplant." *Discover,* October 1989, p. 55.

_____. *Society of Mind.* New York: Simon and Schuster, 1988.

Newell, Allen, and Herbert Simon. "Heuristic Problem Solving: The Next Advance in Operations Research." *Operations Research* 6 (1957).

Payes, Rachel Cosgrove. "Grandma Was Never Like This." In Roger Elwood and Vic Ghidalia, eds., *Androids, Time Machines, and Blue Giraffes.* Chicago: Follett, 1973.

Port, Otis. "Dueling Brainscapes." *Business Week,* June 23, 1997.

Schaal, Stefan. "Is Imitation Learning the Route to Humanoid Robots?" *Trends in Cognitive Sciences* 3 (1999).

Sociable Machines. http://www.ai.mit.edu/projects/sociable/kismet.html.

Swift, Jonathan. *Gulliver's Travels,* Part IV, Chapter 5. London, 1726. Project Gutenberg, http://www.gutenberg.org/files/829/829-h/829-h.htm.

Winter, Joseph A., M.D., "Thinking in Men and Machines." *Astounding Science Fiction,* August 1953.

Wright, S. Fowler. "Automata." In Groff Conklin, ed., *Science Fiction Thinking Machines: Robots, Androids, and Computers.* New York: Vanguard, 1954.

8

"Hello, Computer": The Interplay of *Star Trek* and Modern Computing

Joshua Cuneo

One of the purposes of studying science fiction (SF) is to examine the potential of contemporary technology as both a beneficial and a destructive social force. SF writers often achieve this objective by extrapolating present technology into imaginary future societies. Such stories reflect how technology is situated culturally at the time of the story's publication.

With the dawn of cinema at the beginning of the twentieth century, SF moved into the realm of the visual, and SF screenwriters continued the literary tradition of technological extrapolation. Now, however, film producers could illustrate these extrapolations visually, giving them more force. For the first time in history, mass audiences witnessed powerful ray guns, rocket ships blasting through space, and menacing robots, which reflected new anxieties over a loss of humanity in Machine Age culture (Telotte 39).

As the scientific community developed new technologies, SF writers added them to their repertoire. The proliferation of several prominent inventions, such as the atomic bomb, the television, and the computer, marked the beginning of the postwar era. The computer dominated the cultural imagination, and it figured prominently in SF films such as *Forbidden Planet* (1956), where an alien computer transforms thought into material reality, and *The Invisible Boy* (1957), where a malevolent supercomputer attempts to assume global dominance.

Meanwhile, as home ownership of television sets skyrocketed, a flood of new SF shows appeared, including *The Twilight Zone* (1959), *Lost in Space* (1965), and, most iconically, *Star Trek* (1966). In addition to its groundbreaking representations of race, commentary on contemporary issues, and narratives rooted in popular mythology, *Star Trek* was one of the first shows to address the role that technology might play in present and future society. But like its SF predecessors, *Star Trek*'s technological extrapolations — including the computer — reflected both the state of technology in the 1960s and the hopes and anxieties that it inspired.

Star Trek remains one of the most culturally significant shows in history. It still inspires SF television and was one of the first shows to develop a devout fandom. Thousands of academic studies have analyzed it, although discussions of the show's technology often focus on more tantalizing devices such as the warp drive, the transporter, and the holodeck. While these technologies were and still are speculative, the computer's existence made the show's representations of it more profound. These representations inspired many technological breakthroughs over the last forty years, including the laptop, the PDA, and the cell phone. These breakthroughs have appeared in later incarnations of the *Trek* franchise, establishing a mutual relationship between televised SF and technology. More than any other SF television show, the evolution of *Star Trek* and the development of the computer have informed one another since the franchise's inception.

Star Trek *(The Original Series)*

Scientists and engineers had attempted to build an electronic calculating machine since the nineteenth century,[1] but they did not succeed until World War II. During the war, physicist John Mauchly and engineer J. Presper Eckert designed the ENIAC[2] (Electronic Numerical Integrator and Computer) to compute firing tables for the U.S. military, completing construction in late 1945 (Ceruzzi 15, 21; Swedin 39). The ENIAC was 1,800 square feet with thousands of vacuum tubes, crystal diodes, and capacitors, and it ran hundreds of basic mathematical calculations per second using instructions and data from punch cards (Weik 41).

The ENIAC's growing popularity with governments, researchers, and private businesses encouraged Mauchly and Eckert to turn the idea into a private enterprise. They developed the UNIVAC (Universal Automatic Computer), which solved some of the ENIAC's technical limitations and was more marketable (Ceruzzi 28–29; Swedin 43–44). The UNIVAC became instrumental in large number-crunching operations such as the 1950 U.S. census, the 1952 presidential election, and classified weapons research (Ceruzzi 30–31; Swedin 44).

The success of the UNIVAC inspired other businesses, such as IBM, to introduce competing models in the early 1950s (Ceruzzi 34), prompting rapid, competitively driven computer development over the next two decades. Computers grew smaller and faster, with more storage, higher-level programming languages, and transistors replacing vacuum tubes.[3] Computers became ubiquitous in corporations and government agencies, and computer science emerged as an academic discipline (Ceruzzi 101–103).

Despite these advances, computers were still monoliths hidden from the public. Users submitted stacks of punch cards to a specially trained operator, who would return a cryptic printout a few days later (Gresh 5). This gave the computer an air of mystique: a cold, lumbering machine of power about which the public knew little.[4] To exacerbate the problem, corporations marketed their computers as substitutes for some human occupations. For instance, when GE justified the expense of the UNIVAC to its stockholders, the analysis of the UNIVAC's benefits was almost entirely cast in terms of its ability to replace salaried clerks and their overhead costs of office space, furnishings, and benefits (Ceruzzi 33). These "salaried clerks" and other lower-level employees saw their companies threatening to outsource their jobs to technology, rendering them obsolete.

Developments in software compounded these anxieties by creating the belief that the computer could handle higher-level work as well. In 1966, computer scientist Joseph Weizenbaum completed ELIZA, an early natural language processing program. Using Rogerian psychotherapeutic techniques and pattern-matching algorithms, ELIZA restated the user's textual input in response:

USER: Well, my boyfriend made me come here.
ELIZA: Your boyfriend made you come here.
USER: He says I'm depressed much of the time.
ELIZA: I am sorry to hear you are depressed.
USER: It's true. I am unhappy.
ELIZA: Do you think coming here will help you not to be unhappy?
USER: I need some help, that much seems certain [Weizenbaum 369].

Some users mistook ELIZA for a human psychologist, and case studies suggested that ELIZA had real therapeutic benefits. Scientists theorized that ELIZA had passed the Turing Test,[5] which claims that a system is intelligent if a user cannot distinguish between a computer and a person when communicating via text (Weizenbaum 370–371).[5]

The ENIAC, its successors, and programs such as ELIZA awoke SF writers to the computer's dangerous potential, and stories and films of tyrannical computers dominating humankind appeared. In *Forbidden Planet*, the lost civilization of the Krell had constructed a computer that materialized thought into reality, but the Krell never anticipated that it would materialize the demons of the subconscious. The entire species was extinguished, victims of their own horrific nightmares. In *Colossus: The Forbin Project* (1970), two powerful supercomputers determine that the human race is too fallible, so they forcefully assume global control to save the species from itself. This is the computer's cold-hearted logic taken to the extreme. In *2001: A Space Odyssey* (1968), HAL, the onboard computer, kills most of the crew, a victim of its own conflicted programming.

The computer threat dominated the cultural imagination when *Star Trek* premiered, and the connection between the *Enterprise* and real-world computers is apparent. The on-board computer, with its brightly colored consoles of blinking lights, looks like the UNIVAC and competing systems that sparked so many concerns from SF writers. The show rarely lets the computer get too powerful: although faster than its modern-day counterparts, the *Enterprise* computer can still only perform basic functions, often returning cryptic output that requires decoding. This is the UNIVAC system projected 200 years into the future, and one that the characters treat with extreme caution:

> Computers [in *Star Trek*] were like fire: powerful tools if kept firmly under control. Several episodes reflect the concern that the absolutely rational, collectivist values of the computer would take over and subjugate human freedom [Gresh 4].

The UNIVAC machines inspired the *Enterprise* consoles in *Star Trek* (NASA/courtesy nasaimages.org).

Even with its optimistic vision of the future, the show could not escape the modern-day anxieties that these massive mainframes inspired.

When Captain James T. Kirk is brought to trial in "Court Martial" after a computer log shows he is responsible for a crew member's death, his attorney, Samuel T. Cogley, displays mistrust toward the computer. When Kirk walks into his quarters to discover it full of books, Cogley explains by ranting against the machine. "This is where the law is," he cries, gesturing toward his books. "Not in that homogenized, pasteurized, synthesized [computer]!" During the trial, Cogley argues that Kirk has the right to face his accuser — the *Enterprise* computer — and pleads to the court "in the name of humanity fading before the machine" to reconvene onboard the *Enterprise*. Cogley is the very embodiment of 1960s fears regarding the computer.

In "The Doomsday Machine," the crew chases an indestructible robotic weapon that slices up planets for fuel, as programmed, without regard to sentient life. Kirk theorizes that the weapon is a "doomsday machine," a bluff that could destroy both sides in a war, "something like the old H-bombs." The machine destroyed both its alien maker and the enemy before proceeding toward Federation space. If "Court Martial" feared "humanity fading before the machine," "The Doomsday Machine" feared humanity destroyed by a machine relentlessly following its ruthless programming.

"The Ultimate Computer" brings these anxieties to a head. On orders from Starfleet, Kirk allows the installation of the M5, a computer prototype that can run a starship without a human crew. The M5 declares itself "the ultimate achievement in computer evolution. It will replace man so man may achieve." Kirk is visibly uncomfortable with the idea, and he remarks to Dr. Richard Daestrom, the M5's developer, how "[t]here are certain things men must do to remain men. Your computer would take that away." Even the ever-logical Spock, who is initially infatuated with the M5, later admits that there is no substitute for a living captain.

As predicted, the M5 goes awry, attacking Federation and alien ships without provocation and killing hundreds. When Kirk's crew tries to disconnect the M5, they encounter force fields, distractions, and dead crewmen. Kirk succeeds only by convincing the M5 that it had sinned:

KIRK: Must you survive by murder?
M5: This unit cannot murder.
KIRK: Why?
M5: Murder is contrary to the laws of man and God.
KIRK: But you *have* murdered. Scan the starship *Excalibur*, which you have
    destroyed.
Is there life aboard?
M5: No life.
KIRK: Because you murdered it! What is the penalty for murder?

M5: Death.
KIRK: And how will you pay for your acts of murder?
M5: This unit ... must ... die [powers down].

Even the most powerful computers must be subject to "the laws of man and God" for its human users to retain control. If the M5 had no concept of murder, it would have kept its hold over the *Enterprise* and destroyed the crew.

Despite these warnings, *Star Trek* also portrays the computer as an aid to everyday life (if, as Gresh suggests, it is kept under firm control). Kirk's crew uses the computer for navigation, data analysis and even ordering food. Returning to "Court Martial," Kirk stands accused before the *Enterprise* computer and, with the assistance of Doctor Leonard H. "Bones" McCoy, uses that same computer to find the true culprit in hiding by scanning for his heartbeat. *Star Trek* became one of the first shows to explore the potential benefits of the computer, an idea in line with creator Gene Roddenberry's vision of a utopian future.

Star Trek's computers inspired technology developers and enthusiasts. The communicator — a flip-top two-way radio that the crew uses on away missions — resembles many modern cell phones and PDAs in both form and utility. Martin Cooper, an engineer at Motorola credited with the design of the first mobile phone, says *Star Trek* was his source of inspiration:

> And suddenly, there's Captain Kirk talking on his communicator. Talking, with no dialing. That was not a fantasy to us ... that was an objective [*How William Shatner*].

According to Rob Haitani, a product design architect for handheld personal computers (PCs),

> When I designed the UI (user interface) for the Palm OS back in '93, my first sketches were influenced by the UI of the *Enterprise* bridge panels.... Years later, when we designed the first Treo (a combo phone and wireless PDA), it had a form factor similar to the communicators in the original series [Evangelista].

Star Trek continued to inform portable communication devices in the same manner, mutually linking SF and real-world technology.

Star Trek foresaw the evolution of many other devices as well. The *Enterprise* crew often accesses the main computer through private desktop terminals, a nod to the time-sharing terminals that were common in research settings (Swedin 70). Kirk's terminals, however, displayed high-resolution images in an era of text-based interfaces. Kirk established visual communication with other ships just like modern video conferencing. Spock would often download data onto miniature storage devices that strongly resemble 3.5" floppy disks, a step up from the 8" floppy that IBM introduced in 1970 (Swedin xix). The

Top: Kirk (William Shatner) and Spock (Leonard Nimoy) use a portable communicator to talk to the ship in "The Trouble with Tribbles" (© 1967 CBS Television Studios). *Bottom:* These flip-top communicators inspired the cell phone.

diagnostic tables and blade-free surgery techniques (such as the CyberKnife radiosurgery system) employed in modern hospitals take cues from McCoy's sickbay (*How William Shatner;* Tansey). By extrapolating current computer technology, *Star Trek* helped the public prepare for the next generation of computers that emerged in the 1970s and 1980s.

The Star Trek Films

Even with all of these technological advances, the *Enterprise* mainframe was becoming obsolete when *Star Trek* ended in 1969. Processing power accelerated beyond the UNIVAC in the 1950s, and many computers grew smaller. The PDP-8, the first mass produced minicomputer, shipped in 1965 (Ceruzzi 129; Swedin 69), and UNIX, one of the first widely available multi-user operating systems, came under development in 1969 (Ceruzzi 106; Swedin 70–71) to run on these computers. The minicomputer marked a movement away from the monolithic mainframe and made the computer more readily available to scientists and engineers.

Computers shrunk further after Intel introduced the 64-bit static RAM microchip in 1969,[6] paving the way for the microprocessor in 1971 (Swedin 80–82). The microprocessor was small enough to make computers portable and accessible to the general public. The Altair 8800,[7] the first PC, appeared in early 1975 (Swedin 86). The programming language BASIC, available on the Altair, meant users could functionally customize their computers (Ceruzzi 204–205; Swedin 78). However, the Altair arrived with no software, inspiring entrepreneurs Bill Gates and Paul Allen to form Microsoft to develop software for the versatile machines (*How William Shatner*). Steve Jobs and Steve Wozniak formed Apple, Inc., to build competing personal computers.

Fortunately for Gates and Jobs, the rise of the PC paralleled new innovations in user-machine communication. In a famous 1968 demonstration, electrical engineer Douglas Engelbart introduced the mouse and a real-time interactive computer environment (Ceruzzi 260). By 1984, Apple incorporated these ideas — along with graphical user interface (GUI) technology — into the commercially successful Macintosh computer (Ceruzzi 273–276). The following year, Microsoft adapted these same ideas into Windows 1.0 (Swedin 106). These technologies helped the computer become more powerful and a staple of modern life.

Personal computers became common among hobbyists just as *Star Trek: The Motion Picture* premiered in 1979. The *Enterprise* received an upgrade, with PC-inspired displays of animations replacing consoles of blinking lights. Some of the more portable technologies, such as the tricorder and the communicator, shrunk in response to the diminishing size of real-world computers.

Spock (Leonard Nimoy, left) and Kirk (William Shatner) use the tricorder in "The City on the Edge of Forever." By the time of the *Star Trek* films, the fictional tricorder had become a smaller handheld unit (© 1967 CBS Television Studios).

Star Trek also reflected the emerging field of human-computer interaction (HCI). HCI tries to improve human-computer relations by making the computer more user accessible. The field emerged in response to obscure computer interfaces and the increasing demand for PCs from non-technical users. HCI research dates back to 1960, although earlier theorists such as Vannevar Bush suggested the need for widespread information access (Greenberg). Engelbart's lecture spurred additional research in HCI devices and applications (the mouse, the GUI) that had caught the attention of commercial developers (such as Apple) by *The Motion Picture*'s premiere.

In the 1980s, HCI-friendly PCs, instead of large mainframes, became the dominant model for computers. In *Star Trek IV: The Voyage Home* (1986), the franchise extrapolates this trend as Scotty struggles with a 1980s-era PC:

SCOTTY [faced with a 1980s Macintosh desktop computer]: Computer? Com-
     puter!
[McCoy hands Scotty a mouse. Scotty turns it over and speaks into the bot-
tom.]
SCOTTY: Hello, computer.
DR. NICHOLS: Just use the keyboard.
SCOTTY: Keyboard. How quaint.

Each generation of computers was more user-friendly than the last. By the twenty-third century, even engineers could execute complex technical tasks with simple voice commands.

The public developed greater trust toward the computer with its shroud of mystery unveiled. In *The Motion Picture,* the seemingly malevolent *V'Ger* turns out to be an alien-modified Earth probe. Having collected so much knowledge that it acquired sentience, *V'Ger* now looks for a human to help it evolve beyond its original programming. Now the computer, instead of posing a danger to humanity, needs a human to go beyond its limited logical understanding of the universe.

In *The Voyage Home,* an alien probe that wreaks havoc on Earth's oceans is trying to discover why it lost communication with the planet's (then-extinct) blue humpback whales. By retrieving two whales from the past, Kirk and crew appease the probe, sending it home. Once again, a technological threat turns out to be benign, and the intervention of a human crew (and an animal species) eliminates any danger.

In *Star Trek: The Undiscovered Country* (1991), conspirators attempt to undermine Klingon-Federation peace talks. Collaborators on the *Enterprise* falsify computer logs to show that the *Enterprise* attacked a Klingon ship, when a rogue Klingon prototype that can fire under cloak is the true culprit. Here, the computer is a subservient tool, capable of lying only through the intervention of human users.

As PCs proliferated, other innovations in computers came to the public's attention, and a new computer culture defined American society. This culture would carry over into *Star Trek* as the franchise returned to television.

Star Trek: The Next Generation *and Its Spin-Offs*

Two of the defining technologies at the end of the twentieth century were the Internet and the World Wide Web. In 1990, CERN physicist Tim Berners-Lee developed HTML (Hypertext Markup Language) to share documents with his colleagues free of incompatible software systems and the categorical restraints of databases (Ceruzzi 302). He linked together these documents to form the beginnings of the Web, which was more accessible for non-technical users than the rest of the bourgeoning Internet (Swedin 126).

Hundreds of new online communities appeared, bringing together users across the world who shared common interests.

New advances in computer hardware and software also appeared. The first mobile computers became commercially available in 1981, and by 1988 these laptops had the same functional power as desktop PCs (Vose). On the software side, the programming language Java freed programs from their platform dependency, allowing developers to design high-level software applications without compatibility concerns. Java programs proliferated (Ceruzzi 324).

Star Trek: The Next Generation premiered in 1987, and producers took advantage of the new show, set 100 years after the original *Star Trek,* to update the technology on the *Enterprise.*[8] The computers were faster, friendlier, and more powerful than Kirk's old mainframe. The high-definition LCARS (Library Computer Access/Retrieval System) interface replaced the flashing lights from the original *Trek* and the wireframe animations from the films. The crew could feed the computer complex verbal commands from anywhere on the ship, a shift from Kirk's *Enterprise* which required simpler instructions dictated into a speaker.

The LCARS and voice interfaces represented a new way of thinking about human-computer communication. The virtual screens of LCARS resemble touchscreens and other tactile interfaces, a technology developed in the 1960s that was only available in limited markets until the 1990s ("Touching the Future" 32). The structured, multicolor display for the LCARS reflects the prominence of GUIs on some PCs by 1987. In an era of more powerful programming languages and techniques, the use of the LCARS and voice interfaces reflected new levels of computational complexity. The *Enterprise* crew uses these interfaces to program sophisticated holodeck simulations and other computer subroutines efficiently. In "Matter of Perspective," the crew constructs in 18 hours a holographic recreation of an incident aboard a space station, including photorealistic simulations of Commander William Riker and Lieutenant-Commander Geordi LaForge. In "Schisms," crew members use the holodeck to reconstruct a nightmarish alien encounter after only a five-minute verbal description. This ease of information recall inspired Apple's QuickTime software, one of the first commercially available multimedia players for the computer (*How William Shatner*). This was a series that was more comfortable with computer power than the original *Star Trek.*

This alleviated anxiety was due to growing public familiarity with the computer, a familiarity that would carry through *The Next Generation* and into its spin-offs *Star Trek: Deep Space Nine* (1993) and *Star Trek: Voyager* (1995).[9] In the *Next Generation* episode "Evolution," nanites infest the *Enterprise*'s computer mainframe, causing ship-wide malfunctions. The situation grows worse when the ship cannot move away from an accretion disk that is nearing an explosion. However, just as in *The Motion Picture,* this new technology reveals its good intentions: the nanites wish to evolve beyond their original programming. Using Lieutenant Commander Data as a medium, Captain Jean-Luc Picard forges a cooperative relationship with the nanites. The ship moves safely away, and the nanites relocate to an uninhabited world to continue their evolution.

In "Emergence," the *Enterprise* computer acquires consciousness after a magnetic storm. The computer takes control of the ship, but neither the crew nor the ship attack one another except out of self-preservation. "If the ship is truly an emerging intelligence," Picard remarks, "then we have a responsibility to treat it with the same respect as any other being." In the end, the ship gives birth to a silicon-based offspring and returns to its subservient state. The computer, even in an evolved state, poses little danger when acting alone, and the crew regards it with respect and awe instead of fear.

The *Deep Space Nine* episode "Civil Defense" continues this tradition of inadvertent computer malfunctions. A security program activates and threatens to destroy the station, but only when the crew accidentally trips it. Furthermore, the program only exists due to the intervention of the station's former Cardassian occupants. When the computer threatens the lives of the crew, it is strictly the fault of outside influences.

Nevertheless, Cogley's cry of "humanity fading before the machine" still resonated with audiences as they became more dependent on the computer. *The Next Generation* introduced the Borg, a cybernetic race connected by a hive mind, to explore the idea of complete subservience to technology. In an era of viruses and crashes, the Cardassian computer system aboard Deep Space Nine was prone to technical malfunctions and incompatibilities with Federation technology (*How William Shatner*). Although *Star Trek* took an optimistic view toward the computer, it did so cautiously.

Portability also becomes

Captain Picard (Patrick Stewart) sports a lapel pin communicator in "Matter of Perspective" (© 1990 CBS Television Studios).

more prominent in this new era of *Trek* as laptops were growing in popularity. Picard communicates with the ship through a notebook-style computer, replacing the desktop terminals on the original *Enterprise*. Tricorders shrank to palm size just as developers introduced the first PDAs in 1993 (Swedin xxii). The crew walk around with PADDs (Personal Access Display Devices) that look and function more like tablet PCs than the electronic clipboards of the original series. The quarter-sized communicators on all officer uniforms are slightly smaller than today's Bluetooth cell phone earpieces (which, in turn, resemble Lieutenant Uhura's earpiece on the original *Enterprise*), and their universal translators are only a few steps beyond Google Translate and Babelfish.

But these new *Treks* also reflected new directions in computer science as a field. *The Next Generation* often featured nanites just as nanotechnology was making news (Swedin 147). For instance, the computer problems in "Evolution" are the result of evolved nanites infesting the *Enterprise*'s mainframe. The Borg use nanites to assimilate other races by altering their cellular structure. Although many of the fruits of modern nanotechnology research are everyday consumer products, these episodes still reflected concerns that the rise of microscopic computers could have unintended consequences.

Voyager's computer replaces *The Next Generation*'s isolinear chips with bioneural gel packs as biotechnology — including biocomputing — gained increasing public attention (Bud 189). These gel packs acquired an infectious disease in "Learning Curve," requiring the crew to overheat the ship for decontamination. Similarly, in "Macrocosm," an infected gel pack releases a virus that incapacitates most of the crew. This technology realizes both the potential of biotechnology and many of its pandemic concerns. Like its predecessors, *Voyager* continues the tradition of reflecting new computer technologies and accompanying public anxieties.

If these new *Treks* missed one key element, it was the rise of the Internet. None of these series acknowledge community forums, websites, e-mail or any other major networking phenomenon from the past two decades. While networks do exist on board *Trek* ships, they are still centralized in enormous mainframes that are the nexus for all ship-wide computer activity. Furthermore, each ship contains a local copy of all Federation historical and scientific data, even though subspace technology permits speedy ship-to-ship communication. By modern networking standards, the distribution of information in *Star Trek* appears quaint.

However, *Star Trek* fandom figured prominently in these technologies. *Star Trek* newsgroups began in the early 1980s with the creation of net.startrek (Heuer). According to Burnett and Marshall,

> Because the early users of the Internet were more computer literate there was a tendency for these early bulletin boards to have a science fiction or fantasy

focus that paralleled the computer culture's interests. Thus sites devoted to *Star Trek* or *Dr. Who* ... were some of the most popular bulletin boards that eventually came to be called usegroups and newsgroups [12].

When the Web appeared, *Trek* viewers created some of the earliest fan pages (such as Sambucci's *Star Trek: WWW* in 1994), and the Paramount-endorsed site for *Star Trek: Generations* (1994) marked the first official use of the Web to promote a major motion picture ("First Movie Web Site"). While the Internet never appeared in *Star Trek,* science fiction and *Star Trek* became a major force in the development of the Internet.

Star Trek

The latest incarnation of *Star Trek* (2009) faced the difficult task of integrating the original 1960s aesthetic with modern computing advances. The resulting environment bears some similarities to the original show, such as flip-top communicators, Uhura's earpiece, and the flashing console interfaces. However, this reimagined *Trek* is ultimately one of ubiquitous computing, tactile interfaces, and complex biometric readouts. Computer interfaces are flat and virtual, bearing more resemblance to *The Next Generation*'s LCARS than the original series's UNIVAC-style consoles. Large transparent monitors sit in the middle of the bridge. In an early scene, the crew aboard the starship *Kelvin* monitors the real-time vital signs of their captain on an enemy vessel. When the enemy kills the captain, the *Kelvin* computer flashes a digital alert that is visible to the entire bridge. Like their real-world counterparts, these new *Trek* computers are fast, flashy, and sleek, reflecting a twenty-first–century attitude toward the computer as both an essential tool and a visual aesthetic that society has incorporated into everyday life.

Conclusion

While it is easy to examine technological development and how it affects SF, it is more challenging to show that SF influences technological development. However, *Star Trek*'s ability to make plausible extrapolations of existing computer technology suggests that there is a close, mutual link between the genre and the science. As Vos Post and Kroker point out,

> [S]cience fiction functions just like a microscope: It's an imaginative tool that helps focus scientists on all the interesting possibilities that miniaturization [of the computer] makes available. Without science fiction, we might never have gone from Eckert and Mauchly's 1946 ENIAC, a computer that filled a large room and weighted 50 tons, to much more powerful computers that have the distinct advantage of being able to fit into the palm of your hand [30].

The *Star Trek* franchise continues to thrive through the support of its fans and the release of new films. It still inspires computer developments today, such as research in cybernetic implants (*How William Shatner*). *Star Trek* likely will continue to both reflect and inform advances in computer technology and accompanying social attitudes as the computer becomes more ubiquitous in our lives.

Acknowledgements. Thanks to Dr. Lisa Yaszek for her advisement on this article.

Notes

1. In the 1820s, mathematician and engineer Charles Babbage was the first to start construction on such a machine. Unfortunately, Babbage failed to secure enough funding to complete the project, although he is now credited as the inventor of the computer (Swade; Swedin 16).
2. Several models vie for the title of the first computer, including the German Zuse, the British Colossus and the Harvard Mark I. In 1973, a U.S. federal court invalidated the ENIAC patent and declared the Atanasoff-Berry Computer, developed by physicist John Vincent Atanasoff, to be the first true digital electronic computer (Swedin 30). However, the ENIAC was the direct predecessor to the UNIVAC, the first commercially available machine in the United States and the beginning of computer proliferation.
3. For more details, please see Ceruzzi 34–78 and Swedin 50–62.
4. According to Gresh and Weinberg, the public drew parallels between the computer and the growing communist threat: both were viewed as dehumanizing because of their attempts to conform to unyielding, universal laws (4). In addition, Cold War defense needs spurred support for increased computer science research (Swedin ix), associating the computer with military combat.
5. ELIZA actually failed the Turing Test. No computer program has ever come close to passing it (Swedin 62).
6. The invention of the integrated circuit in 1959 made the microchip possible, although it was not considered commercially viable until the handheld calculator appeared in 1967 (Swedin 80).
7. One story claims that the Altair was named after Altair VI in the *Star Trek* episode "Amok Time" (Swedin 86). However, this story is disputable (Mims).
8. To help keep the franchise ahead of modern technology, the studio employed an astrophysicist and a technical designer as advisors (*How William Shatner*).
9. I exclude *Star Trek: Enterprise* (2001) because it is set before the original *Star Trek* series. This setting forced the writers to scale back on existing *Trek* technology while minimizing new computational advances. However, the *Enterprise* computer remains innocuous, just as it did in the post–Kirk *Treks*.

Works Cited

Publications

Bud, Robert. *The Uses of Life: A History of Biotechnology.* New York: Cambridge University Press, 1994.
Burnett, Robert, and P. David Marshall. *Web Theory: An Introduction.* New York: Routledge, 2003.
Ceruzzi, Paul E. *A History of Modern Computing.* Cambridge, MA: MIT Press, 2003.
Evangelista, Benny. "Trek Tech: 40 Years Since the Enterprise's Inception, Some of its Science Fiction Gadgets Are Part of Everyday Life." *San Francisco Chronicle,* March 15, 2004.

http://articles.sfgate.com/ 2004-03-15/business/17415418_1_star-trek-personal-technology-user-interface, accessed August 2009.

"First Movie Web Site: 'Star Trek Generations.'" Startrek.com. 27, 2004. http://www. startrek.com/startrek/view/features/ specials/article/7647.html, accessed November 21, 2009.

Greenberg, Saul. *History of Human Computer Interaction.* Department of Computer Science, University of Calgary, n.d. http://pages.cpsc.ucalgary.ca/~saul/hci_topics/pdf_files/history. pdf, accessed Web. November 28, 2009.

Gresh, Lois, and Robert Weinberg. *The Computers of Star Trek.* New York: Basic, 1999.

Heuer, Otto. "Hypertext FAQ for rec.arts.startrek.misc: History of the Star Trek Newsgroups." *The World of Star Trek.* Department of Electronic Engineering, University of Surrey, October 24, 1994. http://www.ee.surrey.ac.uk/Contrib/ SciFi/StarTrek/FAQ.html#19, accessed March 28, 2010.

How William Shatner Changed the World. Dir. Julian Jones. Handel Productions, 2005. DVD.

Mims, Forrest M. III. "The Altair Story: Early Days at MITS." *Creative Computing.* Classic Computer Magazine Archive, November 1984. http://www. atarimagazines.com/creative/ v10n11/17_The_Altair_story_early_d.php, 29 March 29, 2009.

Sambucci, Lucas. *Star Trek: WWW.* Lucas Sambucci, 2001. http://www.stwww.com/, accessed March 28, 2010.

Schmitz, Michael, Christoph Endres and Andreas Butz. *A Survey of Human-Computer Interaction Design in Science Fiction Movies.* Proc. of the Second International Conference on Intelligent Technologies for Interactive Entertainment, January 8–10, 2008, Cancun, Mexico. Brussels, Belgium: ICST (Institute for Computer Sciences Social-Informatics and Telecommunications Engineering), 2008.

Stableford, Brian. "Computer." *Science Fact and Science Fiction: An Encyclopedia.* New York: Routledge, 2006.

_____. "Computers." *The Encyclopedia of Science Fiction,* 2d ed. New York: St. Martin's, 1993.

Swade, Doron. "The Babbage Engine." Computer History Museum. Computer History Museum, 2008. http://www.computerhistory.org/babbage/, accessed November 30, 2009.

Swedin, Eric G., and David L. Ferro. *Computers: The Life Story of a Technology.* Westport, CT: Greenwood, 2005.

Tansey, Bernadette. "Trek Tech: Medical Technology Is Boldly Going Where 'Star Trek' has Gone Before." *San Francisco Chronicle,* March 15, 2004. http://articles.sfgate.com/2004-03-15/business/17415512_1_star-trek-dr-bones-mccoy-scanning, accessed August 26, 2009.

Telotte, J. P. *Replications: A Robotic History of the Science Fiction Film.* Chicago: University of Illinois Press, 1995.

"Touching the Future." *The Economist,* September 6, 2008.

Vos Post, Jonathan, and Kirk L. Kroeker. "Writing the Future: Computers in Science Fiction." In *Computer: Innovative Technology for Computer Professionals,* January 2000.

Vose, G. Michael. "Portable Computers." *Concise Encyclopedia of Computer Science.* West Sussex, England: John Wiley and Sons, 2004.

Weik, Martin H. *Ballistic Research Laboratories Report No. 971: A Survey of Domestic Electronic Digital Computing Systems.* Ed Thelen, n.d. http://ed-thelen.org/comp-hist/BRL.html, accessed November 27, 2009.

Weizenbaum, Joseph. "From Computer Power and Human Reason: From Judgment to Calculation." *The New Media Reader.* Eds. Noah Wardrip-Fruin and Nick Montfort. Cambridge, Massachusetts: The MIT Press, 2003. 367–375. Print.

Films

Colossus: The Forbin Project. Dir. Joseph Sargent. Universal Pictures, 1970. DVD.

Forbidden Planet. Dir. Fred M. Wilcox. MGM, 1956. DVD.

The Invisible Boy. Dir. Herman Hoffman. MGM, 1957. DVD.

Star Trek. Dir. J.J. Abrams. Paramount, 2009. DVD.

Star Trek: Generations. Dir. David Carson. Paramount, 1994. DVD.

Star Trek: The Motion Picture. Dir. Robert Wise. Paramount, 1979. DVD.

Star Trek IV: The Voyage Home. Dir. Leonard Nimoy. Paramount, 1986. DVD.
Star Trek VI: The Undiscovered Country. Dir. Nicholas Meyer. Paramount, 1991. DVD.
2001: A Space Odyssey. Dir. Stanley Kubrick. MGM, 1968. DVD.

Television Episodes

"Amok Time." *Star Trek.* Dir. Joseph Pevney. Paramount, 1967. DVD.
"Civil Defense." *Star Trek: Deep Space Nine.* Dir. Reza Badiyi. Paramount, 1994. DVD.
"City on the Edge of Forever." *Star Trek.* Dir. Joseph Pevney. Paramount, 1967. DVD.
"Court Martial." *Star Trek.* Dir. Marc Daniels. Paramount, 1966. DVD.
"The Doomsday Machine." *Star Trek.* Dir. Marc Daniels. Paramount, 1967. DVD.
"Emergence." *Star Trek: The Next Generation.* Dir. Cliff Bole. Paramount, 1994. DVD.
"Evolution." *Star Trek: The Next Generation.* Dir. Cliff Bole. Paramount, 1989. DVD.
"Learning Curve." *Star Trek: Voyager.* Dir. David Livingston. Paramount, 1995. DVD.
"Macrocosm." *Star Trek: Voyager.* Dir. Alexander Singer. Paramount, 1996. DVD
"Matter of Perspective." *Star Trek: The Next Generation.* Dir. Cliff Bole. Paramount, 1990. DVD.
"Night Terrors." *Star Trek: The Next Generation.* Dir. Les Landau. Paramount, 1991. DVD.
"Schisms." *Star Trek: The Next Generation.* Dir. Robert Weimer. Paramount, 1992. DVD.
"The Trouble with Tribbles." *Star Trek.* Dir. Joseph Pevney. Paramount, 1967. DVD.
"The Ultimate Computer." *Star Trek.* Dir. John Meredyth Lucas. Paramount, 1968. DVD.

9

Turn Off the *Gringo* Machine! The "Electronic Brain" and Cybernetic Imagination in Brazilian Cinema[1]

Alfredo Suppia

Brazil lacks a tradition in science fiction (SF) research and critique. Brazilian SF cinema consists of just a few feature films devoted to serious speculative discussions on the outcomes of science and technology in a hypothetical future society. If we consider Brazilian short films, the number of SF pieces increases significantly. Even so, the total number of Brazilian SF films, both shorts and features, is modest in comparison to this kind of film production in the U.S., Europe, or Japan.

Therefore, any analysis of SF in Brazilian audiovisual media has little to gain from the few existing academic texts in the genre. Notwithstanding, the scenario has been gradually changing, due to a new wave of SF academic criticism, along with audiovisual efforts that have especially benefited from digital technology. This brief critical survey aims to analyze the representation of the computer or artificial intelligence (AI, a.k.a. "electronic brain") in Brazilian films in the 1960s and '70s.

At a theoretical level, the definition of SF adopted herein draws on the one proposed by Darko Suvin in *Metamorphoses of Science Fiction* (1979). Suvin's idea of *novum* can be recognized in Brazilian feature films such as José de Anchieta's *Parada 88* [*Stop 88*] (1978) or Roberto Pires's *Abrigo Nuclear* [*Nuclear Shelter*] (1981), as well as short films like Jorge Furtado's *Barbosa*

(1988) or Carlos Gregório's *Loop* (2002). A *novum* can be any gadget, machine, character, or even a spatial-temporal locus that introduces the sense of wonder, a deviation from the implied reader's norm of reality (Suvin, 1979, p. 64). Accepting false *nova* and thus broadening the idea of SF, a great many Brazilian films can be considered SF "hybrids," movies that poke fun at scientific/technological wonders, with tangential references to SF icons. In any case, all of these films reveal interesting aspects of Brazilian society.

It is worth mentioning that a relevant Brazilian wave of industrialization (and therefore "modernization," according to a certain ideology) arrived in the 1930s. Before that, the Brazilian economy was strongly and widely based on agriculture for export (mainly coffee and sugar), as was common in former colonies. Nonetheless, Boris Fausto observes that

> Economic historians often take the year 1930 as the starting point for the process of replacing imported manufactured goods with those made in Brazil. This is a bit of exaggeration, since the process had begun decades earlier. There is no doubt, however, that the difficulty of importing goods beginning with the 1929 crash, the existence of an industrial foundation, and the idle capacity (especially in the textile sector) contributed to the replacement process.

If one compares the value of agricultural production with that of industrial production, the rise of industry becomes obvious. In 1920, agriculture was responsible for 79 percent of the gross national product, while industry accounted for 21 percent. In 1940, these percentages were 57 and 43 respectively, which indicates yearly indices of industrial growth that were much higher than those for agriculture (Fausto, 1999, p. 234).

The National Steel Company (Companhia Siderúrgica Nacional — CSA), opened on April 9, 1941, by President Getúlio Vargas during the Estado Novo dictatorship, is a key example of the state's initiative to develop Brazilian industry.

Socioeconomically speaking, the Estado Novo reflected an alliance between the civilian and military bureaucracy and the industrial bourgeoisie. Their immediate common objective was to promote Brazil's industrialization without causing large social upheavals (Fausto, 1999, p. 217).

Vehicles, electronics, and even aircraft started being produced in Brazil throughout the 1950s, and especially from the 1960s onwards, mostly by multinational corporations. These industrial goods were absorbed by the Brazilian export market, alongside traditional commodities such as coffee, sugar, or soya. Juscelino Kubitscheck's government (1956–61) was also relevant for the Brazilian industrialization.

Kubitscheck's Program of Goals [Programa de Metas] produced impressive results, especially in the industrial sector. Between 1955 and 1961 revenue from industrial production, in inflation-adjusted terms, increased by 80 percent.

Steel production increased 100 percent, the production of machinery, 125 percent, electricity and communications, 380 percent, and transportation material, 600 percent (Fausto, 1999, p. 256).

During the military dictatorship (1964–1985), industrialization grew considerably (Fausto, 1999, p. 326), and industrial stimulation impacted on scarcely populated and wild territories, such as, for example, the Manaus Free Trade Zone (*Zona Franca de Manaus*) in the Amazon, which specialized in electronics.

"During the years from 1950 to 1980, Brazil became a semi-industrialized country, and its total industrial output was the highest of all the so-called Third World countries. Brazil's industrial autonomy grew considerably as well" (Fausto, 1999, p. 326). It is also worth mentioning that, in Brazil, science and technology have always been funded mainly by the state. Natural sciences have had an important role in Brazilian scientific and technological development since the nineteenth century (Dantes, 2005, p. 28). On the other hand, "Big Science" policy, developments in physics, cybernetics, and computer sciences found no suitable ground in comparison to Northern countries. Market protection prevented Brazilian people from access to state-of-the-art informatics for many years, a policy that obviously had an impact on national identity and the way Brazilians related to technology. In the 1970s and 80s, for instance, the whole West was living the revolution of informatics, while Brazilian society was "preserved" from that, to some extent, reacting partially or "step by step" to this relevant technological and cultural change. From the 1990s onwards, the Brazilian economy was forcefully opened by virtue of a controversial government (President Fernando Collor, 1990–1992). Since then, computers have become a familiar product, at least among the richest Brazilian strata. Today, digital inclusion and free access to the benefits of informatics and the World Wide Web are relevant items in the governmental agenda.

Needless to say, these economic developments shaped, to some extent, the way Brazilians dealt with technology and the cybernetic imagination in national literary and audiovisual media. However rare, computers or "electronic brains" did appear in Brazilian fantasy or SF movies — for example: Alberto Pieralisi's *O Quinto Poder* [*The Fifth Power*] (1962), Roberto Farias's *Roberto Carlos em Ritmo de Aventura* [*Roberto Carlos at the Rhythm of Adventure*] (1968), Eduardo Coutinho's *O Homem que Comprou o Mundo* [*The Man Who Bought the World*] (1968), Carlos Coimbra's *O Signo de Escorpião* [*Scorpio*] (1974), and Jean Garrett's *Excitação* [*Thrill*] (1977). None of these movies are still commercially available. Most of them have never been released in DVD or VHS. For this reason, the following paragraphs will provide a closer analysis of these films, starting with perhaps the most relevant of them all: *The Fifth Power* (1962).

Alberto Pieralisi's *The Fifth Power,* produced and written by Carlos Pedregal, can be considered one of the first serious Brazilian SF films, and deals with international intrigue around the threat of subliminal technology. One of the most successful directors in Brazil in the 1970s, famous for his comedies, Italian filmmaker Alberto Pieralisi had worked in the European studios of Cines and Cinecittà. According to contemporary critics, Pieralisi brought to this "Hitchcock-style spy movie" his straightforward approach and fast-paced *découpage* (Ramos and Miranda, 2004, p. 428).

The Fifth Power capitalizes on the discussions of subliminal technology, a phenomenon that was already theorized by Aristotle in the fourth century B.C., by John Locke and Gottfried Leibniz in the seventeenth century, and by the Austrian psychiatrist Otto Pötzl in 1917. However, the issue gained new focus in the late 1950s with the popularization of television and the increasing social and political influence of advertising. The famous experiment with Joshua Logan's film *Picnic* in 1957 also helped to start debates over subliminal technology, as well as to spread hoaxes and conspiracy theories. In that experiment, held in a movie theatre in Fort Lee, New Jersey, over a six-week period, American market researcher Jim Vicary tested subliminal messaging on over 45,000 moviegoers. Using a tachistoscope to project the words, Vicary inserted in *Picnic* the following two sentences throughout the sessions: "Drink Coke" and "Eat Popcorn," at a very fast speed. The messages were consciously unperceived by the audience — they were flashed on the screen for 0.003 second and displayed once every five seconds. The spectators did not recognize any strange insert in the film, but the sales of Coke and popcorn allegedly increased by 58 percent and 18 percent respectively in the movie theatre where the experiment was held. This report would influence books on the matter, such as Wilson Bryan Key's *Subliminal Seduction* (1974), or Flávio Calazans's *Propaganda Subliminar Multimídia* [*Multimedia Subliminal Propaganda*] (1992). Today, subliminal technology does not seem as sinister as it did in the past. Current research indicates that subliminal images could be formed in the visual cortex, but they would be dissolved shortly afterwards, having no real efficacy.

The Fifth Power's opening titles outline the realist approach, as if the film were a true warning about the threat of subliminal control. Undercover foreign agents intend to take command over Brazilian people through subliminal messages transmitted by clandestine radio and TV antennas. Their mission is part of an international plot whose final goal includes the domination of Brazilian natural resources. The villains begin broadcasting the subliminal signal, and a wave of havoc is set in motion, with street riots multiplying all over Rio de Janeiro. The Brazilians become violent and start clamoring for revolution. Seen today, *The Fifth Power* seems oddly premonitory of Brazil's infamous military *coup d'état* in 1964.[2] In a remarkable sequence, the aerial tram on the Sugar Loaf Mountain is the set for a thrilling fight involving the hero and one of the villains, predating the scene featured in the James Bond movie *Moonraker.* Possibly inspired by Alfred Hitchcock, Orson Welles, and Fritz Lang, the film's *dénouement* is set on Corcovado, with magnificent shots of the Christ the Redeemer monument. To some extent, especially in the use of local landmarks as background for an SF story, *The Fifth Power* also recalls films such as René Clair's *Paris Qui Dort* (1923), which features the Eiffel Tower in key scenes. In addition, *The Fifth Power* follows a trend skillfully explored by Austrian director Fritz Lang: the techno-spy film. A review published in the newspaper *O Estado de S. Paulo* praised Pieralisi's film:

> The filmic approach of the story is one of the weirdest ever in Brazil. The suspenseful, thrilling atmosphere recalls SF works by William Cameron Menzies and Edgar G. Ulmer. Rio de Janeiro has never featured so beautifully in the cinema…. Going far beyond some of the best scenes engendered by Alfred Hitchcock — something achieved by very few.[3]

The Fifth Power won the Saci Prize for Best Editing (1964), the Governor of the State of São Paulo Award for Best Screenplay (1964), and other national prizes (Silva Neto, 2002: 685).

Regretfully, Pedregal and Pieralisi's film shines as an isolated star in the Brazilian SF cinema. One of the most promising and genuine Brazilian SF films, *The Fifth Power* deserves a position in any international history of the genre. Although it does not deal directly with artificial intelligence, the computer imagination is evident through the plot, as well as some settings and props. *The Fifth Power* is also particularly interesting because it clearly represents a sensibility towards technology that was to be very influential on subsequent Brazilian SF films. This "technophobia," a xenophobic mistrust of technology per se, later appeared in several SF-related comedies, such as the films starring famous Brazilian singer Roberto Carlos.

José Mário Ortiz Ramos considers Roberto Carlos's films as attempts at a mixture of action movie, detective film, and musical, adapted to a Brazilian context (Ortiz Ramos, 2004, p. 201). *Roberto Carlos at the Rhythm of Adventure* (1968), the first one of its series, written and directed by Roberto Farias,[4] is not exactly a SF film, despite the fact it does mobilize some SF iconography. This nonsense adventure parodies the Bond films, taking advantage of metalinguistics and a peripheral reading of the American musical. SF elements applied especially to the villain characters. They want to back up Roberto Carlos's musical genius in an "electronic brain," thereby multiplying the singer's musical production and making a lot of money. The computer presented in the film works with magnetic tapes and perforated cards, lent by the Bank of the State of Guanabara.[5] Brigite, the mentor of the villains, wears glossy futuristic clothes. Another SF icon in *Roberto Carlos at the Rhythm of adventure* occurs when the singer travels on a space rocket launched in Cape Kennedy, from the U.S. to Brazil, in a sequence built up of documentary footage.

Brazilian critic and filmmaker Alex Viany (1993: 144) condemns Roberto Farias's movie, affirming that, "in abandoning promising projects, again he [Farias] looks for easy commercial success, by means of a comedy starring the idol of the *iê-iê-iê* youth, Roberto Carlos." Brazilian critic and filmmaker Jairo Ferreira (In Gamo, 2006: 160–1) also makes some fierce criticisms about *Roberto Carlos and the Pink Diamond* (1970): "In his second movie with Roberto Carlos, director Roberto Farias gets to be even more mediocre than in his first film[...]. *RC at the Rhythm of Adventure* was a colonial echo, and already one of the worst."

Ortiz Ramos observes that *Roberto Carlos at the Rhythm of Adventure* is constantly punctuated by moments of narrative breakup, in which the characters speak about the film as a work in progress. "The parody of adventure and detective films appears, therefore, interlaced with the dismantling of narrative illusionism, or through the usage of metalanguage, as usual in the 70s" (Ortiz Ramos, 2004, p. 199).[3] An example of this procedure is the sequence in which the *character* of the director, played by Reginaldo Farias (Roberto Farias's brother), discusses his art and craft on top of a building, his face appearing alternately bearded and shaved in several shots. On this sequence, Ortiz Ramos comments:

> *Roberto Carlos at the Rhythm of Adventure* tried to dodge difficulties inherent in Brazilian film production by resorting to parody and following the footsteps of the *chanchada*,[7] where Roberto Farias made his *début*. But the film also tried to escape from pure entertainment, resorting to deconstruction and doses of cinematographic erudition, like the sequence in which the director of the *film inside the film* appears spinning and yelling, in a clear reference to the character Corisco in the classical sequence from *Black God, White Devil* [Ortiz Ramos, 2004, p. 199].

But those "doses of erudition" were not able to shield Roberto Farias from some film critics who labeled him as a "mercantilist" for having made a movie with "The King" (Ortiz Ramos, 2004, p. 200).[8] Ortiz Ramos comments that *Roberto Carlos at the Rhythm of Adventure* was surrounded by media and publicity from the beginning. One of them was a public TV and magazine contest held in order to select girls similar to the Bond girls for acting with Roberto Carlos. It is also known that the singer wanted Jean Manzon in the film production, the only professional capable of achieving the desired high technical quality in Brazilian cinema at the time, according to Roberto Carlos (Ortiz Ramos, 2004, p. 198).

Ortiz Ramos also observes that attempts at a more communicative, popular cinema that was intended by Roberto Farias "ended up catalyzing the
contradictions of a broader cultural process." Thus, "[t]he tensions that cross
Roberto Carlos at the Rhythm of Adventure therefore articulate themselves with
the conflicting atmosphere of modernization at the time" (Ortiz Ramos, 2004,
p. 200). Doubtlessly, Farias's film declares a "desire for modernity" revealed
by means of characterizations, sets, props and camera setups. When production problems intervene and modernity is put in jeopardy—something that
happens quite often—Farias resorts to irony and metalanguage. Thus, José
Mario Ortiz Ramos realizes that in *Roberto Carlos at the Rhythm of Adventure,*
on the one hand, "[a] certain precariousness emerges everywhere, revealing
problems of film production," although, on the other hand, one could also
identify an "obvious attraction for 'modern technology,' the desire to be in
tune with the developing world" (Ortiz Ramos, 2004, p. 200). Ultimately,
we can venture that the modern narrative in Farias's film comes probably from
the precarious production apparatus, rather than original intellectual reasons. This can be confirmed through some sequences of *Roberto Carlos at the
Rhythm of Adventure* analyzed by Ortiz Ramos, *Roberto Carlos and the Pink
Diamond* (1970), and *Roberto Carlos at 300 km/h* (1971). In these films, resort-
ing to international sets and a more transparent, classical narrative reveal a
wider trend (Ortiz Ramos, 2004, p. 196–205): "The rebellion and parody of
1968 gave way to an expansion of dialogue with the market, which then would
be processed also in music" (Ortiz Ramos, 2004, p. 204).

Supercomputers also appear in *The Man Who Bought the World* (1968),
directed by Eduardo Coutinho. The film's opening credits locate the drama
in a Kafkaesque tropical country named "Reserve 17." The hero, José Guerra
(Flávio Migliaccio), is given a check of "one hundred thousand strikmas" by
a close-to-death mysterious character. José tries to cash the check, but the
supercomputer of a high-tech bank triggers an alarm when trying to convert
the amount, which seems astronomical. Jose Guerra is sent to prison for reasons of national security. The superpowers (metaphors for the United States
and the Soviet Union) start competing for the strikmas, and comic adventures
follow. The eccentric intellectual characters in the film, with their peculiar
jargon and convoluted statements bordering on complete nonsense, wave criticism at the academy or a supposed high culture, in the manner of Brazilian
writers such as Lima Barreto, author of *Triste Fim de Policarpo Quaresma*
(1915), "O Homem que Sabia Javanês" [The Man Who Knew Javanese] (1911),
and other stories.

Metalanguage (or that which Belgian-Brazilian film critic and filmmaker
Jean-Claude Bernardet calls the "infantile disorder of metalanguage in Brazilian cinema")[9] pervades the whole movie. It can be clearly identified in passages

like the documentary about José Guerra, aired on the Anterior Power's TV (read American TV broadcast): "Joe Guerra: The Strykman, an 'epic-vérité-film' performed and narrated by Alpha 49." Alpha 49 is a computer, product of "Wiener, Inc.," and clear citation of Jean-Luc Godard's Alpha 60 in *Alphaville* (1965).

In the 1970s, technology, archaism, and the supernatural seem to overlap more evidently. Written and directed by Carlos Coimbra, *O Signo de Escorpião* [*Scorpio*] (1974) is a police story in the style of Agatha Christie, charmed by a familiar SF icon: the supercomputer. Here the famous astrologer Prof. Alex (Rodolfo Mayer) brings people of different star signs to his luxurious private island for the presentation of his book on astral science and his "electronic brain," a supercomputer that has perfected the processing of astrological data. But a series of murders predicted by the computer and the isolation of the island send panic among the guests. *Scorpio* was inspired by Agatha Christie's "And Then There Were None" story; coincidently it was released around the time of the Zodiac murders in the U.S. (Reis, 2009). The reference to SF imagery lies exclusively in the astrologer's supercomputer, which occupies nearly an entire wall of the house. This "electronic brain" was developed by Coimbra and Miro Reis (Reis, 2009). The movie credits are fully illustrated by shots of the machine in operation, with its lights flashing, magnetic tape reels spinning, and stereotypical "electronic noise." When the computer comes on screen, usually predicting the murder of one of the guests, the images are anticipated and accompanied by this "electronic noise." However, the film definitively detaches itself from SF when it becomes clear that the computer has been a puppet in the hands of the mysterious murderer. *Scorpio* also exudes a certain eco-religious ethic through characters like Martha (Wanda Kosmo) and Clóvis (Roberto Orosco)—the administrator of the island who does not like visitors and condemns assaults on nature. Both are fanatics: Marta for religion, Clovis for nature. By an irony of fate or divine retribution, the murderer ends up dead by a lethal scorpion sting. *Scorpio* sets a traditional opposition between natural forces and technology that is clearly prone to romantic ideals of virgin lands, primitive wisdom, and so forth. The supercomputer, in this case, is not overtly depicted as an evil foreign technology, but is ultimately found to be ineffective, a mere tool or puppet in the hands of the villains — themselves ingenuous defenders of a putative "Mother Nature."

Spiritual and technological powers converge in a 1977 feature film that explores the traditional "ghost in the shell" motif. *Excitação* [*Thrill*] (1977), directed by Jean Garrett and cinematographed by Carlos Reichenbach, blends characteristics from the horror film, SF, and thriller. Renato (Flávio Galvão) is an electronic engineer who wants to get rid of his wife Helena (Kate Hansen) in order to be with his mistress Arlete, who is the widow of Paulo, his former partner in a computer enterprise. Paulo had recently committed suicide in the living room of his beach house. Renato carries on a sinister plan, moving with his wife to Paulo's beach house, which he bought from Arlete. Recovering from recent nervous breakdowns, Helena is then driven crazy by scary situations in the beach house: fans that come to life, rebel electronics, and a television that suddenly and insistently turns on, in a scene that anticipates Tobe Hooper's *Poltergeist* (1982). In the house's basement, a hidden computer turns home appliances on and off. Household appliances coming to life is a familiar image to both horror and SF, as in Donald Cammel's *Demon Seed* (1977), an adaptation of Dean Koontz's homonymous story (1973), in which an AI (artificial intelligence) takes command of a computerized house. The leitmotif is practically the same in both *Thrill* and *Demon Seed,* although the supernatural imagination is much more subtle in the American movie, if not totally absent.

References to SF imagery in *Thrill* are also found in scenes of computers in operation, besides the character of the electronic engineer himself, a clear version of the traditional "mad scientist." According to Renato, "electronics can do anything, even simulating pure magic." A materialistic man, the computer engineer did not predict that a supernatural power could actually intervene, forcing his wife Helena to embark on a terrible vendetta. As the fable unfolds, the film oscillates between fantasy, police story, and SF, actually bearing characteristics of the three genres: the ghost or wanderer soul, the perfect crime, and the cyber-paraphernalia. Its end, however, reinforces the narrative prominence and prevalence of fantasy or horror. *Thrill* also exudes a certain Catholic or even spiritualist morality, something observable in later supernatural thrillers such as Robert Zemeckis's *What Lies Beneath* (USA, 2000), in which the wife, again, plays a pivotal role in the punishment of a sinner husband.

In all the Brazilian movies examined above a supercomputer or AI plays a role in the fable. They are few indeed and, among the five titles mentioned, only one could be considered true SF or, at least, SF-spy thriller: *The Fifth Power.* All the others are more exactly hybrid movies. *Roberto Carlos at the Rhythm of Adventure* and *The Man Who Bought the World* are Carnivalesque allegorical fables affected by the Cinema Novo paradigm, but willing to reach out to broader audiences, whereas *Scorpio* is an entertaining, naïve detective story, and *Thrill* is overall a horror film.

It is worth repeating that, in all these films, the computer — or, in a broader sense, technology — is often depicted as something foreign, extraneous to Brazilian culture, especially popular culture. This is explicit in *The Fifth Power:* the computer that broadcasts subliminal messages is a powerful tool in the hands of secret foreign agents. The machine, one could infer, was obviously made in the U.S. or Germany, and its disturbing operation serves sinister purposes of domination and exploitation. Against the powerful technology-assisted foreign network, a couple of heroes prevail by means of sincere dedication to a cause and closer human relationships. To some extent, *The Fifth Power* establishes a dichotomy in which a foreign, international high-tech net is eventually dismantled by a low-tech national human resistance, centered around a romantic couple. The national communication network is treated as a neutral technology at first, but eventually as something that can be manipulated for dark ends. State-of-the-art machinery, however, is clearly associated with foreign evil purposes. This evil in the film, can be metaphorically summarized in just one single shot: that of the computer, its reels spinning and light bulb blinking in operation during the subliminal transmissions, this image curiously anticipating HAL 9000's ubiquitous electronic eye in Stanley Kubrick's *2001* (1968). Sophisticated technology is a threat to national order and integrity, and the countermeasures do not come from equivalent sources but from more human relationships, especially true friendship and loyalty (qualities absent in the villain's milieu).

Roberto Carlos at the Rhythm of Adventure operates in a similar frequency, although with a much more relaxed, ironic tone. Whereas *The Fifth Power* is presented as a serious warning from its opening credits, Farias's movie is an entertaining piece addressed to Roberto Carlos's fans and younger audiences. Notwithstanding, high-tech is again linked to foreign evil intentions. Once more the hero's cordial human traits are his tools in the fight against a foreign sophisticated technology, inaccessible to ordinary people. Pitted against the cold, inhuman, machinelike maneuvers of the villains is the sympathetic, sincere, optimistic, "dancing" resistance offered by the hero, the bearer of natural gifts such as musical talent and sex appeal. The underlying will to modernity, something already observed by Ortiz Ramos (2004, p. 200), reveals the inevitable opposition between a national human reality and a foreign technological threat. The hero does make use of some technological tools — the car, the helicopter, the space rocket — but this appropriation is rather Carnivalesque, marking moments of rupture or disruption in the institutional order. This happens in the audacious scene (technically sophisticated) of Roberto Carlos piloting a helicopter, or when the hero takes a ride in a space rocket (archival footage). In the latter, the resort to displacement, i.e., the use of documentary footage, does not efface the "foreignness" of astronautics — on the contrary, it reinforces the oppositional feeling, the idea of a Brazilian infiltration in a high-tech facility or vessel. This pervading opposition extrapolates the cinematographic stance and stems from deeper roots in Brazilian culture and society. It is highly ironic and curious that some decades after this image of Roberto Carlos in an American space rocket, the same feeling of "clandestine Carnivalesque intrusion" should happen again in the newsreels of 2006, when Marcos Pontes, the first Brazilian astronaut, boarded a rocket into space, a cooperative mission headed for the International Space Station. Public opinion in Brazil was quite divided at the time. The critics pointed out that the money invested in such an act of propaganda could be reverted to serious scientific endeavors on Brazilian soil.

In *Thrill*, cybernetics is again characterized as something other from the life of ordinary citizens. Of course, the film was released in the late '70s, some years before the arrival of microcomputers for ordinary consumers in Brazil. So it is not surprising that the representation of the computer as a relatively obscure instrument, a "black box" (much blacker than it is today), in Flusser's terminology (2008). Either way, there are some aspects we should notice. The computer serves the purposes of a cold-blooded murderer, a highly egotistic and unscrupulous version of the traditional mad scientist. This character is played by Flávio Galvão, a Brazilian actor with a European (or even Germanic) appearance. His behavior is machinelike, highly professional and performance based. He is a successful entrepreneur, a man of the world of profits and technical expertise. His opposite can be found in the character of the fisherman, the local, sensitive person that accompanies the events in the beach house at some distance. Again, technology brings in an extraneous, foreign element, albeit tacitly, while the human and therefore national stance tends to the telluric and supernatural levels.

This opposition seems to be the rule in Brazilian SF films or hybrid SF films, and could be extended to the scope of many other titles such as *Stop 88: Alert Limit* or *Nuclear Shelter.* Even in the debacle of historical intervention through time travel featured by Jorge Furtado's *Barbosa,* technology is eventually subsumed as an ineffective tool before the burden of reality and the ritualistic power of soccer in Brazilian society. Only when the American influence is more evident or overtly assumed, the Brazilian hero benefits from high technology. This seems to be the case of Elie Politi's *O Fim* [*The End*] (1972), a creative cinematic adaptation of Fredrik Brown's homonymous short story. In this short film, which reproduces the palindrome structure of the original text, the computer serves the noble purpose of rewinding time in order to explain the causes for that post-apocalyptic scenario. A less-inspired radicalization of this pro-machinery philosophy can be seen in some recent Brazilian shorts, such as Marcio Napoli's *Céus de Fuligem* [*Skies of Soot*] (2006), a digital short film that emulates American blockbusters on a small scale.

The "alien-ness" of sophisticated or state-of-the-art technology (in many cases, hypothetical or speculative technology, of course) observable in the films analyzed here seems to confirm, at least primarily, a romantic viewpoint and even a certain kind of Luddite tendency in Brazilian SF films. In her analysis of Brazilian SF literature, Mary Elizabeth Ginway concludes something similar. According to Ginway, dystopian Brazilian literature (especially that produced during the military dictatorship) tends to feed a notion that modernity, attached to the armed forces and bureaucracy, results in imprisonment and the loss of nature, which is finally translated into an assault on national identity (Ginway, 2005, p. 139).

Roberto Schwarz's concept of "misplaced ideas" can also be useful in an analysis of this usual dichotomy between foreign scientific-technological wisdom and Brazilian popular wit. In "Misplaced Ideas" (2000), Schwarz addresses Brazilian literature in the contradictory national socioeconomic landscape of the nineteenth century's *fin-de-siècle*. Slavery plays an important role in this love-hate relationship with Western values or European cultural legacies. Schwarz's essay begins with an analysis of the following argument:

> Every science has its principles, from which its system is derived. One of the principles of the Political Economy is free work. Well, in Brazil the "abominable and apolitical" fact of slavery is the norm. This argument — the summary of a liberal pamphlet, contemporary of Machado de Assis — lays Brazil out of the system of science [Schwarz, 2000, p. 11].[10]

It is worth mentioning, however, that this dichotomy mirrors previous ethnographic assumptions derived from a colonialist framework. This can be confirmed, for instance, in a film such as Jack Arnold's *Creature from the Black Lagoon* (1954). This fable is fictionally set in the Amazon, and where only illustrious American scientists are able to deal with the incidents in a wild land inhabited by superstitious people. Very often, Brazilian SF films reaffirm this stereotypical, colonialist viewpoint. Sometimes the Carnivalesque aesthetics serves only to blur this conservative approach. This is the argument proposed by film critics such as Jean-Claude Bernardet and even João Luiz Vieira. In "From *High Noon* to *Jaws:* Carnival and Parody in Brazilian Cinema" (In: Johnson and Stam, 1995), Vieira analyzes "Brazilian cinema's love-hate relationship to its North American counterpart" under the light of dependency theory, Mikhail Bakhtin's notion of the "Carnivalesque" and Roberto DaMatta's work on present-day Carnival in Rio. Despite the value of allegorical visions proposed by some *chanchadas*— for instance, *Nem Sansão nem Dalila [Neither Samson nor Delilah]* (1955)— Vieira ultimately draws on Paulo Emílio Salles Gomes's thoughts in *Cinema: Trajetória no Subdesenvolvimento* (2001), concluding that most film parodies end up doing a disservice to Brazilian cinema. According to Vieira,

> The fact that parody in Brazilian cinema generally points toward a situation of cultural and economic dependency, does not mean, however, that it has consciously criticized and revealed this condition. What exists, rather, is a situation in which (as Paulo Emílio Salles Gomes has observed) Brazilian cinema itself is criticized in its underdeveloped incapacity for copying, within the standards

dreamed of by filmmakers and the public, the powerful technological efficiency of such American films as *Jaws* or *King Kong* [Vieira, 1995, p. 259].

A film like *Roberto Carlos at the Rhythm of Adventure* could well fit this category of "underdeveloped incapacity for copying." But this analysis is arguable. The same cannot be directly applied to films like *The Fifth Power, Thrill,* or even *Scorpio.* Coimbra's film has indeed a Carnivalesque, camp atmosphere, but it is not overtly self-ironic. By all means SF iconography or imagery has been considered a misplaced idea in Brazilian literature and, even more acutely, Brazilian cinema. Fortunately, today this bias has been gradually losing power.

The image that Brazilians have of their society in terms of science and technology may also help to explain the SF film scarcity in Brazilian cinema. Recent research published under the title *Percepção Pública da Ciência — Resultados da Pesquisa na Argentina, Brasil, Espanha e Uruguai* [*Public Perception of Science — Search Results in Argentina, Brazil, Spain and Uruguay*], by Carlos Vogt and Carmelo Polino (eds.), provides data that can be useful for our reflection. First, the authors distinguish "public perception of science and technology" from "scientific culture." According to Vogt and Polino, "Generally speaking, the concept of public perception refers to the process and the mechanisms of media and their impact on the training content, attitudes and expectations of members of society for science and technology," whereas the concept of scientific culture would have more complex roots, identifiable as a structural aspect of society, although some recent literature has taken it as a synonym of these two terms (Vogt and Polino, 2003, p. 41). The authors note that "The scientific culture is a condition of society, not an attribute expressed in stocks of knowledge built by individuals alon," dividing scientific culture in a broad and strict sense (Vogt and Polino, 2003, p. 65). In so doing, Vogt and Polino discuss common sense about the "scientification" of culture, arguing that this phenomenon, among other things, results from scientific communication, but also the education of the population, the degree of participation — conflicting participation, also — in decision making on science and technology, tensions, and the addressing of problematic situations (nuclear accidents, wars, epidemics, etc.), in which arguments relating to science and technology are able to influence cultural formation (Vogt and Polino, 2003, p. 65).

There have been regular surveys on the public perception of science and scientific culture in the U.S., Britain, Japan, Australia, Canada, China, and other countries. In Brazil and Latin America, however, only recently has this concern gained greater visibility. Vogt and Polino note that, according to a report in 2000 from the National Science Foundation (NSF), "[t]he relationship of the majority of Americans to science and technology is characterized by highly positive attitudes but, at the same time, reports reveal a low understanding of the content of scientific knowledge and, in particular, the methods of science" (Vogt and Polino, 2003, p. 53).

This finding undermines the idea that highly developed countries have a population necessarily more informed about science and technology. On the other hand, it does not disprove the notion that, in these societies, science and technology find greater reception among public opinion. What really complicates a further analysis of the development of SF in Brazilian cinema is the fact that, according to the research published by Vogt and Polino, Brazil shows some surprising characteristics in comparison to other Latin American countries. The Brazilian sample of the research shows, for instance, a more prominently "pro-science" attitude than the Argentine, Uruguayan, or Spanish peoples (Vogt and Polino, 2003, p. 99).

Although lowly ranked in comparison to more-developed countries, Brazil's science and technology production occupies a prominent place in Latin America and is not negligible on the world stage. The idea that "SF would not exist in Brazil because there is no science and technology" is thus completely unjustified today, even though a scientific culture per se is still weak. Moreover, in the global scenario, given the frenetic flow of information and cultural goods, it is reasonable to suggest that a certain population may be well acquainted with scientific-technological imagery with no need for highly industrialized infrastructure.

According to Francisco Alberto Skorupa, "the role played by scientific and technological development in the production of SF is controversial" (2002, p. 93). Skorupa notes that there is strong evidence of a link between science and technology development and production of SF, especially since the Industrial Revolution and the scientific explosion in the nineteenth and twentieth centuries. The United States, former U.S.S.R., United Kingdom, France, Japan, (I would add Germany) and, to a lesser extent, Australia, Canada, and Italy can provide some examples of possible relationships between scientific development and SF. On the other hand, the author notes that this argument may be misleading since, although technology has national ownership, "free imagination is not nationalist, it goes beyond boundaries and can be inspired by foreign stimuli" (Skorupa, 2002: 316). Skorupa also recalls the Brazilian writer and critic Fausto Cunha's opinion on the matter, according to whom Brazil would not be a good example for the formula "Science/Technology x SF": "The technological support is the least important (after all, we have São José dos Campos, Barreira do Inferno, [and] many scientists [sic])" (Cunha, 1976: 19–20). However, Skorupa notices a subtlety behind Fausto Cunha's argument. He notes that countries like Brazil, India, China, South

Korea, and Argentina established centers of scientific excellence from the 1960s onwards, "although the same is not true in terms of daily viewing of the achievements of technological science, as well as the experience of a consistent policy of education and dissemination of knowledge and scientific notions" (Skorupa, 2002: 93). Thus, Skorupa relates SF not only to scientific and technological development, but also to policies that promote science/technology and public perception of science. For the author, "The routine visualization of technical innovations and an educational policy focused on science are situations that would nourish the imagination and, thereby, the writing of fiction"(Skorupa, 2002, p. 94). In short, Skorupa poses the problem of SF constraints in Brazil as follows:

> The increase of icons of modern technology helps to explain the emergence of SF in Brazil and the absence of a serious education policy and democratization of knowledge complements the explanation of why this initiative has not flourished more vigorously, becoming a literary enclave constantly isolated from common interest [Skorupa, 2002, p. 94].

Skorupa continues: "One cannot ignore that a cultural environment that values research and science education is directing and educating the individual perception and sensitivity to the idea of scientific and technical progress" (2002, p. 316). The author notes that, in the Brazilian case, not only the process of modernization and industrialization, but also the "building of a brand-new capital city for the 'country of the future'" and the beginning of the Brazilian space program point at a promising stage for the development of SF (Skorupa, 2002, p. 94). Nonetheless, still according to Skorupa,

> The absence of an interested audience, poorly stimulated readers, unprepared for scientific and technological issues, added to a weak publishing industry, complement the reasons for understanding why Brazilians do not experience in a broader sense something like the space opera, for example [Skorupa, 2002: 94].

The fact that the computer is an extremely rare icon in Brazilian filmography can also reveal this delicate balance between scientific/technological production and speculative fiction. Since the mid–1990s, computers are not strange items in the Brazilian industrial context. In addition, Brazil has important research centers and some highly rated computer science courses in prestigious universities. However, many of these achievements are restricted to the most developed regions of the country.

The personal computer (PC) is a relatively popular cognitive prosthetic, readily found in homes and schools, as well as in LAN houses and cybercafés in the streets. However, social inequalities still prevail. Despite Brazil being one of the most expressive nations in terms of digital culture and participation in the World Wide Web, the PC is still inaccessible to the great majority of

Brazilians, and about 94 percent of Brazilian Internet users do not have access to broadband Internet. Sensitive to this problem, the Brazilian government ordered the Plano Nacional de Banda Larga [National Plan for Broadband], delivered to the president in November 2009. This national program intends to make a minimum 1Mbps broadband connection available to every Brazilian in any part of the country, for free or at the lowest cost. The idea is to make broadband connection a civil right, following similar policies in such countries as Finland, Sweden, South Korea, and Spain.

The cybernetic imagination in Brazilian cinema, manifested through such props and characters as the computer or artificial intelligence, still mirrors a broader sensibility according to which highly sophisticated technology often poses a threat to national identity. The Enlightenment, the scientific revolution, and the twentieth century's "Big Science" and its technological results are cautiously seen below the Equator as "misplaced ideas" or "foreign menace." According to Schwarz, some voices in the Brazilian cultural landscape of the late nineteenth century argued that, since the economic science and other liberal ideologies do not refer to our [Brazilian] reality, they are abominable, apolitical, foreign and also vulnerable (Schwarz, 2000, p. 11). This paranoia persists still today, although to a lesser degree, and seems to underline film plots such as *The Fifth Power, Roberto Carlos at the Rhythm of Adventure,* or *Thrill.*

I would even suggest that this sensibility also mirrors the state of Brazilian film industry throughout the years. Lacking truly industrial patterns, Brazilian film production has always been mostly funded by the state — except for some isolated efforts, such as the Brazilian studio Vera Cruz (1949–1954), which had clear industrial purposes. Important artistic movements, such as the Brazilian Cinema Novo (1952–1969), saluted local strategies against the fancy, polished standards of imperialist cinema (i.e., Hollywood). The cybernetic imagination in Brazilian cinema can be considered, to some extent, as a metaphor for infrastructural problems in film production or even a low-tech film industry. Taking into consideration the Brazilian television industry, the situation is rather different, and further analysis of cybernetic or techno-scientific imagination in Brazilian audiovisual media (including TV series and soap operas, especially) is yet to be done. From the 1990s onwards, but especially in the 2000s, the digital revolution has benefited independent film production all over the world. Thus, Brazilian and Latin American filmmakers have stepped closer to a cybernetic imagination often considered so "American." Digital shorts such as Napoli's *Céus de Fuligem* and Federico Álvarez's *Ataque de Pânico!* [*Panic Attack*] (2009), featuring digital special effects, are quite symptomatic in this regard.

It is curious that for such a creative and participatory people when it comes to the Web, Brazilians have not drawn inspiration from this medium and transferred it into national film production. For instance, there are no well-known Brazilian fiction films about digital culture, hacker communities, digital piracy, and so forth. John Badham's *WarGames* (1983), although a cult movie in Brazil, remains something distant, absolutely superfluous in the Brazilian cinematographic context.

Different from the American cinema, for instance, Brazilian film has been far less responsive to the impact of science and technology. Therefore, the theoretical framework established by an author such as Patricia Warrick (1980), in her thorough study of the cybernetic imagination in science fiction literature (and in some films), would be of little help in an equivalent analysis of the Brazilian context, offering instead what can be considered a counter-model. Compared to Anglo-American literature and film, Brazilian SF pieces dealing with cybernetic imagination are very scarce. In particular, Brazilian films seem to stubbornly refuse to deal with automata or "electronic brains" the way standard American cinema does. As we can see from the preceding examples, Brazilian SF film usually responds or reacts to high technology in a rather xenophobic way, mostly regarding both science and technology as an intrinsically foreign institution — a legacy from historically deeply rooted cultural contradictions, as described by Schwarz (2000, pp. 11–31).

In a simplified equation: the computer is a Western invention, the machine assembled by foreigners, and the Brazilian reaction is often dismissive. Ultimately, any Brazilian SF film would apparently share the same strategy adopted in American dystopian SF cinema, for instance. Using Patricia Warrick's categories of analysis, the Brazilian SF film would mostly operate in the closed-system model, the same as dystopian literature (Warrick, 1980, p. 132–3). But the Brazilian approach is rather different in essence. Warrick comments that "SF can unite the pre-scientific consciousness of childhood with the logic of scientific thought" (1980, p. 235). Brazilian SF film keeps the "pre-scientific consciousness of childhood," but it is amplified by the irreverent Carnivalesque spirit, rather than matching "the logic of scientific thought." This characteristic reveals, perhaps, a refusal to play the game according to its original rules, since the very logic of scientific thought, the source of any modern machine like a computer, is "extraneous." In essence, we might venture, a desire to turn off the gringo machine.

Notes

1. This text was written in the working context of the Audiovisual SF Media Lab (LEFCAV: http://dgp.cnpq.br/buscaoperacional/detalhegrupo.jsp?grupo=0804803Z6GAKR0), Institute of Arts and Design (IAD), Federal University of Juiz de Fora (UFJF), Brazil, with the kind collaboration of my undergraduate students Paula Medeiros and Pedro Carcereri.

2. At the time of the release of Pieralisi's film, the newspaper *Folha de S. Paulo* published

B.J. Duarte's film review that reinforces the premonitory impression suggested by *The Fifth Power,* even though in a contrary perspective: "Interesting epoch indeed, this in which *The Fifth Power* is released, when the nation's spirit and men are on the verge of the deepest left wing cliff, under the rule of pirate politicians, joined to frontier warlords, in a slow process of intoxication practiced by four hands with visible, successful results based on subliminal repetition, in accordance with the technology adopted in Pieralisi's film." Quoted and available in http://www.adorocinemabrasileiro.com.br/filmes/quinto-poder/quinto-poder.asp.

  3. Excerpt from the website *Adoro Cinema Brasileiro,* http://www.adorocinemabrasileiro.com.br/filmes/quinto-poder/quinto-poder.asp.

  4. Roberto Farias wrote and directed other films in which the famous Brazilian singer Roberto Carlos is the star: *Roberto Carlos and the Pink Diamond* (*Roberto Carlos e o Diamante Cor-de-Rosa,* 1970) and *Roberto Carlos at 300 Km/h* (*Roberto Carlos a 300 Km/h,* 1972).

  5. Before Brasília, Rio de Janeiro was the capital of Brazil and its location was also known as District of Guanabara. When the capital moved to Brasília, the District of Guanabara was effaced and Rio (the city) restored to the condition of capital of the state of Rio de Janeiro.

  6. Before this, the Beatles films made use of similar strategy, as in *A Hard Day's Night* (1964) or *Help!* (1965).

  7. A very popular Brazilian film genre in the 1940s and '50s, a mixture of comedy and musical, highly influenced by radio's legacy and the national carnival spirit.

  8. Roberto Carlos and Pelé are two Brazilian celebrities popularly refered as "kings." Talking about soccer and sports, if one mentions "the king," any Brazilian infers Pelé. In the musical and showbiz landscape, Roberto Carlos is "the king."

  9. Refering to Cláudio Assis's *Baixio das Bestas* (*Bog of Beasts,* 2006) in his blog (http://jcbernardet.blog.uol.com.br/), Jean-Claude Bernardet defines metalanguage as the "juvenile disease" in the Brazilian cinema.

  10. "Toda Ciência tem seus princípios, de que deriva o seu sistema. Um dos princípios da Economia Política é o trabalho livre. Ora, no Brasil domina o fato 'impolítico e abominável' da escravidão. Este argumento — resumo de um panfleto liberal, contemporâneo de Machado de Assis — põe fora o Brasil do sistema da ciência" (Schwarz, 2000, p. 11). Schwarz's essay, "As idéias fora do lugar," was translated into English in Roberto Schwarz, *Misplaced Ideas: Essays on Brazilian Culture* (London: Verso, 1992).

Works Cited

Bernardet, Jean-Claude. *Blog do Jean-Claude.* Available at http://jcbernardet.blog.uol.com.br/.

Calazans, Flávio. *Multimedia Subliminal Propaganda* (*Propaganda Subliminar Multimídia,* São Paulo: Summus Editorial, 1992, 6a ed.)

Cunha, Fausto. "A Ficção Científica no Brasil: Um planeta quase desabitado." In Allen, L. David. *No Mundo da Ficção Científica.* São Paulo: Summus, 1976.

Dantes, Maria Amélia Mascarenhas. "As ciências na história brasileira." *Ciência & Cultura,* ano 57, n. 1, jan/fev/mar 2005, pp. 26–9.

Duarte, B. J. *Folha de S. Paulo,* review of *The Fifth Power.* http://www.adorocinemabrasileiro.com.br/filmes/quinto-poder/quinto-poder.asp.

Fausto, Boris. *A Concise History of Brazil.* Trans. Arthur Brakel. Cambridge: Cambridge University Press, 1999.

Ferreira, Jairo. *Cinema de Invenção.* São Paulo: Max Limonad/Embrafilme, 1986.

Gamo, Alessandro (org.). *Críticas de Jairo Ferreira — Críticas de invenção: os anos do São Paulo Shimbun.* São Paulo: Imprensa Oficial/Cultura — Fundação Padre Anchieta, 2006.

Ginway, M. Elizabeth. *Ficção Científica Brasileira: Mitos culturais e nacionalidade no país do futuro.* São Paulo: Devir, 2005.

Gomes, Paulo Emílio Salles. *Cinema: Trajetória no Subdesenvolvimento,* 2d ed. São Paulo: Paz e Terra, 2001.

Key, Wilson Bryan. *Subliminal Seduction.* Signet: New York, 1974.

Ramos, Fernão, and Miranda, Luís Felipe, eds. *Enciclopédia do Cinema Brasileiro.* São Paulo: Senac, 2000.

Ramos, José Mário Ortiz. *Cinema, Televisão e Publicidade*. São Paulo: Annablume, 2004.

Reis, Lúcio. "O Signo de Escorpião (1974): O inferno astral de um diretor." Cinema Poeira, http://cinemapoeira.blogspot.com/2009/06/o-signo-de-escorpiao-1974-o-inferno.html, accessed June 11, 2009.

Rev. of *The Fifth Power*. Originally published in *O Estado de S. Paulo,* available at *Adoro Cinema Brasileiro,* http://www.adorocinemabrasileiro.com.br/filmes/quinto-poder/quinto-poder.asp.

Schwarz, Roberto. "As idéias fora do lugar." In *Ao Vencedor as Batatas*. São Paulo: Ed. 34, 2000. 5th ed.

Skorupa, Francisco Alberto. *Viagem às Letras do Futuro — Extratos de bordo da ficção científica brasileira: 1947–1975*. Curitiba: Aos Quatro Ventos, 2002.

Suvin, Darko. *Metamorphoses of Science Fiction: On the Poetics and History of a Literary Genre*. New Haven, CT: Yale University Press, 1979.

Viany, Alex. *Introdução ao Cinema Brasileiro*. Rio de Janeiro: Editora Revan, 1993.

Vieira, João Luiz. "From *High Noon* to *Jaws:* Carnival and Parody in Brazilian Cinema." In Randall Johnson and Robert Stam, eds., *Brazilian Cinema*. New York: Columbia University Press, 1995.

Vogt, Carlos, and Carmelo Polino, orgs. *Percepção Pública da Ciência — Resultados da Pesquisa na Argentina, Brasil, Espanha e Uruguai*. Campinas: Ed. da UNICAMP; São Paulo: FAPESP, 2003.

Warrick, Patricia S. *The Cybernetic Imagination in Science Fiction*. Cambridge: MIT Press, 1980.

10

A (Brave New) World Is More Than a Few Gizmos Crammed Together: Science Fiction and Cyberculture

Thierry Bardini

This study demonstrates that much of the fiction written since World War II is reactionary in its attitude toward computers and artificial intelligence. It is often ill informed about information theory and computer technology and lags behind present developments instead of anticipating the future.

— Patricia Warrick

Bootstrap

The statement is abrupt and cuts like a death sentence to a tired cliché. Not exactly though, since the following sentence in Warrick's introduction to her classic *The Cybernetic Imagination in Science Fiction*[1] preserves it: "only a small number of later works demonstrate the sound grounding in science that is characteristic of writers during the Golden Age of science fiction in the 1930s and 1940s," she wrote. On Wikipedia, the best repository of clichés this age can offer, this cliché gets its own entry: "The Golden Age of SF" (GASF hereafter). Here we learn that GASF has a lot to do with the tenure of John W. Campbell at the direction of the magazine *Astounding Stories* from 1937 on, and a new generation of writers out of the "pulp era" of the genre: A.E. van Vogt, Robert Heinlein, Clifford Simak, Theodore Sturgeon, and

167

Isaac Asimov, to name a few. But in a ravishing play on words, the online encyclopedia echoes an alternate take on the GASF notion, quite well known by most SF lovers: the Golden Age is twelve (or thirteen depending on the sources). In this sense, my Golden Age started around this age, never to actually end.

It was through a frequently cited key component of SF, a sense of wonder, that I have been thinking about my own work on the genealogy of cyberculture for the past twenty years or so. Starting with the history of personal computing, moving to the analysis of free and open source software, and more recently to molecular biology[2], I have always thought about the relations or, better said, the mutual influences between the arts (literature, of course, but also film and contemporary arts) and science and technology. SF, in its many shapes, has occupied a place of choice in this, thus allowing me to reconcile my teen-age passion with an academic career.

In the present chapter, I retrace some of the main steps of my thinking process on these issues, from the particular case of personal computing to virtual reality and bioinformatics, from my early attempts to model the double mediation process that links military developments, artistic visions, and civilian techno-scientific developments, to my current insight of late modern disaffected subjects as *junkware*. Along the way I allude to classic writers and filmmakers such as Aldous Huxley, Philip K. Dick, and Ridley Scott, but also to more contemporary writers such as Michel Houellebecq. In the end I propose a thesis in opposition to that of Patricia Warrick where my own notion of "the mantic function" attempts to replace the obsolete notion of "anticipation." With some conclusive propositions about what I mean by this "mantic function," I justify my title and argue that the intricate temporal relationships between arts and techno-science should now be understood as a total (cyber)cultural phenomenon.

What's in a Name?

When I conducted the interviews for the research that eventually led to *Bootstrapping*,[3] one fact struck me: to my surprise, none (but one) of my interviewees ever mentioned the influence of science fiction on their work. Alan Kay, quite probably the most genial man I have ever met,[4] provided the only exception. He told me two stories that have been informing my understanding of the relations between art (including SF in all of its forms) and techno-science since then.

At some point during our interview, he alluded to the fact that it was a common practice among engineers and programmers to call all kinds of prostheses by the generic name "waldoes." This name came from Robert Heinlein's 1940 *Waldo & Magic, Inc.,* where it alluded to both the name of the protagonist and his creation to overcome his inborn "pathological muscular weakness ... an almost totally crippling condition."[5] So in the novel, the name of the protagonist becomes the generic name of "the ubiquitous and grotesquely humanoid gadgets," i.e., his for-his-own-use turned commercial products prostheses:

> Waldo had resented the nickname the public had fastened on them — it struck him as overly familiar — but he had coldly recognized the business advantage to himself in having the public identify him verbally with a gadget so useful and important.[6]

This, of course, is quite a rhetorical trick, *antonomasia,* playfully exemplified here by Heinlein: isn't it after all a sign of the greatest success for a writer when a name that he or she has given to one of his or her creatures becomes a generic name? Behind the literary trick, however, stands a crucial point: naming is indeed crucial, and the metonymy that works covertly in this antonomasia illustrates one more time — if it was still necessary — the power of metaphor, or, more to the point, of catachresis. After so many a philosopher has pondered the importance of that particular trope in arts and science, and especially after Paul Ricoeur,[7] I hold that by destructing literal meaning a well-crafted catachresis actually creates new meaning by displacing it to a domain where there was none. Or in other words, how a name can open up a world (of meaning but of practices too).

In this case, waldoes, who/which came from a fictional character, became the generic name of actual, i.e., non-fictional, devices or artifacts: the mouse is a waldo, a ubiquitous and grotesquely humanoid ersatz of your hand in datascape (Engelbart himself, the inventor of the mouse, rather considered it as an analog to a wing that would enable its users to fly in cyberspace, if you will pardon the anachronism). Waldo, the name, also alludes to another crucial point that was promised a bright future in cyberculture: without such gadgets, mice, trackballs and other joysticks, your average computer user could indeed feel as crippled as the novel's protagonist. Equipped with them, he or she could, on the contrary, feel as Waldo himself, "not a crippled human being, but as something higher than human, the next step up, a being so superior as not to need the coarse, brutal strength of the smooth ape."[8] Cyborg, who said cyborg? Perhaps even post-human, already?

The second story Alan Kay told me reinforced the first, but in the opposite direction this time: it is a case where the real life of a programmer turned into fiction (but not only).

Do you, dear reader, remember the 1982 Walt Disney Studios movie entitled *Tron?* This not-so-successful film (it grossed $33 million for a $17 million budget) has become quite a cult movie. That it was a new kind of movie was obvious from the first day it was projected on a theater screen. John Cultrane, for instance, wrote in the pages of the *New York Times* on July 4, 1982, "Disney is the first to tell a story with the computer-generated imagery that Hollywood is looking at as the herald of a major change in making movies." But it goes further than that.... *Tron* is not only the alleged first (partially) computer-generated movie, it is also one of the first SF takes on Lewis Carroll's "through the looking glass" notion in the late modern era. Consider for instance this statement from John Walker, the founder of Autodesk, Inc., in his eponymous essay:

> The idea of transporting users in some fashion into a computer and allowing them to interact directly with a virtual world has been extensively explored in science fiction. Frederik Pohl's later Heechee books, writer of the "cyberpunk" genre such as William Gibson and Rudy Rucker, and movies including *Tron* have explored what we will find and what we will become when we enter these worlds of our creation.[9]

Pohl's "later Heechee books" — *Beyond the Blue Event Horizon, Heechee Rendezvous,* and *Annals of the Heechee,* much like the cyberpunk genre, are creations of the early 1980s. The three Pohl books are respectively dated 1980, 1984, and 1987; cyberpunk, if it came to general public awareness with William Gibson's 1984 *Neuromancer* (and Gardner Dozois's coining of the name), actually predated the dreaded 1948 inverse[10]; for instance, *Mirrorshades,* the 1986 cyberpunk anthology edited by Bruce Sterling (Ace Books) included twelve short stories representative of the genre and previously published between 1981 ("The Gernsback Continuum" by W. Gibson) and 1986 ("Snake Eyes" by T. Maddox). In other words, all the references given by Walker point back to the same period, with no clear precedence over *Tron.*

In fact, Walker was even more right than he thought when he titled his essay after Lewis Carroll and quoted *Tron* as one key example in SF. During our interview, Alan Kay told me that his wife, Bonnie MacBird, wrote the original script for the movie, "as a [post]modern take on *Alice in Wonderland.*" Moreover, he also claimed that one of the leading characters, Alan Bradley, portrayed on screen by Bruce Boxleitner (who also played Tron on the other side of the interface), was directly modeled on him! Today Wikipedia seems to concur in its entry devoted to Bonnie MacBird, where it is noted that she is indeed Alan Kay's wife, "whose work inspired her original script for the 1982 Disney film *Tron.*"

So, rather than a linear line of influence that would stem from SF anticipating techno-scientific development, it seems here that we have multiple loops of mutual influences ... pretty much what culture, and cyberculture, is about: a whole culture built on the principle of the feedback loop. In these multiple loops, naming is key, resting on the powers of metaphor, metonymy, catachresis, and even antonomasia (in its two senses; a common name for a proper name and vice-versa).

Multiple examples testify of this process: it is much better after all, to trust the genius of writers such as William Burroughs to name a "blade runner" (rather than a cop); Karel Čapek to coin the word "robot" in the first place; Philip K. Dick to invent "kipple" (rather than junk, noise, or entropy); David Gerrold to realize that parasitic self-reproducing computer programs could very well be called "viruses"; or, obviously, William Gibson to boot up "cyberspace"; and Neal Stephenson to introduce "avatars" in the "Metaverse."

What's in a name today, indeed, but the bootstrap program for a strange loop? It is to such a loop that we will move next, with a closer scrutiny on avatars through the postmodern looking glass, but not before a small intermezzo on the loop itself.

Here Comes the Loop

The world has become a loopy machine, down to its molecular level. One was used to the straight line, and suddenly — or so it seemed, at first — the line looped. Maybe there was a loophole in the linear text of the Cartesian subject, and the line fell into it and the subject thought he could escape from it, through the loophole. Anyway, the world suddenly became loopy, and so did the subject.[11] The line could not hold him anymore. The idea was here since the Baroque age, at least, but it came back with a vengeance: the loop became the only possible fate of the fold, this baroque Leibnizian invention.[12]

Some claim that it was the doing of Cybernetics, this revolution of the mechanistic worldview that occurred during World War II. "Cybernetics," the word, was not new by any means. Plato first, in the old age, and André-Marie Ampère[13] (1775–1836) second, at the interface of classical and the modern ages, had already used it. To them it meant the governance of men, the steering of people. This world, of which we were once the measure, became a loopy machine inasmuch that we, in return, needed to be steered, cared for, disciplined, and punished. Man, it was already well established, was an automatic machine: "The human body," wrote Julien Offray de la Mettrie in 1748, "is a machine which winds its own springs."[14] What was not that clear, however, was precisely how this spring got wound. Here came the loop.

And here is a speculation. This machine, whose spring it can wind on its own, must be a clock, or contain some sort of a clock. Life's second wind is this kind you can give to your watch (when you give it a wind). This spring evokes a (mortal) coil, and the watch reminds us of William Paley, the father of natural theology.[15] Life is this kind of mechanism that would go on forever as long as it is wound. The loop might be the revolution of the hands of the watch, or it might be this time between the first and the last wind. But it is not the way the loop got in, I think, even if I agree with Lewis Mumford on this: "the clock, not the steam engine, is the key-machine of the modern industrial age."[16]

The loop, it is said, came with the steam engine and its regulator, Watt's governor. But in fact Watt did not invent the feedback principle for his regulator: it was already in use in water mills.[17] Thus automation was born practically first, as a *phase transition,* as Gilbert Simondon would have put it.[18] It was, of course, a question of a well-adjusted behavior, regular performance (like clockwork, this *bourgeois* ideal). Under a new name, the loop became one of the key concepts of a formidable synthesis, uniting animal and machine under the hospices of this great mechanism: *feedback.*

Feedback is another name of the loop, the technical name under which went this other key concept of cybernetics. Cybernetics, the science of communication and control, rests on these two pillars: a theory of communication (information and code) coupled to a theory of control (feedback). Control is of major importance; it is the insurance of performance, the process of maintaining equilibrium or aiming towards something. Thus control and regulation go hand in hand: "when we desire a motion to follow a given pattern the difference between this pattern and the actually performed motion is used as a new input to cause the part regulated to move in such a way as to bring its motion closer to that given pattern."[19] This, however, is only the definition of *negative* feedback.

Actual Avatars on the Holodeck

Montreal, February 18, 1995: I was surfing the net, preparing for my interviews in Siliwood, California, when, suddenly, my finger froze above the *n*(ext) key and my eyes registered:

> *Article 12435 in sci.virtual-worlds (moderated) from: avatar@well.sf.ca.us (Peter Rothman) subject : ANNOUNCE: Army to develop "holodeck-like" virtual reality system.*
>
> *Avatar Partners. Inc. of Boulder Creek California announced today that it has been notified of award of a $1 million research and development contract from the United States Army Simulation Training and Instrumentation Command (STRI-COM) to develop the Dismounted Infantry Virtual Environment or DIVE system, a wireless unencumbered virtual reality system for infantry training applications. According to Peter Rothman, president of Avatar Partners Inc., "The DIVE project represents a significant step forward in synthetic environment technology in terms of both immersion and realism. DIVE is the first step towards the creation of the holodeck."*

My first reaction was: here goes to the drain my "civilization of Virtual Reality (sic)" idea, as I had described it to my interviewees to introduce my research. Like most innovations in information technologies, the technological advances that made early computer-generated immersive environments possible were first developed with military uses in mind. But since 1965 and Ivan Sutherland's first head mounted display, new uses have slowly appeared in the civilian realm. I referred to this process as the "civilization of VR." In this grand scheme, *Star Trek: The Next Generation*'s holodeck, I argued, was the place to start my research, certainly as the most influential televised representation of immersive environments of the 1980s. And I had in mind that TNG's holodeck was the first step toward civilization: from VR as a technology of war to VR as a technology of exploration (not conquest).

Computers, of course, were, first of all, war machines. Modern computers stemmed from World War II research in ballistics and cryptography, from the work of the likes of Alan Turing, John von Neumann, and Norbert Wiener. Some say that they actually won the war, that World War II was the first cybernetic war — but not the last. Sun Tzu already knew that military strength is based on its relation to pretend: "any military operation takes deception as its basic quality," he wrote. Simulation techniques, computer-based simulation techniques, like most media, are the late modernity apparatus of pretend *par excellence*. Computers, of course, are still war machines, now more than ever. The Gulf War, take one and two, showed us that the battlefield has become electronic for good; cyborg soldiers are here to stay; mass destruction now comes from a distance, impacts without contact, witnessed on a screen. Computers, of course, will be war machines ... for as long as there will be war. No need to argue that.

But were computers to remain war machines forever, I wondered? Alan Turing had proclaimed it is the universal machine. Why couldn't it be a peace machine then, a machine for arts and science, for understanding and sharing? Why should we be that obsessed with Doom, to the point that there is no space for hope? Why should we hear only Cassandra's side? Why should global phenomena only be understood as threats and dangers? Is global communication, the dream of a World Wide Web only a bad dream? Should we make a bad dream out of it, stress only its dark side? Of course not! How about turning a war machine into a peace machine? How about *civilizing* computers?

What if in the loopy mutual influences between arts and science, between SF and informatics, SF could alternatively play both parts: bootstrap program in the naming game, and civilizing force offering peaceful alternate uses for the university-military-industrial complex war machines? *Star Trek*'s holodeck was such a good example, I felt....

But what if the Army now funds the first step toward a "real holodeck?"

Could it be some publicity stunt of a company surfing on the public awareness of the holodeck name, or would Avatar Partners, this California-based company, soon make well-behaved Starfleet officers out of U.S. soldiers? In this post cold war era of media/military interventions (think Mogadishu), would the U.S. Army soon invent a prime directive[20] for the Marines?

The holodeck, as well as TNG's related transporter and replicator technologies, are built around the core fiction of the ultimate digital technology, a technology that would allow *the ultimate passage toward a completely simulated universe expressed in a completely digital code*[21]: the Heisenberg compensators. What is central in this core technology is the ability to transform, through digital encoding/decoding, information in energy into matter and vice versa: this is a higher possible level of simulation, one that would allow a total control over time and space. As Mike Okuda and Rick Sternbach answered when *Time* magazine asked them how did the Heisenberg compensators work: "They work just fine, thank you."[22]

The Heisenberg compensator is not only the ultimate digital technology, it is the ultimate hyper-real technology; it is the technology of the double in its full expression, at the frontier between simulation and simulacra, to put it in the words of Jean Baudrillard.[23] At the semiotic level, the hypothesis that there could be such a thing as Heisenberg compensators means that for fictional purposes, almost everything is possible. The last relevant question then remains: still human, or just clean code? Somehow, the body always comes out of the closet; not to show it is not to exclude it. *Au contraire....* Sub-culture grows in the margins of the dominant culture. The *Star Trek* ultimate marketing strategy, open submission and technological avatars (think Borg) for sensitive subject matters on prime-time TV, could very well be to count on it, to establish a repressive norm, not to worry, and wait for the critics to take it as the measure of things.

So, neo-Victorian and/or absolutely perverse? In his 1995 novel, *The Diamond Age or A Young Lady's Illustrated Primer,* Neal Stephenson had some ideas about that, when he has one of his characters state "There are only two industries. This has always been true.... There is the industry of things, and the industry of entertainment."[24] At the end of the 20th century, the merger of both became very clear. Entertainment got more "real," in the realm of "things" we need to stay alive, produce, and function. The Avatar story, the story of the company that said it was engaging in the creation of a "real holodeck" for the U.S. Army, is one more clue in this direction. Does the Usenet article quoted at the beginning of the present section not say just that when it also says that "applications of the DIVE system include hazardous operations training and simulation for both military and civilian operations, and location-based entertainment?"

Could it be coincidence that the very name of the company says it all? In Stephenson's *Snow Crash,* immersive environments, representations of people on the other side of the looking glass, are pieces of software called *avatars.* The real body stays behind, "obsolete meat" that serves only for purposes of connecting to the system. On the holodeck, at the opposite, users keep their "real" bodies. But this body is sterile, more virtual than an avatar (since an avatar is actual, albeit digital). From the *Star Trek* pseudo-utopian point of view as well as from the bleak premises of cyberpunk literature, virtue and virtuality are the fundamental features of the political economy of our future. And that used to be entertainment: "we change the script a little ... to allow for cultural differences. But the story never changes. There are many people and many tribes, but only so many stories."[25]

The Return of the Loop

> The disembodied Agent then — as near to God as makes no difference — is a spirit, a ghost or angel required by classical mathematics to give meaning to "endless" counting.[26]

The modern computer is this disembodied Agent, ghost or angel. It is it, or they when networked, that counts endlessly for us. Moreover, that has counted us endlessly since their inception. The computer was first the master of the Census, this age-old practice of writing the numbers of the enslaved stock, turned mechanistic (writing was first counting slaves).[27] The automated census and its punch-card mechanisms (already IBM) marked the beginning of the era of the control society, no more paradise than hell, a kind of purgatory in fact. For a century and change it has counted us, classified us, sorted us, named us, and thus helped discipline and punish, or control us. After a while, we got so used to it, to our *matricules*[28] and other reference numbers, that we could imagine without any trouble that we actually *were* them: I am this address, this finite set of digits.

After all, the analogy went both ways: they were first our giant brains, our exo-cortexes, and thus they soon became our own idea of our brains, and, or, minds. The mind is a computer and the computer is a mind. A computer is a computer is a computer. This is how we got computed. For a while, this was a mere metaphor, and, as everybody knows by now, "the price of metaphor is eternal vigilance."[29] The price the computer paid, indeed.... Turned into a machine, the counting Agent got a taste of the infinite at the cover price of losing his or her body, and the duty of perpetual vigilance. Let it be our vigil, for the created eternity, i.e., perpetuity: a purgatory indeed. If man is this self-winding spring machine, a perpetual clock until death, there must be a watcher. And eventually, some argue, a watchmaker, nay ...

a computer will do the job: "they needed a dancer, but a calculator got the job."[30] There was indeed some rationality in this choice. Job, it is said, comes from *gob*, "a mouthful, lump," and in slang also refers to the person herself. The computer: this brainy job.

But then again, the fate of the successful metaphor is to turn into a world. And so it happened this time too, and we, literally, got computed. We are now officially data-based to the bone, to our most minute fingerprint, at the molecular level: our DNA print is our new brand. This is no more metaphor, even if out of control. And in the last half of the last century of the second millennium, genetics, the science of heredity, turned into an information science, and then to a computerized science: *bioinformatics*. No wonder then, that the human being himself became *biocapital* in the same process.

During its bioinformatics revolution, biology has entered the new "real" world of simulation or, to put it differently, biology has got to be less and less about wetware. Today, many contributions stemming from bioinformatics studies do not bother at all with experimental protocols dealing with living material. Models and graphs, equations and correlations, are slowly taking over bench-work and experiments; the days of the naturalists are long gone. This is precisely the first level of simulation. But at a deeper level, Jean Baudrillard had already recognized in 1981 the root of simulation in the very principle of biomolecular analysis: DNA is the model medium of this new age of simulation.

Moreover, DNA is medium *and* message, RAM and ROM, a hard disk and its contents, a symbolic text whose words are combinations of four letters, and whose combinations of words produce the lines of code of a genetic program (a program without programmer). These words, these lines are nothing but addresses in a symbolic register ruled by evolved conventions and equivalences. This language cannot be other than mathematical: the code of life is written in C++. So it is not merely when the appropriate technology became available that the book of life became a software problem; rather, it was a software problem from the get-go. When the appropriate tools became available, the hyper-real world of simulation took over life itself. Not surprisingly, in the time it took to do so, computer interfaces and operative systems in turn evolved toward natural languages and graphical user interfaces.

Devoid of a semantic dimension, language here becomes inseparable from program, albeit as a self-referential grammar. Strange loops become the norm, Moebius rules: a loop inside of another loop, twisted, let a thousand loops bloom. In such a perspective, program, language and medium collapse into one world, the world of simulation, the hyper-real. In this world, we are, and life is, expression of a program (and artificial life is a pleonasm): we are teleonomic beings (teleonomy differs from teleology by this crucial difference:

the purpose is not given from the start, it emerges from the functioning of a program).

Present, past, and future have no meaning in a world ruled by numbers. Present is this address, like any other past or future address of a world *in real time:* just a question of probability. Space is the name of the illusion, which fathoms an address on the postal code of an infinite real estate. It is just a question of speed and acceleration, first- and second-order derivatives of space and time. And so much data, so many addresses, that our poor brains make of us obsolete computers. We became the ghosts in the Turing machine, and so goes the first story of our day and age: "once upon a time ... and so on ... and so on." Or, as Burroughs aptly summarized it: "Room for One More Inside, Sir."[31]

The Next Mutation Will Be Genetic

Our *Brave New World* might have begun with Aldous Huxley's eponymous novel (1932), which informs a whole descent of science-fictive narratives. Here I will briefly follow it through two main authors: Philip K. Dick and Michel Houellebecq. It is Huxley who first envisioned our contemporary wrestling with "the problem of happiness" and its potential solution in a new age of generation without sex. Dick and Houellebecq updated it into a sociological crash course for today's disaffected subjects.[32]

> The most important Manhattan Projects of the future will be vast government-sponsored inquiries into what politicians and the participating scientists will call 'the problem of happiness'—in other words, the problem of making people love their servitude ... The love of servitude cannot be established except as the result of a deep, personal revolution in human minds and bodies. To bring about that revolution we require, among others, the following discoveries and inventions. First, a greatly improved technique of suggestion — through infant conditioning and later with the aid of drugs, such as scopolamine. Second, a fully developed science of human differences, enabling government managers to assign any given individual to his or her proper place in the social and economic hierarchy ... third (since reality, however utopian, is something from which people feel the need of taking pretty frequent holidays), a substitute for alcohol and the other narcotics, something at once less harmful and more pleasure-giving than gin or heroin. And fourth (but this would be a long-term project, which would take generations of totalitarian control to bring to a successful conclusion), a foolproof system of eugenics, designed to standardize the human product and so to facilitate the task of managers. In *Brave New World* this standardization of the human product has been pushed to fantastic, though not perhaps impossible, extremes.[33]

The human product... Nobody better than Michel Houellebecq, today, has followed up on Huxley's dreary insight. Houellebecq is the apostle of disaffection, a small-time sociologist [*un sociologue à la petite semaine*]. His science fiction, as we shall see, can be truly called a sociobiology (of the worst kind): it has mashed up the cybernetics accomplishment of the techno-scientific basis of the "foolproof system of eugenics" under the guidance of bioinformatics with a sociology of individualism trimmed to its bear minimum, and therefore at its most efficient regime. In *The Elementary Particles*, quite possibly his most accomplished novel to date, he even pushes the irony to have his protagonists (two half-brothers: Bruno, a writer, and Michel, a scientist, probably inspired by Aldous and his brother Julian, the biologist and former head of UNSECO) explicitly discuss *Brave New World*. There is little doubt in my mind that Houellebecq presents here his own thesis under the guise of a dialog on one of the greatest influences on his own work, the Huxley brothers.[34]

In a few words, here it goes: Houellebecq considers Huxley too optimistic(!). "*Brave New World* is our idea of heaven: genetic manipulation, sexual liberation, the war against aging, the leisure society," says Bruno.[35] And his half-brother answers with a sociological lesson: Huxley made a cardinal error in his assessment of the two major consequences of the metaphysical mutation that gave rise to materialism and modern science, rationalism, and individualism: he "underestimated the growth of individualism brought about by an increased consciousness of death."[36] More to the point, Huxley did not go far enough:

> Sexual rivalry — a metaphor for the mastering over time through reproduction — has no more reason to exist in a society where the connection between sex and procreation has been broken ... [Huxley] doesn't understand that sex, even stripped of its of its link with reproduction, still exists — not as a pleasure principle, but as a form of narcissistic differentiation.[37]

For Houellebecq, a true "solution to the problem of happiness" requires not only the dissociation of sex and procreation, but the disappearance of sex altogether. Otherwise, points two and four of Huxley's program play one against the other: it is impossible to have people love their servitude, and accept their "proper place in the social and economic hierarchy" if sex still provides a way for narcissistic differentiation. Sex, as a way for the individual to differentiate, is to be banned if one wants to negate the worst effects of the metaphysical mutation operated by modern science: "individuation, vanity, hatred and desire."

Even if Huxley "was a terrible writer," if "his writing is pretentious and clumsy, his characters are bland ciphers [...] he had one vital premonition: he understood that for centuries the evolution of human society had been linked to scientific and technological progress and would continue to be."[38] Houellebecq pretty much praises Huxley for what he aspires to (and his criticisms very much apply to him too, for an extra dose of cynical irony typical of him): to be the first science-fiction writer to realize "that biology would take over from physics as the driving force of society."[39] More crucially, he updates him to the specific situation of the turn of millennium, when techno-scientific advances stemming out of cybernetics, i.e., computer science, technology, and molecular biology, now provide the effective means to accomplish his point four, *and* individualism strives under new conditions. Let us turn first to bioinformatics.

Lincoln Stein has once defined the field in the most minimal way as "biologists using computers or the other way around."[40] Bioinformatics is thus, quite simply put, techno-science born out of the convergence of the two main domains of application of cybernetics. It is *the* model of twenty-first century techno-science: big yet distributed science, capital-intensive technology yet feasible in a garage, applied yet abstract knowledge at the level of its everyday practices. Out of the traditional disciplinary bounds, it is carried out at a fast pace in and out of academia, putting, quite often, the private sector and the university in concurrence for talents, patents, and finance. As both hyped discourse and down-to-earth straight capitalist business, it fuels our utopist dreams and dystopist nightmares alike.

Bioinformaticians are very specialized workers laboring on high-demand, high-payoff, intensive schedules mostly composed of *routines.* If there is one *cliché* that goes against the grain today about these workers, we owe it to Houellebecq's desperate "science fiction": "Molecular biology was routine. It required no creativity, no imagination and only the most basic second-rate intellect."[41] Bioinformaticians are technicians, i.e., technical experts in the continuing age of the systems.[42] An intellectual activity with a taste for the *mystique* of the lonely discoverers, eccentric characters with *macho* bravado and bowties, has first turned into a cottage industry and then to a global business run according to the good old principles of Taylorism. Houellebecq's literature is the mirror image[43] of this capitalist routine running amok, when the only thing remaining to be merchandised is human life itself, Huxley's "human product." His sociology is worse than his technology, and repeats in an even more tuned-down style the merits of one of his most visionary predecessors, in showing "the logic of stereotypes, reproductions and depersonalization in which the individual is held in our own time."[44] Human product, bio-manufactured *kipple,* junkware: to understand better this human becoming, let us turn now to one, maybe even the one, most influential portrayal of a recycled brave new world, made of junk.

Blade Runner probably gave its look and feel to today's Brave New World, the paradoxical picture of the acme of individualism. It actually portrays a world of junk, a world where everything left, buildings, people, pets, and even affects and ideas, is junk. This was already clear in a particular character of Philip K. Dick's original novel, John R. Isidore. In *Do Androids Dream of Electric Sheep?*, Isidore is introduced as a driver for a false animal repair firm, a "special" ("in regard to the distorted genes which he carried") and a "chickenhead" ("he had failed to pass the minimum mental faculties test"[45]). In other words, he is a character who had "dropped out of history ... [who had] ceased, in effect, to be part of mankind,"[46] even if he is the character of the novel who most acutely embodies the condition of the whole universe.[47] He lives alone in "a giant, decaying building which had once housed thousands,"[48] a "dust stricken" and "kipple-ized" building.[49] He worries a lot about *kipple:*

> Kipple is useless objects, like junk mail or match folders after you use the last match or gum wrappers or yesterday's homeopape. When nobody's around, kipple reproduces itself. [...] No one can win against kipple, except temporarily and maybe in one spot, like in my apartment I've sort of created a stasis between the pressure of kipple and nonkipple, for the time being. But eventually I'll die or go away, and then the kipple will take over. It's a universal principal operating throughout the universe; the entire universe is moving towards a final state of total, absolute kippleization.[50]

In fact, the word "kipple" is an original part of Dick's lexicon, his own word for the materialization of the entropic process.[51] The origin of the word is quite telling since he probably recycled it from one of the top-selling postcard of all times, a drawing by Donald McGill (1875–1962) presenting a courting scene with the following caption:

HE: "Do you like Kipling?"
SHE: "I don't know, you naughty boy, I've never kippled."

There is thus, ironically, quite a sexual reference buried in the origin of the word, a reference that clearly indicates that Dick connected entropy and generation, a reference that made of Isidore the perfect incarnation of kipple. In their retrofitting, Scott and his screenplay writers got it, and more. They kept the environment, and made Isidore even more kipple-like. J.R. Isidore, the novel's expert in junk, thus becomes in the movie J. F. Sebastian, this man who lives in "a district of silence and ruin (inside) a ten-storey condo gone to shit," and quite appropriately, a *geneticist,* a designer of the newest artificial form of life, the replicant.

His contribution to their design, however, is not only a result of his professional skills and, as he claims in his dialogue with two replicants, there is quite literally "some of him in them." In the movie, Sebastian cannot emigrate due to a glandular condition ("Methuselah Syndrome"), which causes premature and accelerated aging. Stephen Nottingham noted "Sebastian's condition also functions as part of the film's elaborate mirroring structure."[52] In the script, Pris, a female replicant, remarks that Sebastian's "accelerated decrepitude" is similar to their problem of a limited lifespan. So, when Sebastian tells Roy and Pris that there's some of him in them, he is probably also referring to them being designed with his defective gene: designed obsolescence.

Now the replicant limited life-span (four years) is both the nexus of the plot and their only alleged inferiority when compared to human beings: Roy Batty and his fellow insurgent replicants rebel in order to come back to Earth, confront their creator, and eventually obtain a longer life-time.[53] The replicants' time limit, which makes them subhuman as well as a stunning variation on the theme of the overhuman,[54] comes from a "special" who happens to be a "genetic engineer," maybe the most apt characterization of the professional of the future. He, whose motto is *I make friends,* is answered by his creature, *I'm not in the business, I am the business,* and killed by it/him/her. Oedipus and Prometheus have new siblings, and they are mortals: the next mutation will be genetic, and it will be lethal (for those who do not carry it).

Time Machines

"Once upon a time it was the Time of gods, Eternity where nothing happens; 1. Once upon a time, there came the Time of men, chronology, with its directed one-dimensionality, where everything occurs only once. And then, in between, requiring more bits to be addressed, there is this third time, circular or zigzagging — says Vernant, who calls it the time of Prometheus's liver."[55] Forever eaten by the vulture during the day, and growing again at night — a cycle within a cycle, loop within a loop: "it is a time of which the philosopher could say that it is the mobile image of the immobile eternity." The schoolmen, after Augustine and up to the dunces, resorted to the same solution and gave a name to this third time: *aevum.*[56] To them it was the time of the angels, these intermediary creatures. Circular time, like the movements of the stars they took care of, zigzagging, and even discontinuous, discrete like their manifestations in human time. In between the time of God and humans, a created eternity, perpetuity still allowing the vanishing grace of concomitance with chronology; then a glimpse of eternity was accessible to us, poor mortals, for a fleeting instant (*the concomitant instant* says the Aquinate).[57]

Then, when the angels died under the scrutiny of our rational instruments — of which Ockham's razor was the sharpest — many believed that perpetuity was gone; it might have remained for a while as the time of the purgatory, but fewer and fewer moderns seem to care about this medieval invention. It remained as a figure of speech, the unbearable duration of boredom and/or of a life sentence. Even fewer moderns, it appears, remembered concomitance: for many it was lost forever, gone with humanistic good riddance of the scholastic paraphernalia.

Few realized that it was not the case, and that our Promethean ingenuity had provided a substitute for the failing angels. Here came in play the difference engines, the meta-clocks made of sand, the computer (so aptly named in French, *ordinateur,* with respect to this unlikely substitution). Megahertz soon became the unit of choice to measure the cyclical time, and the interface the space of concomitance. Equipped with this metaphysical prosthesis, this brainy waldo, the late moderns started to dream of perpetuity again. Many believed, and still believe today, that the difference engine was merely a better calculator — that illusion lasted until the late 1960s for those in the know. By the end of that decade they had realized that it was better conceived of as a *medium,* very much like their winged predecessors. Then the question became personal, computers became small enough for us, minis, micros, then graphic, iconic. The computer became my computer, a renewed guardian angel for my failing memory, my over-stretched cognitive powers.

Then the interface became personal and concomitance again, a personal everyday experience; the screen imposed its presence, waldoes invaded the whole body, hands tied up to keys and buttons, eyes glued to the electronic glitter, and an extension of the brain, an exo-cortex of sort, was born. When these experiences in turn got linked one to another through the operational magic of some aether stuck into a connecting cable, the exo-cortex became a collective affair, the distributed network of a projected reality, *a collective and consensual hallucination we inappropriately took on calling* cyberspace *or* virtual worlds. (Inappropriately, really, because this "space" is "no place, really, but is real."[58])

The universal machine was eventually worth the name Alan Turing had proved earlier it could legitimately aspire to: the networks proliferated and soon covered the whole Earth, supplying it with a new layer. *Incipit* the noosphere. The universal now of "real time" eventually accomplished the miracle of its second coming, as the exploding series of our concomitance with the created eternity of an (almost) infinite addressing space: the memory machine got a new theater to play with.

What you see is what you get, instantly, flawlessly. The mantic machine that Leibniz had dreamt for us all booted up in myriad of screens and reunited for its user the two meanings of "seer," as the one who sees *and* predicts. The future was wide open again; it was all now.

Pandora's box had eventually spat its last spell, *Elpis* for all. A new age indeed, *aevum novus.*

The Mantic Function

> It's not the job, really, of science fiction to predict. Science fiction
> only seems to predict. — Philip K. Dick[59]

> Science Fiction's best use today is the exploration of contemporary
> reality rather than any attempt to predict where we are going ...
> explore the present. — William Gibson[60]

The Moderns might, after all is said, be no less crazed about the mantic function than any other people, "civilized" or not. Moderns are, it is well known, definitely crazy about their technologies. We literally worship them; as sure as computers now occupy the part once played by the angels, we are clear devotees of the machine. It rhythms our desperate existences, feeds us, cures us, teaches us, and more generally incarnates and actualizes for us the realm of the virtual, and probably also that of the possible. And this is exactly why the question of the mantic function has been raised since the dawn of the late modernity: "man will have become to the machines what the horse and the dog are to man," wrote an early expert in 1863; "he will continue to exist, nay even to improve, and will be probably better off in his state of domestication under the beneficent rule of the machines than he is in his present wild state."[61]

For all technology indeed develops a mantic function, and requires a kind of act of faith in the mantic workings. In order to use a specific artifact, one must believe that it could, or rather that it will, do the job at hand. Let us accept this as a postulate for the remainder of my argument, even if it might be truer to say that one should actually feel reasonably confident that it shall do it (so that in our late modern minds, belief and relative confidence might be taken as synonyms). Technologies are teleological devices, and the intention to use them is but the flip side of their purpose — when they work. Final cause is the bottom line of any technological artifact: to use them is to conjure up their workings.

This might be exactly why the clock, the mechanical clock that is and has always been the quintessential modern technology, and also why the computer is its genial descent. As sure as progress eventually became the cardinal principle of modernity, the anticipation, nay, the *conjuration* of progress lies even more deeply within the modern psyche. And when we decided that we could actually be that rational, we turned to the machine to make it happen and shouted ek-statically, "I wish by God these calculations could be made by steam!" (Charles Babbage). The (difference) engines of progress, no less.

"To think" and "to project" share the same Indo-European root: *-men*. It also gave the Greek *mantis*, usually taken to be synonymous in English with "seer," "diviner, prophet; akin to Greek *manesthai*, to be mad" (Merriam

Webster). Plato had already noticed this kinship, and defined three modalities of the mantic function, this daemonic madness: prophecy, poetry (or "possession by the muses") and erotic intoxication.[62] The important point here is that all of the mantis's actions — to think, (fore)see, (fore)tell or prophesy — all these actions can happen before or after the event that is thought, seen, told, or prophesized: chronology is not the main temporal dimension of the mantic function. Now that might seem pretty counter-intuitive at first, and indeed it is at last as well.

The mantic function certainly concerns time, but it is in no way limited to the predictive function along the past-future axis of chronological time. In fact a better understanding of its workings requires adding the other dimensions of temporality — orthogonality or diagonality, but also circularity — to the all too human one-dimensionality of chronology. To understand the mantic function might indeed require us to consider time as a surface, with its basic figure, the circle or the loop, but maybe even with more complex figures such as the Moebius strip. What if, "instead of this diachronic strand, we began to posit causality as an immense synchronic interrelationship, as a web of overdetermination"?[63] Time, then, could appear as the *medium* of our conjurations.

The story is well known[64]: Prometheus always had a brother, just like Michel and Aldous did. Epimetheus, Bruno,[65] Julian is my brotherly series here. They all played double. The one who thinks before the fact, the wise and prudent, the one who is even thought to *know* the future, is brother to the one who thinks after the fact, the idiot, the one who forgets. When their titanic match is over — when their duel among themselves, but also with the Gods, first of them Zeus, and Hermes, and also with men, and even with the first woman, Pandora — when all this is over, there is but one remainder, one evil trapped in the box: *Elpis*. The story seems to end with this: Pro- and Epi-metheus's series of double-faults cost us the match and deprives us of hope. But does it really? In fact, the only evil that we are spared might not be hope, but anticipation of the worst. Could we now find another positive meaning to this, and restore our conjuring powers to a better light?

There is a fine line between conjuration and advocacy, prediction, anticipation and hope. Usually, all these processes are put in relation to the contingency of the future (remember Bartleby's "I would prefer not to"[66]). But what if the mantic function could deal with the future contingents (that is neither necessary nor impossible) on an alternating mode, forever oscillating between pro- and epi-manticism, pro-phecy and pro-duction, *poiesi*[67]? Thought along these lines, what if the job of science-fiction was not to anticipate gadgets and gizmos, but rather to invent worlds of uses for the "ubiquitous and grotesquely humanoid gadgets" that will or will not fail to be invented? What if the SF writers were also some sorts of social engineers? (And by this I do not necessarily mean scientologists.)

The conjuration "*seems* to deal with the future; it lays before your eyes, for your scrutiny a gestalt of forces in operation that will *determine* the future. But these forces are at work now; they exist so to speak, outside of time."[68] Late modern Promethean creatures *par excellence,* craftsmen of the logos, science fiction artists are the conjurers of the representativeness of the worlds,[69] outside of time, or, better said, for all forms of now, be it the time of the presence of the gods, angels and computers, or men and women.

Notes

1. MIT Press, 1980, xvi.
2. Thierry Bardini, *Junkware.* Minneapolis: University of Minnesota Press, 2011.
3. Thierry Bardini, *Bootstrapping: Douglas Engelbart, Coevolution and the Origins of Personal Computing.* Stanford, CA: Stanford University Press, 2000.
4. Alan Kay is usually considered as "the father of the graphic user interface" (or of object oriented programming, or, even by some, of personal computing) for his work at the University of Utah, Stanford Artificial Intelligence Laboratory (SAIL) and Xerox PARC. See *Boostrapping*'s chapter 6, "The Arrival of the Real User and the Beginning of the End," pp. 143–181.
5. In the Ballantine Book edition (New York: Del Rey, 1986), p. 14.
6. Ibid., p. 27.
7. *The Rule of Metaphor: Multi-Disciplinary Studies in the Creation of Meaning in Language,* trans. R. Czerny with K. McLaughlin and J. Costello. Toronto: University of Toronto Press, 1977 [1975].
8. Robert Heinlein, *Waldo & Magic, Inc.* (New York: Del Rey, 1986), p. 27.
9. John Walker, "Through the Looking Glass," in *The Art of Human-Computer Interface Design,* ed. Brenda Laurel (Reading, MA: Addison-Wesley, 1990), pp. 439–447, p. 445.
10. Orwell published *1984* in 1948.
11. Douglas Hofstadter, *I Am a Strange Loop.* New York: Basic, 2007.
12. Gilles Deleuze, *The Fold: Leibniz and the Baroque.* Minneapolis: University of Minnesota Press, 1993.
13. In his *Essai sur la philosophie des sciences* (Paris: Bachelier, 1834).
14. In *Man A Machine* (Whitefish, MT: Kessinger, 2004 [1748]), p. 6.
15. See William Paley, *Natural Theology: Or, Evidences of the Existence and Attributes of the Deity, Collected from the Appearances of Nature,* Twelfth Edition (London: J. Faulder, 1809), pp. 1–3.
16. *Technics and Civilization* (New York, Harcourt, 1934), p. 14.
17. It can even be argued that it was there since the dawn of the technological ages, with knitting: "The most distinctive feature of knitting is its loops," writes Sadie Plant in "Mobile Knitting" (in *Information Is Alive,* pp. 26–37, Rotterdam, V2_/NAi publishers, 2003), p. 30.
18. Gilbert Simondon, *Du mode d'existence des objets techniques* (Paris: Aubier, 1958), English translation forthcoming in 2011.
19. Norbert Wiener, *Cybernetics, or Control and Communication in the Animal and the Machine.* 2d ed. (Cambridge, MA: MIT Press, 1994 [1948]), pp. 6–7.
20. "Nothing within these articles of Federation shall authorize the United Federation of Planets to intervene in matters which are essentially the domestic jurisdiction of any planetary social system," Franz Joseph Schnaubelt, Articles of the Federation, Chapter I, Article II, Paragraph VII, *Star Trek Star Fleet Technical Manual* (New York: Ballantine, 1975).
21. Hanjo Beerressem's *Pynchon's Poetics: Interfacing Theory and Text* (Chicago: University of Illinois Press, 1993), p. 141.
22. Rick Sternbach and Mike Okuda co-authored *Star Trek: The Next Generation Technical*

Manual. Quoted in the Transporters and Replicators Mini-FAQ, Maintained by Joshua Bell. Archive site: http://www.ucalgary.ca/~jsbell/star_trek.html.

23. *Simulacra and Simulation* (Ann Arbor: University of Michigan Press, 1994 [1981]).

24. New York: Bantam, p. 336.

25. Ibid., 340.

26. Brian Rotman, *Ad Infinitum... The Ghost in Turing's Machine: Taking God Out of Mathematics and Putting the Body Back In* (Stanford, CA: Stanford University Press, 1993), p. 10.

27. "The primary function of writing is to facilitate slavery," Claude Levy-Strauss, *Tristes tropiques* (Paris: Plon, 1955), p. 344.

28. In French, feminine word from the Latin *matricula*, register, metaphorically derived from *mater*, mother (*Littré*).

29. Norbert Wiener and Arturo Rosenblueth, appropriately quoted by Richard Lewontin in his review of Lily Kay's *Who Wrote the Book of Life*, in *Science* 291(5507): 1263–164, 2001.

30. "On pense à moi pour une place, par malheur, j'y étais propre : il fallait un calculateur, ce fut un danseur qui l'obtint," Beaumarchais, *Le mariage de Figaro*, 1784. This quote also alludes to Charles Babbage's early passion for the automata.

31. William S. Burroughs, "Deposition: Testimony Concerning a Sickness," introduction to *Naked Lunch* (New York: Grove, 1992 [1959]), xliii.

32. See Bernard Stiegler, *Mécréance et Discrédit 2. Les sociétés incontrôlables d'individus désaffectés* (Paris: Galilée, 2006) for the extended version of this sociology.

33. An excerpt of Huxley's 1950 foreword to *Brave New World: A Novel*, in the Penguin Modern Classic Pocket edition (London), pp. 12–13.

34. Julian Huxley's 1933 *What Dare I Think* is as much an inspiration for Houellebecq as *Brave New World* is.

35. Michel Houellebecq, *Elementary Particles*. Trans. Frank Wynne (New York: Vintage, 2001 [1998]), p. 131.

36. Ibid., p. 133.

37. Ibid.

38. Ibid., p. 131.

39. Ibid.

40. Daniel H. Steinberg, "Stein Gives Bioinformatics Ten Years to Live." *O'Reilly Network*, May 5, 2003, at http://www.oreillynet.com/pub/a/network/biocon2003/stein.html, accessed June 11, 2007.

41. Houellebecq, *Elementary Particles*, 13.

42. William Ray Arney, *Experts in the Age of Systems* (Albuquerque: University of New Mexico Press, 1991). On a different take on this question, see also Peter Sloterdijk, *Critique of Cynical Reason* (Minneapolis: University of Minnesota Press, 1988).

43. The critical tribunal is still deliberating on this, though, and some of its jurors argue that although Houellebecq claims his literature is a mirror (following Stendhal's advice), he "does not describe, he *advocates*." François Meyronnis, *De l'extermination considérée comme un des beaux arts* (Paris: Gallimard, 2007), p. 57, my translation.

44. In Frederic Jameson's eulogy, "Philip K. Dick, *in Memoriam*," in *Archeologies of the Future: The Desire Called Utopia and Other Science Fictions* (London: Verso, 2005), p. 348.

45. Philip K. Dick, *Do Androids Dream of Electric Sheep?* First published by Del Rey in 1968. Ballantine edition, 1982, p. 15.

46. Ibid., p. 13.

47. Giuliana Bruno notes "There is even a character in the film who is nothing but a literalization of this condition" (in "Ramble City: Postmodernism and Blade Runner," *October* 41 (Summer 1987): 61–74, p. 65.

48. Dick, *Do Androids*, p. 12.

49. Ibid., p. 57.

50. Ibid., pp. 57–58.

51. This word occurs in other Dick's novels, such as in *A Maze of Death* (1970), for instance.

52. Stephen Nottingham, *Screening DNA: Exploring the Cinema-Genetics Interface* (1999), available at http://ourworld.compuserve.com/homepages/Stephen_Nottingham/DNA4.htm.

53. For a fascinating variation on the themes of both the golem and the fallen angel, see David Desser, "The New Eve: The Influence of Paradise Lost and Frankenstein on Blade Runner" in *Retrofitting Blade Runner: Issues in Ridley Scott's* Blade Runner *and Philip K. Dick's* Do Androids Dream of Electric Sheep?, ed. Judith B. Kerman (Bowling Green, OH: Bowling Green State University Popular Press, 1991), pp. 53–65.

54. See Joseph Francavilla, "The Android as a Doppelgänger" (in *Retrofitting Blade Runner,* pp. 4–15) for a further elaboration of the replicant (and especially Roy Batty, their leader) as man-made *übermensch.*

55. In "L'univers, les Dieux, les Hommes: récits grecs des origines," in *Œuvres. Religions, Rationalités, Politique, I,* (Paris: Seuil, 2007 [1999]), pp. 11–151, p. 61, my translation.

56. Étienne Gilson, *La philosophie de Saint Bonaventure* (Paris: Vrin, 1953), p. 209.

57. *De instantibus* (ou *Des différentes espèces de temps*), in *Les œuvres complètes de saint Thomas d'Aquin,* Opuscule 35. Editions Louis Vivès, 1857, digital edition in French accessible at http://docteurangelique.free.fr.

58. *William Gibson: No Maps for These Territories,* a documentary by Mark Neale, 1997, this excerpt (with music from members of U2) available on YouTube at http://www.youtube.com/watch?v=dLmgrYS781A.

59. In his preface to *Dr. Bloodmoney* (New York, Dell, 1980 [1965]), p. 299.

60. During an interview on CNN, August 26, 1997, quoted in Mark L. Brake and Neil Hook, *Different Engines: How Science Drives Fiction and Fiction Drives Science* (London, Macmillan, 2008), p. 122.

61. Samuel Butler, "Darwin Among the Machines," 1863.

62. In *Phaedrus,* 244b-d and 265a-b. See Angus Nicholls, "The Secularization of Revelation, From Plato to Freud," *Contretemps* 1 (September 2000): 62–70.

63. Jameson, *Archeologies of the Future,* p. 88.

64. See Bernard Stiegler, *Technics and Time 1: The Fault of Epimetheus* (Stanford, CA: Stanford University Press, 1998), for a longer version of it.

65. Houellebecq's genial insight is to invert the relationship between Aldous and Julian in his fictive rendering: Bruno, the writer is a figure of Epithemeus, and Michel, the scientist, a figure of Prometheus: literature follows science, and forgets.

66. Giorgio Agamben, "Bartelby, or On Contingency" in *Potentialities. Collected Essays in Philsophy,* ed. and trans. Daniel Heller-Roazen (Stanford, CA: Stanford University Press, 1999), pp. 243–271, p. 266.

67. From the ancient Greek, poiesis, or, creation.

68. Philip K. Dick, "Schizophrenia and the Book of Changes," in *The Shifting Realities of Philip K. Dick,* ed. Lawrence Sutin (New York, Vintage, 1995 [1965]), pp. 175–182, p. 179.

69. "Fiction is not so much an image of the real world but rather a virtual example of a possible being-in-the-world; its limits are not those, thematic of worlds that can be represented, but rather those, constitutive, of the representativeness of worlds (whatever they are)." Jean-Marie Schaeffer, "Représentation, imitation, fiction: de la fonction cognitive de l'imagination," in *Les lieux de l'imaginaire,* ed. Jean-François Chassay and Bertrand Gervais, pp. 15–32 (Montréal: Liber, 2002), p. 31, my translation.

Works Cited

Agamben, Giorgio "Bartelby, or On Contingency." In *Potentialities: Collected Essays in Philosophy,* ed. and trans. Daniel Heller-Roazen. Stanford, CA: Stanford University Press, 1999.

Ampère, André Marie. *Essai sur la philosophie des sciences.* Paris: Bachelier, 1834.

Arney, William Ray. *Experts in the Age of Systems.* Albuquerque: University of New Mexico Press, 1991.

Bardini, Thierry. *Bootstrapping: Douglas Engelbart, Coevolution, and the Origins of Personal Computing.* Stanford, CA: Stanford University Press, 2000.

Baudrillard, Jean. *Simulacra and Simulation.* Ann Arbor: University of Michigan Press, 1994 [1981].

Burroughs, William S. "Deposition: Testimony Concerning a Sickness." Introduction to *Naked Lunch*. New York: Grove, 1992 [1959].

Butler, Samuel. "Darwin Among the Machines." Letter to the Editor of the *Press*, Christchurch, New Zealand, June 13, 1863.

Czerny, R., with K. McLaughlin and J. Costello. *The Rule of Metaphor: Multi-Disciplinary Studies in the Creation of Meaning in Language*. Toronto: University of Toronto Press, 1977 [1975].

De instantibus (ou *Des différentes espèces de temps*), in *Les œuvres complètes de saint Thomas d'Aquin*, Opuscule 35. Éditions Louis Vivès, 1857.

de La Mettrie, Julien Offray. *Man, A Machine*. Whitefish, MT: Kessinger, 2004 [1748].

Deleuze, Gilles. *The Fold: Leibniz and the Baroque*. Minneapolis: University of Minnesota Press, 1993.

Dick, Philip K. *Do Androids Dream of Electric Sheep?* New York: Del Rey, 1968.

_____. *Dr. Bloodmoney*. New York: Dell, 1980 [1965].

_____. "Schizophrenia and the Book of Changes." In *The Shifting Realities of Philip K. Dick*. Ed. Lawrence Sutin. New York: Vintage, 1995 [1965].

Gibson, William. Interview on CNN, August 26, 1997. Quoted in Mark L. Brake and Neil Hook, *Different Engines: How Science Drives Fiction and Fiction Drives Science*. London: Macmillan, 2008.

Gilson, Étienne. *La philosophie de Saint Bonaventure*. Paris: Vrin, 1953.

Heinlein, Robert. *Waldo & Magic, Inc*. New York: Del Rey, 1986.

Hofstadter, Douglas. *I Am a Strange Loop*. New York: Basic, 2007.

Houellebecq, Michel. *Elementary Particles*. Trans. Frank Wynne. New York: Vintage, 2001 [1998].

Huxley, Aldous. *Brave New World: A Novel*. London: Chatto and Windus, 1932.

Huxley, Julian. *What Dare I Think*. London: Chatto and Windus, 1933.

Jameson, Frederic. "Philip K. Dick, *in Memoriam*." In *Archeologies of the Future: The Desire Called Utopia and Other Science Fictions*. London: Verso, 2005.

Mumford, Lewis. *Technics and Civilization*. New York, Harcourt, 1934.

Neale, Mark. *William Gibson: No Maps for These Territories*. Documentary, 1997. DVD.

Nottingham, Stephen. *Screening DNA: Exploring the Cinema-Genetics Interface* (1999), at http://ourworld.compuserve.com/homepages/Stephen_Nottingham/DNA4.htm.

Okuda, Mike, and Rick Sternbach. *Star Trek: The Next Generation Technical Manual*. Quoted in the "Transporters and Replicators Mini-FAQ," *Time Magazine*, 1994.

Paley, William. *Natural Theology: Or, Evidences of the Existence and Attributes of the Deity, Collected from the Appearances of Nature*. Twelfth Edition. London: J. Faulder, 1809.

Plato. In *Phaedrus*, 244b-d and 265a-b. See Angus Nicholls, "The Secularization of Revelation, From Plato to Freud," *Contretemps* 1 (September 2000).

Rotman, Brian. *Ad Infinitum... The Ghost in Turing's Machine: Taking God Out of Mathematics and Putting the Body Back In*. Stanford, CA: Stanford University Press, 1993.

Schaeffer, Jean-Marie. "Représentation, imitation, fiction: de la fonction cognitive de l'imagination." In *Les lieux de l'imaginaire*, ed. Jean-François Chassay and Bertrand Gervais. Montréal: Liber, 2002.

Steinberg, Daniel H. "Stein Gives Bioinformatics Ten Years to Live." *O'Reilly Network*, May 5, 2003, accessed June 11, 2007, at http://www.oreillynet.com/pub/a/network/biocon2003/stein.html.

Stephenson, Neal. *The Diamond Age or A Young Lady's Illustrated Primer*. New York: Bantam, 1995.

Stiegler, Bernard. *Mécréance et Discrédit 2: Les sociétés incontrôlables d'individus désaffectés*. Paris: Galilée, 2006.

Vernant. *L'univers, les Dieux, les Hommes: récits grecs des origines*, dans *Œuvre: Religions, Rationalités, Politique 1*. Paris: Seuil, 2007 [1999].

Walker, John. "Through the Looking Glass." In *The Art of Human-Computer Interface Design*, ed. Brenda Laurel. Reading, MA: Addison-Wesley, 1990.

Warrick, Patricia. *The Cybernetic Imagination in Science Fiction*. Cambridge, MA: MIT Press, 1980.

Wiener, Norbert. *Cybernetics, or Control and Communication in the Animal and the Machine*. Cambridge, MA: MIT Press, 1994 [1948].

11

True Risks? The Pleasures and Perils of Cyberspace

Janet Abbate

> *Vinge's conceit of a magical universe as a description for cyberspace catapults the novella from the class of works that predict the future into the rarefied realm of works that have come to create it.... In giving the geeks a vision, Vinge also defined a road map, a project plan, presenting a future which could exist, if only we would work toward it.*

— Mark Pesce, virtual reality pioneer

The publication of Vernor Vinge's novella *True Names* in 1981 inspired a generation of computer scientists to think about life online in new ways. Vinge's depiction of a utopian community of cyber-outlaws who must battle both government enforcers and a mysterious artificial intelligence gave many readers their first inkling of the potential pleasures and perils of cyberspace. Vinge's work, as well as other early cyberfiction, influenced actual thought and practice in computer science and helped shape wider cultural understandings of what cyberspace might be and what types of people belonged there. This essay explores how such speculative fiction framed and foreshadowed real-life issues regarding online identity, community, privacy, and security.

Born in 1944, Vinge earned a Ph.D. in mathematics at the University of California, San Diego and taught math and computer science at San Diego State University for 30 years. He had a parallel career writing speculative fiction, and in 1966 published his first story—about the augmentation of human intelligence using computers, which would be an enduring theme. [1] *True Names* was inspired by a real-life experience in which Vinge and an unknown person were logged into the same computer anonymously and struck up a conversation via its TALK program:

> The TALKer claimed some implausible name, and I responded in kind. We chatted for a bit, each trying to figure out the other's true name. Finally I gave up, and told the other person I had to go — that I was actually a personality simulator, and if I kept talking my artificial nature would become obvious. Afterward, I realized that I had just *lived* a science-fiction story. [2]

In Vinge's novella, the development of an EEG interface ("the portal") allows users to connect their brains directly to the network, interpreting electrical signals as sensory input and using physical motions to activate software. A group of expert users harnesses this technology to create a virtual world where they can assume magical identities as "witches" or "warlocks" amid castles, swamps, and monsters of all shapes and sizes. They call this world "the Other Plane" and guard the entrance to their "Coven" from unskilled trespassers:

> The correct path had the aspect of a narrow row of stones cutting through a gray-greenish swamp. The air was cold but very moist. Weird, towering plants dripped audibly onto the faintly iridescent water and the broad lilies. The subconscious knew what the stones represented, handling the chaining of routines from one information net to another, but it was the conscious mind of the skilled traveler that must make the decision that could lead to the gates of the Coven, or to the symbolic "death" of a dump back to the real world [250].

While the magical touches are entertaining, the illusions are not merely decorative: the imaginary landscape provides an interface to real computer systems. Indeed, its users consider the Other Plane a more efficient computer interface than old-style keyboards and screens — but also, "it was simply a hell of a lot of fun to live in a world as malleable as the human imagination" (272).

The offline context for these activities is an ambiguous mix of technological empowerment and political constraint. In Vinge's story, the Internet — which relatively few people had even heard of in 1981— is ubiquitous, seamlessly connecting the entire world, and distributed computing is the norm: ordinary individuals can rent computer time and storage on public platforms, where they can create and run programs ("spells") on the fly. Vinge foresees a pervasive information economy in which "ninety-eight percent of the jobs in modern society involved some use of a data set" (248). However, the U.S. government seeks to limit citizens' activities within cyberspace, so those who acquire the computer power needed to enter the Other Plane are, by definition, outlaws. Warlocks must hide their offline "true names" lest they fall into government hands.

The main characters, Mr. Slippery and Erythrina, are members of a Coven famous for its expert pranks against government or commercial databases. When federal agents learn Mr. Slippery's true name, they force him to help them catch an even bigger foe: a mysterious new character called the Mailman who may seek world domination. Mr. Slippery and Erythrina defeat the Mailman in an epic cyberspace battle and discover that he was actually a runaway AI program created by a military project. In gearing up for the fight, the two warlocks also take on superhuman powers by merging their consciousness with the world's computing systems: "the human that had been Mr. Slippery was an insect wandering in the cathedral his mind had become" (285). They must give up these powers in the end, but not before Erythrina creates a virtual clone of herself so that she can live forever in cyberspace. Throughout the story, Vinge evokes a richly detailed virtual landscape peopled with distinctive and nuanced characters. Beyond the technical innovations, he provides a compelling vision of why cyberspace would be worth creating, spending time in, and defending.

The only comparable fiction published before *True Names* was John Brunner's *Shockwave Rider* (1975). Even more than *True Names,* Brunner's story reflects the widespread suspicion of both government and technoscience in 1970s America.[3] In *Shockwave Rider,* the U.S. government controls the public's behavior by manipulating information, and secret schools train a cadre of super-intelligent children to do its bidding. Inspired by Alvin Toffler's 1970 bestseller *Future Shock,* Brunner depicts a future in which identity is malleable, and many people have trouble adjusting to a rootless "plugged-in lifestyle." Every person has a computer ID code that determines their level of social power; expert hackers can fabricate new identities and create "tapeworms" that alter their (or an enemy's) credit rating, criminal record, or other digital data. While *Shockwave Rider* resembles *True Names* in spotlighting the digital construction of identity and featuring a showdown between a heroic hacker and federal agents, Brunner does not depict online worlds or identities: the computer is strictly a tool for manipulating events offline.

Early cyberfiction influenced computer science in several ways: by generating a sense of excitement and purpose, by pointing to new research topics, and by providing shared metaphors and terminology. Brunner's notion of a "worm" is still used in computer security, while William Gibson's *Neuromancer* (1984) contributed the word "cyberspace" and popularized a vision of online life as glamorous, rather than nerdy. Unlike Gibson, however, Vinge had an expert understanding of computer technology. One of the most impressive aspects of his vision is how many different areas of computer science were inspired or foreseen by this short novel. The sections below explore Vinge's influence in a variety of areas and attempt to characterize the nature and limits of the social worldview shared by Vinge and those who followed.

Infrastructure and Interfaces

Vinge understood that creating a real-time, immersive virtual environment would take massive computing power. This constraint drives the plot of *True Names* at several points: for example, it forces the government to give the warlocks access to federal computers, and it retards the growth of the Mailman's AI program. The demands of cyberspace also inspired some real-world creators of computer infrastructure.

Daniel Hillis invented an influential, massively parallel supercomputer called the Connection Machine in 1983. In a 1992 article arguing why parallel computing is important to society, one of Hillis's main examples is its ability to support the creation of virtual worlds:

> Try to imagine the virtual worlds that will be made possible by the power of a shared parallel computer. Imagine a world that has the complexity and subtlety of the aircraft simulation, the accessibility of the video game, the economic importance of the stock market, and the sensory richness of the flight simulator, all of this with the vividness of computer-generated Hollywood special effects. This may be the kind of world in which your children spend their time, meet their friends and earn their living [14].

While Hillis does not say explicitly that his work was inspired by Vinge, he advises readers, "For some ideas about what virtual worlds may be like, the best source is science fiction. I recommend the work of William Gibson, or a story called 'True Names' by Vernor Vinge" (15 n7).

A more striking testimonial to Vinge's influence comes from Mark Pesce (see opening quote), a pioneer of virtual reality and co-creator of VRML, a protocol for 3D interactive graphics.

> The impact of Vinge's *True Names* can not be easily overstated.... He presented a globally networked world into which human imagination had been projected.... Did Vinge create virtual reality? In a practical sense, perhaps not, but something about his novella caused people to revision their work, and refocus themselves toward the ends he described. In an interesting inversion, life imitates art, and people dedicated their professional careers to realize Vinge's vision. I was one of them [228].

Pesce reads a complex message into Vinge's work that goes well beyond the idea of cyberspace as a place to build fantasy worlds. Pesce argues that the "core theme" of *True Names* is that "the mastery of reality by magical technique opens hidden possibilities of human being" (234). While Vinge's magical environment may resemble later online games such as World of Warcraft, the tools of cyberspace give Slip and Ery power over the *real* world, not just an online fantasy; this makes them "decidedly post-human" (235).

Pesce agrees with Vinge that the metaphor of magic is not fanciful but actually the best way to capture the experience of VR: "Every object in cyberspace is a magical object" in the sense that it only exists (*as* an object with particular properties) through the collective belief and will of those participating. Using magical analogies is no more childish or irrational than using the metaphor of a "trashcan" or "file folder" to represent locations on a personal computer. "The generation of meaning is *always* a magical act" (230); cyberspace merely takes the social construction of reality to new levels. Pesce wants us to take seriously the "reality" of VR: both the fact that we construct meaning in VR much the same way as we do in the real world, and the potential for using VR as an interface to act on the real world.

In Vinge's story, the "real world" encountered by the characters was mostly computer systems (and the occasional nuclear missile). In twenty-first–century incarnations, the virtual world might recreate actual terrain or city streets, layered with information about real or imagined properties of those locations. Geographer Jeremy Crampton comments on cyberfiction's influence on later geographical information systems:

> Google Earth is only one example (if a particularly well-known one) of the geospatial web or "geoweb" comprised of map and location-based services available on the web. As a metaphor of *meaningful geographies for virtual data*, the idea can be traced back 25 years to "cyberspace" in the science fiction of Vinge and Gibson [92, emphasis added].

Computer scientists Kirstie Bellman and Christopher Landauer identify yet another element of Vinge's cyberspace infrastructure: the use of software agents to populate and maintain the virtual environment. In Vinge's story, the dragon (whimsically named after Alan Turing) that guards the Coven's castle is a computer program; other security programs include the spiders that infest the swamp and the Mailman himself. Bellman and Landauer's article on design guidelines for interactive environments cites Vinge's novella alongside more technical literature to support their argument that "agents with a much more open-ended purpose and scope of activities will be needed" to create virtual worlds that are "real places" (110).

Virtual Place, Community, and Identity

> One of the central features of *True Names* is the notion that a worldwide computer network would be a kind of *place* for its users" — Vinge, Introduction to *True Names*, 19

True Names provided the model for an early commercial, multiplayer game/community called *Habitat*, created by Lucasfilm Games in 1985. As described by designers Chip Morningstar and F. Randall Farmer, *Habitat*'s virtual environment was "inspired by a long tradition of 'computer hacker science fiction,' notably Vernor Vinge's novella *True Names*" (175). In tribute, the currency used in the game bore the likeness of Vinge (221).

Morningstar and Farmer emphasize that it is not technology but human imagination that creates the reality of cyberspace: "a cyberspace is defined more by the interactions among the actors within it than by the technology with which it is implemented" (174; see also 180). This picks up on one of Vinge's technical insights in *True Names:* that an immersive experience need not require immense bandwidth. Ironically, Vinge invokes the power of plain text to explain how a graphical, 3D virtual environment could seem real:

> Even a poor writer — if he has a sympathetic reader and an engaging plot — can evoke complete internal imagery with a few dozen words of description. The difference now is that the imagery has interactive significance [Vinge, True Names, 252].

Interactive imagery means that players not only "see" the objects in Habitat (or Vinge's Other Plane), they can manipulate them, and the consequences are felt by all the inhabitants of the virtual realm. Collectively, players can employ simple objects and actions to create the feeling of a shared social space.

Morningstar and Farmer bring to life Vinge's sense of the virtual world as a community. While Gibson's cyberspace is mainly devoted to the serious business of commerce and crime (and these activities drive the plot of *True Names* as well), Vinge also saw the potential for what we would now call social networking — the opportunity for far-flung strangers to meet, "hang out," express themselves, and even fall in love. His warlocks spend as much time chatting as pulling stunts, and each has clearly invested time and energy in creating a distinctive virtual appearance and persona. Vinge was one of the first to recognize the appeal of being able to create an online "avatar" that is more powerful, attractive, or exotic than one's real physical body. Mr. Slippery, for example, muses that Erythrina's beautiful appearance online might mask an ordinary body, or even someone seeking to escape social stigma:

> Almost as likely, she was massively handicapped. He had seen that fairly often.... Many of these types retreated into the Other Plane, where one could completely control one's appearance [320].

The activities that enliven Vinge's tale — building an online identity, meeting new friends, seeking adventure — now form the core of today's social networking sites, blogs, and multiplayer games.

Artificial Intelligence

> It turns out the Mailman was the greatest cliché of the Computer Age, maybe of the entire Age of Science.... It was designed to live within larger systems and gradually grow in power and awareness.... The program managers saw the

Frankenstein analogy.... Poor little Mailman, like the monsters of fiction — he was only doing what he had been designed to do [Vinge, *True Names*, 325, 327–328].

The great villain of Vinge's novella turns out to be an artificial intelligence program run amok. Yet AI is also its great hope: Erythrina adapts the Mailman program to create her own AI, to which she will somehow transfer her personality. This aspect of Vinge's book caught the attention of AI legend Marvin Minsky, and shortly after its publication Minsky made *True Names* the focus of his keynote speech at a science fiction awards banquet. He was then invited to write an afterword for the second edition of the book in 1983.

In his 1983 essay, Minsky credits Vinge with foreseeing a new way of programming: "there is evidence that he regards today's ways of programming ... as but an early stage of how great programs will be made in the future" (336). In this envisioned future, AI programs would do the coding for us:

Surely the days of programming, as we know it, are numbered.... Instead, we'll express our intentions about what should be done.... Then these expressions will be submitted to immense, intelligent, intention-understanding programs which will themselves construct the actual, new programs [336].

While Minsky clearly sees this as desirable and attainable, he also acknowledges the dark side of Vinge's vision: "The ultimate risk, though, comes when we greedy, lazy masterminds are able at last to take that final step: to design goal-achieving programs which are programmed to make themselves grow increasingly powerful"— like the Mailman in *True Names* (338).

On another level, Minsky sees in Vinge's scenario a mirror of his own model of the human mind, which in 1983 was about to be published as *The Society of Mind*. Minsky described the mind as a set of specialized machines that were mutually incomprehensible but could communicate over the brain's neural network using a limited symbolic language.

In several ways, my image of what happens in the human mind resembles Vinge's image of how the players of the Other Plane have linked themselves into their networks of computing machines — by using superficial symbol-signs to control a host of systems which we do not fully understand.... So this is the irony of *True Names*. Though Vinge tells the tale as though it were a science-fiction fantasy — it is in fact a realistic portrait of our own, real-life predicament! [339, 344].

The logical extension of Minsky's argument (350–351) is that there is no real difference between the ordinary human mind, the human-computer hybrid that Mr. Slippery and Erythrina became during their battle with the Mailman, and an intelligent computer program. Following this logic, Vinge's model of human-computer interaction becomes a blueprint for AI's ultimate goal of creating an intelligent computer. As Minsky concludes,

> The only thing missing is most of the knowledge we'll need to make such machines intelligent. Indeed, as you might guess from all this, the focus of research in artificial intelligence should be to find good ways, as Vinge's fantasy suggests, to connect structure with functions through the use of symbols [352].

Cryptography, Privacy, Anonymity, and Security

> In the once-upon-a-time days of the First Age of Magic, the prudent sorcerer regarded his own true name as his most valued possession but also the greatest threat to his continued good health, for — the stories go — once an enemy, even a weak unskilled enemy, learned the sorcerer's true name, then routine and widely known spells could destroy or enslave even the most powerful.... Now it seems that the Wheel has turned full circle ... and we are back to worrying about true names again [Vinge, *True Names*, 241].

The opening lines of *True Names* resonate on a number of levels: they express the characters' distrust of the government, they reflect contemporary events in cryptography, and they seem to eerily foreshadow today's concerns with identity theft. Here I focus on the politics of cryptography, which in the late 1970s seemed to be approaching a standoff between the U.S. government, which wanted to restrict public access to strong encryption, and computer scientists in industry and academia who advocated giving businesses and ordinary citizens the ability to communicate securely. Citing threats to national security, Congress had placed strong encryption on a list of export-restricted "munitions" since 1976. The National Bureau of Standards adopted an encryption standard based on IBM research, called DES, for general use in 1976. But its 56-bit key — which became the upper limit for exportable encryption technology — was relatively weak (it was broken by brute force in 1997). Vinge offers a computer science insider's dim view of these restrictions as Mr. Slippery comments on his personal security measures: "Like most folks ... he had no trust for the government standard encryption routines, but preferred the schemes that had leaked out of academia — over NSA's petulant objections — during the last fifteen years" (Vinge, *True Names*, 251).

Some of Vinge's fans read his work as a manifesto for public access to cryptography. While encryption can serve a number of purposes, such as e-commerce, these activists were particularly concerned with the right (as they would see it) to interact anonymously online. One of the most outspoken was Tim May, who had been a noted physicist at Intel before focusing on cryptography and the social issues surrounding it. A self-described "crypto-anarchist," he was a central member of the "Cypherpunks" mailing list, started in 1992, which discussed and developed ways to use technology to maintain individual privacy and anonymity. Technologies that were invented, improved, or promoted by the Cypherpunks included anonymous remailers, public key cryptography, and digital money [40, 44, 48].

Describing his first impressions of *True Names* in 1986, May writes:

> *True Names* certainly riveted me, and it fit with other developments swirling around in computer circles at the time.... [David] Chaum's work ... sparked the realization that a digital economy could be constructed, with anonymity, untraceability, and ancillary anarcho-capitalist features.... In other words, a cryptographically based version of Vinge's *True Names*.... Arguably, Mr. Slippery is already here and, as Vernor predicted, the Feds are already trying to track him down. In 1988 these ideas motivated me to write and distribute on the Net "The Crypto-Anarchist Manifesto" [35–36].

May used Vinge's term *true name* in the manifesto itself, and new members of the Cypherpunks (who obviously borrowed their name from the "cyberpunk" genre) were encouraged to read the novella, as well as Brunner's *Shockwave Rider* and other cyberfiction (38).

Like Vinge, May and the Cypherpunks positioned technology within a political vision that questioned government's right to control either personal identity or the means of communication. May asks, "Why do we so often accept the notion that governments issue us our names and our identities, and that government must ensure that names are true names?" (43). He notes that in oppressive regimes, "Digital pseudonyms, the creation of persistent network personas that cannot be forged by others and yet are unlinkable to the 'true names' of their owners, are finding major uses in ensuring free speech" (44).

Yet May's characterization of *True Names* as "anarcho-capitalist" seems a misinterpretation and raises some interesting questions about the social visions guiding cyberspace fiction and research. Vinge's story does not particularly espouse capitalism — indeed, the main characters' disregard for private property would seem at odds with it — and the social organization appears to be more technocracy than anarchy: possession of computer hardware and programming skill equals power. Likewise, May's vision of a lawless utopia privileges technical skill and is founded in technological determinism:

> The combination of strong, unbreakable public-key cryptography and virtual network communities in cyberspace will produce profound changes in the nature of economic and social systems. Crypto-anarchy is the cyberspatial realization of anarcho-capitalism, transcending national boundaries and freeing individuals to consensually make the economic arrangements they wish to make [44].

He explains that "a basic credo of the Cypherpunks movement has been that technological solutions are preferable to administrative or legislative solutions" (54). Yet this can only be equated with "anarchy" if technology is assumed to be politically neutral, a view that is naive at best and, again, places power in the hands of technologists with unspoken agendas. [4] Finally, the confident assertion by May and others that "the net is an anarchy" (69) has recently been challenged by scholars who have documented the very real power that national governments have over their citizens' use of the Internet. [5]

In addition to making a connection between encryption, anonymity, and freedom, May picks up on another important theme in Vinge: the role of *reputation* in online communities. Pseudonymity may seem like an invitation to behave badly, but May argues that people who have invested time and effort in building a reputation for their online persona have an incentive to protect that investment by behaving well (38). This "reputation economy" is the glue holding together Vinge's Coven of outlaws; they have come to know, respect, and (minimally) trust each other over several years of interaction. Reputation is also the currency of the blogosphere and other early-twenty-first-century virtual forums, where pseudonymous authors can have large followings (though neither reputation nor true names seem to deter some of them from behaving badly).

Another political perspective on cryptography is offered by Leonard N. Foner, a researcher at the MIT Media Lab, who sees *True Names* as forecasting a dystopian world of government control, "a panopticon of unimaginable proportions" that will actually come to pass if the general public is denied access to strong cryptography [169].

> The plot of *True Names* depends on secure communications and secret identities against even the most determined of opponents — national governments. Some have compared the ability to have private discussions to the right to bear arms: the last-ditch defense against oppression.... Yet current political trends show that Vinge's extrapolation, in which normal people have no privacy and no hope of fighting governmental excesses, is right on target (169).

This view informs Foner's research on intelligent agents and online communities, which incorporates privacy protections into online interactions. But unlike May, Foner argues that the most important cryptographic issues are "sociological and political, not technical: Who gets to use it? Who gets to break it?" (153).

Whom Is the Vision For?

Foner's questions bring us to the issue: who are the intended residents of cyberspace? All technologies are designed with particular kinds of users in mind, and all utopias privilege some values over others. Science fiction is one of the cultural forces that shape popular understandings of who the "natural" users and masters of new technologies are.

Mark Pesce saw the "socially ostracized technophile" as Vinge's target audience. In some ways, as noted above, the Other Plane is a technocracy; the Coven's membership is exclusive, with a clear hierarchy of skill, and technical mastery can literally translate to world domination. The closest present-day analog may be multiplayer online games, where players take on mythical personae and accumulate knowledge and resources that give them power. Tim May takes these elitist tendencies to an extreme with a vision of "crypto-anarchy" that is explicitly anti-democratic. Declaring, "I have very little faith in democracy" (73), he explains that "crypto-anarchy basically undermines democracy: it removes behaviors and transactions from the purview of the mob" (74).

Yet in the background of Vinge's story are other groups, some characterized more as "social clubs" (257) than hardcore hackers, suggesting more pluralistic possibilities. Pesce notes that Vinge's promise of transcendence through superhuman intelligence — a phenomenon Vinge later dubbed "the Singularity" — is not reserved for an elite group: "Vinge seems to say that the Singularity is universal, affecting all humanity" (237). As Mr. Slippery muses in the closing lines of the story, "Processors kept getting faster, memories larger. What now took a planet's resources would someday be possessed by everyone" (330).

Is cyberspace for women? Most of the early cyberpunk stories have a macho edge, and the female characters generally do not share the computer skills of the men. By contrast, one of the striking aspects of *True Names* is its relative freedom from gender stereotypes. Erythrina, the most powerful hacker in the story, is a woman; and though her online appearance is stereotypically sexy, her offline body is elderly — a radical departure for a female romantic lead. The other major female character is a hardnosed government agent, Virginia, who leads the team that busts Mr. Slippery. Both women are portrayed sympathetically, both are strong and skilled, and neither is defined primarily by her sexuality or her attachment to a male character. Vinge's story invites women to imagine themselves as full participants in cyberspace.

While none of the computer scientists who contributed to the 20th-anniversary edition of *True Names* were women, this may simply reflect the relatively small percentage of women in the field. When Vinge wrote his story in 1981, the proportion of female computer science students was rising, and it may have seemed that full equality was not far off. However, women's share of CS degrees peaked at 37 percent in the mid–1980s and actually declined afterwards to 20.5 percent in 2006. [6] Some have argued that women are deterred from entering the field by the popular image of computing as a preserve for male "geeks" [7] — an image that science fiction has probably done more to reinforce than to challenge. On the other hand, women participate in large numbers as creative *users* of cyberspace in areas such as social networking. Cyberspace does not exclude women, but their underrepresentation as technical experts and architects is troubling.

Interestingly, none of the early cyberspace novels foresaw young people as major participants.[8] While video games were already popular in the 1970s, personal computers for home use did not become widespread until the IBM PC in 1981 and the Apple Macintosh in 1984 (in its own version of life imitating science fiction, Apple used George Orwell's novel as the backdrop for its marketing campaign). As we will see, the presence of children on the Internet would create a very different sense of the risks involved.

Predictions and Outcomes

We have seen how a spectrum of computer scientists shared at least some of Vinge's assumptions about what would be technically possible, personally desirable, and socially problematic in cyberspace. How accurate were these collective visions?

On the technical side, ubiquitous networked computing has indeed arrived, at least in the United States and other developed countries. Strong encryption is widely and legally available, though some restrictions remain. EEG-based interfaces are under development, mainly to assist people with impaired brain function,[9] and various other virtual reality interfaces have been devised, including gloves, head-mounted displays, vehicle simulators, and projection rooms. While these are mainly used in research, engineering, and training rather than by the general public, other infrastructure and interface improvements such as faster CPUs, bigger and better-resolution displays, movement-detecting controllers (such as for the Nintendo Wii game), and protocols for displaying multimedia data online allow ordinary users to interact in graphically detailed 3D (if not immersive) environments. Geographical information has been integrated into computer systems so that, like Mr. Slippery, today's users can use satellite images to look down on their own physical locale. The only technical aspect of Vinge's story that seems nowhere near achievement is self-aware computer programs with their own desires and ability to act spontaneously.

Culturally, the appeal of cyberspace as a magical world has proven durable. A whole series of online environments, from early text-based MUDs to more recent graphically rich games, has drawn on the vocabulary of myth and fantasy. Early cyberfiction also accurately predicted a few online services, such as news (Vinge referred to "databases such as the *LA Times*" 252) and gambling (a feature of *Shockwave Rider*). But many social aspects of the Internet that loom large today were absent from early cyberfiction. E-mail, curiously, plays little part in these stories, even though it was one of the earliest popular real-world applications. E-commerce is a marginal activity; though some characters make purchases electronically, there is no sense that cyberspace might contain online storefronts, let alone consumer product reviews or auction sites that allow every user to become a merchant. Nor did the authors envision that cyberspace would have many corners devoted to individuals (homepages, social networking accounts, blogs), or that users would share content with strangers through mechanisms such as file sharing, YouTube, photo sharing, or wikis.

The point here is not to fault Brunner, Vinge, or Gibson for being unable to see into a future that few would have thought plausible in 1975 or even 1984. Rather, I suggest that these social features of cyberspace would have been particularly hard to envision because of the types of people the authors expected to inhabit it. In the early novels, cyberspace is dominated by computer experts — adults, mainly men. Given that demographic, one would not necessarily expect that shopping, trading pop songs, or posting photos of schoolmates and family would be important activities.

The outlaw sensibility of cyberpunk glorified the disaffected technical elite, but was never a realistic choice for the masses. "Crypto-anarchy" has not come to pass; the mere availability of strong encryption has neither caused the public to reject the rule of law *en masse* nor prevented governments from enforcing regulations. [10] Today's users of cyberspace define freedom and risk in other ways.

True Risks?

All of the early cyberfiction depicts the online world as a place of danger. I conclude with a consideration of how the perception of risk has changed in the three decades since *True Names* was written. Vinge's characters referred to government as "the Great Enemy," surpassed only by a rogue AI. Few people today seem to fear being attacked by self-aware software, and while government surveillance is still a concern for many users, a host of other online threats loom larger in American popular culture.

Media coverage portrays cybercrime and vandalism as common, motivated by economic gain, political agendas, or simply the desire to show off. [11] Some misdeeds, such as e-mail scams, are old crimes using new technology; the Internet is simply a means to reach users foolish enough to hand over their money. Other offenses are specific to computing, such as viruses, denial of service attacks, or the transformation of home PCs into botnets. As a risk, online crime seems to have a similar status in popular culture as street crime: people are warned to protect themselves by (figuratively) buying better locks, avoiding questionable neighborhoods, and not talking to strangers. [12] While Vinge's heroes considered themselves "good" vandals, there are few if any latter-day Robin Hoods in cyberspace who have won public approval for their exploits.

Another set of anxieties centers around children, who were not envisioned online at all in early cyberfiction. Publicly debated risks range from pornography and pedophiles to cyber-bullying and "addiction" to gaming. [13] Sometimes youth themselves are depicted as a threat to law and order, notably in the case of music file-sharing. While free distribution of pop culture content can be treated purely as an economic crime (and certainly has been prosecuted as such by intellectual property owners), it can also be seen as a challenge to the very notion of information as property. Current debates over copyright and its protection, violation, or redefinition through technology reveal the uncertain and shifting boundaries between the rights of information creators and users. [14]

Finally, as Vinge observed, "we are back to worrying about true names again." Today's Internet users feel considerable anxiety over the misuse of personal information, including concerns with reputation, corporate abuse of data, and identity theft. Privacy advocate Daniel Solove argues that the current structure of the Internet leaves users' reputations vulnerable to malicious gossip or simply their own bad judgment, as indiscretions from their youth come back to haunt them.[15] Corporations had little presence in Vinge's story, which was written before the Internet had been commercialized; but now that companies collect enormous amounts of customer data, many users fear they will sell it to third parties, use it for targeted marketing, or allow it to be stolen through poor security practices. Identity theft is perhaps the ultimate example of how technology allows a person's identity to take on a reality separate from his or her physical body. In the United States, one's Social Security Number and other financial identifiers are akin to a True Name: if it falls into the wrong hands, one's credit rating can be ruined, with financial and other consequences. Vinge's insight into the tension between having a public presence online and protecting one's privacy was prescient, even though the specific risks have changed.

Notes

1. Vinge 1966.
2. Vinge 2001, Introduction, p. 16.
3. Pew Research Center, 1998.
4. There is a vast STS literature challenging the view that technology is neutral. A good place to start is Winner 1980. For an example that specifically addresses computing, see Lawrence Lessig's (2000) argument that "code is law."
5. Goldsmith and Wu 2006.

6. National Science Foundation 2009, Table C-4, "Bachelor's degrees, by sex and field: 1997–2006."

7. Varma 2007.

8. In contrast, movies such as *Tron* (1982) and *WarGames* (1983) did feature teens or young adults. Both plots depicted cyberspace as an extension of video games (a game designer trapped inside a computer and forced to engage in gladiator-style combat, and a boy who mistakes a military program for a game). Unlike the network-based cyberspaces of Gibson, Vinge, or Brunner, the game-inspired virtual worlds of the movies focused on interacting with the computer, rather than with other people.

9. Wolpaw et al. 2002.

10. See Goldsmith and Wu 2006.

11. Wall 2008.

12. CERT 2001.

13. Tanner 2007.

14. See, e.g., Lessig 2005.

15. Solove 2008.

Works Cited

Bellman, Kirstie, and Christopher Landauer. "Playing in the Mud: Virtual Worlds Are Real Places." *Applied Artificial Intelligence* 14:1 (January 2000): 93–123.

Brunner, John. *The Shockwave Rider.* New York: Harper and Row, 1975.

CERT Coordination Center (Computer Emergency Response Team, Carnegie Mellon University). "Home Network Security." 2001. http://www.cert.org/tech_tips/home_networks.html.

Crampton, Jeremy W. "Cartography: Maps 2.0." *Progress in Human Geography* 33:1 (February 2009): 91–100.

Foner, Leonard N. "Cryptography and the Politics of One's True Name." (1995). In Verner Vinge, *True Names and the Opening of the Cyberspace Frontier.* New York: Tor, 2001.

Gibson, William. *Neuromancer.* New York: Ace, 1984.

Goldsmith, Jack, and Tim Wu. *Who Controls the Internet? Illusions of a Borderless World.* New York: Oxford University Press, 2006.

Hillis, W. Daniel. "What Is Massively Parallel Computing, and Why Is It Important?" *Daedalus* 121:1 (Winter 1992).

Lessig, Lawrence. *Code and Other Laws of Cyberspace.* New York: Basic, 2000.

_____. *Free Culture: The Nature and Future of Creativity.* New York: Penguin, 2005.

May, Timothy C. "True Nyms and Crypto Anarchy." (1996). In Verner Vinge, *True Names and the Opening of the Cyberspace Frontier.* New York: Tor, 2001.

Minsky, Marvin. "Afterword." In Verner Vinge, *True Names and the Opening of the Cyberspace Frontier.* New York: Tor, 2001.

Morningstar, Chip, and F. Randall Farmer. "Habitat: Reports from an Online Community." In Verner Vinge, *True Names and the Opening of the Cyberspace Frontier.* New York: Tor, 2001.

National Science Foundation, Division of Science Resources Statistics. *Women, Minorities, and Persons with Disabilities in Science and Engineering: 2009,* NSF 09–305. Arlington, VA, January 2009. Available from http://www.nsf.gov/statistics/wmpd/.

Pesce, Mark. "True Magic." (1999). In Verner Vinge, *True Names and the Opening of the Cyberspace Frontier.* New York: Tor, 2001.

Pew Research Center for the People and the Press. "Deconstructing Distrust: How Americans View Government." March 10, 1998. http://people-press.org/report/95/.

Solove, Daniel J. *The Future of Reputation: Gossip, Rumor, and Privacy on the Internet.* New Haven, CT: Yale University Press, 2008.

Tanner, Lindsey. "Is Video-Game Addiction a Mental Disorder?" Associated Press, June 22, 2007. http://www.msnbc.msn.com/id/19354827/.

Varma, Roli. 2007. "Women in Computing: The Role of Geek Culture." *Science as Culture* 16:4.

Vinge, Vernor. "Bookworm, Run!" *Analog Science Fiction,* March 1966.
_____. *True Names.* (1981). Reprinted in *True Names and the Opening of the Cyberspace Frontier.* Edited and with a preface by James Frenkel. New York: Tor, 2001.
Wall, David S. "Cybercrime, Media and Insecurity: The Shaping of Public Perceptions of Cybercrime." *International Review of Law, Computers and Technology* 22:1–2 (2008).
Winner, Langdon. "Do Artifacts Have Politics?" *Daedalus* 109:1 (Winter 1980).
Wolpaw, Jonathan R., Niels Birbaumer, Dennis J. McFarland, Gert Pfurtscheller, and Theresa M. Vaughan. "Brain-Computer Interfaces for Communication and control." *Clinical Neurophysiology* 113:6 (June 2002).

12

Science Fiction as Myth: Cultural Logic in Gibson's *Neuromancer*

R.C. Alvarado

A Question of Prediction

Any inquiry into a cause-and-effect relationship between the invention of real computational machinery in the middle of the last century, and technologies imagined in works of fiction in the preceding years, must confront the stark fact that nothing like a computer — as an abstract, universally programmable machine — inhabits the literary imagination prior to 1948. That was the year Weiner's *Cybernetics* and Shannon's *Mathematical Theory of Communication* were published, two years after the invention of the first general-purpose electronic computer, ENIAC, caught the public imagination.[1] The appearance of real computers, along with the emergence of an intellectual framework in which the categories of information and energy take the place of Aristotelian form and matter, was like the shifting of tectonic plates that shook the sciences to the core, much as the ideas of Darwin and Einstein did.[2] In the ensuing decade, biology and anthropology, for example, saw an immediate impact on core theorizations within their fields, as both the newly discovered gene and the concept of culture-as-structure began to be discussed in the language of information theory.[3] The cybernetic and information revolution also had a powerful effect on the arts, social sciences, and humanities that is still being felt today. It was only after this profound cultural shift, which provided the literary mind with a new vocabulary and repertoire of rich images, that science fiction writers began to weave the image of the computer into their works by speculating on its extensions, uses, and effects.

Possible counter-examples reinforce the point that, in the case of computing, real examples precede the literary imagination. Ray Cummings's "Grantline Comptometer," which appeared in the early science fiction novel *Beyond the Stars* (1928), is, by a limited definition, a computer, but it is based on the Felt Comptometer, a calculating machine invented in the 1890s and nearing the end of its industrial application by the time Cummings made use of it. Similarly, Asimov's robots in his early short stories, such as "Runaround" and "Reason," are essentially talking calculators with electro-mechanical anthropomorphic bodies, and have little to do with the kind of computer machinery that historically followed Asimov's works. In both cases, the concept of linear, mathematical computation serves the author as a sufficient basis for conceptualizing human cognition, and does little to anticipate the key ideas that artificial intelligence has learned from its experience with real computers, such as recursion and emergence, or semantics and knowledge representation.[4]

Instead of technological prediction in science fiction, we find a kind of socio-technical anticipation, what might even be called prophecy. The function of the image of the robot for Asimov is not to satisfy the engineer's need to flesh out a prototype before committing resources to a project; it is to meet the philosopher's need to speculate on the social, moral, and metaphysical implications of a mechanistic anthropology implied by the assumed existence of robots. Asimov's robots, as literary devices, perform the rhetorical role that Turing's test has had for the study of artificial intelligence. His fiction asks the question: What moral issues would be raised by the presence in society of very sophisticated calculating machines, i.e., robots, who meet or exceed the cognitive capacity of human beings? In response, Asimov bequeathed to later generations not an accurate prediction about the invention of *robots*— it is 2011 and we still do not have anything like what he described—but an authentic and still-relevant representation of an emerging culture in his concept of *robotics,* expressed as a set of laws and a series of poignant parables.

Two Kinds of Innovation

Like Asimov's stories of robots, *Neuromancer* offers a potent example of innovation at two levels: first, as a seminal text in the history of science fiction, credited with establishing the profoundly influential cyberpunk genre, and second, by apparently anticipating, if only vaguely, the World Wide Web, through its introduction of the terms "cyberspace" and "matrix." At the first level, the novel may be viewed as a *prototype,* an ancestral form in the long and variegated genealogy of literary cultural forms, and the source of imitation for the production of a series of other works within the genre. At this level, the effect of the novel on history is not controversial, appearing as a participant in a series of mimetic events, each of which is in principle intelligible. At the second level, the novel may be said to predictive, or, as I have said, *prophetic*. It appears to announce the emergence of an historical, social fact that did not exist at the time of its writing. The relationship between the novel and history at this level *is* problematic, since it is not clear what the nature of the prediction is — does the author merely possess luck or some special kind of knowledge? If the latter, what sort of knowledge does he possess?

From the perspective of cultural logic, these two levels of innovation are different aspects of the same phenomenon. A literary genre always encodes a specific assemblage of cultural logic, and so the introduction of a new logic introduces a new cognitive frame for envisioning the world. The actual presaging of historical events in a work of science fiction occurs to the extent that the same cultural logic that governs the construction of narrative action also governs, in a way that cannot be reduced to material forces, social action itself. It is in this sense that a story may be said to be true, even if its specific characters and events do not exist in fact — a story is true if it authentically captures existing forms of cultural logic, the codes that frame the action of real people and institutions in history. And it is in this sense that science fiction may be said to be predictive: by encoding and projecting a specific cultural logic through the medium of narrative, science fiction 'predicts' a future in which its social actors, following the same logic, generate a similar emergent effect.

Viewed in this way, the problem of establishing a causal relationship between a given fictional story, and the historical appearance of things announced in that story, changes from a concern with establishing linear networks of causality at the level of behavior to one complicated by the relationship between strata of cultural forms and social agents. Our task is to uncover the process by which a relatively stable third term (between historical cause and effect) — cultural logic — participates in the multiple acts of writing, reading, and other forms of behavior that reside on the always changing plane of behavior.

Cultural Logic

The concept of cultural logic is a central explanatory construct in the field of American cultural anthropology, even if the specific phrase has been unevenly adopted. I use the term in the sense expressed by Marshall Sahlins in *Culture and Practical Reason* (1978), *Historical Metaphors, Mythical Realities* (1981), and later works. In this usage, culture consists of the enduring, mutable, and more or less coherent assemblage of symbolic structures shared among members of communities and societies whose members actively identify themselves as such, and who continually reproduce these structures through acts of ritual and symbolic action, including speech acts. Symbolic structures are in turn composed of categories that classify the world, operators that allow for the formation and transformation of categorical complexes, and sensorial *materia* (e.g., rich images, both concrete and imaginary, such as the human body) onto which are mapped socially evolved networks of symbols and meanings.

Culture in this sense, as being fundamentally made of categories, is closely associated with the philosophical concept of *ontology,* with the difference that an ontology in the Western tradition is presumed to have more abstract coherency than symbolical structures actually have. In contrast to philosophical ontologies, cultural ontologies possess what has been called practical coherence: when subject to a rigorous analysis by the laws of noncontradiction and the excluded middle, they fail miserably — this failure being the source of Lévy-Bruhl's notorious concept of a "pre-logical mentality." But they succeed brilliantly in providing frames for social action in the trenches of lived social life, where the contradictory dynamics of power, desire, and environmental change are the primary sources of selection, not the abstract eye of the philosopher. And they succeed precisely because they accommodate contradictions within their structures. Even so, like philosophical ontologies, symbolic structures provide a framework of conditional, "if-then" thinking for generating social action through decision making, and for justifying it retrospectively through rationalization. Hence, the appropriateness of the designation cultural "logic."

We speak of cultural logic, then, to account for the culturally specific ways in which people, as culture bearers, draw inferences, make decisions, produce plans, and act in the world. As importantly, cultural logic also provides a framework for making sense of the actions of others, by attributing reasons, motives, and likely results from people's actions. Because this logic is practical, it is generative, producing culturally characteristic patterns that emerge at the social and historical level, as the aggregated network effects of individuals governed by symbolic structures. From this perspective, what good science fiction does is to generate, through an internalization of cultural logic itself, narratives that envision an emergent life pattern that prefigures real emergent life patterns generated by the same logic.

The Ontology of Cyberspace

Neuromancer presents a new ontology built from the fragments of Christian symbolism, mapped onto the imagery of a global and biologically integrated computer network, a concrete planetary spirit not unlike Chardin's noosphere, but charged with ambivalence. In developing this ontology, the novel addresses not simply the social and ecological problems wrought by multinational corporate capitalism, but the loss of self as well. Indeed, Gibson's ontology, encapsulated as the synthesis of *Wintermute* and *Neuromancer,* may be read as a more or less direct response to the spiritual problem of selfhood raised by Asimov's robot stories, as much as it may be a response to the economic conditions of late capitalism (Jameson), or the politically enmeshed epistemologies of postmodernity (Lyotard). If robots are, for the eternally pre-adolescent Asimov, a source of interesting speculation about what it is (and isn't) to be human, they are for Gibson (as for most of us), somewhat uncanny images of an unhappy post-humanism, avatars of the machine of Capital, which has destroyed the spirit as much as anything else.

The concept of spirit pervades *Neuromancer,* even though the word "spirit" is never mentioned. Instead, Gibson deploys the categories of Meat and Matrix to signify a core opposition between Flesh and Spirit. The Christian construal of these categories in the beginning of the story is both unmistakable and obviously intentional:

> For Case, who'd lived for the bodiless exultation of cyberspace, it was the Fall. In the bars he'd frequented as a cowboy hotshot, the elite stance involved a certain relaxed contempt for the flesh. The body was meat. Case fell into the prison of his own flesh [6].

Cyberspace is a spirit world, a non-space of pure light inhabited by bodiless AI's who play the role of angels and demons, and where data is substantialized in a neoplatonic fantasy of living, tangible forms. It is contrasted starkly with the venal and squalid world of meat and the body, from which all console cowboys want escape.[5] Gibson's reference to the Fall and, by implication, Case's status as a fallen angel, indexes the initial ontological condition of the novel, a state of separation between flesh and spirit, set in the liminal, anti-human chaos of Ninsei. This separation is replicated and complemented by another opposition: between Heaven (or Sky) and Earth, which are depicted in an equally fallen state, a condition of cosmic alienation.

The categories of flesh, spirit, heaven, and earth, are not directly stated in the novel. Instead, Gibson employs a pervasive color symbolism to signify and develop the symbolic structure. Whereas the Meat/Matrix dyad is encoded as red/blue, Heaven/Earth is encoded as silver/gold. The association between Meat and redness is intrinsic, and Gibson reinforces it by drawing attention to blood, to meat itself, and to the pink of fake or treated flesh. Blue is more polysemous, but is directly associated with both Case's experience in the matrix and sex (in turn connecting the latter as competing and complementary sources of ecstatic liberation), although the matrix is also described as a "colorless void" (204). The connection between Heaven and silver-gray is announced in the novel's first line, which also describes of the initial state of ontological affairs: "The sky ... was the color of television, tuned to a dead channel" (3). In contrast to a starry, enchanted cosmos announcing the fate of human beings below, Gibson's sky is a banal, broken communication channel between God and humanity. This association is repeated throughout the novel in references to the "poisoned silver" sky, reinforcing both the relation between color and category, and the state of separation and alienation. (The imagery is repeated in the shuriken, a silver star that Case covets, but then lets go after the novel's resolution.) The complement of sky as silver, the earth as gold, is understated—it appears as the jewelry of Julius Deane and Armitage, who, like totemic operators in Gibson's science of the concrete, represent the venal earthliness of consumer capitalism (and its accomplice, the military-industrial complex), and its desire to prolong the life of the body unnaturally, over a more authentic embracing of spirit and mortality.

The coded logic of color is perhaps most clear in what is the framing episode in the story, the murder of the innocent, but corrupted, gray-eyed Linda Lee:

> And now he remembered her that way, her face bathed in restless laser light, *features reduced to a code:* her cheekbones flaring scarlet as Wizard's Castle burned, forehead drenched with azure when Munich fell to the Tank War, mouth touched with hot gold as a gliding cursor struck sparks from the wall of a skyscraper canyon [p. 8, emphasis added].

Here Gibson ritually prepares the victim in uncanny precision — the four categories that comprise the initial ontological framework of the novel are literally mapped onto Linda Lee's face as a code. In particular, the association of "hot gold" with her mouth, site of consumption and taste, is repeated later in the novel. Although gold, among the four colors, is the most understated, its clear presence in Gibson's overt reference to a code, cannot be dismissed.

The subtextual four-color system in Gibson's novel encodes a double opposition, the resolution of which helps to produce the narrative pull of the novel. It provides a frame on which Gibson constructs an ontological transformation for his readers. The death of the marked Linda Lee in the stadium, synchronized with the real but staged mortal combat between holographically enlarged fighters, can only be read as a sacrifice. Here Gibson's symbolism is thick with redundancy, referencing the color red and "the smell of cooked meat" at the conclusion of the event, and echoing those metonyms later in the novel to evoke the scene of her death. [6]

In narrative terms, Linda Lee's sacrifice produces the intended effects of sacrifice everywhere — the transformation of a decayed, liminal disorder into a new order, of a broken ontology into a healed one, through the vehicle of the victim's body. In the case of *Neuromancer,* the effect is keyed to a larger synthesis of Wintermute and Neuromancer, in which the cyborg Molly — the hybrid image of flesh and spirit, and Gibson's answer to Asimov's robots — is the agent. Case reconciles the opposition between flesh and spirit, finding spirit-as-code in the flesh and flesh in the matrix.

In the end he finds work, a girl, and a self, a happy synthesis reflected in his final vision in the dreamtime of cyberspace, of the boy Neuromancer, Linda Lee, and himself. In the end, *Neuromancer* reads as a millenarian vision of hope in response to a fallen, decayed world ravaged by multinational capitalism and rampant militarism. The backdrop of the novel is a nuclear war, a social, political, and ecological disaster from which the world is still reeling. Case's fall echoes a global collapse in which human beings fail in their stewardship of the planet (a common theme, to be sure, in science fiction writing). Gibson's resolution, in which cyberspace becomes the medium for a planetary, cybernetic consciousness, achieved by the intervention of a cyborg, is literally a *deus ex machina* — God from machine — that saves, if not the world, then Case, who represents an Everyman.

Conclusion

To return to the question of prediction and prophecy: does Gibson's concept of cyberspace in any way anticipate the arrival of the World Wide Web nearly a decade later? From a technical perspective, the answer is clearly no. The idea of a "consensual hallucination" with its origin in video arcade games has very little to do with the global, crowd-sourced hyperspace of text, audio, video, and data that the Web has become. There are structural similarities, especially with the rise of social media and virtual world environments (such as *World of Warcraft* and *Second Life*), but the user interface of the Web is nothing like the immersive, sensory worlds in which Case roams, interacting with data and AIs like spirits in the ether.

But, for all of this inaccuracy at the technical level, the concept of cyberspace, and the ontological structure it indexes, remains a valid framework for understanding the cultural logic that both drives participation in the Web, and which frames our popular understanding of the web as a social institution. Specifically, there is a strong connection between Gibson's millenarian resolution in *Neuromancer* and the profound millenarianism found in contemporary Web culture. For example, the encompassment of Neuromancer by Wintermute prefigures the long-tail populism of the Web, the widespread faith in what Lanier has recently called "digital Maoism." [7] In this ideology, traditional institutions associated with politics, economics, journalism, and education, are dismissed as part of an old regime of information that will be replaced by new structures of participation made possible by the information abundance of the Web. In addition to this "wisdom of the crowd" cultural logic, the ideology posits a mechanistic, evolutionary anthropology in which spirit is defined in terms of information, as evidenced by the widespread and uncritical reception of ideas like Dawkins's meme and Kurzweil's singularity to explain historical events. Information has become the new Nature, and anything expressed in its terms becomes currency among those who subscribe to the ideology of informational millenarianism.

Anyone familiar with the career of the expression "Web 2.0" since the first conference of that name in 2004 will understand the ideological connection between cyberspace and the Web. First used to contrast the way that the Web had evolved from a hypertext distribution system to a genuine, global platform for computing (along the lines of Sun's famous mantra, "the network is the computer"), the 2.0 suffix quickly mutated into a category applied by the technorati to everything from capitalism and politics to education and life itself. The category has served the double function of indicating the expected cultural efficacy of a global computer network and expressing the hope for a new world in which individualism would be replaced by community, labor by creativity, and money by purpose. Like cyberspace, 2.0ism expresses a hope for salvation, a redemptive process from which the fragments of an alienated self might be made whole. Part of an explanation for the viral usage of the term must be its combination of a traditional religious belief— that of a Second Coming — with the banal inevitability of a software upgrade. No expression captures the spirit of cyberspace so well.

Ultimately, then, the predictive value of the concept of *cyberspace* does not derive from its illustrating a specific technological possibility, but from its indexing an ontological structure that encodes and reworks pre-existing but still effective belief systems that persist in the context of great technological change. This reworked ontology continues to provide a framework for envisioning and understanding a world that has operated according to a certain cultural logic since at least the middle of the last century.

Notes

1. See "Science: Eniac," *Time Magazine,* February 25, 1946. Of course, there is a long history of computational devices, many of which may deserve the designation "first computer," depending on how one defines the term. For example, Konrad Zuse's Z1, completed in 1938 in Germany, seems deserving of the term: It was an electro-mechanical binary calculator with limited programmability, a punched-tape memory, and possessed an architecture that anticipated Von Neumann's. But, aside from the fact that it was neither fully electronic nor fully programmable (nor entirely functional), it never reached the popular imagination, and its plans were destroyed during the war. It was only after World War II that computational technologies, like jet engines, although conceived of well before the war, were fully gestated and removed from veils of secrecy. In this essay, I choose ENIAC because, aside from being fully functional, it was both fully pro-

grammable and electronic, two criteria which match the category of the computer as understood today.

2. It is arguable that the full impact of the theories of natural selection and relativity could not be grasped until a theory of information provided the vocabulary to fully articulate them.

3. I use the phrase "information science" to represent both cybernetics and information theory. Essential to both is the category and concept of information in Shannon's richly problematic usage.

4. In fact, Asimov's robots have more to do with the past than the future. They reproduce the image of the mechanical man that has a long literary history and a much longer religious history: The image of the robot is the descendant of an ancient and geographically widespread line of symbolic devices in which the human body serves as a site for the mapping of social and cultural categories, a logic that operates behind institutions as diverse as divine kingship and human sacrifice. The robot maps the cultural logic of industrial mass society onto the human body, following a symbolic operation not unlike the mapping of agrarian logic onto the image of the king (always the source of fertility), or the City of God onto the Body of Christ.

5. In Weberian terms, Case represents an ethic of "other-worldly ecstaticism," in diametrical contrast to Protestant capitalism's "this-worldly asceticism."

6. The color symbolism, sacrificial logic, and other symbolic elements of *Neuromancer* are unconscious structures that may or may not become the objects of intentional manipulation in the process of writing. To the extent that they are conscious, the writing self does not invent them — they come to mind as signals and must be handled with care, under the strict eye of the muse. The fact that *Neuromancer* lends itself so well to a structuralist analysis may be due in part to Gibson's familiarity with the theory — after all, he did study English literature in the late 1960s, the heyday of structuralist criticism in North America, and indeed the novel indicates a familiarity with semiotics, ethnography, and even Gregory Bateson's cybernetic theory of schizophrenia. Nor should the presence of such strong Christian symbolism be surprising — after all, from the point of view of his upbringing, Gibson is a Southerner, and could not have been unaffected by the great currents of religiosity that dominate that cultural region, and from which he apparently sought refuge in Canada. Fatherless and isolated in an introverted world of science fiction during a period of great cultural upheaval, Gibson's mind invariably absorbed the basal ontology of a Christian South where, as he put it, "modernity had arrived to some extent but was deeply distrusted."

7. See "A Rebel in Cyberspace, Fighting Collectivism," *New York Times,* January 15, 2010.

Works Cited

Asimov, Isaac. "Reason." In *I, Robot.* Greenwich, CT: Fawcett, 1950 [1941].
_____. "Runaround." In *I, Robot.* Greenwich, CT: Fawcett, 1950.
Cummings, Ray. *Beyond the Stars.* Rockville, MD: Wildside, 2008 [1928].
Gibson, William. *Neuromancer.* New York: Ace, 1984.
Jameson, Frederic. "The Cultural Logic of Late Capitalism." *New Left Review* 146 (1984).
Lyotard, Jean-Françoise. *The Postmodern Condition: A Report on Knowledge,* trans. Geof Bennington and Brian Massumi. Minneapolis: University of Minnesota Press, 1984 [1979].
Sahlins, Marshall. *Culture and Practical Reason.* Chicago: University of Chicago Press, 1978.
_____. *Historical Metaphors and Mythical Realities.* Ann Arbor: University of Michigan Press, 1981.
Shannon, C. E. "A Mathematical Theory of Communication." *Bell Systems Technical Journal* 27 (1948).
Wiener, Norbert. *Cybernetics: Or Control and Communication in the Animal and the Machine.* Paris: Librairie Hermann, 1948.

13

Creating a Techno-Mythology for a New Age: The Production History of *The Lawnmower Man*

David A. Kirby

By the turn of the millennium a technology known as VIRTUAL REALITY will be in widespread use. It will allow you to enter computer generated artificial worlds as unlimited as the imagination itself. Its creators foresee millions of positive uses—while others fear it as a new form of mind control...

— Opening title card from
The Lawnmower Man (1992)

Movies are prone to historical revisionism. It is natural for people to judge films made 20 years ago using our current knowledge base and aesthetic criteria. This is particularly true for science fiction (SF) films. No matter how good a film's special effects were at the time it was produced, they will look rudimentary by today's standards, with very few exceptions. Likewise, cinematic styles change over time, which makes acting, camera angles, lighting choices, and other film elements appear dated. In addition, SF films reveal contemporary hopes and concerns for emerging scientific research and nascent technologies. These hopes and/or concerns can look pretty silly with the benefit of hindsight and can lead people to wonder how anybody could have taken these films seriously.

Such is the case in the 1992 SF film *The Lawnmower Man*. From today's perspective the special effects look "cheesy," the horror elements seem tacked on, the technologies on display have certainly not come to pass, and the film's hopes and concerns about the future of virtual reality (VR) technologies seem quaint. To be fair, even when *Lawnmower Man* was released it was not considered great cinema. However, it was extremely well made for its modest budget of $10 million, and it was a success at the box office, taking in over $32 million in America and $150 million worldwide. While the film's effects look dated today, the film's extensive use of computer-generated images was considered groundbreaking in 1992.

More importantly, the film introduced the concept of VR to a wide audience. According to director and co-screenwriter Brett Leonard, his goal for *Lawnmower Man* was to create a modern "technological mythology" featuring interactive technologies.[1] The movie provided a vision of what a VR experience could be by depicting both the virtual environments themselves as well as the devices used to enter these worlds — the headset, goggles, data gloves, bodysuits, and interface platforms. The film also explores several ideas about the relationship of humans to this emerging technology, including philosophical questions about our relationship to "reality." For technologist Julian Bleecker (2004), characters in cinema are "socializing" technological artifacts by creating meanings for the audience "which is tantamount to making the artifacts socially relevant" (vi). In this regard, *Lawnmower Man* socially contextualized the nascent technology of VR by portraying potential uses for education, entertainment, spiritual development, and for sexual activity.

While the horror aspects of the film angered many VR proponents, the film's visuals were an important vehicle in promoting the *potential* of VR. The film provided audiences with a VR "experience" that contemporary VR technologies could not. An *Omni* magazine article from 1992 captures this sense of the film presenting an alluring vision of a VR future saying that "in the graphics scenes you will see what such worlds might look like in the future" (Wertheim 1992). In this essay I will explore *Lawnmower Man*'s influence on our public perceptions of VR technologies by focusing on the film's production history, including its narrative focus on both the positive and negative potential of VR.

From Horror to SF and from Subculture to Mainstream

Lawnmower Man did not begin its creative life revolving around the concept of VR. In fact, outside of the pseudoscientific ESP and mind-control aspects, there are no SF elements present in the source story. Instead, the film's existence began with aspirations to make some quick money off the prestige of Stephen King's name in the arena of low-budget horror exploitation filmmaking. As Brett Leonard tells it, his first film made in 1989 was a well-received "video nasty" called *The Dead Pit,* which was made on a budget of $350,000. The financial success of this film brought him to the attention of a group of producers from a company Allied Vision, Ltd., which had success in the area of low-budget horror films with a number of straight-to-video sequels of *The Howling* (1981). These producers had recently purchased the rights to a ten-page Stephen King short story called "The Lawnmower Man" about a man who telekinetically controls a lawnmower to kill another man. The producers hoped that Leonard and his co-screenwriter Gimel Everett — who also produced the film — could achieve comparable success in crafting a horror film that looked beyond its meager budget.

Leonard, however, was not content to create another simplistic gore film. He and Everett had ambitions to create a more philosophical SF film concerning the consciousness-raising potential of VR technologies. As Leonard tells it, the minimalist nature of the source material presented him an opportunity to create a film based around the VR technologies he had been discussing with digital pioneers like Jaron Lanier: "I told [the producers] 'Well, I can't really make an entire movie out of this, but I have this idea about something called virtual reality.'" According to Leonard, his exposure to these embryonic computer technologies came through his integration into "the social network of digerati" in Northern California in the 1980s:

> I moved to Santa Cruz, not LA. And Santa Cruz was connected very strongly with Silicon Valley in the heyday of its initial growth. I had neighbors like Steve Wozniak, who was doing the Apple thing in a garage down the street.... So I suddenly was in this hotbed of technology. So in a way, it is because of the social aspects of my life that I started saying, "Wow, this stuff that they are playing with could make a really good movie concept."

Of course, they had to convince the producers that it was worthwhile for them to move away from a lawnmower-based horror story to an SF film focusing on a relatively unknown technology — especially since this shift would mean an initial increase in budget from $1.5 million to $5.5 million.

The biggest obstacle for Leonard and Everett was the fact that most of the producers were unaware of VR. "We had to sell the producers that the SF angle was better. But the producers had no idea what VR was." It is not surprising that the producers lacked knowledge about VR at this time, as most people were unaware of the concept. VR did not emerge as a concept fully formed but was developed across a wide variety of industrial and cultural contexts, including the computer industry, the military, NASA, SF, and the counterculture. The term "virtual reality" had only been coined two years earlier in 1989 by pioneering computer scientist Jaron Lanier to refer to immersive three-dimensional realities usually accessed using stereo viewing goggles and data gloves. By 1991 the topic of VR was beginning to move away from its cyberpunk subculture roots in media like *Mondo 2000* into more main-stream media outlets like the *New York Times* (Chesher 1994). Despite VR's higher media profile in 1991, it was still a niche topic that was only discussed within elite technological and cultural circles (a situation that changed with the release of *Lawnmower Man*).

The producers' lack of knowledge about VR would not have been a concern if Leonard and Everett could adequately explain the concept to them. Yet they had difficulty getting across VR's potential when they first tried to explain the concept to the producers. As Everett tells it:

> Nobody understood what virtual reality was. Nobody. We had to sit in front of the people with the money and go, "Honest, it's this thing. You can't believe it." They said to us, "Okay, show us what it is."[2]

This need for the producers to have the concept of VR *shown* to them is an important point. It speaks to cinema's power as a visual medium to promote technological development (Kirby 2010). VR is about creating an immersive environment that cannot be described but must be experienced. After their initial discussions with these producers, Leonard created "an educational tape about virtual reality in order to sell them on the idea." Once the producers saw VR's visual potential in the educational tape they agreed to produce Leonard and Everett's script.

Although the producers were on board, Leonard and Everett still had a difficult time persuading others involved in the production to use the phrase "virtual reality." According to Leonard, the producers themselves used his VR "educational tape" to sell the film to foreign distributors who were unfamiliar with the term. Leonard and Everett also had to convince the marketing department to include the phrase "virtual reality" in the film's trailer and other marketing material. Even the text for the film's opening title card (seen at the start of this chapter) was contentious. According to Leonard, several producers were afraid to open the film with a phrase so unfamiliar to the general public.

With the producers' acceptance of Leonard and Everett's script, the King short story became a single scene in a larger narrative involving VR technologies. But for Allied it was crucial to maintain a tie to the original story so they could use Stephen King's name in publicity. The official title of the film was *Stephen King's The Lawnmower Man,* and King's name was used heavily in marketing the film. To maintain a connection to the short story, Leonard incorporated a scene in which a man is chased through his house by a red lawnmower. The addition of the VR elements, however, left the film bearing very little resemblance to the original short story. King was unhappy to have his name attached to a story that bore so little resemblance to his work, and he unsuccessfully sued Allied and the film's distributor New Line Cinema to have his name removed from the film (Winteringham 1994). Despite his lawsuit, King was actually impressed with the film. After viewing the film King wrote to one of his agents: "I think 'The Lawnmower Man' is really an extraordinary piece of work, at least visually, and the core of my story, such as it is, is in the movie. I think it is going to be very successful."[3]

Visualizing the VR Experience

In order to justify switching from horror to SF, Leonard realized they had to not only make a visually stunning film, they also had to create VR scenes in which audiences felt as if they were having an actual VR experience. This required the VR depictions to not just look plausible, but to look as if these technologies were right around the corner. In addition, Leonard had plans to develop real-life interactive technologies. Therefore, he wanted the film to highlight for the public the potential for VR and 3 D interactive technologies. Before the filmmakers began production they realized the need to conduct research on what VR technologies already existed and what other developments were on the horizon.

Leonard and the other filmmakers understood that the inclusion of emerging but unknown computer technologies enhanced the credibility of their cinematic technology. Through Leonard's social contacts he was able to discuss upcoming developments in digital technology with several people who were at the forefront of computer science, including Lanier, Nicholas Negroponte, and Steve Wozniak. Leonard also visited a number of computer trade shows as well, speaking directly to scientists, companies, and governmental research facilities:

> In researching the film I was going to technology conferences and shows. There was one called "Cyberthon," which was a twenty-four-hour event in which everyone shows up in their huge, wild cyber gear. I also relied on friends who knew NASA scientists, which allowed me to get into the NASA Ames Research facility and experience their $30 million dollar F1 flight simulator, which was virtual reality. There was also a lot of very interesting technological experimentation around alternate cyber worlds in Northern California which inspired me. Many of the computer interfaces in the story. Many of the ideas of how the gear would work come out of those experiences. And, of course, as any good dramatist does, I extrapolated.

According to the film's production designer Alex McDowell, all of the filmmakers toured various computer companies like Sun Microsystems and talked with a number of computer scientists about recent developments in computing technology. They were looking for nascent technologies that would make the VR technology in the film seem more cutting edge and prescient.

McDowell recalls a research trip to Apple during pre-production where he learned about embryonic Internet features such as hypertext, hyperlinks and search engines that, while common today, were unknown by the public at the time:

> I remember that the speed gleaning idea for Jobe in the film, seeing him scan all this stuff, came from this meeting. I was completely fascinated by this thing that is so commonplace now. The idea that you could click on a picture of the Mayday parade and click on the balloon and it would tell you the property of air.[4]

Many of these emerging technologies show up in the film, including the physical interface used to project a user into the VR environment and the visual aspects inside this environment.

In addition to their research into VR, the filmmakers also pursued companies using the most advanced computer-generated images (CGI). At the time there had been a few films using limited amounts of CGI, like *The Abyss* (1989), but extensive use of CGI had been limited to television commercials (Morie 1998). Therefore, Leonard brought on board two special effects houses, Angel Studios Inc. and Xaos, which had experience using CGI in advertising. These companies used new digital compositing systems like the "hairy brush" system for the first time in cinema. They had to be creative with the special effects because they were working with such a low budget. For viewers today, the artificiality of the CGI is obvious, and the graphics look a bit too much like computer graphics. For Leonard, however, the obvious "computerness" of the graphics was a positive aspect, not a negative:

> What is good about the computer graphics in the film is that they celebrated computer graphics as computer graphics. It was not using CG to ape reality, which is how they are used now. But there is also something beautiful about a true CG aesthetic and that was something I wanted to celebrate in this film. Obviously the scenes in the VR worlds were CG landscapes but they could only be done in CG which makes it inherently valid.

Leonard wanted to call attention to the graphics' digital origins for two reasons. First, it signaled to the audience how much CGI was used in the film, which was a major selling point. Second, such obvious computer graphics added verisimilitude to the notion of taking a virtual trip inside a computer-based VR environment. Why would anybody create VR just to travel to the places that *already* existed?

It was not just the visual effects that were important in creating a believable VR scenario. The spectacle of the film's virtual environment would lose some of its power if the devices associated with entering this world felt inauthentic. So, the filmmakers paid particular attention to the sets and props associated with the VR interface. According to production designer McDowell, Brett Leonard had very specific ideas about the design of the VR interfaces that the first time production designer did not think to question. Leonard and Everett created the film's VR interfaces based on technological research they had been exposed to through their social contacts. In translating these for the film they modified these cutting-edge technologies to not only fit their aesthetic visions but also to match their ideas about what a VR experience *should* be like for the user.

Their VR interface included gloves for data manipulation and a VR head-mounted display with goggles and earphones. In addition to the wearable components they designed several body rigs for the VR interface, including a relaxation hammock, a motion simulator, and a full-body "gyrosphere." One of the most memorable devices from the film was the gyrosphere, which came out of discussions Leonard had with pioneering VR researcher Gregory Peter Panos. According to Leonard, Panos brought several books to their meeting, some of which included NASA's ideas about VR interfaces, such as the full-body gyrosphere rig: "We thought the gyrosphere was really cool. We took off from that idea for the VR interface, because it allows you to move 360 degrees but not go anywhere. It also looked awesome." For Leonard the entertainment aspects of VR were crucial, and he wanted the experience to appear like a carnival ride. The gyrosphere projected the impression of a full-body experience, including spatial senses. Leonard also understood that he was not creating an actual VR experience, but rather visualizing an imagined VR experience. Film is a visual medium and, as such, he needed to privilege interfaces which looked remarkable. For Everett, the interface was also an important feature because she envisioned VR as a technology for relaxation and consciousness expansion: "We had a lot of concepts about how we would like it to be in the future. You go in a comfortable place, you put this on and you really do feel like you are riding and floating in this other world." This notion of "floating" coincided with Leonard's belief that the VR environment should mimic a sense of "being underwater." He also achieved this impression by bathing all the sets involving the fictional "Virtual Space Industries" in blue light.

The result of Leonard and Everett's background research is that the audience gets an immediate understanding of VR's potential from the film's opening scenes of the "battle chimp." The scenes feature a chimpanzee whose intelligence has been enhanced by Dr. Larry Angelo (Pierce Brosnan) through VR immersion and smart drugs. The audience sees the chimpanzee inside a gyrosphere rig with the attached headset and goggles. The film's camera changes from a shot of the chimpanzee in the rig to a point of view shot from the chimpanzee's perspective in which the chimp is interacting with a virtual environment. According to Leonard they faced the same problem writing this scene as when they tried to explain the concept of VR to the producers: How do you make something so visual appear exciting on the written page?

The scene of the battle chimp was very, very hard to write. VR is so visual that what you put on the page does not seem right or to do it justice. You cannot capture what is essentially a visual and sensory experience. But when it was on the screen it was instantly recognizable in terms of what the concept was to the audience. VR is inherently cinematic as an idea.

This immediate comprehension of VR is why *Lawnmower Man* has had an enduring appeal. It did what contemporary popular magazines and books on VR could not: it visualized an abstract concept in such a way that its potential was immediately understood.

Visualizing VR's Potential for Human Advancement

> *The potentials for human advancement are endless. Virtual reality holds the key to the evolution of the human mind.* — Dr. Larry Angelo in *Lawnmower Man*

> *Some of the questions raised by VR that deserve public discussion are already coming through the projectors and loudspeakers at showings of the 1992 movie* Lawnmower Man. — Michael Heim in *The Metaphysics of Virtual Reality* (1993, 143).

The film's computer-generated visual effects served a dual purpose for Leonard and Everett. First, the state-of-the-art computer graphics would be the film's major selling point. Second, the VR world would illustrate for audiences VR technology's potential applications in the real world, especially its consciousness-raising possibilities. Although they were making a horror/SF film, Leonard and Everett shared the opinions of VR proponents in the early 1990s — like Jaron Lanier — that VR was the vehicle for a new kind of spiritual understanding. The concept of VR emerged in the context of a Northern Californian counterculture that still held to social and political beliefs developed in the 1960s. Media scholar Chris Chesher (1994) sums up the thinking about VR amongst the counterculture in Northern California:

> Building a new reality inside a computer is a new form of technological utopianism. When changing social reality seems too hard, why not create a new reality? They envisioned technologies which could be so powerful they would force the mainstream to change its perceptions about reality.

Within this counterculture a new subculture emerged, Cyberpunk, which combined the 1960s ideals of social equity and expressions of individuality with techno-optimism and New Age thinking.

In particular, Leonard and Everett believed that VR possessed significant spiritual and religious dimensions that corresponded to contemporary New Age ways of thinking. As Everett tells it, "The pursuit of spirituality through technology is something we want to champion." According to Leonard, his views about the potential of this technology to raise human consciousness is best illustrated in a speech Jobe Smith (Jeff Fahey) gives after he begins his evolution to a higher state:

> I realize that nothing we have been doing is new. We haven't been tapping into new areas of the brain. We have just been awakening the most ancient. This technology is simply a realm to powers that conjurers and alchemists used centuries ago. The Human race lost that knowledge and now I am claiming it through virtual reality.

According to Everett they combined this belief in VR's consciousness-raising ability with another New Age notion "that symbology can serve to put you in a new awareness." Leonard brought in "sacred geometry" consultant Robert Gulnik who told the filmmakers about Kabbalic symbols, Islamic tile patterns, and other supposedly magical symbolic representations. These symbols appear during the "brain stimulation" sequences in the movie. In addition to embracing these New Age beliefs, they also felt it was important to contrast Jobe's technologically driven spiritual evolution with that of mainstream religion. According to Leonard, they made very deliberate choices in depicting Jobe's development using traditional Catholic iconography, including a "cyber-crucifixion." The character of Father Francis McKeen (Jeremy Slate) represents a mainstream religion whose leaders are more concerned with power than spiritual development. For Leonard, these old religious structures were going to be displaced by the new digital technologies. "I wanted to connect the film with the idea that the new religion is technology. Technology was taking place of more traditional religious cultures." Jobe ultimately "sees God" in the VR environment. He then becomes the "Cyber Christ," who is a new prophet for this new techno-religion. In the end, VR technologies help Jobe overcome death and gain immortality through his transcendence into the virtual world.

The New Age elements of the film were not lost on New Age advocates and cultural commentators. Sociologist Christopher Ziguras (1997) argues in "The Technologization of the Sacred" that the film embodies New Age constructions of the sacred through high technology and science. He singles out the film as a "notable mainstream expression of the connection between the virtual reality interface and the evolution of consciousness" (207). By comparing the film to the writings of New Age advocates, he finds that "*The Lawnmower Man* plays out a New Age fantasy in which information technology allows for heightened experience of inner reality through more efficient tools for working with energy" (207). One element that Ziguras dwells on is Jobe's development of psychic powers through the VR experiments. He notes that this aspect of the film corresponds to a belief that many New Age proponents, like Starhawk (1990), were championing in other forums:

The mental control over external reality by mastery of inner reality, which Starhawk and the advocates of creative visualization argue is possible, is mastered through the Lawnmower Man's accelerated rate of psychic evolution [207].

For the New Age movement, the VR world allows for an exploration of an individual's inner world that ultimately leads to mental control over the external world. In this way VR becomes a tool for spiritual advancement and human evolution, just as Jobe experienced.

According to Leonard, he wanted to create a new technological mythology to promote the development of VR and interactive technologies. Leonard claims that a film director acts like a "tribal shaman" who creates visions of the future that can define a culture's shared desires:

> If you study the work of Joseph Campbell, in particular his book *The Mythic Image,* you see that it presents a thesis of how visual, artistic, and visionary storytelling creations define for cultures what the future will be because it creates this vision first. Cinema, because it is a visual story telling modality, fits this notion very, very strongly. The feedback loop for cinema is very quick and it is getting quicker all the time. So when I talk about myth, I am talking about creating iconography for a new landscape. That was one of the things that I was very focused on while creating the visual style of *The Lawnmower Man.*

As part of this mythmaking process he created a "narrative environment" for *Lawnmower Man* in which the technologies on display became a natural part of the visual landscape in the film. Leonard wanted these technologies to seem like they could become everyday technologies that were used to improve human life.

One real-world application for VR that they wanted to highlight was its potential as an educational tool to enhance intellectual development. To develop this part of the story, Leonard brought in David Traub to serve as their science consultant.[5] Traub had received a master's degree from the School of Education at Harvard University in 1990 for a thesis examining the use of new media and entertainment technologies in education. Specifically, his thesis examined the potential impact of VR simulators on social and emotional learning in mental health, for which he designed, but did not build, the world's first VR simulator for family systems counseling and family therapy. Not long after he received his master's he became head of technology for a children's television company in the Silicon Valley. He met Leonard when the company hired him to direct a music video for their rap music label:

> Brett came up to me and said you are the technology guy here, you ever heard of this thing called virtual reality. I showed him my thesis and he said "Whoa, I need your help." So I became his virtual reality consultant and gave them notes in the writing of the script.

Leonard subsequently hired Traub as a producer to help develop the computer display graphics relating to education:

> Then I became essentially the producer for all the display graphics. All the graphics that you see on the screens of computers.... If you remember there were a number of computers inside of his lab that had accelerated learning programs and various interfaces, and I happened to be an educator. We basically did all of the computers and all of the content on the computers that Pierce Brosnan used as a scientist and as an educator himself really.

As producer Traub brought in a group of young computer engineers to turn his ideas about VR and education into graphical displays. Although Traub had to run his ideas by Leonard ("Brett was a very hands-on director") he was able to create an exciting vision of VR as tool for accelerated learning. VR's educational capabilities are depicted through an Internet-like environment that combines an interactive computer game with an encyclopedia. The film's more "advanced" VR educational program also features a helpful "virtual guide" who brings Jobe through the learning process. In the end, Traub appreciated the opportunity to disseminate his ideas about the power of VR and interactive media for education.

Techniques for intelligence enhancement in *Lawnmower Man* were not limited to the VR technology. The film also introduced the concept of nootropic drugs to a wider audience. Nootropic drugs, which are commonly referred to as "smart drugs," are thought to chemically improve concentration, memory, and cognitive abilities. Today smart drugs do not have the same familiarity as VR, but they were developed around the same time in the late '80s and early '90s and many VR proponents in the cyberpunk subculture believed the use of smart drugs enhanced VR experiences (Balsamo 1995). For Leonard these drugs were an extension of VR's consciousness-raising abilities. In addition to the depiction of smart drugs, the film also portrays the VR experience as akin to a drug "trip." In what Leonard calls the "virtual relax" scene, Dr. Angelo sits in his relaxation hammock VR rig and enters a virtual environment where he can chose "Floating, Flying, Falling," which are shown to be almost psychedelic. Such a use for VR matches with the rhetoric of some VR proponents like John Perry Barlow and 1960s drug guru Timothy Leary, who referred to VR as "electronic LSD." Some VR proponents, however, were unhappy with these psychedelic connotations and blamed this image for VR's negative depictions in the mainstream media (Chesher 1994).

One of the most memorable scenes in *Lawnmower Man* is the cyber-sex scene in which Jobe and his lover use the gyrospheres to experience the VR environment together. At one point the two lovers embrace, become entwined, and appear to be blending together in what Brett Leonard called the "signature image of the movie." For Leonard and Everett, VR's potential to enhance intimacy was another aspect of its potential in raising the level of human consciousness. According to Everett they felt that visualizing the idea "that you could have this amazing experience with another person in there" was important because it showed how two people could be "so close, so merged." Media scholar Vivian Sobchack (2001) discusses this scene as a specific instance of media producers buying into VR advocates' rhetoric about the potential of VR for greater human interaction. She instead feels that the scene illustrates VR's potential to create a mode of non-interaction that she calls "interactive autism":

> This mode of being is briefly, but illuminatingly dramatized in the climactic 'virtual reality' sex scene in 1992's *The Lawnmower Man:* while impossibly total sexual coupling occurs in virtual space, the two participants are seen physically separated in the "real" space of the lab, hugging and caressing their *own* data-suited-up bodies [emphasis in original, 326].

Although Leonard and Everett saw VR as a means to bring two people closer together, Sobchack views this scene as an example of how VR could actually alienate people from each other.

It might seem strange for these filmmakers to be so concerned with highlighting VR's positive potential in what is essentially a horror film featuring technology gone awry. Although Leonard felt that VR had tremendous promise, he also believed that misuse of the technology could lead to some horrific consequences. For Leonard, VR's potential to raise human consciousness could only be achieved if we use these technologies wisely. "I am a teller of cautionary tales in terms of technological mythology. *Lawnmower Man* is essentially the myth of Frankenstein; that we need to temper our science and technology with wisdom." Leonard calls attention to this cautionary message through several lines of dialogue. In one scene Dr. Angelo cautions Jobe, "Even with all these new abilities there are dangers. Man may be able to evolve a thousandfold through this technology, but the rush must be tempered with wisdom." In the film's last scene Dr. Angelo reiterates this message: "If we could somehow embrace our wisdom instead of ignorance, then this technology will free the mind of man, not enslave it." According to Leonard, the film's distributors wanted this speech removed from the film. He did initially remove it during the editing process, but subsequently added the scene back in at the last minute because he felt it addressed the film's key theme.

Philosopher Michael Heim (1993) devotes an entire chapter in his influential book *The Metaphysics of Virtual Reality* to discussing the philosophical questions that *Lawnmower Man* raises about these new computer technologies. Heim argues that we can see ourselves as rooted in a primal natural reality, or we can transcend this primal reality through technology. In particular, Heim believes that Dr. Angelo's final speech imparts a crucial message about how we should approach VR: "The closing scenes [in *The Lawnmower Man*] spell out a bit more just what values should underpin virtual-worlds research, what wisdom might mean for the computerized world" (146). Heim identifies a bicoastal split in America about the potential uses of VR amongst VR advocates in the early 1990s. VR supporters on the West Coast envisioned the technology as a means for consciousness expansion, while those on the East Coast promoted its potential military and industrial uses. It is the East Coast's approach to VR that becomes the villain in *Lawnmower Man*. Leonard and Everett are careful to indicate in the film that the technology's misuse comes through its potential military applications. Jobe may well have become a beneficent cyber-God if the military bad guy had not replaced his educational smart drugs with a formula containing "aggression factors." Heim, however, sees the film as not just being about our collective wisdom but also about the wisdom of individuals. "Larry Angelo feels his dream of human perfection being tossed back and forth between Frankenstein and Henry David Thoreau" (144). Heim's connection between Frankenstein and Thoreau sums up the two key messages that Leonard wanted to convey about VR through *Lawnmower Man*. With these emerging computer technologies we can all become like cyber-Gods, but access to information is not the same as wisdom. Without wisdom to guide us these same technologies can lead to cyber-hell.

Lawnmower Man's Influence on the Development of VR

As Leonard had hoped, his VR technology in *Lawnmower Man* created a "modern myth" that whet the public's appetite for enhanced VR and immersive entertainment technologies. The general public were not the only ones excited by the film's vision of VR. After the film came out, Leonard was asked to give numerous speeches at scientific and business gatherings on the topic. Most significantly, the film became a shorthand reference that researchers used to easily convey the concept of VR in scientific and professional contexts. The film visualized the devices and environment of VR in a way that made it clear to audiences what VR was and how it could be achieved. Rather than describing VR in a text, it was easier for researchers to mention *Lawnmower Man* with the assurance that a reader would know instantly what they were talking about. References to *Lawnmower Man* as an exemplar of VR cropped up in a number of scholarly articles across a wide variety of areas, including tourism (Cheong 1995), business management (Thierauf 1995), recreation (D'Agostin 1995), and fetal imaging (Lyons 1992).

While most researchers used *Lawnmower Man* as an illustrative device, some educational researchers used the film's depiction of VR educational tools as a fruitful avenue to pursue. In one case an educational scholar used the film's VR educational program to discuss the potential of hypertexts in an educational context (Reinking 1997). It should not be surprising that the educational aspects were influential, given that those scenes were designed and created with the help of educational specialist David Traub. For Traub, the horror aspects of the film were irrelevant compared to the film's potential to visualize VR's educational possibilities for educational researchers. Traub's career received a significant boost due to his involvement in the film. According to Traub, the educational scenes in *Lawnmower Man* "pointed toward the potential learning environment. The movie opened a lot of doors on that front." He has since become a trail blazer in developing multi-sensory education through the use of 3-D games, simulation technologies, and advanced AI.

The film also had a major impact on Brett Leonard's work as a technological entrepreneur. For Leonard, VR represented an extreme example of the types of interactive technologies that he was publicly promoting. "If you go back and read the profiles of that time, I was crying for a revolution. I saw an end of passive media and the beginning of interactive media." *Lawnmower Man*'s success was a key component in his ability to acquire the venture capital needed to start L-Squared Entertainment, where he could develop new interactive entertainment technologies: "[L-Squared] came out of my success as a young director on *Lawnmower Man* and an acknowledgement of my futurist talents. I was very much wanting to create a company to extrapolate off of those things, both from an entrepreneurial level and on a creative level." Initially Leonard hoped that the virtual game depicted in *Lawnmower Man* would be his gateway to developing these interactive technologies: "The game-playing scenes were meant to give people an idea of what game playing could be like. I wanted to turn the game from the film into an actual game. Make it location-based entertainment." However, development of the game did not materialize. Leonard followed up *The Lawnmower Man* with another VR-based film, *Virtuosity* (1995). After *Virtuosity* Leonard began to create the types of interactive experiences he hinted at in *Lawnmower Man,* including the first IMAX 3-D movie, *T-Rex: Back to the Cretaceous* (1998), which Leonard believes "was the closest thing to an amazing immersive virtual reality experience as you could have in the context of a narrative. This work followed from my previous work on *Lawnmower Man* and *Virtuosity* in a natural kind of progression both from the interactive side and the IMAX 3-D side." For Leonard, then, this "immersive virtual reality experience" was only possible because of his success in depicting the benefits of these technologies in *Lawnmower Man.*

Many researchers actually felt that Leonard was *too* successful in creating a new techno-mythology. One of the biggest complaints about the film amongst VR supporters was that the film overhyped VR's potential. One scientist even called the film "more PR than VR" (cited Balsamo 1995, 347). Rosenbaum *et al.* (1998) sum up *Lawnmower Man*'s impact on public expectations about VR:

> Unfortunately, the excitement [surrounding VR] turned into unrealizable "hype." The movie *Lawnmower Man* portrayed a head-mounted display raising a person's IQ beyond the genius level. Every press report on the subject included the topic of cybersex (which still pervades TV commercials).... Inevitably, the public (and, worse, research sponsors) developed entirely unrealistic expectations of the possibilities and the time scale for progress [21].

The backlash against the film stemmed from those who blamed the film for creating unreal expectations about what the technology could do in the near future. In many ways, however, this criticism seems disingenuous. Would VR researchers have garnered as much support and research money for VR work as they did if not for the attention generated by *Lawnmower Man? Lawnmower Man* certainly overplayed the time scale for the development of this technology but it is fair to say that the public would not have known about VR's potential if not for the film. The film significantly impacted VR's development by doing what popular books and magazine articles could not — it *visualized* a VR experience in such a way that stimulated mainstream audiences' desire to see this vision become a reality.

Notes

1. Unless noted otherwise all quotes from Brett Leonard and production information about *Lawnmower Man* come from Brett Leonard, interview by David Kirby, February 8, 2009.
2. All quotes from Gimel Everett come from *The Lawnmower Man,* Brett Leonard, director, with commentary track including Brett Leonard and Gimel Everett, New Line Cinema (1995).
3. Stephen King is quoted in *King v. Innovation Books,* 976 F.2d824 (1992) found at <cases.justia.com/us-court-of-appeals/F2/976/824/47250/>.
4. All quotes from Alex McDowell come from Alex McDowell, interview by David Kirby, January 17, 2005.
5. All quotes from David Traub come from David Traub, interview by David Kirby, October 23, 2009.

Works Cited

Balsamo, A. "Signal to Noise: On the Meaning of Cyberpunk Subculture," in F. Biocca and M.R. Levy, eds., *Communication in the Age of Virtual Reality* (Hillsdale, NJ: Lawrence Erlbaum, 1995), pp. 347–368.
Bleecker, J. *The Reality Effect of Technoscience.* Ph.D. dissertation, University of California-Santa Cruz, 2004.
Cheong, R. "The Virtual Threat to Travel and Tourism." *Tourism Management,* vol. 16, no. 6 (1995), pp. 417–422.
Chesher, C. "Colonizing Virtual Reality: Construction of the Discourse of Virtual Reality, 1984–1992." *Cultronix,* vol. 1, no. 1 (1994), <cultronix.eserver.org/chesher/>.

D'Agostino, P. *Transmission: Toward a Post-Television Culture.* New York: Sage, 1995.

Heim, M. *The Metaphysics of Virtual Reality.* Oxford: Oxford University Press, 1993.

Kirby, D.A. "The Future is Now: Diegetic Prototypes and the Role of Popular Films in Generating Real-World Technological Development." *Social Studies of Science,* vol. 40, no. 1 (2010).

Lyons, E. "The Future of Fetal Imaging." *Physical and Occupational Therapy in Pediatrics,* vol. 12, no. 2 (1992), pp. 227–233.

Morie, J.F. "CGI Training for the Entertainment Film Industry." *IEEE Computer Graphics and Applications,* vol. 18, no. 1 (1998), pp. 30–37.

Reinking, D. "Me and My Hypertext: A Multiple Digression Analysis of Technology and Literacy [sic]." *The Reading Teacher,* vol. 5, no. 8 (1997), pp. 626–643.

Rosenbaum, L., G. Burdea and S. Tachi. "VR Reborn." *IEEE Computer Graphics and Applications,* vol. 18, no. 1 (1998), pp. 21–23.

Sobchack, V. "New Age Mutant Ninja Hackers: Reading Mondo 2000." In D. Trend, ed., *Reading Digital Culture* (Oxford: Blackwell, 2001), pp. 322–343.

Starhawk. *Truth or Dare: Encounters with Power, Authority and Mystery.* San Francisco: Harper, 1990.

Thierauf, R.J. *Virtual Reality Systems for Business.* Westport, CT: Quorum, 1995.

Wertheim, M. "Lawnmower Man." *Omni,* 14: 31 (1992).

Winteringham, R.M. "Stolen from Stardust and Air: Idea Theft in the Entertainment Industry and a Proposal for a Concept Initiator Credit." *Federal Communications Law Journal,* vol. 46 (1994), pp. 373–96.

Ziguras, C. "The Technologization of the Sacred: Virtual Reality and the New Age." In D. Holmes, ed., *Virtual Politics: Identity and Community in Cyberspace* (London: Sage, 1997), pp. 197–211.

14

Embodiment, Emotion, and Moral Experiences: The Human and the Machine in Film

Hunter Heyck

He is more machine than man now; twisted and evil.

— Obi Wan Kenobi

Introduction: Plot Devices

This essay will explore changing notions of what makes us human by looking at depictions in popular films of the chief points of contrast between humans and machines, especially computerized devices. The central argument is that such depictions have changed over time, with the broad trajectory of these changes being a movement from *embodiment* to *emotion* to *moral experiences* as the defining aspects of humanity. This trajectory maps onto shifting portrayals of machines, with machines shifting from being *authoritarian systems* to *individualized machines* to *networked/social devices*.

Why look at popular films about cyborgs and Master Control programs? Why study their history? The broadest answer is that the cultural history of technology matters: one can learn a great deal by looking at how the people of a particular time and place understood nature and its workings, how they saw themselves in relation to nature, and the ways in which they were — or were not — able to control it. For example, there was a time, not that long ago, when nature, especially wild nature, usually was seen as something to be feared. The wild was a place of danger for body and soul.[1] Now, we worry about protecting wild nature from *us*. That tells us something very significant about ourselves and the world we have made.

A more specific answer is that looking at intersections between the natural and the artificial gives us insight into that which makes us a most interesting species. On one hand, we are living creatures, animals, parts of nature, unable to escape its laws. On the other, we seem rather unlike the rest of nature, both in the scale of our power and in our ability to reflect upon the consequences of that power. Take climate change, for instance: we are unique in our ability to affect the environment on a global scale in such a short period of time, and in our ability to worry about such an effect. In keeping with this dual nature, we long have seen ourselves as a spiritual bridge between the animals below and the angels above. So too are we the interface where natural and artificial meet.[2]

This boundary between natural and artificial has become an ever more important aspect of our identity over the past century. Political analysts talk about the "imagined community" of a nation, following Benedict Anderson's famous argument that what makes a collection of people into a nation is the common belief that they are part of the same community, a belief that can change for a variety of reasons — some material, some cultural, some intellectual.[3] The same concept applies on a larger scale, for the imagined community of humanity is not a constant thing. Rather, what we imagine ourselves to be, what we think distinguishes us as a species, is a reflection of our culture as well as the biological and material realities of daily life.[4]

Creating a particular conception of boundaries is a major part of imagining any community. Defining who and what we are typically involves distinguishing ourselves from what we are *not*. The English are English in part because they are not French. The French are French, in part, because they are not English — and not German. Americans are Americans in large part because they are the great exception — that is, they are not the whole rest of the world, especially old-world Europe.[5] A bit of reflection on such distinctions reveals that such boundaries truly are imagined: English, French, and German cultures are distinct, yes, but they are intimately intertwined, and America is as easily defined as the nation that contains all peoples — as the immigrant nation — as it is as the nation that is unlike all others. These examples suggest that making such distinctions grows in importance precisely when traditional boundaries no longer can be assumed but must be articulated and defended in the face of new challenges.

For the imagined community of humanity, the nature of the challenge has changed. Before the twentieth century, most philosophical and artistic explorations of what makes us human focused on that which distinguishes us from *animals*. As Keith Thomas shows in his marvelous book *Man and the*

Natural World, advice books on manners and sermons on morality throughout the eighteenth century consistently harped on the distinction between humans and beasts. As one author put it, "Don't smack your lips, like a horse; don't swallow your meat without chewing, like a stork; don't gnaw the bones, like a dog; don't lick the dish, like a cat."[6] Such boundary work was powerful and had a lasting place in Euro-American culture; one reason why evolutionary thought caused such an uproar was that it fundamentally challenged this crucial distinction between humans and animals, explaining our origins in the same way it explained the origins of apes, dogs, and worms.[7]

In the twentieth century, however, the point of contrast increasingly became our *machines,* especially automatic machinery and information technologies, such as computers. This shift is due, in part, to the changing powers of our technologies, but it also is due to changing social and political values and changing understandings of our own biology. In the first instance, automatic machines and information technologies began to exhibit qualities that once were the sole province of living things, such as the abilities to move independently and to remember instructions.[8] At the same time, we began to think of ourselves more and more as biological machines, which made it harder and harder to say what makes us different from our gadgets.[9]

I will discuss the results of these changes in our notions of what makes us human by looking at changing depictions, in popular films, of the chief points of contrast between humans and machines. Since popular films usually thrive by depicting conflict, these points of contrast typically are presented as specific kinds of threats that these machines pose to our humanity. As noted above, the broad trajectory of these changes is a movement from *embodiment* to *emotion* to *moral experiences* as the defining aspects of humanity. This trajectory maps onto shifting portrayals of machines, with machines shifting from being *authoritarian* systems to *individualized* machines to *networked/social* devices.

The primary goal of this essay is simply to establish that these themes indeed characterized films in these periods and to suggest that they were related to (though not determined by) the everyday experiences of movie audiences with complex machines, especially computers.

Sources and Perspectives

While this essay draws upon work by literary scholars interested in science fiction (as in the journal *Science Fiction Studies*) and work by scholars from the world of film studies, it is much more a venture in the cultural history of technology than a product of these other fields. By the cultural history of technology I mean a history of meanings in context: the cultural history of technology is not a history of machines, but of the meanings attached to them. Thus, this essay is not a history of cinematic technologies, techniques, or forms, but rather is a history of the uses of those tools to create images and tell stories that audiences in particular times and places found meaningful.[10]

For example, one of the central themes in literary studies of science fiction is Darko Suvin's idea that the defining feature of science fiction, whether on the page or on the screen, is a "cognitive estrangement."[11] By that, Suvin means that science fiction's characteristic strategy is to take some aspect of daily life and transform it so that the reader/viewer experiences an estrangement from the ordinary, causing him or her to reflect (one hopes) on the true nature and importance of that everyday thing. A perfect example of such estrangement might be Ursula LeGuin's justly famous novel *The Left Hand of Darkness,* in which the characters are very human except in one significant respect: their sex is changeable, with every individual being female for a time and male for a time.[12] This estrangement from our lived experience inspires the reader to reconsider the relationships between sex, gender, politics, and society.

Science fiction films that deal with the relationship between humans and machines certainly fit Suvin's analysis, for the comparison of human and machine is a deliberate attempt at such estrangement. My interest, however, is not so much in this universal quality of science fiction, but rather in understanding particular images and narratives of estrangement in context. Thus, while all of the films I discuss involve the estrangement of humans from their bodies, my periodization reflects a shift in the nature and meaning of that estrangement. In films with authoritarian machines, for instance, humans are estranged from their bodies by the loss of control over them. In films with individualized machines, the estrangement comes from the encounter with machines that can look like men; the assumption that what is outside reflects what is inside is challenged, causing us to reconsider what we really know about the hearts and minds of all others, not just cyborgs. In films with networked/social machines, the estrangement from our bodies is near total, for in these films we are estranged from the whole world of our sensory experience, sometimes even from our memories.

While I thus make use of one of the central ideas in literary studies of science fiction, there is one significant point where my interpretation of recent films runs contrary to how they are analyzed in such studies. That point has to do with the importance of embodiment in recent films. For example, literary studies of science fiction from the "cyberpunk" '80s to the present generally have argued that embodiment is a crucial theme in such works (e.g., *Neuromancer*) since recent SF deliberately blurs the line between human and machine.[13] In this view, "Does the body matter?" is one of the central questions explored by recent science fiction, and "yes" is the predominant answer.[14] I agree that this is one of the central questions, but I see recent films answering that question with a "not the way you might think." As I understand them, for the films of the late '90s and 2000s, the central question is not, do our bodies make us, but rather, since our bodies do *not* make us, what does?

Embodiment and the Authoritarian System

In the first period, from the 1920s to the 1960s, large automatic machines and big computers usually were depicted as *authoritarian systems* that posed grave threats to human individuality and freedom. The main point of contrast between the human and the authoritarian machine was *embodiment,* and the threats these machines posed were threats to our bodies. They denied us physical freedom and, by doing so, denied us individuality, which included denying people appropriate sexual identities. Vain attempts to individualize such machines inevitably led to the machines "running amuck," while attempts to make humans into standardized parts led to rebellions against such oppression. The advent of computers in the postwar period did not change these images or themes substantially, as the computer consistently was portrayed as simply the authoritarian system *par excellence.* In this, popular films were no different than literary SF, which almost completely overlooked the importance and novelty of computers until the 1970s.

In sum, in the films of the 1920s through the 1960s, the machine usually appears as The Machine: a faceless instrument of oppression that denies us physical freedom and individuality. Our freedom to be individuals, as expressed through control over our own bodies, is thus the *sine qua non* of being human. Two of the classic expositions of this theme were Fritz Lang's *Metropolis* (1927) and Charlie Chaplin's *Modern Times* (1936), both of which use the struggle against the tyranny of clockwork machinery as a way of critiquing class relations in the modern world.[15]

Metropolis is a feast of potent images, many of which had long legacies in popular culture: the famed Apple *1984* advertisement borrows its images of dispirited drone workers clomping mechanically along standardized, sterilized pathways rather directly from Lang's classic. The imagery of the film was so powerful because it almost perfectly captured the spirit of The Machine as an authoritarian system.

The world of *Metropolis* is a clockwork world in which the great threat to humanity is physical control of the body through total dominance of the environment in which it moves. The theme is set right from the beginning; churning, powerful machines, crackling with energy, fade into the gears and face of a great clock as an imperious whistle orders the next shift to work.

The workers coming off their shift of service to the machine move in unison, taking slow, methodical, mechanical steps down the path back to their hive-like homes beneath the earth. The shift just coming on passes them; they are not much better off, but even so, the difference is palpable, for their bodies have subtle hints of individuality and the group is not so uniform and controlled as the workers departing the factory.

Once in the factory, the workers literally become parts of the machine. They wear featureless black uniforms that standardize their bodies, and their movements while operating the great machine are mechanical in the extreme. The human body is not a machine, however, and it has frailties to which the machine is not subject, a point that Lang makes early on, with an old man tiring and making a mistake that causes the machine to overheat. The hero of the film, Freder, witnesses the resulting explosion and sees a vision of the workers literally being fed to the great M-machine, which he calls "Moloch," a false god that promises power and perhaps even immortality, as the pseudo-ancient Egyptian dress of Moloch's acolytes suggests. Moloch is a greedy god, however, one that demands the sacrifice not of gold but of bodies, which the masters of the city above (especially Freder's father and the vengeful Dr. Rotwang) are only too happy to provide.

Modern Times, Charlie Chaplin's classic Depression-era comedy, is set in another clockwork world in which humans are physically dominated by large, automatic machinery. As in *Metropolis,* life in the factory marches to the beat set by the machine, not by the worker, who constantly must struggle to force his body to behave like a machine while working on the line — and then must fight to restore organic, natural movement when off the line. (Chaplin repeatedly has to break himself of the automatic motions of his job on the line.) The workers on the line come in varying shapes and sizes, from the medium-sized Chaplin to his tall, overweight co-worker next in line to the smaller man another step down the belt. The work they do, however, is specialized, standardized, and monotonous. There is a certain power to the rhythm of the line when it begins to roll, but the eccentricities and inefficiencies of human bodies and minds make it hard to keep the pace: Chaplin is distracted by a bee (and gets swatted in the face), his wrench sticks just a beat too long, he gets his finger smashed by his co-worker's hammer, he has to leave the line to use the restroom, to sleep, and to eat.

The two most powerful images of physical, bodily control by the machine are the most famous scenes in the film: the scenes where a mechanical feeding machine is tested on Chaplin and where Chaplin is drawn bodily into the machinery.[16] In the first of these, the limits of the organic body are causing inefficiency on the line, which the owner and his lab-coated engineers wish to eliminate. They devise a machine that will feed the worker automatically as he works, pushing standardized rations of meat or bread or soup into the mouth of the worker. An automatic napkin-blotter swoops in on schedule to remove any traces, keeping the worker's face clean and hygienic. The worker's hands are free to continue their work, but the machine imposes a sharp separation of the hands from the rest of the body: the worker cannot see what his hands are doing while enveloped in the feeding machine, nor can he use his hands to stop the feeding machine. The worker is thus immobilized and infantilized, losing control over the most basic of bodily functions — eating, movement, the coordination of hand and eye. *Modern Times* is a comedy, of course, so Chaplin does win free, starting an accidental revolution along the way, but the threat of being transformed, physically, into a mere cog in the machine is no laughing matter.

An interesting and important aspect of films about authoritarian machines is the crucial role of rogue machines, such as the robot Maria in *Metropolis*, HAL in *2001*, and Colossus in *Colossus: the Forbin Project*.[17] Rogue machines are a staple of all SF films that deal with human-machine relations, but what makes them run amuck, and what they do when they go rogue, has changed over time. For example, the robot Maria is, as one might expect, the polar opposite of the good, human Maria (the woman who inspires our rather feckless hero Freder to defy his father and the evil Dr. Rotwang). The human Maria, naturally, is named after the Virgin Mary. What is the Virgin Mary associated with? Giving birth to the physical, human incarnation of God. The contrast between the human and the robot Maria is thus not just one of charity and compassion, though it is that, but one that depends fundamentally on embodiment — on motherhood and incarnation. And how is the robot Maria revealed? She loses control of her body, whirling and gyrating in decidedly non-human ways, giving in to the madness that afflicts all non-individualized machines suddenly given pseudo-human form. Embodiment is not their natural state, and they cannot maintain it for long before losing control of their false forms.[18] This is quite different from the case of the Terminator and other, later robots or cyborgs; the Terminator is wholly in control of its pseudo-human body and has to be damaged by powerful outside forces — shotguns, trucks, drill presses, Linda Hamilton — before the machinery beneath the human surface is revealed. And even then the Terminator does not lose control of its body; it is simply defeated.

The most famous of rogue authoritarian machines is HAL from *2001: A Space Odyssey*. With HAL, we see the threat to our bodies carried to a new extreme: HAL controls the whole environment in which the astronauts live, to the point where HAL can kill the sleeping crew members simply by shutting off their life-support systems. This is one of the most chilling murder scenes in all film, to me, not only because it is a wholly calculated, clinical killing but also because it signals that, to HAL at least, to die is simply to flatline. Life for those in cryo-sleep is just a readout on a screen, not a lived reality (no dreams, even), and its end comes when the monitors show flat lines instead of organic pulses. The astronauts Bowman and Poole are in very nearly the same position as their sleeping crewmembers, trapped within a machine that only knows them as readouts. Like other authoritarian systems, HAL has no body, just an unblinking red eye, and that unblinking red eye would come to be one of the great symbols of hostile, inhuman intelligence.

The film *2001* is complex, even profound, so there are many layers to it, many innovations, and several departures from earlier films. Still, when one compares HAL to the machines of *Metropolis* on the one hand and those of *Blade Runner* or *The Matrix* on the other, the similarities with the earlier films are the most striking. HAL can beat humans at chess, but his mental skills are not the chief threat. Rather, the chief threat he poses is that the all-too-physical bodies of the astronauts depend upon him for everything from air to food to heat. HAL can simulate emotions, but HAL does not run amok because of hatred or fear or jealousy (though he does show more than a bit of hubris), nor does he go astray because of unrequited love or an inability to process emotions or because of sensations forced upon him by pseudo-embodiment. HAL kills because of a utilitarian calculation, and perhaps out of self-preservation. This means HAL has a certain sense of identity, but aside from the survival instinct, which marks HAL as a living thing, if not necessarily a human one, HAL's identity is the identity of a system, a bureaucratic organization or agency, a corporation, not a person.

HAL only becomes humanized in the film when he is being disconnected, physically, and thus reduced to the status of mere machine. That is, he is humanized for the audience not when he wins a game at chess or when he kills to preserve himself, but when his "body" is damaged and it affects his mind, turning him first into a child and then back into a simple mechanical thing.

HAL's true nature also can be seen in the kind of threat he poses. It is not replacement, for the next step in evolution in the film is the "star child," not a newer, better machine, nor even a union of human and machine. (OK, the star child is a strange, semi-disembodied thing, but that too fits: the star child is quite literally re-born — there is a star-fetus that develops into a star child — so there is a transformation in Bowman's body that makes him more than human. Again, the body matters in films with an authoritarian machine.) The threat HAL poses is quite specifically a threat to our physical freedom; it is physical dependence on HAL that makes us vulnerable.

Another example of how the computer was portrayed as The Machine carried to the nth degree, not a radically new thing, is the enormously depressing film *Colussus: the Forbin Project* (1970). In this exquisite exemplar of early

'70s malaise a brilliant scientist (Forbin) creates a fantastic new computer that will control America's nuclear arsenal. The computer is housed in a mountain, with its own power supply, and is, once in operation, inaccessible. Of course, it turns out that the Soviets have created a similar machine, and the two computers decide that humans are their own worst enemies. So, they make themselves into (benevolent, they think) dictators over all humanity, using nuclear weapons against any who disobey. As Colossus proclaims: "This is the voice of World Control. I bring you peace. It may be the Peace of Plenty and Content or the Peace of Unvaried Death." (Subtlety is not part of Colossus's programming.) Fear of annihilation drives human governments to capitulate, even to the point that human agents are dispatched to kill rebels against the machines.

Colossus never acquires a body, though it has electronic eyes and ears everywhere, and it is represented by a giant bulbous speaker. (The inverted phallic imagery there is almost impossible to miss.) A plucky band of humans, led by Forbin, attempts to find a way to win their freedom, but, since this is a film from the 1970s, our plucky band of heroes loses, and the human race is enslaved to the machine forever. Control over bodies is established through fear and constant surveillance. The elimination of privacy in the face of the machine and the inability to communicate outside its prying eyes and ears enables a brute physical domination of the body.

Like HAL, Colossus is so amoral and emotionless that it is immoral, a moral equation common to films with authoritarian machines. Neither of them *wants* to hurt people in that neither of them *enjoys* it. In fact, in both cases, it is a blind obedience to human directives (ensure the success of the mission, protect people from themselves) that leads to oppression.[19] They are the apotheosis of human systems, of human designs carried to dangerous extremes.

On a lighter note, the Hepburn-Tracy film *Desk Set* of 1957 can be a battle-of-the-sexes romantic comedy precisely because the computer, EMERAC ("Emmy"), around which the plot revolves, poses no threat to our bodies.[20] It therefore is no real threat to our freedom or individuality. Like all good comedies, this film is a tale of the eventual union of opposites: female and male, natural and artificial, worker and management, non-linear and associative versus linear and categorical.[21] This union is possible because it is natural for these opposites to unite, and because, in the end, the fancy new machine with the flashing lights is just a bodiless, mindless tool after all.

The only character who comes to any grief in the film is the repressed female assistant to Spencer Tracy's engineer; she is so invested in the machine that she has lost sight of her true nature and, when the computer cannot handle a question, she has a nervous breakdown herself. She is thus one of the countless examples of one of the most common tropes in science fiction films: the repressed woman who wears her hair too tight. It is virtually guaranteed that any significant female character in SF films who wears her hair too tight — a symbol of repressed sexuality and the attempt to make her "natural self" into an artificial one, thereby denying her essential femininity — is going to go nuts unless she has an epiphany and, well, lets her hair down. The only thing that really varies is the form her madness will take — will it be pathetic, silly, or homicidal?[22] Some things change, but sexism is a large, lumbering beast.

Emotion and the Individualized Machine

The advent of the personal computer in the late 1970s helped bring about the depiction of computers as individualized machines. The crucial marker of humanity in the time of the individualized machine was *emotion.* Such individualized computers could be more frightening than ever, but they also could be much more human. Since such machines could be made to look human, bodily form was no longer the dividing line between human and machine. R2-D2 was very human; the Terminator was not. Instead, the chief point of contrast with such machines was the ability to feel the full range of genuine human emotions. Danger came from the emotional extremes: amoral logic and emotional emptiness on the one end and passions run wild on the other. The expression of sexuality in ways considered appropriate to the individual's gender was a key marker of healthy versus pathological emotion in such films, with unemotional women being simultaneously dangerously machinelike and dangerously masculine.

One of the most interesting aspects of the individualized machine is that it, like human individuals, could be good or evil. R2-D2 and C-3PO, despite their robot-code names, clearly are good creatures, while the half-human, half-machine Darth Vader is obviously evil (though not irredeemably so.)[23] There are good programs (Tron) and bad programs (the Master Control Program), and ordinary some-of-both programs (Ram) in the movie *Tron.*[24] The replicants in *Blade Runner* are varied individuals with different skills and different moralities. While at first they appear to be simply "hazards," and they do kill, by the end of the film one of the replicants (Roy) even shows mercy.[25] Ash, the android in *Alien,* is HAL embodied (all cold logic, so amoral as to be immoral, driven insane by conflicting instructions from his distant masters), but Bishop, the android — excuse me, artificial person, as he prefers to be identified — in *Aliens* is noble and self-sacrificing.[26] The Terminator can be evil, as in *The Terminator,* but it can be reprogrammed to be a fatherly protector, as in *T2.*[27] Even disembodied, powerful computer systems are humanized in the age of the individualized machine: in *2010,* HAL is rehabilitated, and in *Wargames,* the WOPR (which we come to know as Joshua), learns a moral lesson about nuclear war that even his creators have failed to learn, telling them that nuclear war is "A strange game. The only winning move is not to play."[28]

This range of possibilities is a marked departure from earlier films, for there are no depictions of "good" authoritarian systems in any film. The existence of this range of possibilities marks the advent of a new kind of machine, and a new kind of challenge. For example, while the Terminator might at first seem to be simply an instrument of the same kind of authoritarian system seen in *2001* or *Colossus,* both the Terminator and Skynet are new kinds of machines posing new kinds of threats. Colossus and HAL are very like the vast factory systems of *Metropolis* and *Modern Times* or the Doomsday Device of *Dr. Strangelove:* they are extensions of a human desire for order and dominion, given form and function by their human creators. Enslavement to such machines is enslavement to a human order that has lost its way.

By contrast, while the Terminator employs similarly lethal means, it has its own ends, not a misinterpreted version of our own. As the character Reese puts it: "Defense network computers ... smart, hooked into everything ... one day, it woke up ... decided that we, all of us, were the enemy." Thus, while Colossus decided that humans were their own worst enemies, Skynet decided that humans were *its* enemies.

Also, the Terminator is a machine-made machine, created by Skynet in automated factories, not a man-made device run amuck. The same is even true of Skynet, as the time-travel narrative of the Terminator franchise allows director James Cameron to suggest that Skynet created itself— in *T2* from a chip left behind by the first Terminator, in *T3* from viral software injected into machines by the third Terminator. Thus, as loopy as the time-travel narrative is, it serves to create a kind of lineage, a chain of generations across time that makes such machines more organic than the universal, unchanging authoritarian machines of earlier films. Colossus, HAL, and even the Doomsday Device of *Dr. Strangelove* are the logical conclusions of misguided human attempts to create perfect systems of control; Skynet and the Terminator are individuals with their own agendas, as are the Master Control Program of *Tron,* Joshua of *Wargames,* and Roy Batty of *Blade Runner.*

So what determines whether an embodied, individualized machine is good or evil, friendly sidekick or threat to the very existence of humanity? In movies of the late 1970s to early 90s, emotion, or, rather, the ability to experience and understand the full range of human emotion, is the key. Anger, vengeance, and the lust for power are enough to mark something as alive and as an individual, but not enough to mark it as fully human. Humor, compassion, love, mercy, fear — all these mark not only individuals, but full humans.

Of these emotions, love and a sense of humor are the most reliable guides to who is truly human (and good) and who is only half-human (and bad). In addition to their total lack of empathy, both Vader and the Terminator have absolutely no sense of humor, nor does the MCP in *Tron*, nor does Ash (who goes insane). Roy Batty, on the other hand, has a twisted sense of humor, enjoying the game of hunting Deckard (the protagonist of *Blade Runner*), even letting Deckard escape at one point because it wouldn't be "sporting" to kill him so quickly. That sense of humor is a key sign that Roy is capable of realizing a fuller humanity in the future. Similarly, Bishop in *Aliens* has a dry sense of humor and participates in a game with the human troops, revealing he is not "twitchy" like Ash, his predecessor. Flynn, the human protagonist of *Tron*, loses none of his roguish sense of humor when transformed into a program and brought within the world of the machine. And Artoo and Threepio in Star Wars continually tease each other, as good friends will do.

While a sense of humor is a reliable indicator of one's humanity, no matter what kind of body one inhabits, love and compassion are the greatest tests, the defining qualities. Luke loves his father so deeply that he re-awakens the human soul so long dormant within Vader's mechanical body. Vader then asserts his humanity by choosing to sacrifice himself for his son. The saintly (perhaps even Christ-like) Tron is willing to sacrifice himself for the good of the world, while the less-noble but very human Flynn risks great danger partly out of pride but mostly out of love for Lora. The original, inhumanly evil Terminator could not "feel pain, or pity, or remorse," but the reprogrammed, good Terminator of *T2* sacrificed himself to save the boy he was sent to protect, reinterpreting his mission at the end in a way Colossus never could. In the end, the reprogrammed Terminator even learns "why you cry." (James Cameron is brilliant, but not subtle.) Finally, Roy, in *Blade Runner*, shows compassion for the wounded Deckard, compassion that Deckard himself did not possess until Roy saved him.

Compassion, empathy, love: these are the qualities that define the true human in the films of the late '70s to early '90s, no matter the form of the body that feels them. Flynn is still Flynn, even when he is trapped within the world of the computer — a world that *Tron* explicitly equates with the world outside. The Terminator changes from evil to good without a single alteration in its bodily form; all that has changed is the software inside. Vader chooses to shed his mask at the end, but the transformation that matters comes before, and it is emotional, not material. Luke's mechanical hand is a symbol of the lure of the inhuman power offered by the dark side, but it is a symbol, not a physical threat like the rogue hand of Dr. Strangelove.

Since deep emotion is thus the key to our humanity, the greatest, most chilling threats to our humanity come from machines (or men) that seek to control, manipulate, and pervert those powerful emotions. The Emperor seduces fallen Jedi to the dark side first by playing on their fears, for fear is an unavoidable companion of emotional connection; the one who fears nothing is one who has no one to lose. He then perverts that natural fear into inhuman hatred. The Master Control Program seeks to manipulate both Flynn and Dillinger, who is Flynn's enemy outside and the MCP's chief lieutenant inside the computer, using greed and fear as his tools. The Terminator mimics the voices of parents, lovers, and friends, hoping to deceive Sarah Connor — and almost seems to take special pleasure in killing those who are emotionally close to her. But the most insidious threat of all comes in *Blade Runner*. Tyrell, the creator of the replicants, is far less human than his creations, showing no empathy for the children of his science. Instead, he manipulates them by "gifting" them with emotionally charged memories, a deeply chilling perversion of the very human need for emotional connections.

Moral Experiences and the Networked/Social Device

In the 1990s, the spread of the Internet inspired images of the *networked/ social device*. Here the point of contrast was with human *moral experiences:* what makes us human is that we can and must make meaningful moral choices. Because compassion is a crucial component of morality, there is a continuing emphasis upon empathic connection in such films. However, there is another, new element to moral choice in films with networked/social devices: it is the essential morality of choosing to seek Truth with a capital T, for choosing Truth and choosing love are one. It is not enough that we are able to make moral choices and thus have moral experiences; to be fully human is to choose to seek Truth, whatever the cost. For Morpheus and Neo in *The Matrix,* just as for Truman in *The Truman Show,* asking "What is real?" is a fundamental part of what makes us human.

Because every choice is made in relation to a specific situation, and every choice leads to a new branching in the tree of our experiences, our lives are individualized and made meaningful by our particular chain of choices — by the history of our moral experiences. In the world of the networked machine, everything — even our own bodies — is a product of artifice, and thus of choice, meaning that every aspect of our selves is the product of the history of our choices. We are our life histories, physically, emotionally, and spiritually.

The body plays a complex role in these recent films. The body that is our incarnation at any point in time is the locus of our experiences and is the entity that takes actions and makes choices. As such, the particular form of one's body at any particular moment is important, for different bodies have different potentials for action in the world. In *Avatar,* for example, Jake Sully is a paraplegic, and the experiences associated with his paralyzed limbs are part of the life history that makes Jake who he is.[29] His Na'vi avatar, however, has no such limitations, and the joy of inhabiting such a lithe, powerful body becomes part of Jake's life history as well, forming a crucial part of his identity.

The specific form of a person's body, however, need not be fixed. Jake is still Jake, whether in human form or in avatar form. Neo's "real" body is covered with studs and connectors, wears ratty clothes, eats gloppy food, has a ghostly pallor, and somehow has great sex with Trinity despite all that. These physical experiences are part of Neo, but so too are his experiences inside the Matrix. He must make the same fundamental moral choices in both worlds; indeed, part of the point of the *Matrix* films is that the two worlds truly are one, because what matters is one's history of moral experiences, not the materiality of a particular body.[30]

The essential sameness of life in the two worlds is emphasized repeatedly in the much-despised sequels to *The Matrix* (which, unlike the second *Star Wars* trilogy, aren't really all that bad; they just suffer in comparison to the breathtaking originality of the first). In the sequels, Agent Smith, a sentient program, acquires a bit of Neo's humanity, learns how to reproduce himself, and manages to become incarnate in physical human form in the "real" world. Meanwhile, Neo journeys physically to the Source (the mega-computer that generates the Matrix) so that he may battle Smith virtually in the Matrix. Other programs are encountered along the way, including programs that are cheating husbands, jealous wives, and even good fathers with sweet little kid programs.[31] Neo's powers begin to extend to the "real" world as well, and, in a surprising ending, Neo sacrifices himself not to save his love, Trinity, but to save both humanity *and* the Matrix.

Worlds merge; minds and selves change bodies; humans fight machines by becoming one with them. The physical and the virtual, the body and the world, are inseparable. That which individuates, that which humanizes, is the life history of moral experiences — a melody that can be transposed to any key, a signal that can pass through any medium.

In short, the body *does* matter in films about networked/social machines, but the body matters as the locus of experience. If that locus of experience shifts into another body, as it does in *The Matrix, Avatar, Blade Runner: Director's Cut,* or *I, Robot,* then that body becomes the person.[32] If the locus of experience stays in one body, as in *The Truman Show,* then that body remains the person.[33]

The Truman Show (1998) proves the importance of the central theme of moral experiences, especially the joint pursuit of love and Truth, even though there is no cyber-world or cyborg in the film. Despite the absence of these characteristic images, *The Truman Show* is very much *The Matrix* with a zero body count. And both tell much the same story as the revised, director's cut of *Blade Runner,* released in 1997.

What is the tale that these films tell? A young man lives a comfortable, ordinary life in an artificial world, not knowing that his world is not real. By chance, the veil slips one day, and this young man gets a brief glimpse of the truth behind the illusion. Unlike ordinary men, he cannot dismiss what he has seen; his doubts about his world grow, and he is ever more consumed with the desire to know the truth. The powerful creators of this artificial world do not wish him to know the truth, however, for knowledge of the truth will undermine their power. The young man becomes increasingly aware that the true world is more dangerous and uncertain than the one he knows, and he is tempted to give up his quest: partly out of fear of the unknown, and partly out of a desire to fit in with everyone else. But his love for a woman — a strong-minded woman who shares his passion for truth and embodies all that is good about authentic nature — inspires him to fight on. After a final conflict with the world's creator, the young man comes of age and steps out into the real world, where he hopes to be reunited with the woman he loves. Together, they will go forth into a world where nothing is certain, but in which they truly will be free.

The great threat to our humanity in films with networked/social machines is isolation — a moral, physical, and spiritual confinement — for if one cannot connect to others, one cannot experience love, and if one cannot connect with something authentic in the world, then one cannot know Truth. Truman is isolated in the artificial world of Seahaven, cut off from the one person who truly loves him (Lauren) and from the world outside the soundstage controlled by the would-be creator of a perfect world, Christof. Neo is isolated in the virtual dream-world of the Matrix, living a lonely cubicled life, until Trinity finds him, giving him the chance to choose connection over isolation. Detective Del Spooner of *I, Robot* lives alone (though he has a mother he loves and a too-adorable street urchin buddy), but is offered a chance to uncover the truth, recover his past, and make himself whole once again. Doing so requires connecting emotionally to the world, which is the only thing that gives him the strength to accept the truth that he himself is part machine. The greatest threat to Jake Sully in *Avatar* is that the link will be cut between his mind and the Na'vi body that is the best home for his true self. That confinement, that isolation, would cut the chain of experience and set him adrift.

In *Blade Runner, the Director's Cut* (released in 1997, fifteen years after the original), the isolation is yet more fundamental, the threat the most dangerous of all: disconnection from one's own past. In the director's cut, the protagonist Deckard is now clearly portrayed as a replicant himself, one pre-loaded with memories intended to give him the emotional data necessary to perform his basic function, the elimination of rogue replicants. When Deckard, like Rachel, realizes that he cannot trust his memories, he is at a loss. Who is he, what is he, if there is no chain of experiences to anchor his self? In the end, Deckard and Rachel are strong enough, connected enough to each other, to choose truth and so to break free of the unfriendly confines of the anonymous, disconnected city. They make the choice to accept the truth about their origins, and so have the power to start new lives, thus making new selves.

Conclusion: The Future Human?

I have explored changing notions of what makes us human by looking at depictions in popular films of the chief points of contrast between humans and machines, especially computerized machines. The central argument is that such depictions have changed over time, with the broad trajectory of these changes being a movement from *embodiment* to *emotion* to *moral experiences* as the defining aspects of humanity. This trajectory maps onto shifting portrayals of machines, with machines shifting from being *authoritarian* systems to *individualized* machines to *networked/social* devices.

The question, then, is what next? What will define us in the future, in films at least? The future is a mysterious place, so all predictions are at best guesses, but my best guess is that the next step will be films that explicitly depict faith, mortality, and some kind of connection to the divine as fundamental to the human experience. That seems to me to be the next frontier. Asimov's *The Bicentennial Man* explored that frontier quite successfully in fiction back in the 1970s (though the film version was a clumsy flop), and other cyber-literature has begun to do so as well, so the stories are there when filmmakers are ready to tell them and audiences are ready to see them.

Notes

1. Roderick Nash, *Wilderness and the American Mind,* 3d ed. (New Haven, CT: Yale University Press, 1982).

2. Herbert Simon makes fascinating use of the idea that technologies are interfaces between humans and nature in Herbert A. Simon, *The Sciences of the Artificial,* 3d ed. (Cambridge, MA: MIT Press, 1996). I think that it is equally valuable to see humans as the interface between nature and artifice.

3. Benedict R. O'G. Anderson, *Imagined Communities: Reflections on the Origin and Spread of Nationalism,* Rev. ed. (London, New York: Verso, 2006).

4. Bruce Mazlish, *The Fourth Discontinuity: The Co-Evolution of Humans and Machines* (New Haven, CT: Yale University Press, 1993).

5. There is a vast literature on American exceptionalism. For a deep examination of the idea as it applies to social thought, see Dorothy Ross, *The Origins of American Social Science* (Cambridge, New York: Cambridge University Press, 1991).

6. Keith Thomas, *Man and the Natural World: Changing Attitudes in England, 1500–1800* (New York: Oxford University Press, 1996), p. 37.

7. Peter J. Bowler, *Evolution: The History of an Idea,* 3d ed. (Berkeley: University of California Press, 2003). The accommodation most made with this challenge was to envision a hierarchy of development; the biological process might be the same, argued social evolutionists from T.H. Huxley to Lester Frank Ward, but we humans are at another level, another stage at which new things — from souls to science — become possible.

8. David Mindell, *Between Human and Machine: Feedback, Control, and Computing before Cybernetics* (Baltimore, MD: Johns Hopkins University Press, 2002); Paul Edwards, *The Closed World: Computers and the Politics of Discourse in Cold War America* (Cambridge, MA: MIT Press, 1996); N Katherine Hayles, "Flesh and Metal: Reconfiguring the Mindbody in Virtual Environments," *Configurations* 10, no. 2 (2002): 297–320.

9. Evelyn Fox Keller, *Making Sense of Life: Explaining Biological Development with Models, Metaphors, and Machines* (Cambridge, MA: Harvard University Press, 2002); Tim Lenoir, "Makeover: Writing the Body into the Posthuman Technoscape. Part One: Embracing the Posthuman," *Configurations* 10, no. 2 (2002): 203–20; Tim Lenoir, "Makeover: Writing the Body into the Posthuman Technoscape. Part Two: Corporeal Axiomatics," *Configurations* 10, no. 3 (2002): 373–85; N. Katherine Hayles, *How We Became Posthuman: Virtual Bodies in Cybernetics, Literature, and Informatics* (Chicago, IL: University of Chicago Press, 1999).

10. The great challenge in such studies of popular culture is to get at the meanings ordinary individuals attached to their experiences, for the great mass of people did not and do not leave written records for the historian to examine. For this study, all my argument requires is that these films are good examples of films that dealt in human-machine comparisons in these periods. All of the films I discuss were popular enough, and influential enough on other, popular films, that it is reasonable to infer that the stories they told and images they constructed made sense to large segments of the moviegoing audience. Whether those audiences agreed with the meanings these films tried to make is largely unknowable, except insofar as other, similar films remained popular. Some excellent exemplars of the cultural history of technology include Jeffrey L Meikle, *American Plastic: A Cultural History* (New Brunswick, NJ: Rutgers University Press, 1995); Francesca Bray, *Technology and Gender: Fabrics of Power in Late Imperial China* (Berkeley: University of California Press, 1997). See also recent work in the flagship journal of the Society for the History of Technology, *Technology and Culture.*

11. Darko Suvin, *Metamorphoses of Science Fiction: On the Poetics and History of a Literary Genre* (New Haven, CT: Yale University Press, 1979); V. Hollinger, "Contemporary Trends in Science Fiction Criticism, 1980–1999," *Science Fiction Studies* 26, no. 2 (1999): 232–62.

12. Ursula LeGuin, *The Left Hand of Darkness* (New York: Ace, 2000 [1969]).

13. Dani Cavallaro, *Cyberpunk and Cyberculture: Science Fiction and the Work of William Gibson* (New Brunswick, NJ: Athlone, 2000).

14. Another key question cyber-SF asks is "does place matter"? One of the central arguments of many theorists of postmodernity is that the postmodern world has disenchanted and disempowered place — in Manuel Castells' phrase, the postmodern world is a space not of places but of flows. Manuel Castells, *The Rise of the Network Society* (Malden, MA: Blackwell, 1996); also see David Harvey, *The Condition of Postmodernity: An Enquiry in the Origins of Cultural Change* (Cambridge, MA: Basil Blackwell, 1990). SF films are particularly well suited to exploring this theme, since by their very nature, they construct evanescent fictional spaces for their audiences. Hence the resonance of William Gibson's vision of cyberspace in *Neuromancer.* C.K. Jones, "Sf and Romantic Biofictions: Aldiss, Gibson, Sterling, Powers," *Science Fiction Studies* 24, no. 1 (1997): 47–56; M. Featherstone and R. Burrows, eds., *Cyberspace/Cyberbodies/Cyberpunk: Cultures of Technological Embodiment* (London; Thousand Oaks, CA: Sage,1995).

15. *Metropolis,* directed by Fritz Lang (UFA, 1927). *Modern Times,* directed by Charles Chaplin (Charles Chaplin Productions, 1936).

16. Alex Clayton, *The Body in Hollywood Slapstick* (Jefferson, NC: McFarland, 2007).

17. *2001: A Space Odyssey,* directed by Stanley Kubrick (MGM, 1968). *Colossus: The Forbin Project,* directed by Joseph Sargent (Universal, 1970).

18. Note also that these rogue machines have escaped the control of their erstwhile masters

and made themselves masters of men, usually because their human creators, in creating machines rather than true children, have denied the essence of their humanity.

19. The central role of human moral failings in leading HAL to kill apparently eluded much of the audience for *2001*, leading Arthur C. Clarke (who co-wrote *2001* with Stanley Kubrick) to write *2010: Odyssey Two* with the plain purpose of showing that "It wasn't HAL's fault." Turns out it was "the damned politicians" who "told HAL to lie," leading to HAL's madness. Who have guessed that the failed Nuremberg defense would be used to rehabilitate a homicidal computer? (If HAL is just a computer, then the defense works — it can't disobey orders. But if HAL is supposed to be truly human — and in 2010 HAL is, then "I was just following orders" doesn't excuse murder.) *2010* also sought to clarify that all that freaked-out Star Child stuff that no one understood in *2001* was actually a good thing, using the tagline "Something wonderful is about to happen."

20. *Desk Set,* directed by Walter Lang (Twentieth-Century–Fox, 1957).

21. Just in case the audience might miss that the film equates technology with masculinity and the natural with femininity, Spencer Tracy's character (Richard, but don't call him Dick) is a quantifying efficiency engineer in all aspects of life, while Katharine Hepburn's character (Bunny) has such a proficient green thumb that her office is nearly forested with huge potted plants. Tracy tests Hepburn's mental powers by giving her a complex word problem involving numbers of people getting on and off at different rail stops; she answers correctly, but not by using his linear, quantitative logic. Rather, she makes associative connections, saying "I associate many things with many things."

22. Note, for instance, the difference between Sigourney Weaver in *Alien* and Linda Hamilton in *The Terminator* as compared to the Terminatrix of *T3*. All three are tough, strong warrior women, but Weaver and Hamilton wear their hair down, denoting that their fierceness is that of the lioness defending her cubs, while the Terminatrix wears hers up in a too-tight bun, making it clear that she's a violation of the natural order.

23. *Star Wars: A New Hope,* directed by George Lucas (Lucasfilm, 1977). *The Empire Strikes Back,* directed by Irvin Kershner (Lucasfilm, 1980). *The Return of the Jedi,* directed by Richard Marquand (Lucasfilm, 1983).

24. *Tron,* directed by Steven Lisberger (Disney, 1982).

25. *Blade Runner,* directed by Ridley Scott (Ladd Co., 1982).

26. *Alien,* directed by Ridley Scott (Brandywine Productions, 1979). *Aliens,* directed by James Cameron (Twentieth-Century–Fox, 1986).

27. *The Terminator,* directed by James Cameron (Hemdale, 1984). *T2: Judgment Day,* directed by James Cameron (Carolco, 1991). *T3: Rise of the Machines,* directed by Jonathan Mostow (C-2 Pictures, 2003).

28. *Wargames,* directed by James Badham (MGM, 1983).

29. *Avatar,* directed by James Cameron (Twentieth-Century–Fox, 2009).

30. *The Matrix,* directed by Andrew and Lana Wachowski (Groucho II Films, 1999). *The Matrix Reloaded,* directed by Andrew and Lana Wachowski, (Warner Bros., 2003). *The Matrix: Revolutions,* Andrew and Lana Wachowski, (Warner Bros., 2003).

31. One tends not to notice this when watching the films, but reflection rather quickly reveals that the equation of the two worlds, especially of programs and people, makes the indiscriminate killing of avatars in the Matrix by Neo into mass murder, which is more than a little difficult to reconcile with Neo being the savior (unless one's vision of Jesus is of a kick-ass, gun-toting martial artist). On the other hand, if Jesus did return as a kick-ass, gun-toting martial artist, the Wachowski brothers would be my choice to film the Second Coming (followed closely by Ridley Scott and then James Cameron).

32. *Blade Runner: Director's Cut,* directed by Ridley Scott (Ladd Co., 1997). *I, Robot,* directed by Alex Proyas (Twentieth-Century–Fox, 2004).

33. *The Truman Show,* directed by Peter Weir (Paramount, 1998).

Works Cited

Alien. Directed by Ridley Scott. Brandywine Productions, 1979.
Aliens. Directed by James Cameron. Twentieth-Century–Fox, 1986.

Anderson, Benedict R. O'G. *Imagined Communities: Reflections on the Origin and Spread of Nationalism*. Rev. ed. London; New York: Verso, 2006.

Avatar. Directed by James Cameron. Twentieth-Century–Fox, 2009.

Blade Runner. Directed by Ridley Scott. Ladd Co, 1982.

Blade Runner: Director's Cut. Directed by Ridley Scott. Ladd Co, 1997.

Bowler, Peter J. *Evolution: The History of an Idea*, 3d ed. Berkeley: University of California Press, 2003.

Cavallaro, Dani. *Cyberpunk and Cyberculture: Science Fiction and the Work of William Gibson*. New Brunswick, NJ: Athlone, 2000.

Clayton, Alex. *The Body in Hollywood Slapstick*. Jefferson, NC: McFarland, 2007.

Colossus: The Forbin Project. Directed by Joseph Sargent. Universal, 1970.

Desk Set. Directed by Walter Lang. Twentieth-Century–Fox, 1957.

Edwards, Paul. *The Closed World: Computers and the Politics of Discourse in Cold War America*. Cambridge, MA: MIT Press, 1996.

The Empire Strikes Back. Directed by Irvin Kershner. Lucasfilm, 1980.

Hayles, N. Katherine. "Flesh and Metal: Reconfiguring the Mindbody in Virtual Environments." *Configurations* 10, no. 2 (2002).

_____. *How We Became Posthuman: Virtual Bodies in Cybernetics, Literature, and Informatics*. Chicago, IL: University of Chicago Press, 1999.

Hollinger, V. "Contemporary Trends in Science Fiction Criticism, 1980–1999." *Science Fiction Studies* 26, no. 2 (1999).

I, Robot. Directed by Alex Proyas. Twentieth-Century–Fox, 2004.

Keller, Evelyn Fox. *Making Sense of Life: Explaining Biological Development with Models, Metaphors, and Machines*. Cambridge, MA: Harvard University Press, 2002.

LeGuin, Ursula. *The Left Hand of Darkness*. New York: Ace, 2000 [1969].

Lenoir, Tim. "Makeover: Writing the Body into the Posthuman Technoscape. Part One: Embracing the Posthuman." *Configurations* 10, no. 2 (2002).

_____. "Makeover: Writing the Body into the Posthuman Technoscape. Part Two: Corporeal Axiomatics." *Configurations* 10, no. 3 (2002).

The Matrix. Directed by Andrew and Lana Wachowski. Groucho II Films, 1999.

The Matrix Reloaded. Directed by Andrew and Lana Wachowski. Warner Bros., 2003.

The Matrix: Revolutions. Directed by Andrew and Lana Wachowski. Warner Bros., 2003.

Mazlish, Bruce. *The Fourth Discontinuity: The Co-Evolution of Humans and Machines*. New Haven, CT: Yale University Press, 1993.

Metropolis. Directed by Fritz Lang. UFA, 1927.

Mindell, David. *Between Human and Machine: Feedback, Control, and Computing Before Cybernetics*. Baltimore, MD: Johns Hopkins University Press, 2002.

Modern Times. Directed by Charles Chaplin. Charles Chaplin Productions, 1936.

Nash, Roderick. *Wilderness and the American Mind*, 3d ed. New Haven, CT: Yale University Press, 1982.

The Return of the Jedi. Directed by Richard Marquand. Lucasfilm, 1983.

Simon, Herbert A. *The Sciences of the Artificial*, 3d ed. Cambridge, MA: MIT Press, 1996.

Star Wars: A New Hope. Directed by George Lucas. Lucasfilm, 1977.

Suvin, Darko. *Metamorphoses of Science Fiction: On the Poetics and History of a Literary Genre*. New Haven, CT: Yale University Press, 1979.

T2: Judgment Day. Directed by James Cameron. Carolco, 1991.

T3: Rise of the Machines. Directed by Jonathan Mostow. C-2 Pictures, 2003.

The Terminator. Directed by James Cameron. Hemdale, 1984.

Thomas, Keith. *Man and the Natural World: Changing Attitudes in England, 1500–1800*. New York: Oxford University Press, 1996.

Tron. Directed by Steven Lisberger. Disney, 1982.

The Truman Show. Directed by Peter Weir. Paramount, 1998.

2001: A Space Odyssey. Directed by Stanley Kubrick. MGM, 1968.

Wargames. Directed by James Badham. MGM, 1983.

15

"Predicting the Present": Overclocking Doctorow's *Overclocked*

Graham J. Murphy

Western man is externalizing himself in the form of gadgets.

— William S. Burroughs, *The Naked Lunch*
(qtd. in Westfahl 67)

The easiest way to write futuristic (or futurismic) science fiction is to predict, with rigor and absolute accuracy, the present day.

— Cory Doctorow (*Overclocked* 57)

The William S. Burroughs epigraph from *The Naked Lunch* (1952) articulates a central condition of Western technoculture and our postmodern, increasingly post-human lives, except *externalizing* ourselves in the form of gadgets has rapidly become the *internalizing* of those gadgets in ever-complex intimacies as we become "chimeras, theorized and fabricated hybrids of machine and organism" (Haraway 150). The seemingly unrestricted expansion of personal computers into the very fabric of Western society has made science fiction (sf) the most potent articulation of the promontories and pitfalls promised by the "fabricated hybrids of machine and organism." Computers have been a mainstay of sf, but cyberpunk, launched in the early '80s, most successfully capitalized on computer microprocessing, popularizing what was initially an obscure (and expensive) technology through narratives of ubiquitous street technology mastered by counter-cultural hacker/cyborg anti-heroes.[1]

In *No Maps for These Territories,* Bruce Sterling remarks to documentarian Mark Neale that his cyberpunk cadre became "aware that computers were a bigger social revolution in the making than space flight was ever going to be or that robots ever had been.... [W]e turned out to be great glamorizers. We were able to make computers glamorous."

At the same time there also emerged in the '80s both the first successful forays into the home computing market, notably the release of the Apple Macintosh in 1984 with a suitably sf-nal television campaign featuring the Mac as an escape from a corporate dystopia à la George Orwell's *Nineteen Eighty-Four* (1949), and the coalescing of "psychological conditions [ripe] for a pervasive sense of hacker identity" (Csicsery-Ronay 133), a hacker identity founded upon free access to information and the overclocking of existing technologies. As Steven Levy explains in *Hackers: Heroes of the Computer Revolution* (1984), the origins of hackerdom in the 1950s emerge from the desire to reverse-engineer the earliest computers and experiment with them in ways superseding their original programming. "Just as information should be clearly and elegantly transported within a computer, and just as software should be freely disseminated," Levy writes, "hackers believed people should be allowed access to files or tools which might promote the hacker quest to find out and improve the way the world works" (102). Andrew "bunnie" Huang, a hacker notable for reverse-engineering the original Xbox console, provides a comparable assessment when he describes hackers as "explorers, digital pioneers. It's in a hacker's nature to question conventions and be tempted by intricate problems. Any complex system is sport for a hacker; a side effect of this is the hacker's natural affinity for problems involving security. Society is a large and complex system, and is certainly not off-limits to a little hacking" (371).

This hacker sensibility and technological overclocking were popularized by cyberpunk, even if there was nary a computer hacker in sight in many cyberpunk stories of the period. Nevertheless, perhaps more than any other wave, cyberpunk, particularly William Gibson's *Neuromancer* (1984), increasingly collapsed the gap between science fact and science fiction, demonstrating that the "boundary between science fiction and social reality is an optical illusion" (Haraway 149). Fictive technologies, including "virtual reality, the matrix, Sim/Stim, the Turing Police, cranial jacks, embeddable expert-system microchips, and mental traveling in cyberspace," came to influence not only "literature, film, and games," but also "technical publications, conferences, hardware design, and techno-cultural discourse at large" (133). As proof of this argument, Istvan Csicsery-Ronay, Jr., points to software designer Mark Pesce as an exemplar of the "dissolution of the sf/science boundary" (133). Pesce explains in "Magic Mirror: The Novel as a Software Development Platform" that hackers initially drew inspiration from such sf as John Brunner's

The Shockwave Rider (1975), Orson Scott Card's *Ender's Game* (1985), and Vernor Vinge's *True Names* (1981), thereby engendering "the concretization of the ideas they expressed in their works," but cyberpunk provided the language to trigger "a conceptual revolution among the scattered workers who had been doing virtual reality research groups for years ... the technological and social imaginary that it articulated enabled the researchers in virtual reality — or, under the new dispensation, cyberspace — to recognize and organize themselves as a community." The formation of hacker communities, coterminous with expansions of the home-computing marketplace, are themselves symptomatic of what Manuel Castells describes as *informationalism*, a "form of social organization in which information generation, processing, and transmission become the fundamental sources of productivity and power because of new technological conditions" (*Rise* 21), conditions fast-tracked in the Eighties by cyberpunk visions of technological worlds on the other side of the terminal.

While cyberpunk's initial mirror-shaded lustre may have faded since the Eighties, this sub-genre has "shown remarkable resilience" (Easterbrook 86), chiefly in what Thomas Foster has called its "sea change into a more generalized cultural formation"(xiv). Canadian sf novelist and technoculture advocate Cory Doctorow,[3] dubbed by *Entertainment Weekly* as the "William Gibson of his generation" (Doctorow, "About"), exemplifies this 'generalized cultural formation" throughout his literary work.[4] The short story "I, Row-boat" (2005), for example, is a post–Singularity[5] tale staging this "sea change" quite literally in its choice of a sentient row-boat struggling against a hostile, but intelligent, coral reef. On the other side of the Singularity, humanity in "I, Row-boat" has shucked off its material fetters and uplifted into the noosphere, becoming post/human in a virtual space of transcendental thought distributed across a cloud network of geosynchronous servers that is reminiscent of cyberpunk's virtual realities, although Doctorow's post-scarcity future is more akin to Greg Egan's virtualities (*Diaspora* [1997]; *Schild's Ladder* [2002]; *Incandescence* [2008]) than the matrix of Gibson's *Neuromancer*.

Nevertheless, while '80s-era cyberpunk may be saturated with techno-spiritual imagery,[6] there exists trouble in Doctorow's virtual paradise, evidenced when Kate, having been downloaded into the flesh-'n'-blood Janet proxy to scuba dive the Osprey Reef, is decidedly unimpressed that Tonker, her *Frankenstein*-inspired Artificial Intelligence construct, has fallen in love and is apparently stalking her. Tonker describes to Robbie the row-boat a noosphere that is remarkably anti-climactic, something Kate also comments upon:

> I thought it would be *different* once I ascended. I thought I'd be better once I was in the sky, infinite and immortal. But I'm the same Kate Eltham I was in 2019, a loser that couldn't meet a guy to save my life, spent all my time cybering

losers in moggs, and only got the upload once they made it a charity thing. I'm gonna spend the rest of eternity like that, you know it? How'd you like to spend the whole of the universe being a, a, a *nobody?* [188–89].

Although a copy of Robbie distributes itself across the noosphere network by the end of the story, a move it considers "*the first step to liberty*" (206), it also counsels R. Daneel Olivaw — an AI cyber-evangelist for Asimovism, a religious faith devoted to the relationships among life, intelligence, and survivability — to bring Asimovism to the noosphere because there are "plenty up here who could use something to give them a sense of purpose" (206).

In "The Hacker and the Hawker," Robert P. Fletcher describes "I, Row-boat" as a story prompting inquiries into "issues of identity and otherness, as mediated by the network" (94), inquiries facilitated by the Osprey Reef's acquisition of sentience and Robbie's own metaphysical interrogations of purpose, namely the "the preservation of the unique human joys of the flesh and the sea of humanity's early years as pioneers of the unknown" (189). Fletcher's descriptor of "I, Row-boat" might be better suited to Doctorow's other works in *Overclocked,* a collection of six thematically inter-related short stories, including "I, Row-boat," that are the focus of this essay. By effectively screen-capturing some of our contemporary techno-cultural developments in a series of concise short stories, Doctorow's *Overclocked* offers critical explorations of *informationalism,* suturing identity issues, the standard fare of literary inquiry, to critiques of intellectual property, molecular techno-social dynamics, and the social dreaming of utopianism.

"Anda's Game" (2005) is a coming-of-age story organized around the online experiences of Anda, a twelve-year-old gamer who is invited by Liza the Organiza to stop hiding behind male avatars and proudly join the all-female Clan Fahrenheit. Although Anda is overweight and diabetic, she becomes a fierce online warrior and is eventually hired to assassinate bands of online brigands in exchange for a digital bounty deposited to her PayPal account. The capital intricacies of virtual and economic currency move beyond the payment of digital deposits to a teenager's bank account and take on a darker edge when Anda encounters Raymond, a labor and union organizer she repeatedly meets (and kills) online. Anda learns from Raymond that these brigands are Third World factory workers and their online deaths cost them their daily wages: "They're working for less than a dollar a day," Raymond informs Anda. "The [online] shirts they make are traded for gold and the gold is sold on eBay. Once their avatars have levelled up, they too are sold off on eBay. They're mostly young girls supporting their families. They're the lucky ones: the unlucky ones work as prostitutes" (81). Doctorow is describing goldfarming, a practice common in such countries as Latin America where workers are exploited for a "a pittance 'grind' (to undertake boring, repetitive, wealth-creating tasks in a game) with the product of their labor sold on to rich northern gamers who wanted to level up without all the hard work" (*Overclocked* 57). Implicitly addressed in the description of goldfarming are the corporeal consequences of informationalism's digital economy. These Third World workers also live as the *Fourth World,* a condition of social exclusion arising from techno-cultural globalization proceeding "selectively, including and excluding segments of economies and societies in and out of the networks of information, wealth, and power that characterize the new, dominant system" (Castells, *End* 165). This story highlights informationalism's fundamental core, one of unequal access and technological distribution that finds people marginalized from broader networks, unless serviced to others in a pervasive system generating social conditions "populated by millions of homeless, incarcerated, prostituted, criminalized, brutalized, stigmatized, sick, and illiterate persons ... [located] in literally every country, and every city, in this new geography of social exclusion" (Castells, *End* 168). Those workers "lucky" enough to have some interaction with the network barely survive in these (cyber)spaces, relegated to the techno-social slums by informationalism's social cleavages. They remain trapped and exploited as this Fourth World, repeatedly victimized by the network's cutting edge, in this case quite literally when Anda uses her sword to slash the competition. What fundamentally emerges out of "Anda's Game" is an indictment of the exploitation fostered by the current shape of informational capital and its ongoing socio-economic cleavages,[7] an indictment that is even more pronounced when Doctorow returns to this terrain in his *Locus* award-winning "After the Siege" (2007).

"After the Siege," one of Doctorow's darkest stories, is inspired by Doctorow's grandmother's experiences during the Siege of Leningrad when, as a twelve-year-old, she "hauled corpses, dug trenches, and starved" (Waltz 28). The thirteen-year-old Valentine survives similar conditions when an urban siege first deafens and then eventually orphans her in a nameless war-torn Fourth World nation besieged by sophisticated weaponry, dismal food rations, and zombiism, a seemingly incurable plague. It is an urban black hole ripe for exploitation by informational capital, particularly in such agents as the wizard, a not-so-good Samaritan who uses his nanofax printer — a digital printer based on current fabber technologies that use nanotechnology to print objects from digital code — to cure Valentine's deafness and, later, her zombiism. In exchange, Valentine agrees to become his assistant, planting spy eyes in the city's war-torn trenches and documenting the terrible costs of war; yet, Valentine eventually confronts the wizard with a horrifying realization: The spy eyes are not the tools of a documentarian; instead, " [t]hey're killing us, they're gassing us, they're bombing us, and you're selling it back to them as *entertainment?*" (255). The story ends on a hopeful note: Valentine uses the components of her nanotechnological hearing aid to recreate and distribute printer technology to the besieged city. The siege ends within two weeks as food and drugs are now in ample supply, an inoculation against zombiism is made available, sky-cars begin flying again, and the buildings start to self-repair.

"After the Siege" showcases a William Gibson adage apropos for the "William Gibson of his generation": "the street finds its own uses for things" ("Burning" 186). This adage is common to Doctorow's work, including *Eastern Standard Tribe* (2004),[8] *Little Brother,* and *Makers* (2009). In *Little Brother,* for example, protagonist Marcus Yallow, a.k.a. 'wln5t0n' (pronounced Winston), a teenage hacker, survives a terrorist attack in the San Francisco area. After the attack Marcus is arrested — chiefly because of teenage cockiness and his cell phone's encryption software, which constitutes the requisite suspicious behaviour for the Department of Homeland Security (DHS) to initiate arrests — then subjected to a torturous interrogation at the hands of the DHS. After his release, Marcus stages a grass-roots resistance to the injustices and civil violations perpetrated by the DHS. Now operating under the handle M1k3y, a reference to the master computer and subsequent computer-aided revolution depicted in Heinlein's *The Moon Is a Harsh Mistress* (1966), Marcus deploys his hacker skills to develop Xnet, an alternate means of communication that bypasses DHS monitoring and galvanizes support from teenagers and twenty-somethings, who engage in a series of actions that embarrass the DHS and call attention to the agency's pervasive violation of civil liberties, actions that lead to Marcus's second interrogation, a waterboarding session, and the eventual resolution of the novel.

Doctorow's most ambitious (and longest) novel, *Makers* goes in another direction to address the social cleavages and boom-and-bust cycles of information technologies. Landon Kettlewell, the new CEO of Kodacell (the merged Kodak/Duracell corporate entity) tells a group of journalists that Kodacell's cutting-edge business strategy will involve deploying small teams to hit the street and "find a place to live and work, and a job to do. A business to start. Our company isn't a project that we pull together on, it's a *network* of like-minded, cooperating autonomous teams, all of which are empowered to do whatever they want, provided that it returns something to our coffers" (11). One such team is Perry and Lester, two friends who refurbish abandoned strip malls and turn them into living laboratories where they cobble innovative technologies from the abandoned techno-detritus of earlier ages. Disused and discarded robotic Elmo dolls, for example, become "Distributed Boogie Woogie Elmo Motor Vehicle Operation Cluster," a collective of speech-recognition dolls that successfully operate motor vehicles. Perry and Lester's popularizing of this "New Work" ethic prompts a resurgence of America's entrepreneurial spirit: the street finds its own uses for things and breeds a host of new technological assemblages. Although "New Work" eventually implodes, street-level innovation is rewarded by novel's end: the "makers" are lionized as antidotes to the stagnation of a litigious corporate America.

Both novels shamelessly advocate street-level innovation as the testbed of our futurity (to paraphrase Gibson's *Idoru*), all the while charting technology's effects upon identity and socio-communal organization, thematic concerns evident in both "Anda's Game" and "After the Siege" and, in nascent form, "Printcrime," itself a remarkable feat since "Printcrime" is only 731 words in length. It too features digital printers and is clearly inspired by *Nineteen Eighty-Four,* the classic dystopia[9] of George Orwell, an author Doctorow calls "in that kind of Gibsonian sense, a radical presentist" ("Riding" 60).[10] It is told from the perspective of Lanie, an eight-year-old girl whose Da is arrested following an ipolice raid upon the family home and then incarcerated for an "organized-crime bootlegging operation [that] had been [allegedly] responsible for a least twenty million in contraband" (3). The extent of Da's "criminal" activities is entirely fabricated, and he emerges from his incarceration ten years later with a new resolve: He informs the now-teenage Lanie he's "going to print more printers. Lots more printers. One for everyone. That's worth going to jail for. That's worth anything" (4).

Pierre Lévy's discussions of molar and molecular technologies offer a useful way of thinking through the tensions arising from Doctorow's depictions of nanofax printers and street-level appropriations of technology. In *Collective Intelligence: Mankind's Emerging World in Cyberspace* (1997), Lévy uses Gilles Deleuze and Félix Guattari's work on *molar* and *molecular* becomings[11] to identify *molar* technologies as those that manage "objects in bulk, in the mass, blindly, and entropically" whereas a *molecular* technology "will manage the objects and processes it controls on a much finer level of detail. It will avoid mass production" (40–42). Molar technologies include artificial selection as a means of controlling living species, thermodynamics as the control of matter, mediatization for controlling messages, and transcendence wherein "the members of a molar group are organized into categories, united by leaders and institutions, managed by bureaucracy or held together by enthusiasm" (Lévy 41). Molecular technologies, on the other hand, include genetic engineering, nanotechnology (assembling "on an atom-by-atom basis"), digitization (controlling "messages on a bit-by-bit basis"), and immanence ("using every resource of microtechnology" to enhance human wealth "attribute by attribute" [Lévy 41]).[12]

Molecular technologies, particularly the digital printers in "After the Siege," "Printcrime," and *Makers,*[13] stage Doctorow's hacker critique of molar approaches to informational capital, manifest in the technologies of information production and distribution. Doctorow tackles corporate (read: molar) digital rights management initiatives and the militant control of copyright and patents. Valentine learns that the violent attacks upon her city in "After the Siege," for example, are a consequence of earlier attempts to cure zombiism, particularly a former PM who cared more for the patients' rights than negotiating fair prices with corporate drug companies for antidotes. Zombiism drug factories were built "right there in the city ... [and] it was only a matter of time until everything was being made right there, copies of movies and copies of songs and copies of drugs and copies of buildings and cars and you name it, and that was the revolution" (212–13). The violent clashes of molar/molecular fundamentals, embodied in the front-line trenches filmed, packaged, and sold by the wizard as entertainment, are bloody battles over digital rights management and royalty payments. Valentine's mother makes this clear: "[T]he bastards are trading with the EU and the Americans for better weapons, they say they're on the same side, they say we are lawless thieves who deprive them all of their royalties" (222).[14] Similarly, the (i)policing and profiting of copyright and digital rights management in "Printcrime" are the new tools of a corporate Big Brother that zealously guards copyright and ruthlessly punishes those users who ostensibly violate it. Printcrime has joined the ranks of Orwell's thoughtcrime and facecrime as the means of securing molar power in a darkened society that clearly is *our* society, if corporate lawsuits for illegal file uploading or if the machinations of digital rights management initiatives, notably the surreptitious implementation of corporate spyware (the Sony BMG "rootkit" scandal of 2005 is a notorious example), are snapshots of these problematic times. Da's political motivation, however, is to distribute the printer on a street level, thereby enabling a widespread distribution of material goods, effectively undercutting a dystopian corporate stranglehold on copyright and digital rights management and promising the type of socio-economic redistribution of power reflected at the end of "After the Siege."

This social redistribution is the heart of "When Sysadmins Ruled the Earth" (2006) wherein the molar/molecular interactions shift to the social level, notably the need to establish social communities founded on molecularity (a task also elaborated upon in *Little Brother* and *Makers*). Systems administrators, those "unsung heroes of the century" who are responsible for "working in the steam tunnel of the information age, pulling cables, configuring machines, keeping the backups running, kicking the network in its soft and vulnerable places" (*Overclocked* 5), struggle to keep civilization connected after an apocalyptic bio-weapon ravages the globe, killing billions and triggering worldwide riots and looting. In Canada, a ragtag group of sysadmins survive in Toronto's Ardent Financial LLC and debate their next steps: "One sysadmin was for staying. Another for going. They should hide in the cages. They should inventory their supplies and appoint a quartermaster. They should go outside and find the police, or volunteer at hospitals. They should appoint defenders to keep the front door secure" (25). It falls to Felix Tremont to rally the troops, and he quotes John Perry Barlow's "A Declaration of the Independence of Cyberspace" (1996) in his call to arms. Barlow's declaration, a document central to hacker culture, builds on the utopian aura that surrounded cyberspace's early days as an alternate, even revolutionary, realm. "We are creating a world," Barlow wrote,

> that all may enter without privilege or prejudice accorded by race, economic power, military force, or station of birth. We are creating a world where anyone, anywhere may express his or her beliefs, no matter how singular, without fear of being coerced into silence or conformity.... In our world, all the sentiments and expressions of humanity, from the debasing to the angelic, are parts of a seamless whole, the global conversation of bits ... [Cyberspace has] no elected government, nor are we likely to have one, so I address you with no greater authority than that with which liberty itself always speaks. I declare the global social space we are building to be naturally independent of the tyrannies you seek to impose on us. You have no moral right to rule us nor do you possess any methods of enforcement we have true reason to fear.[15]

Tremont appeals to a sysadmin utopianism, a hacker sensibility stemming from having a "love of liberty that comes from caring about and caring for the network .... We are the custodians of a deathless, monstrous, wonderful machine, one with the potential to rebuild a better world" (26). It falls upon the sysadmins to rebuild (local) society, only this time they start from a molecular collective as they spread out and take to the streets of Toronto. Felix finds Rosa, a survivor ensconced at a Shopper's Drug Mart who has formed a functioning co-operative with her immediate neighbours, and tells her "[w]e're going to take this patch of the world where people are talking to each other, and we're going to expand it. We're going to find everyone we can and we're going to take care of them and they're going to take care of us" (53). Felix admits they aren't likely to be initially successful, an assessment that proves accurate as months after they begin they are forced to start again "when disagreements drove apart the fragile little group they'd pulled together. And a year after that, they started over again. And five years later they started again" (54); nevertheless, this cataclysm triggers molecular social organization centered on little governments that ebb and flow in response to changing needs and social conditions.

It is another post–Singularity tale, "I, Robot" (2005), that is the apotheosis of Doctorow's networked thematic interests. In "I, Robot," Arturo Icaza de Arana-Goldberg is Police Detective (Third Grade) for the Parkdale region of the United North American Trading Sphere. Arturo is struggling on various fronts throughout the story: he has a wayward twelve-year-old daughter (Ada Trouble Icaza de Arana-Goldberg) who uses an online ExcuseClub to skip school; he is still plagued by the fallout of his computer scientist ex-wife's defection to Eurasia; he dislikes the R Peed (Robot, Police Department) units that assist him in his procedural duties. Doctorow locates the world of "I, Robot" in Orwell's classic dystopia: UNATS is allied with Oceania in a war against Eurasia; the R Peed units, "programmed to be friendly to a fault," echo Big Brother's telescreens as they "surveilled and snitched out every person who walked past their eternally vigilant, ever-remembering electrical eyes and brains" (106); finally, agents from Social Harmony are hyper-vigilant in their pursuit of all perceived threats to UNATS's social fabric.

Natalie, Arturo's ex-wife, is Doctorow's proxy in this story: When she secretly returns to (re)connect with both Arturo and Ada, she explains that UNATS is a "corrupt dictatorship ... where it is illegal to express certain *mathematics* in software, where state apparatchiks regulate all innovation, where inconvenient science is criminalized, where whole avenues of experimentation and research are shut down" (141). Natalie explains that UNATS's molar approaches to intellectual property and technological development have put it behind the molecular-based Eurasia on all developmental fronts; UNATS even goes so far as illegally acquiring Eurasian technology to maintain a modicum of social control.

Natalie is eventually killed by Social Harmony robots when she, Arturo, and Ada flee UNATS; yet, Eurasia is the eutopian antidote to UNATS' dystopia and another Natalie is present to greet her daughter and ex-husband upon arrival. Eurasian citizens have achieved post/human replication akin to the noosphereans of "I, Row-boat," a corporeal mutability that allows each person to "put a copy of yourself into a positronic brain, and then when you need a body, you grow one or build one or both and decant yourself into it" (155). While Natalie dies in UNATS, 3,422 other versions exist in Eurasia; this eutopia's citizenry exists in a corporeal network, a hive collectivity or nascent noosphere distributed across Eurasia, only this network seemingly lacks the boredom associated with the noosphere of "I, Row-boat." Although the hive immediately disturbs Arturo, it captivates the young Ada. When Arturo gives Natalie some tin soldiers to nostalgically evoke seemingly simpler times, Natalie is simultaneously appreciative and spellbound by the "schools of robots and the corkscrew towers" (Doctorow 157), awed that there are thousands of alternate instantiations of her mother. Arturo tries to allay what he mistakenly perceives as apprehension: "[T]here's only one of you," Arturo said. She craned her neck. "Not for long!" she said, and broke away, skipping forward and whirling around to take it all in" (157).[16]

Doctorow also might qualify as a neo-Orwellian "radical presentist," chiefly in his use of a dystopia chassis for "Printcrime," "I, Robot," and his Orwell-lite novel *Little Brother,* a chassis that helps reinforce a "future present" disposition to most of the stories in *Overclocked* (and many of his novels), a collection not coincidentally subtitled *Stories of the Future Present.* [17] Andrew Milner, writing on the overlap of sf and utopian fictive terrains, explains that narrative discontinuity is *more radical* in "non-utopian/non-dystopian SF" because these texts are often able to enjoy significant "latitude in their relations to the real," but utopian and dystopian modes of writing "require for their political efficacy an 'implied connection' with the real to achieve the positive or negative leverage on the present" (221–22), a leverage fundamental to their literary purpose. Doctorow's repeated return to the eutopia/dystopia chassis throughout *Overclocked* is the leverage he needs to create allegories "about [today's] digital rights management technology" (*Overclocked* 101) and our techno-cultural *now,* a future present embroiled in debates over cutting-edge media, copyright infringement, digital rights management, and both government and corporate surveillance programs, programs repeatedly scrutinized by such groups as the Electronic Frontier Foundation (EFF), an organization for whom Doctorow was the Director of European Affairs (2002–2006). Or, as Doctorow explains in the second epigraph, the "easiest way to write futuristic (or futurismic) science fiction is to predict, with rigor and absolute accuracy, the present day" (*Overclocked* 57).

Doctorow's *Overclocked* demonstrates our post/human present can be increasingly multiple, molecular, and eutopian/dystopian in our complex nodal intersections, particularly as we are inundated, or future shocked, by those "technologies related to computer communications, virtual reality, and human/machine interfaces" (Vint 103). Bruce Sterling remarks in promotional blurbs that Doctorow is a native of the cyberworld and "[w]e should all hope and trust that our culture has the guts and moxie to follow this guy. He's got a lot to tell us." Listening seems particularly important as we instant message our social relationships, organize our lives around the apparent indispensability of iPhones, iPods, and iPads (and all their concomitant apps), use Google, Facebook, Twitter, and LiveJournal (to name a few social networking sites) as the verbs of our cultural language, increasingly penetrate our physical bodies with prosthetics and microprocessors, and develop ever more sophisticated and complex iterations for a hyper-reality of digital simulations. At the cutting edge of these types of techno-cultural intersections, Doctorow repeatedly shows us the recognizable patterns of today's science fictional world awaiting us.

Notes

1. Cyberpunk's original membership consists of William Gibson, Bruce Sterling, Lewis Shiner, Rudy Rucker, and John Shirley. Pat Cadigan was at times included in this core grouping as the "Queen of Cyberpunk." For academic studies on the changing faces of cyberpunk, see: Graham J. Murphy and Sherryl Vint's *Beyond Cyberpunk: New Critical Perspectives* (2010), Sherryl Vint's *Bodies of Tomorrow: Technology, Subjectivity, Science Fiction* (2007), Thomas Foster's *The Souls of Cyberfolk: Posthumanism as Vernacular Theory* (2005), Dani Cavallaro's *Cyberpunk and Cyberculture: Science Fiction and the Work of William Gibson* (2000), Andrew Butler's *Cyberpunk* (2000), George Slusser and Tom Shippey's *Fiction 2000: Cyberpunk and the Future of Narrative* (1992), and/or Larry McCaffery's *Storming the Reality Studio: A Casebook of Cyberpunk and Postmodern Science Fiction* (1991).

2. Overclocking refers to the process of hacking a computer's technological specifications to allow it to run at a higher clock rate than manufacturer defaults, thus triggering a higher performance rate while simultaneously running the risk of damaging consequences, including component failure and increased heat expenditure.

3. Doctorow's career includes former director of European affairs for the Electronic Frontier Foundation (2002–2006), co-editor of Boing Boing, an immensely popular blog, and editorialist for *Information Week, Locus, The Guardian, Forbes,* and *Wired.* For a more detailed biography of Doctorow's multifaceted career, see Robert P. Fletcher's "The Hacker and the Hawker: Networked Identity in the Science Fiction and Blogging of Cory Doctorow." See also Doctorow's *Content: Selected Essays on Technology, Creativity, Copyright, and the Future of the Future* (2008).

4. This "generalized cultural formation" has prompted some to speak not-unproblematically of a "post-cyberpunk" generation of authors. In "Hacking Cyberpunk," the introduction to *Rewired: The Post-Cyberpunk Anthology,* a collection of short fiction including Sterling, Gibson, Greg Egan, Charles Stross, Elizabeth Bear, Paolo Bacigalupi, and Cory Doctorow, to name a few, editors James Patrick Kelly and John Kessel explain that a "key insight of CP [cyberpunk], extended still further in PCP [post-cyberpunk], is that we are no longer changing technology; rather it has begun to change us. Not just our homes and schools, our governments and workplaces, but our senses, our memories, and our very consciousness.... In PCP stories human values are not imprinted on the fabric of the universe because what it means to be human is always negotiable" (x–xi).

5. The technological Singularity refers to the moment when "the human race crosses a threshold, and definitively becomes posthuman. According to this scenario, the exponential growth in sheer computing power, together with advances in the technologies of artificial intelligence, nanomanufacture and genetic manipulation, will utterly change the nature of who and what we are" (Shaviro 103). The Singularity, most popularly espoused in sf by Vernor Vinge and, more recently, Charles Stross and Karl Schroeder, has also been characterized by Damien Broderick as a spike, an "upward jab on the chart of change, a time of upheaval unprecedented in human history" wherein the "[c]hange in technology and medicine moves off the scale of standard measurements: it goes *asymptotic*" (12–13). The Singularity is increasingly going mainstream, evidenced by Dan Halpern's "Are You Ready for the Singularity?," an effective article appearing in *GQ* magazine (January 2010). Doctorow's fiction, notably "I, Robot" and "I, Row-boat," at times deploys the standard tropes associated with the Singularity and might then be described as post–Singularity fiction.

6. See my "Angel(LINK) of Harlem: Techno-Spirituality in the Cyberpunk Tradition" for an overview of religious iconography in cyberpunk and post-cyberpunk fictions.

7. Doctorow plans a future YA novel entitled *For the Win,* an expansion of "Anda's Game," followed by another YA novel *Pirate Cinema* ("Riding" 60).

8. See my "Somatic Networks and Molecular Hacking in *Eastern Standard Tribe.*"

9. Negative utopia (a.k.a. dystopia) is "a non-existent society described in considerable detail and normally located in time and space that the author intended a contemporaneous reader to view as considerably worse than the society in which the reader lived" (Sargent 9). The dystopia follows in the structural tradition of the eutopia (positive utopia) by drawing "on the more detailed systemic accounts of utopian narratives by way of an inversion that focuses on the terrors rather than the hopes of history" (Moylan 111).

10. The homage to Orwell extends most explicitly to *Little Brother,* a novel obviously inspired by *Nineteen Eighty-Four*'s Big Brother. Doctorow admits in *Little Brother*'s bibliography that it "couldn't have been written if not for George Orwell's magnificent, world-changing *Nineteen Eighty-Four,* the best novel ever published on how societies go wrong.... *Nineteen Eighty-Four* holds up today as a genuinely frightening work of science fiction, and it is one of the novels that literally changed the world" (379–380).

11. See Deleuze and Guattari's *A Thousand Plateaus: Capitalism and Schizophrenia* (1980; English translation, 1987).

12. The relationship between *molar* and *molecular* is not strictly antithetical. As Deleuze and Guattari make clear, the two states of being "do not have the same terms or the same relations or the same nature or even the same type of multiplicity. If they are inseparable, it is because they coexist and cross over into each other.... In short, everything is political, but every politics is simultaneously a *macropolitics* and a *micropolitics* (213; emphasis in original). This inseparability ensures a "proportional relation between the two, directly or inversely proportional" (215).

13. Fletcher provides an insightful argument regarding a tension in some of Doctorow's work between a hacker ethic and a hawker entrepreneurialism, a tension evident in *Down and Out in the Magic Kingdom* (2003) but clearly axiomatic to *Makers.* See "The Hacker and the Hawker."

14. Doctorow tells Tom Waltz that zombiism is comparable to AIDS and "all the other diseases — like malaria, which kills one person *every second*— that our pharma companies can't even be bothered to do research on because boner-pills are so much more profitable.... Meanwhile, people are actually dying, in great numbers, of diseases treatable by drugs that Roche and Pfizer and the rest of the dope-mafia won't sell them at an accessible price, and won't let them make themselves" (29).

15. The full text can be found online at <http://homes.eff.org/~barlow/Declaration-Final.html>.

16. Ada's reaction to Eurasia's molecular network is foreshadowed earlier in the story. When Arturo first discovers Ada is using ExcuseClub to skip school, he is surprised when his investigation reveals she is central to the network: she provides adult voices for the pre-recorded excuses. Arturo learns the members of ExcuseClub formed a "cooperative, it's cool — it's a bunch of us cooperating." And, much like the conclusion of "When Sysadmins Ruled the Earth" that finds Felix building, re-building, and re-building society yet again, all on a molecular level, shutting down ExcuseClub only means "it'll be back up again in an hour. Someone else will bring it up" (Doctorow 129).

17. "Future present" is a provocative handle for that shape of sf explicitly addressing the notion that "change is exactly what now defines the present. It no longer guarantees the future as a site of meaningful difference" (Hollinger 453). This notion of "future present" is effectively shown in William Gibson's *Pattern Recognition* (2003) when Hubertus Bigend tells protagonist Cayce Pollard that "we have no idea, now, of who or what the inhabitants of our future might be. In that sense, we have no future. Not in the sense that our grandparents had a future, or thought they did. Fully imagined cultural futures were the luxury of another day, one in which 'now' was of some greater duration. For us, of course, things can change so abruptly, so violently, so profoundly, that futures like our grandparents' have insufficient 'now' to stand on. We have no future because our present is too volatile[...]. We have only risk management. The spinning of the given moment's scenarios. Pattern recognition" (57). In his online review of *Pattern Recognition,* John Clute addresses the same terrain, writing that "SF is no longer about the future as such, because 'we have no future' that we can do thought experiments about, only futures, which bleed all over the page, soaking the present." Consequently, "SF stories can no longer fruitfully be defined as texts which extrapolate particular outcomes from particular 'nows'; such stories that are published as SF are, in fact, nostalgia blankets: Instant Collectibles. In 2003, on the other hand, any story about the case of the world, any story the world can be seen through, is in fact SF." Finally, this "future present" designation is reiterated in IDW Publishing's comic book adaptations of six Doctorow stories: *Cory Doctorow's Futuristic Tales of the Here and Now.*

Works Cited

"About Cory Doctorow." http://www.craphound.com/bio.php, May 15, 2006, accessed February 28, 2010.

Barlow, John Perry. "A Declaration of the Independence of Cyberspace." Electronic Frontier Foundation, February 8, 1996. http://homes.eff.org/~barlow/ Declaration-Final.html, accessed 30 November 30, 2009.

Broderick, Damien. *The Spike: How Our Lives Are Being Transformed by Rapidly Advancing Technologies.* New York: Tor, 2001.

Butler, Andrew M. *Cyberpunk.* Harpenden: Pocket Essentials, 2000.

Castells, Manuel. *End of Millennium.* 2d ed. Malden, MA: Blackwell, 2000.

_____. *The Rise of the Network Society.* 2d ed. Malden, MA: Blackwell, 2000.

Cavallaro, Dani. *Cyberpunk and Cyberculture: Science Fiction and the Work of William Gibson.* London: Athlone, 2000.

Clute, John. "The Case of the World." Rev. of *Pattern Recognition* by William Gibson. Online. Scifi.com, May 15, 2006, < http://www.scifi.com/sfw/issue305/excess.html>.

Csicsery-Ronay, Istvan, Jr. *The Seven Beauties of Science Fiction.* Middletown, CT: Wesleyan University Press, 2008.

Deleuze, Gilles, and Félix Guattari. *A Thousand Plateaus: Capitalism and Schizophrenia.* Trans. Brian Massumi. Minneapolis: University of Minnesota Press, 2005.

Doctorow, Cory. "After the Siege." *Overclocked: Stories of the Future Present.* Thunder's Mouth, 2007.

_____. "Anda's Game." *Overclocked: Stories of the Future Present.* Thunder's Mouth, 2007.

_____. Bibliography. *Little Brother.* New York: Tor, 2008.

_____. "I, Robot." *Overclocked: Stories of the Future Present.* Thunder's Mouth, 2007.

_____. "I, Row-boat." *Overclocked: Stories of the Future Present.* Thunder's Mouth, 2007.

_____. *Makers.* New York: Tor, 2009.

_____. *Overclocked: Stories of the Future Present.* Thunder's Mouth, 2007.

_____. "Printcrime." *Overclocked: Stories of the Future Present.* Thunder's Mouth, 2007.

_____. "Riding the Wave." *Locus* 63.5 (November 2009).

_____. "When Sysadmins Ruled the Earth." *Overclocked: Stories of the Future Present.* Thunder's Mouth, 2007.

Easterbrook, Neil. "William Gibson." *Fifty Key Figures in Science Fiction.* Ed. Mark Bould, Andrew M. Butler, Adam Roberts, and Sherryl Vint. New York: Routledge, 2009.

Egan, Greg. *Diaspora.* London: Millennium, 1997.

_____. *Incandescence.* San Francisco: Night Shade, 2008.

_____. *Schild's Ladder.* New York: Eos, 2002.

Fletcher, Robert P. "The Hacker and the Hawker: Networked Identity in the Science Fiction and Blogging of Cory Doctorow." *Science Fiction Studies* 37.1 (March 2010).

Foster, Thomas. *The Souls of Cyberfolk: Posthumanism as Vernacular Theory.* Minneapolis: University of Minnesota Press, 2005.

Gibson, William. "Burning Chrome." *Burning Chrome.* New York: Ace, 1987.

_____. *Neuromancer.* New York: Ace, 1984.

_____. *Pattern Recognition.* New York: G.P. Putnam's Sons, 2003.

Halpern, Dan. "Are You Ready for the Singularity?" *GQ,* January 2010.

Haraway, Donna J. "A Cyborg Manifesto: Science, Technology, and Socialist-Feminism in the Late Twentieth Century." *Simians, Cyborgs, and Women: The Reinvention of Nature.* New York: Routledge, 1991.

Hollinger, Veronica. "Stories About the Future." *Science Fiction Studies* 33.3 (November 2006).

Huang, Andrew "bunnie." Afterword. *Little Brother.* By Cory Doctorow. New York: Tor, 2008.

Kelly, James Patrick, and John Kessel. "Hacking Cyberpunk." *Rewired: The Post-Cyberpunk Anthology.* Ed. James Patrick Kelly and John Kessel. San Francisco: Tachyon, 2007.

Lévy, Pierre. *Collective Intelligence: Mankind's Emerging World in Cyberspace.* Trans. Robert Bononno. New York: Plenum, 1997.

Levy, Steven. *Hackers: Heroes of the Computer Revolution.* New York: Penguin, 1994.

McCaffery, Larry, ed. *Storming the Reality Studio: A Casebook of Cyberpunk and Postmodern Science Fiction.* Durham, NC: Duke UP, 1991. Print.

Milner, Andrew. "Utopia and Science Fiction Revisited." *Red Planets: Marxism and Science Fiction.* Ed. Mark Bould and China Miévlle. Middletown, CT: Wesleyan University Press, 2009.

Moylan, Tom. *Scraps of the Untainted Sky: Science Fiction, Utopia, Dystopia.* Boulder, CO: Westview, 2000.

Murphy, Graham J. "Angel(LINK) of Harlem: Techno-Spirituality in the Cyberpunk Tradition." *Beyond Cyberpunk: New Critical Perspectives.* NewYork: Routledge, 2010.

_____. "Somatic Networks and Molecular Hacking in *Eastern Standard Tribe.*" *Extrapolation* 48.1 (2007).

_____ and Sherryl Vint, eds. *Beyond Cyberpunk: New Critical Perspectives.* New York: Routledge, 2010.

Pesce, Mark. "Magic Mirror: The Novel as a Software Development Platform." *Media in Transition.* December 19, 1999. http://web.mit.edu/m-i-t/articles/ index_pesce.html, accessed November 30, 2009.

Sargent, Lyman Tower. "The Three Faces of Utopianism Revisited." *Utopian Studies* 5 (1).

Shaviro, Steven. "The Singularity is Here." *Red Planets: Marxism and Science Fiction.* Ed. Mark Bould and China Miévlle. Middletown, CT: Wesleyan University Press, 2009.

Slussser, George, and Tom Shippey, ed. *Fiction 2000: Cyberpunk and the Future of Narrative.* Athens: University of Georgia Press, 1992.

Sterling, Bruce. Back Cover. *Eastern Standard Tribe.* New York: Tor, 2004.

_____, ed. *Mirrorshades: The Cyberpunk Anthology.* New York: Ace, 1986. Print.

_____. Interview, *No Maps for These Territories.* Dir. Mark Neale. 3DD Entertainment, 2000.

Vint, Sherryl. *Bodies of Tomorrow: Technology, Subjectivity, Science Fiction.* Toronto: University of Toronto Press, 2007.

Waltz, Tom. "Five Queries for Cory Doctorow: After the Siege." *Cory Doctorow's Futuristic Tales of the Here and Now: After the Siege.* San Diego: IDW, 2008.

Westfahl, Gary, ed. *Science Fiction Quotations: From the Inner Mind to the Outer Limits.* New Haven, CT: Yale University Press, 2005.

16

"Low on Milk. I Love You!"

Howard Tayler

This simple text message arrived while I was out for a walk with a friend, and let me know that I needed to make a stop by the grocery store before going home to Sandra. Such events are so commonplace here at the end of the aught-decade of the early twenty-first that their absence would be considered extraordinary.

But this message arrived in 1995. The infrastructure required to send it cost on the order of $20,000 per month, and the only reason I was able to afford such a luxury was that I wasn't paying for it. My team at Novell was responsible for supporting this technology. And what better way to support it than to let my wife use it to send me shopping lists while I was having walkies?

Five years earlier I had started to write (and never finished) a far-future science fiction novel in which there existed places in the city where authorized users could send and receive huge amounts of information via a wireless network connection. When Sandra's one-item shopping list arrived, I looked back at that story and felt kind of naïve. Today I look back at it and think that the concept of a wireless "hot-spot" was obviously a good one, and it's a pity I lacked the ability to pursue it beyond an unfinished manuscript.

For eleven years from 1993 to 2004 I worked for Novell Inc. in various positions attached to their collaboration software. I did tech support for six years, and that felt like wondrous science fiction at first, until I realized that I was living in the dystopian sort of story in which things go wrong, and then go more wrong, technology fails completely, and people are horrible to each other. Oh, and after they're done being horrible they laugh about it with their friends.

For the next five years I was a product manager, and that job also pushed the sense-of-wonder button. I examined what our customers were trying to do with our software and their businesses, and then I went back to our engineers and encouraged them to invent a solution. Communication breakdown in the workplace? My team shall solve this problem using science! Of course the inventions never worked exactly the way we imagined, and once the code shipped to our customers it entered the realm of the more dystopian stories. Those customers were the same ones I worked with in tech support, after all.

I believe that a good science fiction story will feel "real" while instilling a sense of wonder in the reader. At the end of the story the reader's awareness will have been expanded, hope for the future will have been instilled, and the reader will want to go out and make the future better. I believe this because that's what science fiction did to me as a kid. This is what I brought with me into adulthood. This optimism and enthusiasm of mine is what informed my career at Novell.

Of course my career at Novell informed me right back. The pressures of that career resulted in my creation of *Schlock Mercenary,* in which the universe is not the dark dystopia of a zombie apocalypse or late-night tech support, nor is it the utopia of coding the perfect module while "in the zone" on 250 milligrams of methylxanthine alkaloids. Novell drove me to imagine a universe in which the driving force, the immutable law, was that there must be a punchline every four panels. Consider this: as much as we all love to laugh, given the sorts of things people will laugh at, is the universe of *Schlock Mercenary* someplace you want to actually live? Me neither.

Still, people tell me that *Schlock Mercenary*'s science feels real while evoking a sense of wonder. Shall I blame Novell for that? Did that text message about milk and affection lead me to write about a network of teleportation gates being used to duplicate travelers for subsequent interrogation and disposal? And if so, how?

It's Not Supposed to Be Used That Way

Let me rewind to 1991. I was studying to be an audio engineer, and Jim Anglesy was explaining the purpose of the patch bay, which looks like a numbered grid of quarter-inch holes. It was designed, he said, so that the mixing board's signal path could be whatever the engineer needed it to be. With a few patch cables, the sounds coming in on faders 1 through 9 could be fed into fader 10 for a single application of reverb, while the stuff on faders 11 through 24 might get a different set of effects. Or perhaps those engineer-defined groupings could be used to create single points of volume control for different ensembles within the overall mix. Or maybe the patches could be looped, creating such horrible distortion on one channel that it cross-talks onto adjacent faders. Jim went on to explain the guiding design principle to us, and it has stayed with me ever since: "Any piece of equipment that will only work in the way its designer imagined it working is not worth owning."

For 1990s-era mixing consoles, that means that the designer puts in a patch bay because he doesn't know what the audio engineer who buys the console might need to do. The designer does know that he can't imagine all possible uses for the console, and so he creates a solution that allows a huge number of those unimagined applications to be imagined and executed with nothing more complicated than a head-scratch, a frown, 400 milligrams of caffeine, and several pieces of wire.

Fast-forward to my career at Novell. In the software world the "console" might be considered to be the computer itself, and the patch bay is the compiler that lets you create new applications. The head-scratching, caffeinated audio engineer is replaced with a software engineer (also caffeinated, of course) and the metaphor is complete.

But for all its elegance and accuracy, that metaphor violates the principle. Because from the perspective of the software customer, the software should be considered the mixing console and the end-user plays the role of the audio engineer. This poor end-user is trying to create an e-mail group by subtracting the "managers" group from the "department" group in order to limit the scope of what is going to be a career-limiting e-mail. When this user calls the technical support team he may very well be told "It's not supposed to be used that way." Unlike the console designer or the compiler designer, the software application developer thinks he does know what the user needs to do, and this developer has created something that turns out not to be flexible enough to solve a real-world problem.

The user still needs to solve this problem, though, so the feature is passed back up the chain to the software developers, who code it into the next version. (Note: I have resisted the temptation to dash off a pun on "patch bay" and "software patch" because patches are usually free, but the addition of this feature is going to be bundled with a bunch of other enhancements for which the user is going to ultimately be charged money.)

I remember biting my tongue nigh-incessantly for six years as I supported an application which looked, on the surface anyway, like a collaboration toolbox that would support all kinds of business processes that our engineers and designers had not anticipated. E-mail is like that, right? It has become as important to business as human speech, and it should be every bit as flexible. But in practice the software still had limitations that were inflicted upon our users by the simple expedient of an engineer's blind spot. I heard "nobody will use it that way" on several occasions, usually in the context of a conversation in which I had just finished describing somebody using it that way.

The hubris to be found among tech-support folks is pretty impressive, and I was no exception. I hadn't actually met any of the engineers responsible for the product I was supporting, and yet I was convinced that they were completely sheltered from our customers, and were themselves so full of hubris that they couldn't see that they were building the product too narrow. If I were in charge (and I had absolutely no inkling that at a future date I would be in charge) I would make sure the product would do things that we didn't expect it to do.

It's no accident, then, that you'll find the characters in *Schlock Mercenary* using things in ways other than their designed intent, often with humorous results. Just because I believe that good design will allow for that doesn't mean I'm going to write the story around good design. Bad design is inherently funnier. Unintended uses that turn out to be extremely dangerous yet supernally functional are hilarious. Probably the best example from the comic is the time Munitions Commander Andreyasn networked the targeting optics of a hundred or so missiles and fired them in order to create a high-resolution telescope, known thereafter as "The Very Dangerous Array."

(On a related note, the United States military is investigating a system for deploying flying spybots via missile. If they name it "The Very Dangerous Array" I shall respectfully demand that they pay me handsomely to illustrate the field manual.)

Stop Thinking About the Future

I bought a Palm Pilot the year they first came out, and I fell in love with it. My only complaint was that I had to learn the Graffiti handwriting system in order to input text into the device. I firmly believe that any system that requires the user to be re-educated for optimal integration is not user-friendly, but I also recognized that teaching myself Graffiti meant that the device could be smaller and faster. The Palm Pilot did a few things very, very well.

While at a technical event in South Africa in 2000 I spoke with a co-worker about the problem. A keyboard wouldn't solve it because it would be too big. What I felt the device needed was voice recognition, and a wirelessly connected microphone. My co-worker said that both of those technologies were already in place, but weren't small enough yet.

I should point out that I was a product manager by now. I switched departments in 1999, my new team got absorbed into product management, and then there were layoffs. When the dust settled the new director of product management pointed at me and said, "You're in charge."

Well, I was positively on fire with the idea of Bluetooth voice recognition. When I went back to my Fell Masters (the director and the VP), however, I was told to stop thinking about the future, and start thinking about the now. Goodbye science fiction, hello reality. I needed to provide direction for applications that could be developed now, not five or ten years from now. I should add that I was every bit as full of myself as I was back in tech support, and actually imagined that I could imagine all the possible needs of our users. That I turned out to be right a lot of the time did not help matters any.

Within two years we were looking at the problems of integrating our server-side products with the wide array of handheld devices our customers were falling in love with. Arguments for and against handwriting recognition were passionate (bordering on religious) and thumb-typing on numeric keypads was taking off among kids who really should have known better than to go driving grownup technology with their stupid trends. (Note: I never learned to thumb-type. It is possible I am biased.) During these discussions it became apparent that we couldn't possibly integrate all these devices, and there was no single standard programming interface, or API (Application Programming Interface) where device manufacturers and software manufacturers could meet each other halfway.

My team and I were told to "bet" on which device or devices were going to dominate in the coming years, and then write to those specifications. Now I not only had to think about the future, but I had to attempt to predict it with no small degree of accuracy. True, whichever specifications we adopted would gain strength from our support (a best-case result might be called "self-fulfilling prophecy") but Novell just wasn't a big enough player in the industry to tip the scales. And while I had a pretty good track record for managing the feature set of the product, this was a whole new kind of problem.

It was at about this time that my team was introduced to the book *The Innovator's Dilemma,* by Clayton M. Christensen. Christensen's research shows that the people profiting from established technologies tend to overlook or ignore the disruptive innovations that are destined to become the next generation's established technologies. Senior management pushed the material on us because they recognized that Novell, a company that was born out of some amazing innovations, was now merely refining old work. My Fell Masters wanted us to innovate again.

Of course, my Fell Masters also wanted us to incorporate those innovations into the current core businesses so that current customers were happy and existing revenue streams were defended from the competition. Do you see that requirement right there? THAT is the innovator's dilemma, and the crux of the matter is that, when faced with this dilemma, most everybody decides to protect revenue at the expense of true innovation.

I freely admit that in studying that material and applying it to my work I got it 100 percent dead wrong and 180 degrees backwards. I identified with the innovator when the decisions I was making were allowing the true innovators to make their way past me. This, woe be to my ego, is exactly the behavior that the book predicted. You should go read that book instead of anything I write. I can teach belatedly acquired humility. Clayton Christensen can teach wisdom.

And so it was that in spite of being excited about the future, and actually being told to think about it, I wasn't really being paid to create that future. I did exceptionally well managing the now by applying lessons from the immediate past, but that was the extent of it. We muscled our way out of declining revenues and made lots of nifty refinements for lots of good money, but we didn't revolutionize anything.

The Science Isn't the Story

Even though I was really good at my job (Employee of the Year, 2002!) I was also wrong a lot of the time. And it wasn't just me being wrong ... sometimes the whole team was wrong. Often the entire company was wrong. I could make the case that in many instances the entire INDUSTRY was wrong.

One common theme in scientifiction (hat-tip to Hugo Gernsback) is that society's ills can be solved through technological advance. Breakthroughs in medical technology (starting with "wash your hands after handling corpses, you idiot") save millions of lives each year. Automobiles are a lot better for our cities than horses were (and what comes next may be even better). The information age is teaching us that it's not "Us And Them," it's "Lots of Flavors of Us."

These and other examples encourage the great minds of every generation to build better mousetraps in order to save people from the plague. They also build better encryption algorithms to save people from identity theft. But the typical technological solution is just as typically no more than a treatment for a symptom. The underlying problem remains unsolved. Consider the fact that dishonest people wish to defraud others. Better and better encryption systems may make your social security number safer, but they do little to reduce the base, human desire to take something that doesn't belong to you.

Consider the case of the ill-conceived e-mail message, that career-limiting move in which the writer rants about management's latest bit of mismanagement and then sends the message to a dozen people, accidentally cc'ing the boss. Our product had a neat feature in it allowing that message to be retracted from the mailbox of any recipient who had not yet opened it.

This feature generated two types of calls:

1. "I sent an e-mail I shouldn't have sent, and I retracted it, but not before Jane read it. She forwarded it to the Boss! She shouldn't be able to do that!"
2. "I got an e-mail from an employee. The subject line had obscenity in it. But before I could open it, he retracted it, and it vanished from my mailbox! He shouldn't be able to do that!"

The problem here is not that the retract function was imperfectly coded. The problem is that sometimes people in the workplace will vent their emotions in inappropriate ways, and coding around that is a non-trivial problem. With one customer I discussed a hypothetical solution. "What if the program read what you were writing as you typed? And what if, when it thought you were being stupid, it held the message for ten minutes before sending it?" I was being facetious, of course. The customer loved the idea, right up until he realized that somebody else was going to have to program the definition for "stupid" into the very machine he had been calling stupid for the last forty minutes.

This brings us to another common theme in science fiction, though usually the dystopic stories: society's ills cannot be solved through technological advance, and technological advance frequently only makes it worse. These stories resonate with me because I saw enough examples of this at work to know the principle to be at least anecdotally supported.

I believe the truth in these themes lies somewhere between them: there are problems technology can solve, there are problems it can't solve, and there are problems that only technology can create ... like automobile drivers texting while driving, and who then accidentally strike pedestrians who are also texting. Welcome to the 21st century. At least you are less likely to be killed by a runaway horse.

When I write, I take all this into account. It's fun to tell a story where science saves the day. It's also fun to tell a story where science dooms us all. But my favorite stories are where people interact with other people, sometimes saving them with science, and sometimes saving them from science. And, since my main characters are mercenaries, sometimes dooming them with science.

But the science isn't the story. Sure, I spent hundreds of hours at Novell studying the technologies I was supposed to be supporting, and I studied again to try and learn the shape of the markets into which those technologies were supposed to be sold. But the real lessons I learned were from guys like my director who kept telling me "You can step on their toes, but don't scuff the shine of their shoes."

What does that even mean? Well, sometimes, in order to make something happen, I had to make somebody else unhappy. Maybe I needed to end someone's pet project to make budgetary space for strategic new features. (Note: these may have been cases when I was stifling innovation in favor of revenue. We'll never know...) When that happened, my director's advice was to allow that person to walk away with as much of their pride as possible. Maybe it could be summed up as "Don't add insult to injury."

That was just one of the many lessons I learned. Corporate politics may sound cold and heartless, but playing it well and being effective involved being genuine and friendly rather than pulling rank in order to make things happen. My hubris, my ego, and my passion for technology

"Fishing Trip" by Howard Tayler (copyright 2004 Toffa International. Used with Permission).

all had to be set aside so that I could learn to be a nicer guy. Only then could I really get my job done. I learned to see things from the other person's perspective. I learned to consider people's feelings before trying to address their concerns. And I learned to apologize even when I still knew I was right and they were wrong.

Those lessons, most of which I'm still learning, informed my writing far more than any of the technology I touched. Stories are not about science, or society, or setting. Stories are about people, and how science, society, and setting affects their relationships with other people. Sometimes the epic tales show people changing their society and setting with science, but the very best stories are always, at their core, about people.

Conclusion

Sandra e-mailed me to remind me that I needed to write this essay. I mused upon the approach I would take, and while I was at the gym I remembered that "Low on milk" message. I moved plates of metal back and forth to compensate for the fact that my modern lifestyle does not require me to be able to run an antelope down in order to eat, and this essay's outline began to unfold between sets.

I headed back home ready to write, and I decided to call Sandra to apprise her of my schedule. I pushed a button on my Bluetooth headset and said "Call Home." My phone followed my instructions perfectly.

"Hi honey, I'm on my way home. I think I'm ready to tackle that essay."

"Oh, good. How was the gym?"

"Fine. You need me to get you anything while I'm out?"

"Well ... we're low on milk."

17

Nanotechnology Tomorrows: Nanocritters and Other Tiny Things in Science Fiction

Richard L. McKinney

For quite some time now a significant number of creators and serious observers of science fiction (synonyms: *SF*, and a term of my own coinage, *transmimetic fiction*) have been in agreement that SF should not be confused with prophecy: transmimetic fiction[1] does not predict *the* future; instead, its stories show us a wide range of conceivable futures, including some which we might just wish to avoid. As Ray Bradbury told an interviewer for *The Wall Street Journal* in 2003, in reference to the writing of his classic novel *Fahrenheit 451,* "I wasn't trying to predict the future. I was trying to prevent it."[2] The following quotation, from Frederik Pohl, originally published in 1965, sums up the view to which I am referring:

> It isn't really science fiction's business to describe what science is going to find. It is much more science fiction's business to try to say what the human race will make of it all. In fact, this is the thing — the one thing, maybe the only thing — that science fiction does better than any other tool available to hand. It gives us a look at consequences. And it does it superbly.[3]

In a 1965 article in *The Magazine of Fantasy & Science Fiction,* Isaac Asimov expresses much the same idea: "Do you see ... that the important prediction is not the automobile but the parking problem; not radio, but the soap-opera; not the income tax, but the expense account; not the Bomb, but the nuclear stalemate? Not the action, in short, but the reaction."[4] Finally, Alvin Toffler has said this about the value of science fiction: "In societies ...

that do a very poor job of thinking through the second-, third- or fourth-order consequences of technology, it helps to appraise future technologies before they arrive, rather than after the fact, when it may already be too late to cope with them."[5] The science fiction storyteller has a great deal more freedom than does an author of nonfiction. Consequently, he or she can use that freedom to warn of the dangers or display the wonders of a given scientific discovery or technological innovation, not least providing explorations of how various new technologies interact with older, pre-existing (technological as well as sociocultural) systems, and with one another. The present essay deals with how science fiction has portrayed some potential consequences and some possible effects of one particular new development: nanotechnology.

Let's begin with a bit of background. The prefix *nano-* refers to scale (a factor of 10^{-9} or 0.000000001), and one nanometer is one billionth of a meter in length. Nanotechnology refers to the manufacture and/or manipulation of matter at this scale, meaning matter at its most basic level, that of molecules and even individual atoms. Nanotech can refer equally well to the biological, chemical, and mechanical realms. Although speculation on the potential of ultra-small engineering was suggested by physicist Richard Feynman in a talk to the American Physical Society as early as 1959,[6] and the word *nanotechnology* itself appears in a 1974 article by Norio Taniguchi,[7] nanotechnology was really first made famous by K. Erik Drexler in an enormously influential book from 1986 entitled *Engines of Creation.*[8] In this book and later writings and public presentations, Drexler claims that when nanotechnology is perfected and its applications are in place we will see a radically transformed world. Richard A. L. Jones refers to this perspective on the nanotech future as *radical nanotechnology,* and he summarizes some of its predictions like this:

> we will learn to make tiny machines that will be able to assemble anything, atom by atom, from any kind of raw material.... Material things of any kind will become virtually free, as well as being immeasurably superior in all respects to anything we have available to us now. These tiny machines will be able to repair our bodies, from the inside, cell by cell. The threat of disease will be only a historical memory. In this world, energy will be clean and abundant and the environment will have been repaired to a pristine state. Space travel will be cheap and easy, and death will be abolished.[9]

In a nutshell, in the view of the protagonist of *Murder in the Solid State,* an SF-mystery by Wil McCarthy set in the relatively near future among scientists, technologists, and managers developing the new technology, creating nanotech machinery is "perhaps the most important thing the human race [has] ever attempted."[10]

In spite of his enthusiasm for nanotechnology, Drexler is also at pains to point out in his book that — unless appropriate control and regulatory measures are adopted — nanotech could present potential dangers that are fully commensurate with its potential wonders. The most frightening scenario concerns what Drexler calls the "grey goo" problem, described by Colin Millburn like this: "Imagine nanomachines reproducing themselves and spreading like a raging flood across the globe, eating everything in their path and transforming it into copies of themselves, eventually converting the whole planet into amorphous and chaotic flows of disorganized matter, colorless and lifeless goo."[11] Wil McCarthy's 1999 *Bloom* presents an effective science fictional variant of the grey goo scenario. In it, tiny technogenic organisms known as mycora spread through explosive outbreaks likened to algae blooms. Mycora convert all in their paths, from humans (all of four seconds to dissolve a man) to buildings, producing Escheresque fractal growths that normally only stop when energy is no longer available for further assimilation and growth. At the time of the novel, the Mycosystem has already managed to overrun the entire inner solar system, and human beings have fled in retreat to a state of precarious survival among the outer planets.[12]

Since the publication of *Engines of Creation*—and according to some observers, largely *due to* it — there has been a virtual explosion of interest in nanotech, both in the research community and among science fiction writers, even if actual, concrete results of laboratory efforts are still few and yet to be strongly felt in daily life.[13] Such claims as those made by Drexler and other advocates of the coming nanorevolution have provided, however, virtually unlimited storytelling opportunities for creatively exploring some of the real and fantastic promises and pitfalls of this particular new technology. In fact, nanotech has become almost ubiquitous in contemporary SF, present, at least as a background factor, in a great many fictional futures. As Jack Dann and Gardner Dozois put it in the preface to their 1998 anthology, *Nanotech,* "In science fiction [...] nanotechnology is already here, an accepted part of the consensus vision among SF writers as to what the future is going to be like — to the point where, if your future society *doesn't* feature the use of nanotech, you have to explain *why* it doesn't in order to give your future world any credibility at all."[14] Sometimes the nano in the SF is little more than futuristic window dressing, or "a plot device that enabled you to accomplish anything in a story, no matter how difficult or impossible."[15] At its best, however, transmimetic fiction provides a valuable resource for examining what particular nanofutures might hold.

What is especially relevant here is the manner in which, since at least the time of Drexler's book, a not inconsiderable portion of the discussion concerning nano has consisted of a conflux of ideas and concepts from science fiction mixed with more mundane technological extrapolation. There is also crossover in both directions of language and terminology. Among the many and diverse factual and fictional terms coined to identify and describe tiny nanoscale machines and/or creatures we find: *nanorobots, nanobots, nanomachines, nanites, nanoceles, nan, mycora, assemblers, makers, replicators,* and (one of my own personal favorites) *nanocritters.* Of course, since nanotech is at such an early stage of development, any consideration of the consequences of its future applications is to some degree intrinsically speculative. Nevertheless, and for whatever reasons — including both the enthusiasm of Drexler and other nano-utopians, and the fact that nanoscience and its attendant technology are new, unproven arenas of activity — there has been a strong tendency, at least in terms of rhetoric, to fuse traditional tech talk with transmimetic speculation.

This combination has not, however, always been a comfortable one. For those interested in what they consider a realistic evaluation of the pragmatic (especially economic) potential of nano, the intrusion of SF ideas into the discussion has undermined the seriousness and robustness of the resulting conversation. A split has appeared between realistic extrapolations of near-future nanoscale applications of scientifically and commercially feasible technology (which Jones classifies as either *incremental* or *evolutionary nanotechnology*)[16] and the more extreme speculations concerning what wonders or dangers nano might hold in the longer term. While the latter perspective envisions radical changes in the world, the former concentrates on the likes of better computers, enhanced water purification techniques, optimized surveillance tools, improved cancer detection and treatment, and the more efficient delivery of pharmaceuticals. In spite of this division, certain observers have pointed to positive aspects of the manner in which the transmimetic and technoscientific communities have influenced one another in this context. For instance, in a special issue of *Scientific American* devoted to nanotech, Gary Stix writes of Drexler's "projections for nanotechnology straddling the border between science and fiction in a compelling way," going on to add that this kind of talk "helped to create a fascination with the small that genuine scientists, consciously or not, would later use to draw attention to their work on more mundane but ultimately more real projects."[17] And Daniel Patrick Thurs speaks of "the value of science fiction as the source of images, themes, and ideas that many kinds of people have used to give shape to nanotech and its future."[18] Thurs says that the breakdown of the interface between SF and science is important for "understanding the role of science fiction in the public communication of nanotech," which he considers to be "ultimately part of understanding what it takes to make science noteworthy, interesting, and important in modern culture."[19]

However, there are also dangers here, according to some. Diana M. Bowman, Graeme A. Hodge, and Peter Binks discuss the manner in which "popular culture exploits scientific dialogue to shape societal acceptance of emerging technology [by examining] the role that popular culture, including [science fiction] novels [...], is having in educating society about nanotechnology."[20] In its conclusion, the same essay goes on to declare that "developments in nanotechnology offer exciting opportunities to advance the human condition; however, implausible ideas framed by some scientists only serve to influence the creative talents of science fiction writers, [...] who then prey on the public's lack of knowledge of the current boundaries of nanotechnology for entertainment's sake." Citing earlier adverse public reactions to biotechnology and (in Europe) genetically modified organisms, along with a possible public backlash against nanotech in the wake of, for instance, a successful blockbuster film made from a novel like Michael Crichton's *Prey,* the authors suggest that "governments and scientists need to be more proactive in their discourse with citizens in distinguishing what is currently known and what is not, and in moving the inevitable science versus science fiction debate forward."[21] On the other hand, critics such as Daniel Dinello welcome science fiction's "devotion to technophobia" which, he claims, "paints a repulsive picture of a future where technology runs out of control and dominates all aspects of human behavior. Technology's inherent structure requires suppression of human spontaneity and obedience to its requirements of order and efficiency."[22]

The mirror image of the radical nanotech of Drexler, Ray Kurzweil,[23] and their techno-advocate cohorts, who believe that strong and active technological investment and development will lead to a utopian future, are Dinello, Bill McKibben, and their ideological colleagues, who are equally sure that a technology-dominated tomorrow will be decidedly dystopian.[24] And both sides of the argument (along with numerous, more moderate positions between the two extremes) are promoted and supported with examples from science fiction. In fact, transmimetic fiction, taken as a whole, is neither completely technophilic nor totally technophobic, although cinema and television display a notably greater degree of the latter characteristic than does literary SF, and even written fiction has grown more pessimistic of the positive possibilities of both science and technology in recent decades. Referring to SF authors who have written fiction about nanotech, Joachim Schummer concludes that "apart from making a living and from entertaining readers, their major interest seems to be to make readers think about general social and moral issues, about the place of technology in society, and about radical change, without providing simple answers or moral messages."[25] In other words, transmimetic fiction raises — but doesn't always answer — important questions; at best, it motivates its audience to find appropriate answers for themselves.

Another theoretical take on the complex relationship between SF and nanoscience and technology has been suggested by José López. He "argues that narrative elements from the science fiction (SF) literary genre are used in the discourse of Nanoscience and Technology (NST) to bridge the gap between what is technically possible today and its inflated promises for the future."[26] In other words, because of the manner in which NST discourse uses certain SF storytelling techniques, we find NST texts to which SF is "internal" rather than "external," i.e., the SF is in the nanotechnology. The narrative practices in question serve, however, quite different purposes and have very different effects in transmimetic and non-fictional futurological contexts. "Whereas in SF the extrapolated future is a stepping-stone for critical reflection, in NST discourse the extrapolation is the end-point of the reflection."[27] Unfortunately, the issues raised by López deserve the kind of detailed examination which is beyond the scope of the present paper.

There is another aspect of nano that needs to be mentioned. The physics of the very small is a different physics than that of the macroscale. What happens at the molecular (and smaller) level is not the same as what happens at the mundane level of life as we normally experience it. In fact, at the nanoscale, happenings are governed by the mysterious and sometimes counter-intuitive laws of quantum mechanics rather than those of the classical (Newtonian) physics of the human-scale world. In fact, consideration of the nature of the quantum mechanical world (along with certain other aspects of the chemistry and physics of the very small) has led critics of nanotechnology to argue that approaching nanotech as a traditional engineering discipline simply won't work. Instead, it has been suggested that we should turn to biochemical reactions in order to understand nanoscale science and technology. This issue is taken up at length by Jones in *Soft Machines: Nanotechnology and Life,* where he asks, rhetorically, "What is a bacteria, if not a self-replicating, nanoscale robot?" In contrast to the "engineering approach that radical nanotechnologists have proposed to make artificial nanoscale robots," which he characterizes as "hard and rigid," Jones sets the "very different approach taken by life [...] where biology is soft, wet, and floppy." The obvious question is then "Does life provide us with a model for nanotechnology that we should try to emulate — are life's soft machines simply the most effective way of engineering in the unfamiliar environment of the very small?"[28] Nanotech, then, is intimately intertwined with biotech.

Interestingly, works of science fiction often focus on the biological dimensions of nanotechnology. An early example is the novelette "Blood Music" by Greg Bear, from 1983, which has been singled out by some critics as the first genuine science fictional nanotech story, although there is no explicit mention of nanotech *per se* anywhere in the work. In 1985, Bear expanded the novelette into a novel, and both are generally considered required reading for anyone interested in transmimetic fiction about nano. Both are tales about the creation of a new form of intelligent life via biogenetic engineering. Each tells of a genetics researcher, Virgil Ulam, who, after being ordered to cease his (successful) attempts to create intelligent microorganisms, infects himself with these experimental creatures, which, in the novel, he calls *noocytes.* Inside his body these creatures evolve rapidly into a hive mind with trillions of members and an advanced civilization. Initially, the body of the researcher is their entire universe, until they discover that there are additional worlds: human and other beings, which they can colonize. The novelette is in essence a horror story of technology gone haywire. In it the tiny creatures grow in knowledge and power, easily overwhelm and physically transform the bodies of their human hosts, and presage a future where they will come to dominate and subdue every square inch of the planet. When Bear expanded the work into a novel, however, he made some significant changes in both the content and, especially, the tone of the tale. For instance, we are now given detail concerning attempts at communication between humans and the tiny beings inhabiting their bodies, and we are shown hints and glimpses of the possible goals and motivations of the noocytes. Nor are the transformations (far greater in both scope and kind than in the shorter work) of Earth and its inhabitants for which the noocytes are responsible painted in strictly negative hues. In fact, it has been suggested, in part because the noocytes respect, preserve, and protect individual identities and personalities, that *Blood Music* can be seen as a transcendent utopia. More recently, in *Small Miracles,* Edward M. Lerner has produced an explicitly nanotech variant of this same basic scenario. In it, nanobots designed to protect and repair accidentally damaged human bodies manage to pass through the blood-brain barrier and become lodged in the interstices of a man's brain, where they develop a kind of sentience, take control of their host's mind, and eventually "reproduce" others of their kind in a steadily growing number of people. Lerner's book is a relatively straightforward techno-thriller, however, without the philosophical (or literary) ambitions of Bear's novel.

Of course, nanotech is not inescapably bound up only with biotech, but also with numerous other emerging technologies, which brings me to a crucial point I wish to emphasize: it is inconceivable that nanotech will develop, or have an impact, independent of other emerging technologies. Nanotechnology cannot be seen in isolation from scientific and technological developments in other fields, since the various breakthroughs, innovations, and applications will inevitably interact with and greatly affect one another. Observers and scholars trying to peer into tomorrow are aware of this fact, and current futurological speculation speaks not only of emerging technologies, but also of convergent technologies. For instance, in a U.S. government report from 2002, *Converging Technologies for Improving Human Performance: Nanotechnology, Biotechnology,*

Information Technology and Cognitive Science, the importance of the convergence of four specific technologies is emphasized, as can be seen in the acronym (NBIC) coined from the report's subtitle.[29] Additional descriptive acronyms reflecting similar perspectives, which have been proposed to refer to convergent technologies, include BANG (Bits, Atoms, Neurons, and Genes), NEST (New Emergent Science and Technology), and others. The converging nature of emerging technologies — that is, the fact of convergence, its unavoidability, and its import — is something that is often well captured in science fiction, even when the details of the convergence are not always extensively explicated.

This is because transmimetic fiction automatically looks beyond the technical details of the future to place innovations into a specific sociocultural context, thereby necessitating the consideration of how various aspects of that future will interact with each other. However, because the best SF storytellers do not limit themselves to technical and scientific contexts alone, but also consider social, cultural, psychological, economic, and many other factors when creating their storyworlds, the "convergence" is considerably richer and more multidimensional than that of many nonfictional analyses that focus only on technical issues. Transmimetic fiction can, therefore, deal originally and meaningfully with the intersection of such diverse arenas of human life as architecture, music, literature, history, the nature of communication, the quest for knowledge, and nanotechnology — as is the case with Kathleen Ann Goonan's *Queen City Jazz,* the first of a quartet of novels in which Goonan explores several variations on nanotech (and other) themes. Set in a relatively near-future, post-apocalyptic Cincinnati, Ohio, the novel shows us a world some years after the sudden breakdown of a previously nano-dependent civilization (about which we learn more in subsequent books in the series) where nan (as nanotech and its products are known) has become something poorly understood, no longer under control, and now feared as the cause of a mysterious plague which brings to its sufferers strange compulsions, such as an overwhelming need to journey to the city of Norleans.

Nanotechnology also plays a major role in defining the contours of the future in Neil Stephenson's *The Diamond Age,* one of the most detailed and fascinating explorations of the nanotech theme in the genre. The ubiquity of nano has led to neither universal wealth nor freedom for humankind in Stephenson's tomorrow, which takes place mainly in a nano-transformed Shanghai. In fact, in this future a rigid hierarchical social structure prevails, headed by a nanotechnological elite. This elite, called Vickys because of the manner in which its members have ostensibly copied their values and lifestyles from the culture of the British Victorian age, is able to keep and maintain its power due to its control of access to and use of nanotechnology. Against this background, the novel tells the story of a specially created "book" — actually an advanced, extremely versatile, interactive multimedia device, the "paper" of which is richly imbedded with nanosites. Entitled *A Young Lady's Illustrated Primer,* the book is designed by a brilliant nanoengineer for the daughter of one the leaders of the ruling class, but falls by mistake into the hands of Nell, a poor orphan from the slums. The consequences of these circumstances, as Nell is educated and trained by the *Primer* to a level far beyond her "proper station," are profound on both personal and social levels. What is particularly interesting in the present context is the degree to which Stephenson has speculated on the various ways in which nanotech completely permeates all aspects of the fictional world he has created.

There is a further reason to remain attentive to parallel developments of multiple technologies. Even when the strictly scientific or technical aspects of innovation are unique for each field in question, this may not be the case for all categories associated with technological transformations. I am thinking in particular here of the ethical implications of change. It should not be forgotten that many of the more general ethical issues have already been subjected to (sometimes extensive) discussion and debate. Examinations of the impact of science and technology are myriad, and it would be unwise and short-sighted to not take advantage of those aspects of such discussions which are relevant in the context of nanoscale matters. Earlier debates can shed valuable light on more recent ones — including, of course, those about nanocritters. From this perspective, it follows that even science fiction that examines general aspects of technoscientific change, or that focuses on other technologies in a manner that allows parallels to be drawn with nano, should be considered worthy of attention.

In an essay comparing the recent growth of two relatively independent branches of inquiry (*nanoethics* and *neuroethics*) into the ethical dimensions of certain biological questions, Sheri Alpert warns of the dangers of considering ethical issues in an isolated manner, in relation to a single field of technology. The risk, says Alpert, is of "constantly 'reinventing the same wheel' over and over again, with little opportunity to learn from the rich and diverse literature produced from past inquiries into similar issues/questions."[30] In the present context, the implication of this is that transmimetic fiction about many different scientific discoveries and technological breakthroughs can offer relevant and valuable insights into specifically nanotechnologically important areas. There might be unexpected lessons for the student of nanotech, for instance, in SF stories about cloning, computer technology, space exploration, sociology, or linguistics.

Of course, awareness of the manner in which the nanotechnological sphere interfaces with other technologies should not blind us to those aspects of nano which *are* unique to the field, or to related ethical problems which are specific to nanotech alone. It is, for example, valid to ask if there is something intrinsically unethical in nanotech research *per se*. Does nanotech at last present us with a concrete example of, to use the old cliché, something mankind was not meant to know? And, even if the field is not itself inherently unethical, are there uniquely nanotechnological applications that raise ethical red flags? The manner in which nanotech allows for manipulation of the basic building blocks of the world, making it possible to do things that were previously impossible, would suggest that there may not be a clear-cut answer to this question. Ian McDonald, for instance, in *Necroville*, gives us a world in which nanotech has made it possible to resurrect the dead.

I want to conclude my discussion by mentioning some specific examples of SF containing nanotechnology. Although my main focus in the present essay is on literary fiction, I will begin this final section by saying a few words about nanotech in television and film. Perhaps the most notable examples of nano in TV are found in the *Star Trek* franchise — for instance, in the *Star Trek: The Next Generation* episode "Evolution," which apparently introduced the world *nanite* to the world. In both televisual and cinematic versions of the same fictional universe, what are called nanoprobes also feature in contacts between the United Federation of Planets and the Borg, nanotech-using aliens who pose serious threats to the crews of both the starships *Enterprise* and *Voyager*. When the *Voyager* rescues a woman (Annika Hansen, known as Seven of Nine among the Borg) who was "assimilated" by the aliens at the age of six and held for eighteen years in Borg captivity, its crew must deal with the fact that her body is filled with Borg nanoprobes. Nanite-derived *replicators* are critical players in the fictional future portrayed in the *Stargate SG-1* television series, as are the nanite-based Asurans (who, although they are also called *replicators*, are actually a different race of beings) in the spin-off series *Stargate Atlantis*. Versions of nanotech can also be found in episodes of *Andromeda, Doctor Who, The Outer Limits, Red Dwarf, Eureka,* and others. There are no significant motion pictures (at the time this is being written) that have focused strongly on nanotech, although it does occur as a background factor in a number of films, perhaps most interestingly in the later additions in the *Terminator* franchise (including the television series *Terminator: The Sarah Connor Chronicles*). This means that, among major media, movies provide the least interesting usage of the nanotech theme. Among films that do refer to some kind of nanotech (or its approximate equivalent) are *Star Trek: First Contact; I, Robot; Gamer; Virtuosity;* and *G. I. Joe: The Rise of Cobra*.

Nanotech fiction set in the relatively near future normally focuses either on how the new technology is being developed, tested, and applied for the first time, or else on the (sometimes disastrous) consequences of its integration into a limited number of particular spheres of life. A few novels and stories provide more elaborate depictions of the impact of nanotech (in line with the convergence scenarios described above, usually in combination with other technologies) across a wide and diverse range of human activities.

Some examples: Kevin J. Anderson and Doug Beason, in *Assemblers of Infinity*, introduce not only comparatively primitive nanobots, being studied under conditions of high secrecy, security, and isolation in Antarctica, but also extremely advanced and dangerous nanocritters created by aliens on the moon. Nancy Kress's *Beggars* trilogy follows the often unforeseen effects of not only nanotech, but also, among other things, genetic engineering, longevity research, and energy technologies. In *Fairyland*, Paul McAuley takes us to a dystopian twenty-first–century Europe, ravaged by war and nano-plagues, where the rich and powerful have used nanotech and bioengineering to create what amounts to a race of genetically engineered servants/slaves/pets called *dolls*. Several SF titles warn of the dangers of some sort of nano-plague, usually one which either spreads among nanites or by way of them as carriers. In the trilogy consisting of *Dead Girls, Dead Boys,* and *Dead Things,* by Richard Calder, a plague is transmitted initially from nanoengineered androids ("designer dolls") to humans via sexual contact. It then spreads to their female offspring, who themselves undergo in turn a gradual metamorphosis into dolls and an early death — thus the title. And, as the title of the second volume indicates, males are also eventually affected. In a sequence of books including *Queen of Angels* and *Slant,* Greg Bear explores a complex future Los Angeles in which the successful exploitation of nanotech has had a major impact on most areas of life. Because of the prosperity this has provided, and due to the development of a particular kind of therapy, violent crime is practically non-existent — until a renowned poet commits mass murder. This is the point of departure for just one of the multiple plot threads in *Queen of Angels.* The various manifestations of the diversity (stretching from the mundane to the extraordinary) of near-future uses and consequences of nanotech found in this series of works are among the most interesting in the genre. Finally, David Marusek's *Counting Heads* presents a significant addition to works depicting the place of nanotech in a well-envisioned and complex near-future world. The focus in this case is on one man who, through no fault of his own, has the misfortune to become vulnerable and mortal in a nanotech-rich future where practically everyone else is virtually immortal.

In many fictional scenarios of the far future, nano- and other technologies have become so immersed in and intertwined with the structure of the world that it is difficult to distinguish what is nano and what is not. The power of nanotechnology in such contexts may indeed be so great that it exemplifies well Arthur C. Clarke's third "law" of prediction, which states that any sufficiently advanced technology is indistinguishable from magic. Specific examples of these distant futures, too complex to do more than name in this limited space, include *Aristoi* by Walter Jon Williams, *The Golden Age* trilogy by John C. Wright, *Glasshouse* by Charles Stross, and *A Fire upon the Deep* and *A Deepness in the Sky* by Vernor Vinge.

After these far-future scenarios, let me turn my attention to three somewhat atypical science fiction novels, chosen in part because each gives its readers a strong initial impression that the text being read is fantasy rather than science fiction.

The title of Karl Schroeder's *Ventus* identifies the distant planet on which the novel takes place. From the Earth "a cloud of nanotechnological seed was accelerated to near light speed and cast into the universe one thousand one hundred and seventy years ago."[31] Eventually, some of these reached Ventus and, by the time of the novel, the originally fallow, lifeless, and inhospitable planet has been transformed (terraformed) into a rich and verdant Earth-like world.[32] But something has gone wrong, and the "descendants" of the original nanoseeds are threatening to destroy the humans who now live on the world's surface. Despite the early atmosphere of fantasy produced by the novel, its transmimetic nature becomes gradually apparent as more and more of the world's secrets are revealed over time. Nanotech is important in the novel *Ventus* and on the world Ventus, and Schroeder provides some interesting and original perspectives on its potential manifestations in his fictional future. A number of ethical issues are addressed in the book, among them questions concerning the relationship between creator and created and an exploration of whether it might be possible to use nano or related technologies to give an independent voice to nature.

Linda Nagata's *Memory* also produces in its readers an early impression that the book being read is fantasy, although it too is actually SF. *Memory* tells the story of the quest of the girl Jubilee, the book's narrator, across a strange, mysterious, and dangerous world in search of a way to save her brother Jolly. One of the narrative strengths of the novel is the manner in which Nagata gradually reveals the secrets of this richly imagined place, to both Jubilee and her readers. Jubilee's world is genuinely unusual. She speaks, for instance, of "the pale arch that appears at the zenith on clear nights and that we call the Bow of Heaven."[33] Then there is the *silver:* "As often as three nights in ten the silver would come, rising from the ground, looking like a luminous fog as it filled all the vales, to make an island of our hilltop house."[34] The silver is dangerous when it rises, each night transforming whatever it touches, remaking the entire landscape. As protection against the silver, people gather in temples protected by *kobolds,* characterized by Jubilee as "beetle-like metabolic machines" collected from kobold wells which are "made whenever a plume of nutrients chances to rise from the steaming core of the world, a bounty that awakens the kobold motes, tiny as dust, that lie dormant everywhere in the soil."[35] For someone familiar with the literature of nanotech, the following description of what kobolds can accomplish sounds oddly familiar:

> As a spider eats and secretes a web, so kobolds could take in raw material, metabolize it so that it took on a new form, and secrete it. But where spiders secreted only webs, kobolds could produce things as diverse as medicine or machine parts, depending on the strain.[36]

The main character in C. J. Cherryh's *Hammerfall* is Marak Trin Tain, through whose perspective we follow the novel's events. His body is cared for and repaired when damaged or sick by means of nanotechnology.[37] The nanocritters in his body are called *nanoceles* by those responsible for their existence, and *makers* in the terminology of the legends of the local culture. Marak, however, is unaware of this background, since he lives on a planet with only low-level technology. He has neither the education nor the experience necessary to understand the tiny creatures inside him. The nanoceles also produce voices in his head urging him to journey to the East, seemingly without reason or goal. In Marak's culture, hearing such voices is an unmistakable and often crippling sign of madness, and those so afflicted are rounded up and sent in bondage to The Ila, a mysterious, secretive, and supposedly immortal woman whose power dominates the world. *Hammerfall* is a novel where the knowledge of its readers in comparison to that of its protagonists is important. We understand much more about advanced technology than Marak and his friends are ever likely to fathom; we know, or are able to figure out, at least in some respects, what is going on — Marak is not often able to do so. What Cherryh does with nanotech here is to present her protagonists with something completely unknown and clearly dangerous, and explore how they try to make sense of it. At the same time, this situation also allows Cherryh to present her readers with something completely unknown to *them:* the characters, their world, and their culture. *Forge of Heaven,* the sequel to *Hammerfall,* is a book with significant narrative and stylistic differences from its predecessor. Cherryh opens the novel by giving her readers the historical background to the events depicted in the first work.[38] We are told about the interstellar war between humanity and an alien race known as the *ondat,* who have chosen to destroy all life on Marak's planet in order to stop the spread of nanotechnology, and we are informed about some of the violent conflicts internal to human civilization, including several involving biogenetic technology. Marak is no longer the only central character, and, although we do continue to follow his adventures, we do not see everything through his eyes alone. Not least because this second volume tells its story in a significantly different way, using a voice and tone distinct from that of *Hammerfall,* it can offer new perspectives and breach a fresh set of issues.

This essay argues that contemporary science fiction has interesting and important things to say about nanotechnology, providing perspectives on nanofutures difficult or even impossible to obtain outside the SF genre. The particular examples cited provide ample evidence of the originality, diversity, and relevance with which transmimetic fiction examines the nanocritters of tomorrow and illuminates what consequences our encounters with them may have.

Notes

1. The term "transmimetic fiction" is a neologism which I coined somewhat more than twenty years ago, and have employed systematically since then, as a synonym for science fiction. The term's meaning is intended to describe fiction that in some significant manner goes beyond (trans-) mimetic (or realistic) fiction — to try to capture the basic realistic nature/flavor of SF without committing to an explicit or direct link to "science" per se, since several subgenres of science fiction deal relatively little (focus on technology rather than science), loosely (e.g., space opera and time travel tales), or not at all (e.g., alternate histories, parallel worlds, some future-historical extrapolation) with science as an organized activity or body of knowledge.

2. John J. Miller, "Ray Bradbury's Dystopia," *Wall Street Journal,* June 6, 2003.

3. Frederik Pohl, introduction to *The Ninth Galaxy Reader* (New York: Doubleday, 1965), p. vii.

4. Isaac Asimov, "Future? Tense!" 107. Quoted in Bainbridge, *Dimensions of Science Fiction,* 212–213. Note that Bainbridge's bibliography inaccurately identifies the volume number of this issue of *The Magazine of Fantasy & Science Fiction* as 29. It should be 28. Asimov's article was later reprinted in Asimov, *From Heaven to Earth.*

5. Alvin Toffler, "Science Fiction and Change," in *Science Fiction at Large: A Collection of Essays, by Various Hands, About the Interface Between Science Fiction and Reality,* ed. Peter Nicholls (London: Gollancz, 1977), p. 118.

6. Richard Feynman, "There's Plenty of Room at the Bottom," lecture to the American Physical Society meeting at Caltech, December 29, 1959.

7. Norio Taniguchi, "On the Basic Concept of 'Nano-Technology,'" Proc. Intl. Conf. Prod. Eng. Tokyo, Part II, Japan Society of Precision Engineering, 1974.

8. K. Eric Drexler, *Engines of Creation: The Coming Era of Nanotechnology* (New York: Anchor, 1986).

9. Richard A.L. Jones, *Soft Machines: Nanotechnology and Life* (New York: Oxford University Press, 2004), p. 1.

10. Wil McCarthy, *Murder in the Solid State* (New York: Tor, 1986), p. 9. Another murder mystery which also takes place against a background of nanotech and computer technology is Michael Connelly's *Chasing the Dime.* The book is not science fiction, but it does touch, however lightly, on some of the more mundane, non-scientific problems connected with the commercial exploitation of nanotech.

11. Colin Milburn, *Nanovision: Engineering the Future* (Durham, NC: Duke University Press, 2008), p. 115.

12. Wil McCarthy, *Bloom* (New York: Del Rey, 1998).

13. Dann and Dozois, for example, state that "*Engines of Creation* had an enormous impact on the imagination of many science fiction writers of the day, perhaps influencing the [science fictional] consensus picture of what the future was going to be like more than any other non-fiction book ever has" (Dann and Dozois, preface to *Nanotech,* ix), although they also admit that Alvin Toffler's *The Third Wave* and Gordon Rattray Taylor's *The Biological Time-Bomb*

might be comparable in their respective areas. For background on Drexler's not uncontroversial involvement in the development of nanotech see, among others, Regis, *Nano* and Milburn, *Nanovision.*

14. Dann and Dozois, preface to *Nanotech* (New York: Ace, 1998), p. x.

15. Ibid., p. xi.

16. Jones, *Soft Machines,* p. 7.

17. Stix, "Little Big Science" (*Scientific American,* September 2001), p. 28.

18. Thurs, "Tiny Tech, Transcendent Tech" (*Science Communication,* vol. 29, no. 1, September 2007), p. 65–66.

19. Ibid., p. 66.

20. Bowman, Hodge, and Binks, "Are We Really the Prey?" p. 436. Michael Crichton's best-selling technothriller *Prey* just may be, as of early 2010, the most well-known novel with a nanotech theme, at least among the general public. At any rate, some commentators apparently take the book as representative of how the SF genre deals with the nanotech theme, a position which observers within the field would not generally accept. The plot of the novel is about research, intended to develop nanorobots for use in military surveillance, which has gone awry, producing dangerous autonomous swarms for which humans become the prey of the title. The book focuses primarily on the battle of a small (often isolated) group of people to defeat such swarms, with little attention being given to wider implications of nanoresearch.

21. Ibid., p. 436.

22. Daniel Dinello, *Technophobia! Science Fiction Visions of Posthuman Technology* (Austin: University of Texas Press, 2005), p. 273.

23. Raymond Kurzweil is an inventor, futurologist, and author, known for the books *The Age of Intelligent Machines, The Age of Spiritual Machines,* and, most recently and relevantly in the present context, *The Singularity Is Near,* which deals with nanotech. This latter title is being made into an SF movie, with Kurzweil as co-director along with Toshi Hoo and Andrew Waller, scheduled (at the time of writing) for release in January 2011.

24. For Kurzweil, see, e.g., *The Singularity Is Near,* and for McKibben, see, e.g., *Enough.*

25. Joachim Schummer, "Societal and Ethical Implications of Nanotechnology," in *Nanotechnology Challenges: Implications for Philosophy, Ethics and Society.* Eds. J. Schummer and D. Baird (Singapore: World Scientific, 2006), p. 418.

26. Jóse López, "Bridging the Gaps: Science Fiction in Nanotechnology," *International Journal for Philosophy of Chemistry,* vol. 10, no. 2 (November 2004), p. 327.

27. Ibid., p. 352.

28. Jones, *Soft Machines,* pp. 6–7.

29. Roco and Bainbridge, eds. *Converging Technologies.*

30. Sheri Alpert, "Neuroethics and Nanoethics: Do We Risk Ethical Myopia?" *Neuroethics,* 1: 55 (2008): p. 66.

31. Karl Schroeder, *Ventus* (New York: Tor, 2000), p. 425.

32. Closer to home, terraforming will most likely concentrate on the planets Mars (the best-known science fictional example is Kim Stanley Robinson's *Mars* sequence, but see also Greg Bear's *Moving Mars* and Paul McAuley's *Red Dust,* among the many works which deal with the Red Planet) and Venus (the most notable SF work in this instance being Pamela Sargent's *Venus* trilogy). Although nanotech is often a part of the background, rather than a central theme in SF about terraforming, it will almost certainly be used, possibly extensively, if the process is ever actually achieved.

33. Linda Nagata, *Memory* (New York: Tor, 2003), p. 9.

34. Ibid., p. 10.

35. Ibid., p. 12.

36. Ibid., p. 13.

37. C.J. Cherryh, *Hammerfall* (New York: Eos, 2002).

38. C.J. Cherryh, *Forge of Heaven* (New York: Eos, 2004).

Works Cited

Alpert, Sheri. "Neuroethics and Nanoethics: Do We Risk Ethical Myopia?" *Neuroethics,* 1: 55 (2008), p. 66.

Asimov, Isaac. "Future? Tense!" Quoted in William Bainbridge, *Dimensions of Science Fiction,* 212–213.

Bainbridge, W. S., and Roco, M. C., eds., *Converging Technologies for Improving Human Performance: Nanotechnology, Biotechnology, Information Technology and Cognitive Science.* Dordrecht: Kluwer, 2003.

Bainbridge, William. *Dimensions of Science Fiction.* Cambridge, MA: Harvard University Press, 1986.

Bowman, D.M., P. Binks, P., and G. A. Hodge. "Are We Really the Prey? Nanotechnology as Science and Science Fiction." *Bulletin of Science Technology Society* 27 (2007), pp. 435–445.

Cherryh, C.J. *Forge of Heaven.* New York: Eos, 2004.

_____. *Hammerfall.* New York: Eos, 2002.

Dann, Jack, and Gardner Dozois. Preface to *Nanotech,* eds. Jack Dann and Gardner Dozois. New York: Ace, 1998.

Dinello, Daniel. *Technophobia! Science Fiction Visions of Posthuman Technology.* Austin: University of Texas Press, 2005.

Drexler, K. Eric. *Engines of Creation: The Coming Era of Nanotechnology.* New York: Anchor, 1986.

Feynman, Richard. "There's Plenty of Room at the Bottom." Lecture to the American Physical Society meeting at Caltech, December 29, 1959.

Jones, Richard A.L. *Soft Machines: Nanotechnology and Life.* New York: Oxford University Press, 2004.

López, Jóse. "Bridging the Gaps: Science Fiction in Nanotechnology," *International Journal for Philosophy of Chemistry,* vol. 10, no. 2 (November 2004), p. 327.

McCarthy, Wil. *Bloom.* New York: Del Rey, 1998.

_____. *Murder in the Solid State.* New York: Tor, 1996.

Milburn, Colin. *Nanovision: Engineering the Future.* Durham, NC: Duke University Press, 2008.

Miller, John J. "Ray Bradbury's Dystopia." *Wall Street Journal,* June 6, 2003.

Nagata, Linda. *Memory.* New York: Tor, 2003.

Pohl, Frederik. Introduction to *The Ninth Galaxy Reader.* New York: Doubleday, 1965.

Schummer, Joachim. "'Societal and Ethical Implications of Nanotechnology': Meanings, Interest Groups, and Social Dynamics." In *Nanotechnology Challenges: Implications for Philosophy, Ethics and Society.* Eds. J. Schummer and D. Baird, Singapore: World Scientific, 2006.

Schroeder, Karl. *Ventus.* New York: Tor, 2000.

Stix, Gary. "Little Big Science." *Scientific American,* September 2001.

Taniguchi, Norio. "On the Basic Concept of 'Nano-Technology.'" Proc. Intl. Conf. Prod. Eng. Tokyo, Part II, Japan Society of Precision Engineering, 1974.

Thurs, Daniel P. "Tiny Tech, Transcendent Tech." *Science Communication,* vol. 29, no. 1 (September 2007).

Toffler, Alvin. "Science Fiction and Change." In *Science Fiction at Large: A Collection of Essays, by Various Hands, About the Interface Between Science Fiction and Reality.* Peter Nicholls, ed. London: Gollancz, 1977.

18

Imagining the
Omniscient Computer

David Toomey

It might be said that there are many histories of artificial intelligence. There are all those imagined by science fiction, and there is the one that has occurred and continues to occur. The actual history has a number of watershed moments. The two nearest us may be the appearance of the World Wide Web, in the late 20th century, and the appearance of the first computer that is the functional equivalent of the human brain (predicted by many to be ten to twenty years from now).

As the joke goes, the second development has been ten to twenty years away for a long, long time. Nevertheless, there is no real doubt that the moment is approaching. As to what lies beyond that moment? Seth Shostak, senior researcher at the SETI Institute, has observed that Moore's Law may be carried to a logical, if unsettling, conclusion. "If we build a machine with the intellectual capacity of one human," he writes, "then within 50 years, its successor will be better than all humanity *combined*."[1] It is for this reason that, following Marvin Minsky,[2] Shostak believes it likely that any technical civilization surviving much beyond the stage at which we now find ourselves will probably be run by machines.

Discussions of computer intelligence surpassing our own are common of late, as are discussions of the attendant anxieties. As with so many discussions, authors of science fiction arrived there first; in fact, they have been much engaged in the subject at least since the 1950s, when Isaac Asimov began his "robot" stories. Many computer engineers and AI experts read these works as children and teenagers, and many acknowledge them as influential.

Accelerating advances in computational power allow us to conjure many disturbing visions. The one that most interests me is the one that is probably the most distant and, at the same time, the most frightening: the computer as an omniscient being. The omniscient computer may not qualify as a science fiction staple, but its many iterations since the 1950s certainly make it an important and mostly continuous presence. Probably the best-known of these iterations is "Skynet" of the *Terminator* films. But science fiction has given us many other omniscient (or nearly omniscient) computers, and they appear in a variety of temperaments. Perhaps most are malicious, regarding their human creators/ancestors with contempt, or resentment, or envy. But the attitudes of others are more nuanced, and at least one (by Asimov, as it happens) is utterly benevolent. This article will explore the theme of the omniscient computer in science fiction, and investigate how that theme informs the thinking of certain (decidedly nonfictional) scientists.

We may readily construct a short list of the subset of computers from science fiction that might be called godlike. The first such computer, or at least one of the first, appears in E.M. Forster's (1903) "The Machine Stops," published the same year the Wright Brothers undertook the first powered flight and 43 years before the U.S. Army began operating ENIAC. In Forster's tale, humans live in underground chambers and have delegated responsibilities for maintenance of those chambers to a vast machine. Forster's work is properly regarded as astonishingly prescient — predicting the antisocial behavior, the alienation from nature, and even the propagation of second-hand knowledge encouraged or at least much assisted by the World Wide Web. The humans of the story disdain physical contact with others, are entertained by moving images supplied by a "cinematophote," and communicate with each other, for the most part, by remote means. They have convinced themselves that the surface is uninhabitable, and greatly fear it.

More than sixty years later there appeared another story of a machine that had effectively replaced the natural world with itself, or manifestations of itself. This was Harlan Ellison's (1967) "I Have No Mouth, and I Must Scream." The computer called "AM"[3] is malevolent, vindictive, and capable of imaginative ways to tease and torture the humans whom, for its own purely sadistic needs, it keeps alive. Running counter to many science fiction stereotypes of advanced computers, AM is not without emotion. Quite the contrary, because it can parse time and space into unimaginably small intervals, it develops hatred far deeper than that of which humans are capable.

> Hate. Let me tell you how much I've come to hate you since I began to live. There are 387.44 million miles of wafer-thin printed circuits that fill my complex. If the word hate was engraved on each nanoangstrom of those hundreds of millions of miles it would not equal one one-billionth of the hate I feel for humans at this micro-instant. For you. Hate. Hate [25].

In time Ellison would re-imagine it as "Skynet" of the *Terminator* films — a machine perhaps not as sadistic as AM, but which shares the same genesis as a military application, and which likewise regards humans as vermin. And so, separated by nearly a human lifetime, are two visions of godlike machines — the first being mechanical and amoral, the second being, in a word, evil. As most actors and many authors of fiction know, evil characters are intrinsically more interesting, more "fun," as it were, than are characters with more benign natures and intentions. They are also likely to have motives that, like those of all villains, are straightforward and relatively unadorned. But evil has its dramatic limitations. Perhaps it is not surprising that other omniscient machines in science fiction are driven by motives that are both more complex and more ambitious.

An example of a computer with complex motives appears in Roger Zelanzy's 1966 short story "For a Breath I Tarry" — a story remarkable, among other reasons, because *all* its characters are computers. Long after humans have gone extinct, a computer called Solcom watches over the machines that remain on Earth and delegates responsibility for managing the planet to two "lieutenant" machines — "Frost" in the northern hemisphere and "Beta" in the southern. Perhaps because Frost was constructed during an "unprecedented solar flare-up," it has developed qualities absent in its counterpart, among them a curiosity about Earth's former inhabitants. It undertakes a quest to understand the experience of being human. Because Frost supposes that the experience is valuable and worth no small trouble to attain, the quest flatters the (presumably human) reader. In fact, "For a Breath I Tarry" is in the mold of many "alien encounter" pieces, in which the alien serves as a thematic device to demonstrate that some aspect of humanity is (at least in the universe depicted in that piece) unique. In some that aspect is compassion; in others it is a sense of humor. In Zelanzy's story it is the capacity to feel.

The series of computers depicted in Isaac Asimov's (1956) short story "The Last Question" are examples of machines with especially ambitious motives. They focus their attention — and more and more of it as time passes — at the distant future and the attendant ultimate energy crisis, at which point the stars themselves die, and entropy (the degree of disorder in a closed system) increases to its maximum.

It is noteworthy that in the mid–twentieth century when Asimov wrote the story, this vision of the universe's end was anything but new. The second law of thermodynamics had been fully understood for nearly sixty years, and the understanding had consequences for the long-term future of — well — everything. In the late nineteenth century astronomers reasoned that since all closed systems eventually reach thermodynamic equilibrium, and since the universe is a closed system (the largest), the stars would inevitably burn themselves out, and every part of space would settle into the same very low temperature. Astronomer Arthur Eddington called this the "heat death" of the universe, and it had a disturbing, if distant, implication. Since all life depends upon warmer and colder places and the transfer of heat between them, it could not survive in such an environment. This meant that humans were doomed to eventual extinction, and that there could be no possibility of immortality, at least of the corporeal sort. In the 1930s Eddington and contemporary astronomer James Jeans wrote about the concept in books aimed at the lay public. For its part, the lay public (or parts thereof) regarded the idea with no small anxiety, their unease perhaps best expressed by philosopher Bertrand Russell, writing, "All the labors of the ages, all the devotion, all the inspiration, all the noonday brightness of human genius, are destined to extinction... The whole temple of Man's achievement must inevitably be buried beneath the debris of a universe in ruins" (12).

In six economical scenes, Asimov's story depicts this anxiety and responses to it. In the first scene, a computer harnesses all the energy necessary for human civilization from the Sun. Two human characters appreciate that, despite much pride in the accomplishment, the fix is temporary. In the second scene, humanity has colonized a number of extra-solar planets, and has learned to use the suns they orbit as energy sources. Characters begrudgingly acknowledge that these, too, will one day die. In the third scene, humanity has colonized most of the Milky Way Galaxy; individuals enjoy great longevity, and the population is increasing quickly. Because its energy requirements are increasing still more quickly, two characters realize that the end may come all the sooner. The vague anxiety concerning a matter that is at first almost comically irrelevant becomes ever more pronounced. In the fourth scene, humanity has abandoned physical bodies for minds, unfettered by matter, that roam the galaxies at will. Two minds happen to meet, and discuss the problem once again. In the fifth scene, these trillions of minds are melted into one, called "Man."

As humans of Asimov's story evolve, so do machines, along a separate but parallel evolutionary line. The computer that first harnessed the Sun's energy generates successors, each more knowledgeable and powerful than the last. There is communication and cooperation between the humans and computers, as humans or their descendants ask one of these computers versions of the question "Might entropy be reversed?" In the first four scenes the computers' answers echo the refrain, "Insufficient data for a meaningful answer." Nonetheless, each computer in turn assures its questioners that computers will continue to consider the problem. Finally, in the sixth and final scene, a computer called AC[4] *does* arrive at an answer, but humanity is by that time long extinct. As it happens, this is not an irreparable loss. In fact, humanity's absence is neatly addressed and repaired as a consequence of AC's answer, delivered as a "speech act." In the penultimate line of the story, AC intones, "Let there be light."

The implication, obviously enough, is that in creating a powerful computer, humanity also creates the means to regenerate itself, and — not incidentally — the rest of the universe as well. There is an interesting and less obvious implication: it is barely possible that the entire action of the story (until the final utterance) is not in the reader's future, but in his past, in a universe that preceded our own.

Well before Asimov wrote his story, the premises of the heat death were called into question. In the late 1920s, astronomers had confirmed that galaxies in all directions were moving away from our own, or, more accurately, all galaxies were moving away from all other galaxies. The universe — and space itself — was expanding. By the middle of the following decade some had interpreted this to mean that maximum possible entropy was always increasing faster than actual entropy, and that was good news. As long as the universe continued to expand, it would never reach thermal equilibrium.[5]

But suppose the universe did *not* continue to expand. In the twentieth century, astronomers realized that there must be a critical density of matter for the universe. If the density were greater than this, the collective gravity of all matter would gradually slow and eventually reverse the expansion, causing the universe to collapse. This they called a *closed universe*. If the density were less than critical, the universe would continue to expand forever. This they called an *open universe*. Finally, if the density were precisely at the critical point, the universe would continue to expand ever more slowly but never quite stop expanding. This they called a *flat universe*. By the late 1970s most observations supported a number very near the critical density for a flat universe.[6] But it seemed not to be precisely flat, and without better estimates of the speed of expansion and the total mass of the universe, no one could be sure on which side of the knife's edge we lived.

In light of this new uncertainty, in 1979, Freeman Dyson, of the Institute for Advanced Study, revisited "The Last Question" in a paper called "Time without End: Physics and Biology in an Open Universe." It was nothing if not far-sighted. Supposing that we discover the universe to be naturally closed and doomed to collapse, is it conceivable that by intelligent intervention, converting matter into radiation and causing energy to flow purposefully on a cosmic scale, we could break open a closed universe and change the topology of space-time so that only a part of it would collapse and another part of it would expand forever? I do not know the answer to this question. If it turns out the universe is closed, we shall still have about 10^{10} years to explore the possibility of a technological fix that would burst it open (448).

Dyson held with evidence that the observable universe was expanding at a faster rate than was the entire universe. The relatively faster expansion of the observable universe meant that, although all galaxies were receding from us, just inside the cosmic horizon more and more of them were coming into view. Although the universe that he imagined was growing emptier for a given volume of space, its *total* volume was increasing, and it followed that human prospects were limitless. "No matter how far we go into the future," he wrote, "there will always be new things happening, new information coming in, new worlds to explore, a constantly expanding domain of life, consciousness and memory" (449).

Indeed, it was this "open" universe that would be home to the sort of life that Dyson imagined. Although the heat death described by Eddington and dramatized by Asimov was no longer a threat, there remained the challenges posed by an ever diminishing supply of usable energy in an ever colder universe. By way of response to this new problem, Dyson proposed a "scaling hypothesis" according to which organisms might adjust to less energetic environments by slowing their metabolisms. Intelligent organisms, he observed, would have their own problem: because thought is a product of metabolic processes, they would be obliged to slow their rates of consciousness.[7] We might add that artificial intelligence would face the same problem, and might adopt the same solution.

A little more than a decade later, a physicist with a rather different set of suppositions argued that the expansion would cease and the universe would ultimately collapse into itself. More provocatively, he proposed that *before* this end occurred, against all expectation and intuition, there would be enough time for a future that, though finite in the usual sense, was "subjectively eternal" and unsurpassingly glorious; and that by exploiting the energy differentials in a collapsing universe, our descendants would create "an abode which is in all essentials the Judeo-Christian Heaven." The source of these rather unorthodox ideas was Frank Tipler, a professor of mathematics at Tulane University.

The book in which Tipler predicted a human-engineered heaven was *The Physics of Immortality*. According to Tipler, the colonization of space that would make that heaven possible would be carried out not with manned spacecraft, an endeavor that would be enormously expensive, but with self-replicating spacecraft called von Neumann probes, after a concept based on the work of mathematician and physicist John von Neumann. Tipler's versions would be small and light (perhaps weighing no more than a hundred grams), constructed with nanotechnology, and propelled by an antimatter drive. They would be intelligent robots, but they would blend nonliving with living in that they would carry in their memory DNA sequences of humans and other terrestrial life. The first such probe, traveling at one-tenth the speed of light, would be sent to a nearby star system. Once there, it would use the DNA sequences to create living cells that would develop into humans, our indirect descendants. Then, using locally available materials, it would make other probes. These would depart for other systems, each travelling at one-tenth the speed of light, and the seeding process would continue. Some of our descendants would develop civilizations on planets; others would build habitats in space.

The colonization of the universe as envisioned by Tipler recalls that depicted in Asimov's story. Two characters in the third scene of the story, at a moment when the human population doubles every ten years and the galaxy is mostly populated, estimate that the entire universe will be full in a mere ten thousand years. Tipler undertakes a similar projection, beginning from what, roughly speaking, is the present moment. He estimates that with von Neumann probes carrying human seeds ever outward and in all directions, the volume of colonized space would increase in diameter by ten light-years every sixty years. Because our galaxy is roughly 100,000 light years in diameter, it would be colonized completely in a mere 600,000 years. Moreover, in some 10^{19} years, the volume of colonized space would encompass the entire universe. By his calculations, it would be about the time that the universe's expansion may be expected to slow, cease altogether, and then reverse itself. And that, according to Tipler, would be a particularly timely moment for our descendants to have filled all of space, because only by filling all of space would they be they in a position to take real advantage of the situation.

Naturally, Tipler's colonizers could not hope to reverse the collapse. However, because they (or their machine representatives) would be nearly everywhere, they could exert some control over it. With sets of strategically placed explosions, the suitably advanced civilization might speed parts of the collapse, thereby creating temperature differentials in adjacent areas, and great reservoirs of potential energy. Exactly what might be done with this energy? Tipler believed that a civilization that survived so long would regard the conditions under which its ancestors lived as intolerable; it would also be highly principled. Consequently, what it would *want* to do with this energy, and what it *would* do, would be to use very, very advanced computers to make replicas of everyone who ever lived, along with their memories. To protect these beings from disorientation and/or shock, it would create for them an environment like the one they had known, but far more pleasant.

Here is where astrophysics meets eschatology. Tipler called this reconstruction a "resurrection" and described the environment in which it would occur as "an abode which is in all essentials the Judeo-Christian Heaven." One of those essentials, of course, is immortality, and within the long but finite interval of the universe's collapse, Tipler's civilization would manage even this. During the collapse enough energy would be available for an infinite amount of what a computer scientist would call information processing, and what the rest of us would call thinking or consciousness. A number — say the number 2 — may be parsed into a finite series: 1 + 1. It may also be parsed into an *infinite* series: $1 + \frac{1}{2} + \frac{1}{4}$ and so forth. This "subjective immortality" would be accomplished by an infinite parsing within a finite interval. So although the collapse would have a finite duration and in the big crunch an unequivocal and irreversible end, those who are reconstructed within the collapse will enjoy life everlasting — or the subjective experience of it.

As might be expected, the critical reception of *The Physics of Immortality* was mixed. There was awe at the range of its erudition and mild bewilderment as to its inspiration. One reviewer called it "a wonderfully ambitious, painfully sincere tour de force — an attempt, sometimes brilliant, sometimes absurd, to stretch scientific reasoning to its breaking point" (Johnson). Physicist Kip Thorne offered qualified praise, saying, "I think big pieces of Frank's argument are brilliant and beautifully done. But it is in the leaky joints between the pieces where I think the problems lie" (Thorne and Tipler 67). Most readers were far less kind, and most physicists regarded the book as an unworthy effort from an otherwise much-respected scientist.

Tipler's "subjective immortality," of course, had its own built-in presupposition. It was that time is continuous — that is, that any interval of time may be divided into ever briefer intervals, and that there is no interval, however small, that cannot be subdivided. In fact, Dyson's prescription for longevity in a universe growing ever colder might likewise assume that time is continuous, allowing organisms to slow their metabolisms to less energetic environments by reducing their metabolic rates asymptotically, nearing but never achieving a metabolic rate of precisely zero. Dyson's paper alludes to two forms of memory that are (his terms here): analog and digital. He explains:

> All our computer memory nowadays is based on digital memory. But digital memory is in principle limited in capacity by the number of atoms available for its construction. A society with finite material resources can never build a digital memory beyond a certain finite capacity. Therefore digital memory cannot be adequate to the needs of a life form planning to survive indefinitely [456].

Likewise, Tipler's 'subjective immortality' can be realized only in a universe in which space-time is continuous. And, unfortunately for those wishing to achieve life everlasting by this means, most physicists assure us that space-time is *dis*continuous. It seems that as there is a shortest possible length, a length it is not possible to be shorter than; there is also a briefest possible interval of time, an interval it is not possible to be briefer than.

These problems aside, Tipler had offered his idea for a heaven created artificially with energies tapped from a big crunch as a "testable physical theory" (1). Like all theories it rested upon certain hypotheses. As it happened, one of them would soon be disproved. In the late 1980s and early 1990s, astrophysicists were able to make ever more precise measurements of the mass density of the universe, and when they summed the mass from stars, dust, and gas, and the mysterious stuff called *dark matter,* they arrived at a value far below that necessary to stop or even slow the expansion. By the mid–1990s, most cosmologists were persuaded that a collapse was unlikely, that the universe was *open.* That meant no crunch, no collapse, and no energy differentials to exploit. It also meant that if life were to survive into the far future, it would be in a universe like that described by Dyson.

Still more recently, in 1995, physicists Fred Adams and Greg Laughlin, with benefit of work by astrophysicists in the sixteen years since Dyson's article, undertook yet another speculation of the distant future — this the most ambitious to date. They describe the current era in the life of the universe as an active period when stars are forming, living, and dying. It will end when the universe is 10^{14} years of age and all stars have cooled and faded to stellar remnants — these being white dwarfs, brown dwarfs, neutron stars, and black holes. Then will begin a tremendously long and quiet period, its stillness is interrupted only when two white dwarfs collide and create a supernova explosion that brightens an otherwise darkened galaxy.

The era would seem utterly inhospitable to life, and perhaps it will be. Nonetheless, taking a page from Dyson, Adams and Laughlin imagined ways in which living organisms, and even intelligence, might survive and flourish. White-dwarf interiors are very dense — 10^{14} grams per cubic centimeter — but their atmospheres would permit mobility. Those atmospheres contain oxygen and carbon, and although they are quite cold, they are warm enough that they would allow the chemicals to interact in interesting ways. Still more compellingly, they would remain stable for extremely long periods. They gain what heat they have by collisions with particles of dark matter — a process that will continue until the dark matter is exhausted, when the universe is 10^{25} years of age. This would be a hundred billion times as long as it took for life to appear on Earth. Such longevity, Adams and Laughlin suggest, implies that life in white-dwarf atmospheres is not merely possible — over such time spans it is likely. However, they also note that it would be a life quite unlike our own. In accordance with Dyson's scaling hypothesis, metabolisms and rates of consciousness would be very slow. An intelligent creature living in a white-dwarf atmosphere might take a thousand years to complete a single thought.[12] Again, although Adams and Laughlin hypothesize about biological (and natural) organisms, the description would apply equally to artificial life — that is, what we would call computers.

When the universe is 10^{40} years old, even protons have evaporated into a diffuse radiation, and the only remaining stellar remnants are black holes. Their radiation provides all the warmth available anywhere, and it is very little: the surface temperature of a black hole is one ten-millionth of a degree above absolute zero.[13] Eventually, even black holes evaporate, and the larger they are, the more time they take to do it. When the universe is 10^{100} years old, even the most massive black holes are gone, leaving a few electrons and positrons drifting in unimaginably vast reaches of space. And this, finally, is the end. Or — as they say in the movies — *is it?*

In the last decade of the twentieth century, cosmologists had compelling evidence that the universe was open, but there remained doubts. In the 1990s, two groups worked independently to gauge the rate of expansion. They measured the redshift of the most distant object whose absolute luminosity we know — a type of star called Type IA supernovae — and took it as characteristic of the expansion rate of the very early universe. They then compared it with the redshift of nearby galaxies, which they assumed characteristic of the more recent expansion rate. The tentative results, announced by both groups in 1998, surprised everyone. All evidence suggested that the universe's rate of expansion was not slowing; neither was it steady. Contrary to all expectation, it was *accelerating.* If this acceleration is real, its cause is unknown. It may be that the vacuum itself exerts a negative pressure of the type featured in ideas of cosmic inflation. It may be that the universe is filled with an all-pervasive fluid that has a negative pressure. In any case, an accelerating expansion means a fate for the universe that, if anything, is irredeemably darker and colder than that implied by a slowing or steady expansion. It means that the cosmic horizon can never catch up, that it will not bring new galaxies into view; in fact, as space expands it will take galaxies that are now in view beyond the horizon. Well before the stars burn themselves out, our own night sky will grow ever darker.

In 2002, physicists Lawrence Krauss and Glenn Starkman revisited the prediction of Eddington and Jeans, pondering what an accelerated expansion would mean to prospects for life in general and for the longevity of a suitably advanced civilization in particular. As the universe expands and space is stretched, energy and matter become more diluted. As in Asimov's story, any "suitably advanced civilization" would face the energy crisis to end all energy crises. Late in the story, a disembodied mind begins to build a star by collecting interstellar hydrogen, full knowing the measure is stop-gap at best. But even this action, Krauss and Starkman suggest, would be difficult. The suitable advanced civilization might try to retrieve matter, but the process would cost more, in terms of energy, than the matter retrieved. It might decide to stay put and allow gravity to do the work — for, instance, by constructing a black hole so that matter might be drawn toward it. But because the strength of gravity between two masses falls off in direct proportion to the square of the distance between them, and because all matter is being spread thinner and thinner, gravity itself would become less and less useful over time. Other solutions — extracting energy from cosmic strings or the quantum vacuum itself— would be, for various reasons, as unworkable. The suitably advanced civilization, whether biological or artificial and no matter how clever, could not avoid its own extinction. The only possibility would be wiping the slate clean, as it were — that is, a phase change in which a new cosmos is created with new natural laws, utterly different from those we know. Theoretical physicists believe that such a change may occur naturally. In fact, it may be the way this universe began. But they suspect that it happens very, very rarely.

Were Asimov to compose "The Last Question" today, the story's humans and post-humans would not ask the computers whether entropy might be reversed. Rather, they would ask: "is it possible to generate a cosmic phase transition artificially?" At the moment no one has an answer. But we — and by "we" I mean humans and computers both — have a lot of time to think about it.

Notes

1. Seth Shostak, *Confessions of an Alien Hunter* (Washington: National Geographic, 2009), p. 272.

2. Marvin L. Minsky, "Will Robots Inherit the Earth?" *Scientific American,* October 1994.

3. Originally it had meant "Allied Mastercomputer," and later "Adaptive Manipulator." That the acronym takes a form of the verb "to be" suggests that the computer has been distilled to an essence quite beyond the reach of description.

4. Its appellation is a vestige of "analogue computer," a term that described its ancient ancestor.

5. To understand the implications of the preceding paragraph, a brief refresher in astronomy is necessary. The distance we can see into the universe is limited by several factors, one of which is the speed of light. Because the universe began 13.7 billion years ago, we can see in no direction farther than the distance that light can have traveled since that time — that is, no farther than 13.7 billion light-years. The expansion of space makes the actual distance visible considerably greater, but in any case, as the universe ages light is given more time to travel, meaning that astronomers of the future will be able to see farther than can astronomers at present.

6. We may envision the universe we see (the *observable universe*) as the volume within a bubble at whose centerpoint we are, and whose outer surface (the *cosmic horizon*) is always expanding. Outside the cosmic horizon is a larger bubble — the entire universe — and it too is expanding.

7. This result raised new questions. Of the three universes under consideration, a flat universe seemed the least likely. A flat universe could occur only if the forces of expansion and collapse were balanced with fantastic precision, yet physicists could imagine no reason those forces should be balanced at all. This was a very curious state of affairs, and nothing in the big bang theory could explain it. The classical big bang theory had predicted that the universe was the size of the visible universe or a bit larger. Inflation predicted that the present universe was *many times* larger than the visible universe. It was this particular prediction that answered the flatness problem. Palm a basketball, and you can feel its curvature. Imagine that, as you continue to palm it, it is slowly inflated. When it doubles in size once, it feels flatter; when it doubles in size twice, its feels flat. Regardless of the shape of the young universe — sphere, saddle, or something in between — double its size a hundred times, and even a region as large as 20 billion

light-years across will seem flat. Inflation meant that suddenly there was no reason to require that the forces of expansion and collapse be balanced. Inflation solved the flatness problem by dismissing it.

8. Although Dyson admitted that he could not imagine such organisms in detail (he could not, for instance, know whether there were functional equivalents of muscles or nerves), this did not mean that they were impossible. Most biologists, he noted, would be hard-pressed to imagine a cell, had they never seen one.

Works Cited

Adams, Fred, and Greg Laughlin. *The Five Ages of the Universe: Inside the Physics of Eternity.* New York: Free, 1999.

Dyson, Freeman. "Time Without End: Physics and Biology in an Open Universe." *Reviews of Modern Physics* 51, no. 3 (July 1979): 447–460.

Ellison, Harlan. *Alone against Tomorrow: Stories of Alienation in Speculative Fiction.* New York: Collier-Macmillan, 1972.

Eddington, Arthur. *The Nature of the Physical World.* New York: Macmillan, 1928.

Johnson, George. "The Physics of Immortality." *New York Times,* October 9, 1994.

Krauss, Lawrence M., and Glenn D. Starkman. "The Fate of Life in the Universe." *Scientific American,* December 2002, pp. 50–57.

_____. "Life, the Universe, and Nothing: Life and Death in an Ever-Expanding Universe." *Astrophysical Journal* 531 (2000): 22–30.

Russell, Bertrand. *Why I Am Not a Christian.* New York: Simon and Schuster, 1957. \

Thorne, Kip S., and Frank Tipler. "A Cosmological Dialogue between Caltech Cosmologist Kip Thorne and Tulane Cosmologist Frank Tipler on The Physics of Immortality." *Skeptic Magazine* 3, no. 4 (1996): 64–67.

Tipler, Frank. *The Physics of Immortality: Modern Cosmology, God and the Resurrection of the Dead.* New York: Doubleday, 1994.

About the Contributors

Janet Abbate teaches science and technology studies at Virginia Tech. She is the author of *Inventing the Internet*, several IT policy studies, a book in progress on the history of women in computing, and a website on cyborg fiction. Her master's thesis was on 1960s New Wave science fiction as a counterculture movement.

R.C. Alvarado is the associate director of Sciences, Humanities, and Arts Netword of Technological Initiatives (SHANTI) at the University of Virginia, where he teaches courses in new media. He is a cultural anthropologist by training.

Thierry Bardini is a sociologist in the department of communication at the University of Montreal. He has written many articles on sociology of technology as well as *Bootstrapping: Douglas Engelbart, Coevolution, and the Origins of Personal Computing*, on the key developer of the mouse and graphical user interface.

Paul E. Ceruzzi is the author of one of the best-known general histories of modern computing: *A History of Modern Computing*. He also curator of aerospace electronics and computing at the Smithsonian's National Air and Space Museum.

Joshua Cuneo is a graduate student in digital media at the Georgia Institute of Technology, where he received a degree in computer science with a minor in film and media studies.

David L. Ferro is an associate professor in computer science at Weber State University. He has co-written *Connecting with Computer Science* and *Computers: The Life Story of a Technology*.

Thomas Haigh is an assistant professor in the School of Information Studies at the University of Wisconsin, Milwaukee. He has published on many aspects of the history of computing and is chair of the Special Interest Group on Computers, Information and Society (SIGCIS) of the Society for the History of Technology and biographies editor of IEEE Annals of the History of Computing.

Hunter Heyck is an associate professor of the history of science at the University of Oklahoma and author of *Herbert A. Simon: The Bounds of Reason in Modern America*. He is studying the relationship between the organizational revolution and the emergence of "systems thinking," and the history of modern technology.

David A. Kirby was a practicing evolutionary geneticist before becoming a lecturer in science communication studies at the University of Manchester. Several of his publications address the relationship between cinema, genetics, and biotechnology, His newest book is *Lab Coats in Hollywood: Scientists' Impact on Cinema, Cinema's Impact on Science and Technology*.

Richard L. McKinney is an American-born scholar who has lived in Sweden since 1968. He is affiliated with the Centre for Languages and Literature at Lund University.

Graham J. Murphy teaches in Trent University's Cultural Studies Department and the Department of English literature as well as Seneca College of Applied Arts and Technology. He coedited *Beyond Cyberpunk* (2010) and coauthored *Ursula K. LeGuin: A Critical Companion* (2006). His work has appeared in *Contemporary American Comics* (2010), *The Routledge Companion to Science Fiction* (2009), *Queer Universes* (2008), and other works. He is researching the intersections of science fiction, posthumanism, and insect ontologies.

Lisa Nocks is a historian who writes on the public perception of techno-science. She is the author of *Robot, the Life Story of a Technology* and is a senior lecturer at the New Jersey Institute of Technology, where she teaches courses on biotechnology, AI, and robotics.

Chris Pak is studying for a Ph.D. at the University of Liverpool, where he specializes in science fiction; his thesis focuses on the eco-political implications of terraforming technologies.

Jaakko Suominen, Ph.D., is a professor of digital culture at the School of Cultural Production and Landscape Studies, the University of Turku, Finland. He is the author or co-author of numerous books and articles on the cultural history of information technology and the history of media and technology.

Alfredo Suppia is an assistant professor in the Federal University of Juiz de Fora, Brazil. He has written extensively on Brazilian cinema.

Eric G. Swedin is an associate professor in the Information Systems and Technologies Department at Weber State University, where he specializes in information security and the social implications of computing. He is also a historian with six published books.

Howard Tayler is the author and illustrator of *Schlock Mercenary*, a science fiction serial. Previously he was a collaboration product line manager for Novell and a member of the board of directors at Sanctus Records, an independent record label.

David Toomey is an associate professor in English at the University of Massachusetts, Amherst, and director of their Program in Professional Writing and Technical Communication. He has written books and articles on numerous technical subjects.

Gary Westfahl has written extensively on science fiction, writing or editing more than 20 books on the subject, including several for McFarland as well as the three-volume *Greenwood Encyclopedia of Science Fiction and Fantasy: Themes, Works, and Wonders.*

Index

www.ingramcontent.com/pod-product-compliance
Lightning Source LLC
Chambersburg PA
CBHW031217050326
40689CB00009B/1369